LEON BATTISTA ALBERTI'S

HYPNEROTOMACHIA

POLIPHILI

*   *

*

THE MIT PRESS | CAMBRIDGE, MASSACHUSETTS | LONDON, ENGLAND

LEON BATTISTA ALBERTI'S

HYPNEROTOMACHIA

POLIPHILI

* *
*

RE-COGNIZING THE ARCHITECTURAL BODY IN THE EARLY ITALIAN RENAISSANCE

LIANE LEFAIVRE

First MIT Press paperback edition, 2005

© 1997 Massachusetts Institute of Technology

This book was set in Bembo by Graphic Composition, Inc., and was printed and bound in the United States of America.

Library of Congress Cataloging-in-Publication Data

Lefaivre, Liane.

Leon Battista Alberti's Hypnerotomachia Poliphili : re-cognizing the architectural body in the early Italian Renaissance / Liane Lefaivre.

p. cm.

Includes bibliographical references and index.

ISBN 0-262-12204-9 (HC: ALK. PAPER), 0-262-62195-9 (PB)

1. Colonna, Francesco, d. 1527. Hypnerotomachia Poliphili. 2. Alberti, Leon Battista, 1404–1472—Authorship. 3. Colonna, Francesco, d. 1527—Authorship. I. Title.

PQ4619.C9Z76   1997

853'.3—DC20

96-40960

CIP

10 9 8 7 6 5 4 3 2

FOR A.T.

CONTENTS

*

ILLUSTRATIONS

✳

ACKNOWLEDGMENTS

*

This book would not have been possible without the help of a number of people. Douwe W. Fokkema provided guidance and a framework. Christian Klamt read the text and made many valuable suggestions. Arpad Orbàn contributed much to the Latin translations. George Szanto and Louis van Delft helped shape the work in its earliest stages. Giuseppina Saccaro and Eugenio Battisti invited me to present the work for the first time at a conference they organized in Rocca di Papa and Ravello some years ago.

Léonce Laget, the Parisian bookseller, provided background about the book market. Werner Oechslin xeroxed texts for me from his own library of rare books. Harald Hendrix helped with Italian references. Badi al-Abed translated the Arabic in the *Hypnerotomachia,* and Benjamin Brest the Hebrew. Daniel Schlaepfer explained his *boîtes magiques.*

The book benefited in different ways from conversations with Christine Boyer, Cathy Lang Ho, Phyllis Lambert, Marilyn Matz, Mary Otis Stevens, and Elka Spoerri; Denis Bilodeau, Stathis Eustathiadis, John Heintz, Luca Molinari, Peter Scriver, Tatiana Spinari, and Ian White. I owe Santiago Calatrava the use of the term *extra-vagare.* Most valuable were the insights and knowledge shared with me by my anonymous reader for the MIT Press who commented on the Latin, as well as by Howard Burns, Joop Doorman, the late Richard Pommer, Myra Nan Rosenfeld, Johanna Maria van Winter, and, at the last moment, Wolfgang Jung and Arthur Steinberg. The late Robin Evans and Mark Jarzombek commented on parts of the text. James Ackerman was particularly generous early on in the book's conception. Richard Ingersoll gave repeated stimulating criticisms.

For the MIT Press, Alice Falk copyedited the text with swift and meticulous precision. Ori Kometani designed the book with imagination. Matthew Abbate provided skillful management help. Roger Conover's constant and resourceful support, both intellectual and personal, was invaluable.

I am grateful to them all. My most precious debt is to Alex Tzonis. The present book is an echo of a conversation he brought me into some time ago about architectural history, creativity, theory, cognition, cognitive history, and criticism, and many other things besides, or at least it has tried to be. I dedicate it to him.

LEON BATTISTA ALBERTI'S

HYPNEROTOMACHIA

POLIPHILI

*　　*

*

METAPHORS AND MENTAL LEAPS: TOWARD A COGNITIVE HISTORY OF ARCHITECTURE

CULTURAL INNOVATION AND MODERNIZATION ARE INCREASingly topical in architectural history. An approach one might call cognitive is beginning to develop in response to the need to understand historical moments of intense cultural creativity and the mechanisms that brought them about.[1] The focus of such research necessarily falls on the ways in which innovation and modernization occur—on patterns of reasoning and conceptual systems. Of special interest is the role that precedent knowledge, metaphor, and analogy play.

The early Italian Renaissance is an especially significant moment to study. It is the time when much of our own contemporary culture together with its attitude toward innovation—in particular with regard to architecture, one of the leading expressions of culture in early modern society—was determined. What the great historian Jacob Burckhardt wrote nearly one hundred and fifty years ago in *The Civilization of the Renaissance in Italy* still holds true: the "civilization" of the Renaissance is "the mother of our own, and [her] influence is still at work among us."[2]

To such a focus, the *Hypnerotomachia Poliphili,* written in the second half of the fifteenth century or quattrocento, is central. Few people have attempted an exhaustive reading of this book, which is visually ordered and pleasurable but written in a tortuous, almost Joycean style. And those who have read it have not placed it in the context of a rather improbable set of contemporary texts, including the medieval patristic writings and Leon Battista Alberti's *De re aedificatoria.* Even less has it been seen as a complementary text to those others; least of all has it been seen as a complementary text to the totality of Leon Battista Alberti's oeuvre, let alone attributed to him. However, the attribution to Alberti is not as important as the elucidation through this new reading of the *Hypnerotomachia Poliphili* of how innovation occurred in the early Renaissance, using on the one hand precedents and on the other metaphor and analogy.

Innovation and modernity were crucial issues in the quattrocento. Leon Battista Alberti was the first architectural theoretician to formulate a wholly new approach to precedent rules and knowledge, working within a broader cultural debate between authority and a new approach to reality. The revolutionary novelty of Alberti's reasoning is twofold. First, instead of accepting the authority of antique precedents as found in texts and buildings, he submitted them to rational, critical, empirical inquiry.[3] Second, once such precedents were proved unacceptable he did not dismiss them; instead, he turned them into raw material to be recombined into new designs. Certainly by stripping them of their previous absolute value and subjecting them to critical evaluation, he opened the door to subsequent debates that led to relativism. In other words, ancient texts and beliefs could now be used in ways that were creative rather than imitative. For Alberti, this meant the architect was free to draft precedent knowledge and rules in the search for new solutions.[4]

Alberti's reconfiguration of architectural knowledge and reasoning by reevaluating the role of precedent in design constitutes a conceptual revolution. It separates him from his intellectual forerunner, Vitruvius, who tended to rely in most cases on the authority of precedents, and it constitutes a major epistemic break within Western culture. The *Hypnerotomachia* is key in documenting how this new kind of creative reasoning as invented by Alberti was structured. Longer than *De re aedificatoria* and composed some eighteen years later, it is itself an unprecedented combination of novel and architectural treatise, written in an invented language combining vernacular Italian with Greek and Latin. Its main theme is new thinking. Not many creative people make their own mental activity a subject of study. Among the ones who do, most report the importance of dreamwork, that realm where the authoritarian "no" of conventional life is no longer valid, where thought experiments are free to unfold and mental leaps occur.[5] Alberti seems to have been among those who decided to dedicate a whole book largely to the reflection on his own creativity in a plot that unfolds in a dream.

In this creative dreamwork, precedents do not associate with each other in a totally arbitrary way. Alberti proposed a means to constrain this process, by placing his formula of recombinant design under a higher-standing imperative: *concinnitas,* based on the metaphor of the body. The concept of *concinnitas* is inextricably linked with a new cultural value: finding pleasure in the material world and, reciprocally, aiming for pleasure, no different from the erotic kind, in designing or in making an artificial world. The significance of the *Hypnerotomachia* is that it links this reflection on creative design process with the process of establishing a new value for designers: what came to be considered later the aesthetic value. In this respect, of most importance in the study of the *Hypnerotomachia* is investigating the function of the metaphor of the building as a body and the unbridled eroticism that metaphor introduces into the architectural experience. Indeed, the buildings encountered by the hero of the story are all embodiments of his beloved, to whom he is passionately attached, and whom he seduces, in the form of a building.

This is the point at which the present study moves beyond the microhistory of Alberti's life, opening up to a much broader horizon of interpretation. I examine the gradual eroticization of the body and its role in the aestheticization of architectural thinking that culminates in the *Hypnerotomachia Poliphili*. The analysis is based on a large, heterogeneous group of writings, including poems, biographies, songs, novels, travel journals, memoirs, letters, diaries, and plaques on walls, written from the end of the eighth century to the time of the *Hypnerotomachia*. At the beginning of this period the body is considered as the source of all evil, the *radix omnium malorum*. By its close, the body is accepted as the highest good, the *summum bonum*.

This re-cognition of the body was key to reconfiguring architectural thinking from archaic to modern, from authoritarian to creative. The renewed metaphor of the building as a body permitted thinking the unthinkable. In particular, it acted to sanction the abandonment of a "cold," prohibitive paradigm in favor of one open to reformulation. Because the body metaphor was a "basic" metaphor at the time, it encapsulated and subsequently generated a universe of thinking about architecture.

The study of the *Hypnerotomachia* and the metaphor of the architectural body embedded in it says something about how knowledge is represented and categorized. The body is a map, a description of the world and a way of prescribing acts in that world. It carries within it a site of prohibitions and imperatives. The new, erotic body becomes a means of pulling together and reorganizing knowledges that would otherwise have been impossible to associate. In its turn toward the metaphorical representation of the mentality of *eros mundi* and *libido aedificandi,* the metaphor of the erotic, humanist architectural body made it possible to conceive the new architectural world to come.

Renaissance humanism is a long, enduring phenomenon, which extends to our own
time and perhaps onward for some time to come. By definition, it has no end.
It was invented by free thinkers, a way of thinking in the making, open-
ended, taking risks and looking forward in its attempt to formulate a better future without losing sight of those parts of
the past that are worth preserving. This humanism
is encapsulated in Alberti's own motto, *Quid*
tum ("what next"), and possibly exemplified more than in any
other text in his *Hyp-*
nerotomachia
Poliphili

.

1

*

THE READ *HYPNEROTOMACHIA*, OR THE
HYPNEROTOMACHIA AS KNOWLEDGE

I N MANY WAYS THE *HYPNEROTOMACHIA POLIPHILI* IS NON-descript.[1] Published in 1499, it is modeled on the idyllic pastoral, bucolic *romanzo d'amore,* a tradition that had peaked over a century earlier with its universally acknowledged master, Giovanni Boccaccio, whose works included *Filostrato* (1339), *Teseida* (1339–1340), *Ninfale fiesolano* (1340s), and *Amorosa visione* (1342).[2] It is an anachronism. It adds nothing new to the amorous imaginary. It brings together all the stereotypical characters traditionally associated with what was by then a highly stylized genre: the enamored hero and the indifferent heroine, attended by scores of stock characters—nymphs, naiads, satyrs, gods, goddesses, and demigods—who, all too predictably, sing, dance, give advice, and in general eagerly officiate whenever there is opportunity for the lovers to engage in a rite of union. Its settings bow to the invariable formula of verdant glades, babbling brooks, and enclosed gardens. As for the plot, it too conforms to the conventions of the genre's time-worn topoi—the lover's unrequited love, his quest to win the heart of the heroine, love's triumph, the blissful union.

The action takes place in a dream. The book opens on the hero, Poliphilo, who has spent a restless night because his beloved, Polia, has shunned him. At the break of the day he is to embark on his love quest, he falls into a deep slumber and his "hypnerotomachia," or, as it can be roughly translated, "struggle for love in a dream," begins.[3] The action is particularly absurd, however, even by the norms of the genre. Poliphilo is transported inside a wild forest. He gets lost, escapes, and falls asleep again. He awakens in a second dream, dreamed inside the first. Within it, he is taken by some nymphs to meet their queen. There he is asked to declare his love for Polia, which he does. He is then directed by two nymphs to three gates. He chooses the third, behind which he finds his beloved. They are taken by more nymphs to a temple to be engaged. Along the way they witness five triumphal processions celebrating their union. Then the lovers are taken to the island of Cythera by barge, with Cupid as their boatswain; they see another triumphal procession. The narrative is interrupted, and a second voice takes over, as Polia describes the erotomachia from her own point of view. This takes up one-fifth of the book, after which the hero resumes his narrative. They are blissfully wed, but Polia vanishes into thin air as Poliphilo is about to take her in his arms.

Readers have found the single most extraordinary feature of the story to be the series of buildings and gardens that the hero keeps encountering throughout the narrative. Among them are a *boschetto* (a garden planted to look like wilderness), a palm grove, a temple, a pyramid, a triumphal arch, a hippodrome, a propylaeum (the gateway to a temple), a palaestra (a Greek or Roman building, smaller than a gymnasium, for athletic training; it consisted of a large, square court flanked by covered porticoes, baths, and rooms for massages), a *xystus* (a roofed colonnade for exercise in bad weather) or *peridromos* (a colonnaded promenade), a *hypaethron* (a court or enclosure open to the sky), a *euripus* (a ditch around an arena or a circus to keep the wild animals from escaping), two colossi, a gigantic building in the shape of an elephant carrying an obelisk on its back, a bridge, a bathhouse, a *chambre verte,* a palace in the form of a temple, a picturesque landscape, a pergola, an aquatic labyrinth, three nymphaea, two circular-plan temples, some ruins, a grotto, a barge, an immense garden that covers an entire island, and an amphitheater.

These architectural surroundings and design artifacts in which the plot of the *Hypnerotomachia* unravels are described at such length that they take up more than half the book. Two hundred pages out of 370 are exclusively devoted to architectural descriptions. No fewer than 78 of the first 86 pages are occupied by the painstakingly minute detailing of the *boschetto,* the palm grove, the giant pyramidal building, the bridge, the octagonal baths, and the palazzo. Indeed, the great pyramidal building alone monopolizes almost 50 pages: and of these, 5 pages, in turn, record nothing but the measurements of the triumphal arch that serves as its entrance. The temple of Venus fills an additional 18 pages, the *nymphaea* and the aquatic labyrinth 12, the ruins 35. Descriptions of various landscapes and the gardens run to close to 60 pages, the gardens on the island of Cythera alone absorbing 36 of them. Of the remaining 150 or so pages of Poliphilo's tale, 63 are occupied with the description of chariots in the triumphal arches, 14 with the food and place settings at what surely must be the most copious banquet ever described, 4 with a ballet, 20 with music, and 20 with the ceremonial rituals at a temple. The descriptions of precious stones, gems, and metals consume 8 pages. Finally, 60 pages are taken up with the description of botanical lore; they constitute a veritable encyclopedia of every plant known during the Renaissance. A mere 30 pages at most are left to the actual action of the love story, to its dialogue and inner monologue, and to the devices usually associated with the genre.

So knowledgeable are the descriptions of architecture and its attendant arts that they have conferred upon the *romanzo* of *Hypnerotomachia Poliphili* the additional character of an architectural encyclopedia and textbook—what was referred to at the time as a *trattato.*

*   *   *

For the last five hundred years, since the *Hypnerotomachia* was first published, scholars have tended to shrug off the novel as a mere corollary to the architectural treatise. Leonardo Crasso, the patron of the original publication, barely mentions it in his dedicatory introduction to the book addressed to Guidobaldo da Montefeltro in 1499. The same is true of its generally recognized French translator, the literary figure Jean Martin. In his dedication to the Conte de Nantheuil he passes it over in silence, and he mentions it only incidentally in his "Avis aux lecteurs" in the same edition. Jacques Gohorry, responsible for several editions of the book during the sixteenth century in France, in his comments of 1561 is equally impassive. Tommaso Temanza and Leopoldo Cicognara, the two main commentators of the eighteenth and early nineteenth century, give it no notice at all.[4]

But the novel has never suffered more than at the hands of modern academic scholarship.[5] Albert Ilg, in the first doctoral dissertation devoted to the topic, entitled *Ueber den kunsthistorischen Werth der Hypnerotomachia Poliphili* (On the art-historical value of the *Hypnerotomachia Poliphili*), sees it as nothing more than an amusing but secondary device for holding together the vast tracts of learning the book contains.[6] Benedetto Croce, one of this century's most prominent philosophers and Renaissance scholars, wrote that "if this book had not been so serious and so long and boring, it might have been interpreted as a caricature of humanism." William Ivins, the famous American historian of printmaking, dismissed it as a "dull unreadable romance"; Roberto Weiss, the Renaissance historian, as a "serious runner-up for the most boring book in Italian literature." In the words of Italian scholar Francesco Fabbrini, it represented no less than "the complete dissolution of an entire literary world," that of the Renaissance *romanzo d'amore*.[7]

Scholars have dismissed the *Hypnerotomachia Poliphili* as derivative. Domenico Gnoli, another Italian Renaissance scholar, deemed it a "freewheeling remake" of Boccaccio's *Amorosa visione,* from which whole episodes "seem to be stolen"; French philologist Claudius Popelin, a "pedantic amplification" of Boccaccio's *Ameto, Fiammetta,* and *Corbaccio;* and Charles Ephrussi, a French scholar, a "direct imitation" of the *Roman de la rose*.[8] Fabbrini reviled it as an unimaginative derivative of Dante's *Divina commedia,* separated from its famous model by an "incalculable abyss" thanks to its "vacuity," "serious formal deficiencies," "general defects of the imagination," and lack of both "freshness" and "vitality."[9] Scholars have looked beyond the great prototypes in search of the sources of the *Hypnerotomachia.* For Fabbrini, again, the primary source lay in the *Fimerodia* (fourteenth century), a mediocre work by Iacopo da Montepulciano, which narrates a vision in which the hero's love is unrequited. As in the *Hypnerotomachia,* the two lovers meet in church and, like Polia, the heroine wants to devote herself to the goddess of chastity, Diana. The same sumptuousness informs the architecture: precious marbles, marble monuments. The *Fimerodia* contains a marvelous island, with the same richness in flowered glades and fabulous triumphal chariots. There is even a marble wolf and a great, reflecting diamond elephant in the story.[10] Worst of all, perhaps, the turn of the century scholar and author Vladimiro Zabughin claimed the *Hypnerotomachia* was really nothing but a thinly disguised plagiarism of an anonymous, obscure, and mediocre fourteenth-century *Life of Saint Patrick*.[11]

If modern academic scholarship has discovered much to fault in the *Hypnerotomachia* from the literary point of view, it has, conversely, always held it in high esteem as an architectural treatise. With good reason: its date of completion, 1467, makes it one of the first treatises of the Renaissance, along with that of Leon Battista Alberti (1440s), Antonio Averlino, called Filarete (1451–1464), and Francesco di Giorgio Martini (1478–1501),[12] as well as translations of Vitruvius by Fra Giocondo (1511) and Cesare Cesariano (1521). Its date of publication, 1499, makes it the second to appear in print after Leon Battista Alberti's

De re aedificatoria at the famous press of Niccolò di Lorenzo Alemanno in Florence (1485).[13] And its 172 woodcut engravings, 88 of which represent buildings, make it the first illustrated printed architectural book in history.[14] Finally, its many reissuings and translations make it by far the most popular architectural book of the Renaissance, outstripping Alberti, Fra Giocondo, and Cesariano in terms of reprints and reissuings, at a time when even major architectural books, such as Filarete's and Francesco di Giorgio's, remained unpublished.

But the *Hypnerotomachia* had even greater significance. The editio princeps has the distinction of having been printed in Venice at the press of none other than Aldus Manutius. Aldus was a humanist scholar himself and counted among his friends the likes of Pico della Mirandola and Erasmus.[15] The bulk of his production was aimed at the humanists and scholars attached to northern Italian universities such as Padua and Ferrara, and the Aldine selection of titles is the most scholarly one of the Italian Renaissance. Most of his publications were in Latin or Greek, with the notable exceptions of Cardinal Bembo's *Li asolani,* Dante's *Divina commedia,* Petrarch's *Cose volgari,* Sannazaro's *Arcadia,* and the *Hypnerotomachia Poliphili.*

Aldus published Latin works by the classic authors along with ones by humanists. His first Latin text, in fact, was by his contemporary humanist Cardinal Bembo, *De Aetna* (1495). Among his other publications celebrated at the time were Angelo Poliziano's *Opera* (1498), Reuchlin's *Oratio* (1498), and Niccolò Perotti's *Cornucopia* (1499). The classic authors appeared later—the *Opera* of Virgil and of Horace in 1501, followed by the works of Juvenal, Martial, Cicero, Lucian, and Statius in that same year. Ovid's *Metamorphoses, Heroides,* and *Fasti* followed in 1502, then Catullus, Tibullus, Propertius, Origen, Cicero, Caesar, Cato, Quintilian, Lucretius, Valerius Maximus, and Horace between 1503 and 1508.[16] Erasmus's *Adagia* appeared in 1508.

Primarily, however, the reputation of the Aldine press rested on its role in introducing and disseminating classical Greek culture and contemporary Greek scholarship.[17] Before its inception, only a dozen Greek books had been printed in Italy. It is known that Greek was Aldus's abiding love, that he spoke Greek at home, and that he hired Greeks at his press. In his famous "Rules of the Modern Academy," which dictated the code of behavior to be followed at his press, Aldus required that those who set the type and corrected proofs speak only classical Greek, or be fined.[18] The first five books he published were in Greek, starting with Musaeus's *Hero and Leander.* His introduction to this Byzantine satire, which he mistakenly took for an ancient Greek one, is indicative of his enthusiastic philhellene spirit:[19] "I wanted the most ancient of poets, Musaeus, to be the first precursor of Aristotle and of the other great geniuses that I am about to publish, and this because this little poem is at the same time most pleasing and eloquent, and especially because you will see how happily Ovid was inspired by it in the letters written from Hero to Leander."[20] He went on to publish the satirical Byzantine play by Theodoros Prodomus, *Galeomyomachia,* "the battle of the cats and the rats," which in its preface he compares to a Hellenistic work he erroneously believed to be by Homer (*Batrachomyomachia,* or "the battle of the frogs and rats") as another precursor to the works of ancient Greece to follow.[21]

The press was renowned above all for its editions of classical Greek texts, especially for the five volumes of Aristotle's works published between 1495 and 1498, the first complete edition in Greek. It published the Greek grammars of Theodore Gaza and Constantine Lascaris and that of the Italian humanist Urbano Valeriani, along with a selection of earlier grammatical writings and a dictionary by Giovanni Craston.[22] The list of literary works consists largely of recommended introductions to Greek language and style, some of them dedicated to contemporary teachers. These include Hesiod, selections from the Greek gnomic poets, the comedies of Aristophanes, two treatises on pharmacology by Dioscurides and Nicander, Theophrastus's *History of Plants* and *Causes of Plants,* and Theocritus's *Idylls.* Aldus published the editiones principes of Thucydides, Herodotus, Xenophon, Sophocles, and Euripides. The Aldine edition of Iamblichus was a full series of short works by various Neoplatonist writers—Proclus, Synesius, Psellus, Alcinous, Speusippus, and Xenocrates—translated by Marsilio Ficino, the Florentine philosopher. In addition, Aldus published Plutarch, Homer, Demosthenes, and Aesop.[23]

One of the features of the *Hypnerotomachia* that has attracted the attention of scholars has been its use of the famed Aldine "Roman" type font, invented by Nicolas Jenson[24] but distilled into an abstracted ideal by Francesco Biffi da Bologna, a jeweler who became Aldus's celebrated cutter. This font—generally viewed as originating in the efforts of the humanist lovers of belles-lettres and renowned calligraphers to re-create the script of classical antiquity—appeared for the first time in Bembo's *De Aetna,* mentioned above. Recut, it appeared in its second and perfected version in the *Hypnerotomachia* (fig. 1).[25] The font that you are reading at this moment—Bembo—is its direct descendant.

1. EXAMPLES OF FONTS FROM THE *HYPNEROTOMACHIA POLIPHILI* (1499; RPT. NEW YORK, 1976).

Hora ͂qſta ſpectatiſſima ſtatua lartifice táto definitaméte la expſſe, che ueraméte dubitarei tale Praxitele Venere haueſſe ſcalpto. La ͂qle Nichomede re degli Gnidii cóparádola (come uola, la fama) tutto lo hauere dil ſuo populo expoſe. Et quanto uenuſtaméte belliſſima lui la expreſſe, tanto che gli homini iſacrilega cócupiſcétia di ͂qlla exarſi, il ſimulachro maſturbando ſtuprorono. Ma quáto ualeua æſtimare dritaméte arbitrai tale imagine mai fuſſe cuſi perfecta di celte, ouero di ſcalpello ſimulata, che quaſi ragioneuolmente io ſuſpicaui, in queſto loco de uiua eſſere lapidita & cuſi petrificata.

POLIPHILO INCOMINCIA LA SVA HYPNEROTO
MACHIA AD DESCRIVERE ET LHORA, ET IL TEM·
PO QVANDO GLI APPARVE IN SOMNO DI RITRO·
VARSI IN VNA QVIETA ET SILENTE PIAGIA, DI·
CVLTO DISERTA . DINDI POSCIA DISAVEDVTO,
CON GRANDE TIMORE INTRO IN VNA INVIA ET
OPACA SILVA.

2. EXAMPLES OF CAPITALS.

3. EXAMPLES OF DECORATED INITIALS.

Technically Biffi's achievement consists in having carried out a reduction in the relative weight of the lower cases, creating what the renowned English printing historian Stanley Morison has called a superbly harmonious effect,[26] further enhanced by the introduction of a delicately proportioned font of capitals. Bibliophiles and historians of printing, such as Morison and George Painter, admire the rounded and strong outline of the *Hypnerotomachia* font, "tall in uprights and firmly seriphed, both bold and delicate, equally dark and radiant in its blacks and whites."[27] Aldus's biographer, Martin Lowry, points out that the capitals of the *Hypnerotomachia* have a relative height and weight governed by the 1:10 proportion recommended by Feliciano and only partially reduced to 1:9 by Pacioli (fig. 2).[28] Equally admired is the particular care lavished on the decorated initials (fig. 3). Some are in hatchwork, while others, still finer, are decorated in strapwork or tendriled foliage and flowers.[29]

Appearing after a domination of the Gothic, when fonts inspired by classical calligraphy were still novel,[30] this font is considered the most modern in appearance of fifteenth-century types and marks a watershed. The fact that it survives today after half a millennium

4. Hebrew and Arabic fonts and woodcuts.

as a standard in Western typography makes the *Hypnerotomachia* one of the most significant contributions of the Renaissance to the history of printing.[31] Adding to this typographical tour de force, the book also contains prototypical Greek fonts, one of the earliest examples of Hebrew type, and what are the first Arabic passages in the history of European publishing (fig. 4).[32]

The 172 woodcuts of the *Hypnerotomachia* are at least as well studied as the font.[33] The book is unique in being the only illustrated book to have been published by Aldus.[34] Yet the identity of the designer and cutter is unknown. The letter *b* appears on two of the woodcuts (fig. 5), but it has been unclear whether this is the signature of either.[35] In any event, their anonymity is not exceptional. Sander lists no fewer than four hundred illustrated books published in the last ten years of the fifteenth century in Venice alone, and we know next to nothing about their individual illustrators.[36] Most are mediocre. This is no doubt because, as

5. TWO WOODCUTS BEARING THE INITIAL *B*.

we know from Arthur Hind, in the late fifteenth century woodcuts for books were still considered an inferior art form, especially compared to illuminations, but indeed among the visual arts in general. Federigo da Montefeltro, one of the most famous collectors of manuscripts of the period, excluded all printed books from his renowned and extensive library,[37] and the presentation copy of Dante (Florence, 1481) preserved in the National Library, Florence, is without its celebrated woodcut illustrations.[38]

The *Hypnerotomachia* is one of the two Venetian illustrated books that does stand out for its great quality; the other is the Malermi Bible, named after its Italian translator, which was printed in 1490 and reprinted in 1493 by Giovanni Ragazzo for Lucantonio Giunta with 373 woodcuts.[39] The images of the *Hypnerotomachia* are far superior. They are distinguished by their design in the same classicizing "stil nuovo"[40] as the high art of the time. Sculpted by a woodcutter,[41] their original designs have been associated above all with Andrea

6. Poliphilo fleeing the dragon.   7. Example of female beauty.

Mantegna who, more than any other figure, shaped the new classicizing style in engraving.[42] However, they also recall the work of Fra Giocondo, Vittore Carpaccio, and Gentile Bellini.[43] Scholars have even been tempted to see the influence of the young Raphael, an attribution that is difficult to support as Raphael was sixteen years old at the time.[44]

Hind saw the new classicism evidenced in the *Hypnerotomachia*'s illustrations as consisting in a mastery, on many levels, of the details of classical artifacts—vases, clothes, and so on; a remarkable facility for architectural design; and a fine sense of rhythm in figure drawing, as shown especially in Poliphilo and the dragon (fig. 6). He points out that certain of the illustrations also disclose a knowledge of the work of Botticelli.[45] Aby Warburg noted the similarity to that painter, above all in the representation of nymphs with flowing hair and billowing gowns (fig. 7), which gave the composition the dynamism of antique bas-reliefs and of the works of Botticelli.[46] Poppelreuter was struck by the "youthful genius," "fantasy,"

ſipunculo per ilquale emanaua laqua della fontana per artificio perpe.
tua in la ſubiecta concha.

    Nel Patore dunque di queſto uaſo prominua uno pretioſiſſimo mó
ticulo, mirabilmente congeſto di innumere gemme globoſe preſſamente
una ad laltra coaceruate, cum inæquale, o uero rude deformatura, lepidiſ
ſimamente il móticulo ſcrupeo rendeuano, cú corruſcatióe di uarii fulge
tri di colore, cum proportionata eminétia. Nel uertice, o uero cacumine
di queſto monticulo, naſceua uno arbuſculo di mali punici, di tronco, o
uero ſtipite & di rami, & ſimilmente tutto queſto compoſito di oro prælu
cente. Le foglie appoſitie di ſcintilláte Smaragdo. Gli fructi alla granditu
dine naturale diſperſamente collocati, cum il ſidio doro iſchiantati larga
mente, & in loco degli grani ardeuano nitidiſſimi rubini, ſopra omni pa
ragonio nitidiſſimi di craſſitudine fabacea. Poſcia lo ingenioſo fabro di
  queſta inextimabile factura & copioſo eſſendo del ſuo diſcorſo
  imaginario hauea diſcriminato, in loco di Cico gli grani cum
   tenuiſſima bractea argentea. Oltra di queſto & ragioneuol
    mente hauea ficto & alcuni altri mali crepati, ma di
    granelatura immaturi, oue hauea cópoſito cum im
    probo exquiſito di craſſi unione di candore orienta
    le. Ancora ſolertemente hauea ficto gli balau
    ſti facti di perfecto coralio in calici pieni di api
    ci doro. Vltra di queſto fora della ſum
    mitate del fiſtulatamente uacuo ſtipite
    uſciua uno uerſatile & libero ſty
    lo, il cardine imo delqua
    le, era fixo in uno ca
    po peronato, o ue
    ramente firma
    to ſopra il medio
    dellaxide. & aſcendeua
   per il peruio & inſtobato trunco.

8. Text in the form of a cup.

"romantic enthusiasm for the antique," emphasis on "representations of naked female beauty," and generalized celebration of "pagan nakedness" in the illustrations.[47]

    However, scholars find the greatest artistic merit of the book in neither typography nor woodcuts separately,[48] but in the overall composition of text and image into a harmonious whole, which allows the eye to slip back and forth between textual description and corresponding visual representation with the greatest of ease—a rarity even today. Besides displaying a remarkable level of visual culture and clarity, the *Hypnerotomachia* must also be seen as an extraordinarily adventurous and inventive example of book design. It is the first ever experimental montage of fragments of prose, typography, epigrams, and pictures and constitutes an extraordinary visual-typographical-textual "assemblage" of a type not repeated until the avant-garde books of the 1920s and 1930s in Russia, Italy, and France. Among its feats of typographical ingenuity, the form of antique goblets and drinking cups described in

9. Triumphal processions.

the text is reproduced in the layout of the text on the page (fig. 8).[49] It also contains, I believe, the first examples of double-page spreads in publishing history. To convey graphically the great length of four triumphal processions, the illustrations spill over from one page onto the next (fig. 9).

Small wonder there is a widespread consensus among scholars that the *Hypneroto-machia* is the most hauntingly beautiful of all the illustrated incunabulae, perhaps the most beautiful book of all time.[50] With its thirty or so copies still in existence in private and public collections, it is surely one of the most sought after.[51] It is ironic, as Ivins notes, that what has become the pride of any collector fortunate enough to own a copy was originally an economic fiasco.[52] Ten years after it was issued, its sponsor, Leonardo Crasso, applied for a ten-year extension of his copyright, arguing that the enterprise had cost him hundreds of ducats, a staggering capital investment for the period, and he had hardly sold any copies. A possible

TERTIVS

reason is that the *Hypnerotomachia* fell victim to the economic recession that followed a defeat of the Venetians by the Turks. In early 1499 the business community was rocked by a series of bankruptcies. Crasso himself blamed "the times, and the troubles caused by war" for his financial woes.[53] A cash shortage overtook the city, which severely affected presses; many were forced to close. By 1500 the number of presses and publications had declined sharply, and by 1501 book production had dropped to half the normal annual output of the previous ten years. Furthermore, the *Hypnerotomachia* was priced at one ducat, exceptionally high in relation to other *romanze* and close to the price of one volume of Aldus's Aristotle edition— which, at between one and a half and three ducats, was one of the most expensive publications of the time.[54] Lowry sees the bad timing of the book as almost unequaled in the annals of publishing.[55] Ivins speculates that this work, now an extremely rare work of art, may even have been "remaindered" shortly after publication.[56]

ce ligatura alla fistula tubale, Gli altri dui cũ ueterrimi cornitibici con
cordi ciascuno & cum gli instrumenti delle Equitante nymphe.

   Sotto lequale triũphale seiughe era laxide nel meditullo , Neleq̃le glj
rotali radii erano ínfixi , deliniamento Balustico ,gracilíscenti seposa
negli mucronati labii cum uno pomulo. alla circunferentia . Elquale
Polo era di finissimo & ponderoso oro, repudiante el rodicabile erugi
ne,& lo incẽdioso Vulcano ,della uirtute & pace exitiale ueneno. Sum
mamente dagli festigianti celebrato,cum moderate , & repentine
riuolutiõe intorno saltanti,cum solemnissimi plausi , cum
gli habiti cincti di fasceole uolitante ,Et le sedente sopra gli trahenti centauri . La Sancta cagione,
& diuino mysterio ,inuoce cõsone & car-
mini cancionali cum extre
ma exultatione amo-
rosamente lauda
uano.
**
*

EL SEQVENTE triũpho nõ meno mirauegliofo dl primo. Impo
che egli hauea le q̃tro uolubile rote tutte,& gli radii,& il meditullo deſu
sco achate,di cãdide uéule uagamẽte uaricato. Ne tale certamẽte gestoe re
Pyrrho cũ le noue Muse & Apolline í medio pulsãte dalla natura ípsso.

   Laxide & la forma del dicto q̃le el primo, ma le tabelle erão di cyaneo
Saphyro orientale,atomato de scintillule doro , alla magica gratissimo,
& longo acceptissimo a cupidine nella sinistra mano .

   Nella tabella dextra mirai exscalpto una insigne Matróa che
dui oui hauea parturito,in uno cubile regio colloca
ta,di uno mirabile palluccio,Cum obstetrice stu
pefacte, & multe altre matrone & astante
NympheDegli quali usciua de
uno una flammula, & delal-
tro ouo due spectatissi
me stelle.
**
*

Sopra de questo superbo & Triumphale uectabulo, uidi uno bian‐
chissimo Cycno, negli amorosi amplexi duna inclyta Nympha filiola
de Theseo, dincredibile bellecia formata, & cum el diuino rostro obscu‐
lantise, demisse le ale, tegeua le parte denudate della igenua Hera, Et cū
diuini & uoluptici oblectamenti istauano delectabilmente iucundissi‐
mi ambi connexi, Et el diuino Olore tra le delicate & niuee coxe collo‐
cato. Laquale commodamente sedeua sopra dui Puluini di panno do‐
ro, exquisitamente di mollicula lanugine tomentati, cum tutti gli sum‐
ptuosi & ornanti correlarii opportuni. Et ella induta de uesta Nympha
le subtile, de serico bianchissimo cum trama doro texto præluccente
Agli loci competenti elegante ornato de petre pretiose.
      Sencia defecto de qualunque cosa che ad incremen‐
to di dilecto uenustamente concorre. Summa
mente agli intuenti conspicuo & dele
ctabile. Cum tutte le parte che
al primo fue descripto
di laude & plau
so.
❋

EL TERTIO cæleste triumpho seguiua cum quatro uertibile rote
di Chrysolitho æthiopico scintule doro flammigiante, Traiecta per el‐
quale la seta del Asello gli maligni dæmonii fuga, Alla leua mano gra‐
to, cum tutto quello chò di sopra di rote e dicto. Daposcia le assule sue in
ambito per el modo compacte sopra narrato, erano di uirente Helitro‐
pia Cyprico, cum potere negli lumi cælesti, el suo gestáte cœla, & il diui‐
nare dona, di sanguinee guttule punctulato.
      Offeriua tale historiato insculpto la tabella dextra. Vno homo di re‐
gia maiestate isigne, Oraua in uno sacro templo el diuo simulacro, quel
lo che della formosissima fiola deueua seguire. Sentendo el patre la eie‐
ctione sua per ella del regno. Et ne per alcuno fusse pregna, Fece
una munita structura di una excelsa torre, Et in quella cum
soléne custodia la fece inclaustrare. Nella qua‐
le ella cessabonda assedédo, cum ex‐
cessiuo solatio, nel uirgi
neo sino gutte do
ro stillare
uede
ua.
❋

TRIVMPHVS

Dionysia petra,cũ macule í ni
gritudine rubéte, el Nume trita

oléte. Il tertio de optía Medea, í fusco aureo colore diffemiato,cũ el Ne
ctareo fapore.Lo ultío đ ptiofa Nebride,al Nume dicata,Nel nigro exi
mio colore bianco & uiride immixtamente coeunte. Nella cóchula de
gli ꝗli,una Pyramidale flámula, di foco fextiguibile continua ardeua.
Per laꝗle luculétia le eximie opature & expſſi, p lo reflexo del flámicu
láte lũe,p li fulguráti lapilli ꝑtiofiſſimi pfeuerátemte fpectare nó ualeua.
Circa dlꝗle diuino triúpho, cũ multa & foléne fupftitióe & maxía pó
pa & religióe Infinite Nymphe Mænade cũ li foluti & fparfi capilli.Al
cũe nude cũ amiculi Nymphei dagli humeri defluéti, & tale Nebride,
cioe ídute depelliceo uariato đ colore di damule,fenza laltro fexo, Cym
baliſtrie, & Tibiciarie, faceuão le facre Orgie, cũ clamori uociferádo , &
thyaſi,ꝗle negli Trieterici, cũ thyrfi di fróde di cóifere arbore, & cũ fron
de uitine iſtrophiate,fopra el nudo cíſte & coróate faltatorie,pcuréte feꝗ
ua ímediate el triúpho fíléo feniculo lo afello eꝗtáte, Pofcia retro a ꝗſto
eꝗtáte ímediate uno Hirco horricome de facrifica pópa ornata feſtiua
méte códuceuáo. Et una đ ꝗſto fectaria, uno uiminaceo Váno geſtaua,
cũ defordíato rifo,& furiali geſti,cũ ꝗſto ueterrimo & fcó rito, ꝗſto ꝗrto
triúpho adoriaméte extolleuano, Et có uenerádo difcorfo Euibache ad
alta uoce,cófufaméte exclamádo gli Mimalloni.Satyri.Bacche.Lene.
Thyade.Naiade.Tityri.nymphe,celebrabondi fequiuano.

LA MVLTITVDINE DEGLI AMANTI GIOVENI, ET DILLE DIVE AMOROSE PVELLE LA NYMPHA APOLI PHILO FACVNDAMENTE DECHIARA, CHI FVRO. NO ET COMEDAGLI DII AMATE. ET GLI CHORI DE GLI DIVI VATICANTANTI VIDE.

LCVNOMAI DIT ANTO INDEFESSO E LO
quio aptamente fe accommodarebbe,che gli diuini ar
chani difertando copiofo & pienamente poteſſe euade
re & ufcire.Et expreſſamente narrare,& cum quanto di
ua pompa,indeſinenti Triumphi,perenne gloria, feſti
ua lætitia,& fœlice tripudio,circa a queſte quatro iuiſi
tate feiuge de memorando fpectamine cum parole fufficientemente ex
primere ualeſſe. Oltra gli inclyti adolefcentuli & ſtipante agmine di ínu
mere & periucunde Nymphe,piu che la tenerecia degli anni fui elle pru
dente & graue & aſtutule cum gli acceptiſſimi amanti de pubefcente
& depile gene. Ad alcuni la primula lanugine fplendefcéte le male in
ferpiua delitiofe alacremente feſtigiauano . Molte hauendo le facole fue
accenfe & ardente . Alcune uidi Paſtophore. . Altre cum drite haſte
adornate de prifche fpolie. Et tali di uarii Trophæi optimaméte ordinate

The English version of 1592 was published under the title *The Strife of Love in a Dreame* at the press of Simon Waterson in London, dedicated to Sir Philip Sydney, and probably translated by Sir Robert Dallington.[57] While the text is a fine example of the exquisitely crafted and charming prose of the Elizabethan period, it represents only about a third of the original and contains many errors of translation, beginning with the first sentence.[58] The illustrations, also subject to many eliminations, are by a mediocre hand (fig. 10). Apparently the book went almost unnoticed, for it was reprinted only once, in the same year, nor has its influence been mentioned in any scholarly publication.

In spite of these inauspicious beginnings, the book went on to become a spectacular success. Indeed, it turned into something of a cult book in sixteenth-century Italy and was reedited by Aldus's sons in 1545. But it is in France that the book had its greatest success. There its publication probably shaped to a great extent the sensibility of the arts of the French Renaissance under the reign of Francis I (1515–1547). His mother, Louise de Savoie, had

10. ILLUSTRATION FROM THE ENGLISH EDITION (*THE STRIFE OF LOVE IN A DREAME* [1592; RPT. NEW YORK, 1976]).

given him a manuscript version of the text, made around 1510, as a wedding present, and it is known that he owned a copy of the original.[59] *Le songe de Poliphile* was published at the press of Jacques Kerver in Paris in 1546; it was reprinted twice in folio editions, in 1554 and 1561, and in quarto in 1600. The translation is usually attributed to Jean Martin, whom Joachim du Bellay unhesitatingly called the equal of Ronsard[60] and who also translated into French the anonymous *Peregrino,* the *Horoappollo,* Ariosto's *Orlando furioso,* Cardinal Bembo's *Azolani,* and Jacopo Sannazaro's *Arcadia.* However, it is also possible that he only amended and improved a translation actually done by Monsieur de Lenoncourt. Many editions followed Kerver's, making the book more popular in France than in its native Italy.[61]

The engravings of the French edition in 1546, adaptations of the edition of Aldus, also anonymous, are generally attributed to Jean Cousin (engraver and writer, 1490–1561) or to Jean Goujon (sculptor and architect, ca. 1510-ca.1569)[62] and are also held to be the apogee

11. Same image in Italian and French editions (*Le songe de Poliphile* [1546; rpt. Paris, 1963]).

of French book illustration. They are without doubt technically superior to the originals: the lines are more supple in the outlines, faces, and clothes; the bodies are less stocky and chunky, more elongated and elegant; and there is more emphasis on corporeality thanks to the increased use of hatching (fig. 11). The representation of space reveals a complete mastery of perspective, which the Italian does not (fig. 12). In fact, the French adds twelve entirely new perspectival images of buildings and gardens that were presumably beyond the reach of the inferior Italian technician (fig. 13).[63] Finally, the more rationalist Parisian edition contains two geometrical representations, one of a garden and the other a complex breakdown of a triumphal arch in terms of its proportional system (figs. 14, 15), described in the text, which the Venetian forgoes. Nevertheless, the French edition can only be considered an incremental improvement to the Italian, and the original is universally preferred for its immense visual culture and ingenuity, as well as for the inventiveness of its design principles.

12. ELONGATED FRENCH BODIES.

ΠΑΝΤΩΝ ΤΟΚΑΔΙ

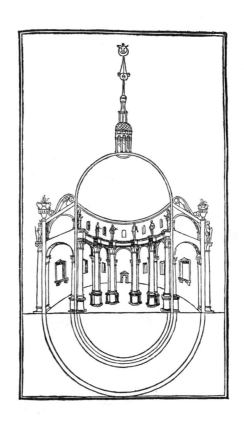

13. PERSPECTIVE IN THE ITALIAN AND FRENCH EDITIONS.

However impressive the formal qualities of the *Hypnerotomachia,* they have not lessened the admiration of its scholarly attributes, which equal those of any Aldine work. There is a long tradition of looking at it as a learned tract, frequently lauded as a prodigious display of classical architectural erudition. As early as the seventeenth century, François Blondel (1618–1686), the head of the Académie royale d'architecture under Louis XIV, referred to it as one of the two most useful amateur books for the study of architecture.[64] Similarly, André Félibien (French architect and author, 1619–1695), in his *Dissertation touchant l'architecture antique et l'architecture gothique* (1699), compared it to Vitruvius's *Ten Books,* claiming that although Vitruvius supplied the mechanics of architecture, the *Hypnerotomachia* had revived the spirit of antiquity; and since its descriptions were all based on ancient buildings, they could be used with as much confidence as the actual works of the Greeks and the Romans.[65] In the eighteenth century, Tommaso Temanza, a Venetian engineer and author of a biographical study of famous architects, and Francesco Milizia, one of the most influential of the early European functionalists in architecture, ranked the author of the book among the greatest architects of all time (although later, in his *Memorie degli architetti antichi e moderni,* Milizia passed from extreme admiration to outraged contempt).[66] Popelin found in it the same level of learning as in the first generation of humanist scholars. In this century, Julius Schlosser's monumental synthetic work on the artistic literature of the Renaissance placed the *Hypnerotomachia* within the great tradition of architectural treatises.[67]

Indeed, looked at as providing a precedent knowledge base, it is the most systematic and richest work of the Renaissance. To begin with, the *Hypnerotomachia* demonstrates total mastery of all the specialized technical and classical Vitruvian terminology. As we have seen, from the very first pages of the book the reader is treated to an exhaustive enumeration of the building types constructed in antiquity. Furthermore, within three pages, the reader is confronted with an onslaught of the terms that Vitruvius used to describe the different parts of classical architcture: highly specialized terms such as *abacus, anteride, anta, aerostyle, cariatida, cauliculo, cimatio, denticulo, echino, elcie, enthesis, epistylo, eustylo, hypaetrio, hypothrachelia, mutulo, paegma, picnostylo, plinthide, plinto, pulvinato, scalmo, scotia, sima, terebratione, thoro, troclea,* and *zophoro.*[68] Another indication is the book's practice of referring each and every building to its classical precedent. The description of the temple crowned by the pyramid ends with the evocation of the Mausoleum of Halicarnassus; the obelisk leads to the obelisks of the Vatican, of Alexandria, and of Babylon; the description of a labyrinth inside the peripteral temple ends with the Lemnian labyrinth, which had 150 columns and whose architects were Zmilis, Rhoecus, and Theodorus, all natives of Lemnos; the paving of a hall is compared with the mosaic floor or *lithostrote* of Palestrina; the fictive amphitheater leads to the amphitheater of Ephesus, the Coliseum in Rome, and the amphitheater of Verona; the account of the temple of Venus ends with the Pantheon; and a palace is compared to the Gordian villa on the Via Palestrina because of its innumerable columns.[69] In fact, even the work's mistakes reflect the

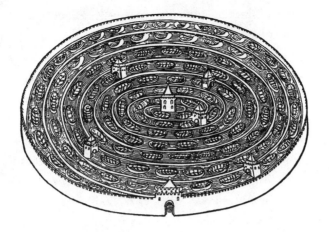

14.   Garden as aquatic labyrinth, added to the French edition.

15.   Proportions of the triumphal arch, added to the French edition.

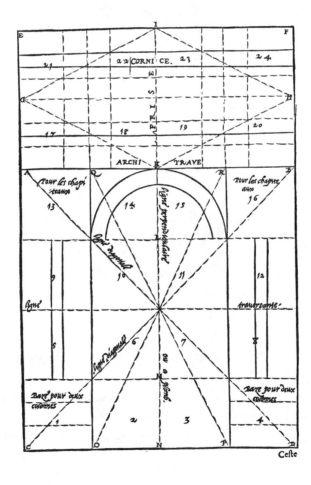

most advanced architectural knowledge of the day. For example, it claims that the amphitheater has two vases at the entrance like "the temple of Jupiter in Athens." According to Popelin, who relies on Pausanias, the correct allusion is to the temple of Zeus at Olympia.[70]

What learned references the book does not itself provide have become the object of intense and painstaking research. Many scholars have focused particularly on the antique philological sources of its great architectural erudition. Besides Vitruvius, these authors include Pliny, Herodotus, Diodorus Siculus, Pausanias, and Pomponio Mela.[71] Pliny is the most often quoted, with five hundred passages attributable to him. Thus Huelsen claims that the description of the Mausoleum of Artemisia in Pliny's *Natural History* was the model for the pyramid of the *Hypnerotomachia,* while Pozzi finds a partial model in Pliny's description of the Mausoleum of Halicarnassus.[72] Pozzi has traced the labyrinth under the same pyramid back to the labyrinth of Porsenna, as also described by Pliny, and Popelin derives the strange twirling nymph on the top of the obelisk from the figure of the rotating triton on the top of the Tower of Andronicus Cirrhestes in Athens, as described in Vitruvius.[73] Emanuela Kretsulesco-Quaranta, an Italian scholar specializing in the *Hypnerotomachia Poliphili,* claims that the hieroglyphs inside the base of the pyramid can be traced to the hieroglyphs in the *Horoappollo,* which appeared in manuscript form in Rome in 1419 (later translated into Latin by Lorenzo Valla); Pozzi suggests that the Medusa on the front of the pyramid might be inspired by Pausanias's mention of a Medusa's head that guards the Acropolis of Athens.[74] Such implicit references reveal a degree of architectural erudition quite stupendous for the time.

Renaissance authors, too, may have served as sources for the architecture of the *Hypnerotomachia.* Pozzi sees the obelisk on the top of the pyramid as deriving from a passage from Flavio Biondo's description of the Mausoleum of Augustus, because it is surmounted by two obelisks. Pozzi also believes that Biondo's description of the same mausoleum as "an immense building, closely nestled between mountains," underlies the conception of the pyramid in the *Hypnerotomachia,* which similarly nestles between mountains.[75] The *Hypnerotomachia*'s love of ruins can of course be interpreted as the echo of the topos earlier found in Master Gregorius's *De mirabilibus urbis Romae* (twelfth century) and in Fazio degli Uberti's *Dittamondo* (composed between 1318 and 1360), which give free vent to an unlimited admiration for the remnants of the antique city;[76] in Dante's *Convivio* (late thirteenth century), where he decries the current irreverence for the ruins of Rome; in Petrarch's many *Lettere* in which he insists on the superiority of the ancient city over the contemporary one; in Biondo's invectives of the early fifteenth century against time ravaging the antique city of Rome;[77] and in Poggio Bracciolini's description of the ruins of Rome (1430) and Manuel Chrysolaras's *Comparison of Old and New Rome* (1411).[78] The aquatic labyrinth, with its waterways instead of footpaths, has been connected with Filarete's labyrinth of Sforzinda (described in his *Trattato di Architettura,* composed between 1451 and 1464).[79] Finally, the two colossi mentioned in the book have their roots, again, in Flavio Biondo: in *Roma instaurata* (the first guide to Rome that aimed at archaeological exactitude, composed in 1446), he describes "two colossal statues . . . which lay on the ground, with what remained of their body, the chest . . . the head and parts of the arms." Pozzi has argued that the anatomy of the colossi might instead be related to John Ketham's *Fasciculus medicinae* (published in Venice in 1493); Maurizio Calvesi, a scholar of the Italian Renaissance, makes the speculative suggestion that it answers Poggio Bracciolini's text—which compared Rome to a gigantic cadaver, killed off by misfortune and dug out on all sides ("prostata jacet instar gigantei cadaveris corrupti, atque undique exesi")—substituting the cured state for the pathological and suggesting ancient wisdom as the remedy.[80]

The one great contemporary philological influence that scholars have detected on the *trattato* in the *Hypnerotomachia,* however, was the most erudite of all the humanists, the figure most responsible for systematizing and canonizing the architectural knowledge base that would shape architectural thinking for the next five hundred years: Leon Battista Alberti. Alberti felt that one of the great problems of his own treatise on *De re aedificatoria* (completed in 1450) was to establish a clear terminology that would substitute Latin neologisms for words of Greek origin. Thus "entasi" becomes *venter,* "massima entasi" becomes *ventris diametrum,* "plinto" becomes *latastrum,* "scozia" becomes *obiculus,* and the various moldings are described as *fasceola, gradus, rudens,* and so on.[81] In addition, Alberti invented other terminology, from *arula* to *torque,* all of which are to be found in the *Hypnerotomachia.* There they intermingle with the Vitruvian terms, often on the same page, as is the case in *De re aedificatoria.*

A meticulous analysis of the *Hypnerotomachia* has found that it employs the same terminology as Alberti, gives to buildings the same measurements and proportions as Alberti, and uses the same antique sources as Alberti. Many passages repeat Alberti's words.[82] For example, "Ergo *rimari omnia, considerare, metiri,* lineamentis picturae colligere nusquam intermettebam" ("I never stopped exploring, considering, and measuring eveything and comparing the information through line drawings"; VI.1, p. 155) reappears in the *Hypnerotomachia* when a nymph, Logistica, informs the hero that "Poliphile, te in questa parte commando, perche avido sei di tanta disquisitione, imperoche *omni cosa rimare, considerare et metire* laudabile se presta" (h7).[83] Pozzi and Casella have found ninety-seven similar instances in which whole passages from *De re aedificatoria* are plagiarized! Even the complaints and opinions of the *Hypnerotomachia* are the same as Alberti's. "We said," Alberti writes, "we would do everything possible to express ourselves in correct, comprehensible Latin. But where the current terms are lacking, we are obliged to coin new ones." So too in the *Hypnerotomachia:* "It is obvious that in our times the vernacular, proper, and native terms of the art of building have disappeared along with the true men now dead and buried" (b4).[84] They quote from identical sources: from Pliny about the Colossus, from Philostratus's *Life of Appolonius of Tyana* about the royal basilica of Babylonia, from Eusebius of Cesarea about the temple of Jerusalem.

The *Hypnerotomachia*'s description of the palazzo of Queen Eleutherillida, which the narrator compares to "the Gordian structure on the road to Praeneste, of which two hundred columns were divided into an equal number of Numidian, Claudian, Simidian, and Tistean" (f3), repeats a passage from the *De re aedificatoria*. Here Alberti mentions that "the Gordian family, for example, built a house on the road to Praeneste with two hundred columns, all of the same size and style, of which, as ———— recalls, fifty were of Numidian marble, fifty of Claudian, fifty of Simidian, and fifty of Tistean" (IX.1, p. 292).[85] Even their misquotations are the same: for Vitruvius an architect must know music; for Alberti and the *Hypnerotomachia,* the work of the architect is similar to a musical composition.[86]

More startlingly, the *Hypnerotomachia* makes the same mistakes Alberti does. Alberti writes "Sannitico" instead of "Psammetico," the Egyptian architect mentioned by Herodotus, and so does the *Hypnerotomachia*. Alberti uses "Hippari" instead of "Hypanis" and so does the *Hypnerotomachia*.[87] Indeed, those Latinisms are found only in these two books.

So great is the mark of Albertian learning in the book that Popelin assumes that Alberti could have been the author's teacher and his guide to the Roman antiquities; at the least, he believes the author must have read *De re aedificatoria*. Calvesi goes so far as to claim that all the architectural culture of the book derives from Alberti's writings.[88] Emanuela Kretsulesco-Quaranta speculates that Francesco Colonna must have based the *Hypnerotomachia* on an initial idea of Alberti's that he developed into the book with the help of the classicists Domizio Calderini and Gaspare da Verona after Alberti's death.[89] Not everyone was equally impressed with the presence of Alberti in the text, however; one critic argued that because of the great learning in the *Hypnerotomachia,* only one person could have composed it: the polymath Felice Feliciano.[90]

Scholarly studies on the book's knowledge have also focused on the archaeological basis of its descriptions. Most concentrate on the importance of the antique remains in the historical center of Rome, lying between the Orti Salustiani and the Via Appia and between the Circus Maximus and the Roman Forum, as precedents on which the *Hypnerotomachia*'s buildings are based.[91] Giehlow observes that the equestrian statue on Poliphilo's way to the pyramid is inspired by the one of Marcus Aurelius located near the Lateran.[92] He also connects the colossus in the book to the actual colossus whose head and hand still lay near the Colosseum in the mid-fifteenth century.[93] Three scholars agree that the antique Roman frieze at the church of S. Lorenzo fuori le Mura, portraying as it does a *buchranium* or ox skull, an open chest, an amphora, a helm, a plate, and a dolphin twisted around an anchor, was an important source for the hieroglyphics on the sculpted pediment that serves as a base for the sculpture of the elephant.[94] Huelsen traces back a statue of Venus described in the book to the relief on a sarcophagus that was in the church of S. Maria di Monterone in Rome in 1500; the medallion on the throne of the queen, bearing the emblem of a haloed youth gazing upon an eagle with outstretched wings, to a bas-relief on an altar originating from Palmyra called "Sol Sanctissimus," now conserved in the Museo Capitolino in Rome. In addition, he links the three graces adorning the wellhead in the temple of Venus to a group of three graces in the Casa Colonna in Rome that were later transferred to the house of Piccolomini, the future Pope Pius II.[95] Giehlow finds resemblances in one of the obelisks in the book, surmounted by a sphere, with the Vatican Obelisk, which was believed in the Renaissance to contain the ashes of Caesar in the ball at the top and to be his tomb.[96] As for the reclining nymph adorning the baths in the *Hypnerotomachia,* she can be traced to the notorious sculpture that Pico della Mirandola was shocked to find in Bramante's garden design for Julius II in the Cortile del Belvedere. It had been in the collection of the renowned Roman collector Girolamo Maffei at the end of the fifteenth century and was acquired by Pope Julius II around 1502.[97]

On a larger scale, Donati identifies the model of the round temple of Venus in the book as the Mausoleum of Bacchus, renamed Santa Costanza in the Christian period, because it is a rotonda made up of concentric rings of columns carrying a series of arches.[98] The round church of S. Stefano is a more obvious potential source for the same fictional building. Its restoration under Nicholas V is usually attributed to Alberti, who wrote about the building in Book VII of his *De re aedificatoria* as the "round basilica." The source for the octagonal baths, according to Calvesi, is "la rotonda" of Albano near Rome, with its centered octagonal plan capped with a cupola, surrounded by eight niches and laid with a mosaic floor with an aquatic theme of tritons and marine animals.[99] Again, Rome offered a number of hippodromes that might have served as prototypes for the one mentioned in the *Hypnerotomachia,* notably the hippodrome/garden located on the Palatine Hill in ancient times. Kretsulesco-Quaranta claims that the name "Polyandrion" given to one of the temples in the book is borrowed from an antique temple of the same name located on the Elysian Way.[100]

Maurizio Calvesi has devoted a great deal of his book on the *Hypnerotomachia* to the thesis that the antique site of Praeneste, which was called Palestrina in the Renaissance, the seat of the Colonna dynasty just southeast of Rome, is the basic inspiration for most of the buildings in the work. According to him, the pyramid is copied from the spectacular and gigantic site of the temple of Fortune there, which occupies the entire face of a mountain. The temple is framed by mountains, in particular the lower part of the sanctuary, which, inscribed inside the ramps, takes on a triangular appearance. He believes that the view from the palm grove onto the pyramid described at the beginning of the book is in reality the view of the ruins of Palestrina from the Via Appia at Velletri, both being planted with palm trees.[101] He also assimilates the round temple of Venus to the Rotonda of the Santuario Prenestino, which has a cycle with a well in the middle, and the cyborium.[102] The mosaics in the two grottoes at Palestrina, too, are analyzed. In the eastern hall is a great landscape of the Nile valley (now in the Museum of Palestrina) and in the western grotto delightful marine motifs still remain, which Calvesi thinks might have influenced the mosaic wall and ceiling inside

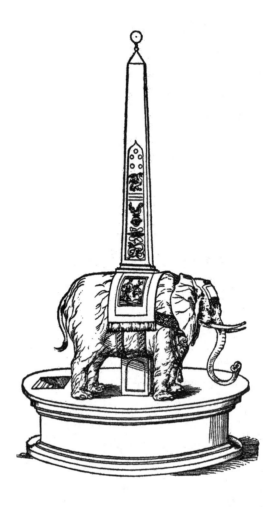

16. THE ELEPHANT (FRENCH EDITION).

the peripteral temple at the base of the pyramid. Furthermore, he claims the Polyandrion is an allegorical representation of the Santuario Prenestino.[103] And Kretsulesco-Quaranta points to a final connection: there is a Medusa's mask on the lip of an ancient well in the upper sanctuary of Palestrina in which she detects the possible inspiration for the Medusa's head on the face of the pyramid.[104]

Hadrian's Villa at Tivoli is another certain source for the *Hypnerotomachia*. The buildings of the *Hypnerotomachia*, like those at Tivoli, are in a garden setting. Just as Hadrian had the idea of reproducing the buildings of antiquity that he had seen on his conquests, so the author does in the dream setting of the *Hypnerotomachia*. The architectural pieces, as have been shown, are fragments taken from the Palatine Hill, Palestrina, and various other symbolic monuments of Rome and the antique world.

Although Rome and its immediate environs are the major archaeological sources for the buildings of the *Hypnerotomachia,* there are signs of an expertise in the antique Roman and Etruscan sites on the Italian peninsula. Giehlow argues that part of the book's knowledge of hieroglyphs rests on a trip to Ravenna.[105] In addition, the monolithic temple of Venus could be seen as deriving from the church of Santa Maria della Rotonda in Ravenna, the ancient tomb of Theodoric, which has a monolithic dome thirty-four feet wide. Pozzi connects the octagonal *thermae* to the drawing by Feliciano-Marcanova of the Baths of Diocletian.[106] Popelin and Heckscher have traced the elephant back to a similar sculpture of a huge, late antique, possibly Roman elephant, carved out of black lava with white marble tusks and carrying an octagonal Egyptian obelisk, which stands as part of a fountain in the Piazza del Duomo in Catania in Sicily (fig. 16).[107] However, as Heckscher points out, although the elephant is composed of antique pieces, it was not assembled in its present form until the eighteenth century, by the architect Giovanni Battista Vaccarini.[108]

Finally there are a few architectural descriptions of the Greek and Hellenistic architecture of Asia Minor and Greece; first noted by Jacob Burckhardt, these lead him to infer that the author had made voyages to the Orient.[109] Albert Ilg noted that the author of the book possessed an archaeological erudition worthy of Ciriaco d'Ancona, the Italian merchant who traveled extensively in Greece and Asia Minor and whose travel notebooks full of drawings and descriptions of antique sites make him the founder of modern archaeology.[110] Charles Mitchell has in fact observed a resemblance between the Polyandrion and its surrounding ruins in the *Hypnerotomachia* and drawings from a manuscript of Ciriaco d'Ancona, owned by Felice Feliciano, that depicts the Polyandrion at Delos drawn on site. This suggests that the author knew of Ciriaco's travel notebooks, and perhaps knew their owner, Feliciano.[111] The Medusa's head, as Mitchell has argued, could have been influenced by the Medusa's head on the temple of the Hadrian at Cizicus, documented by Ciriaco d'Ancona. Similarly, the golden grapevines on the roof of the temple of Venus could also come from Ciriaco's drawing of the temple of Cizicus, whose portico with five columns was decorated with grapevines.[112] The gigantomachia on the plinth of the pyramid can be seen as deriving from the frieze of the Parthenon describing the victory of the Greeks over the Persians, a monument that very few Italian humanists besides Ciriaco would have known first-hand. The same is true of the Mausoleum of Halicarnassus, which is described in the *Hypnerotomachia.*

Far from being limited to architecture, the astounding level of erudition in the *Hypnerotomachia* extends to other fields. No person, no place, no thing is presented without reference to classical mythology, classical geography, classical art. The story offers its own interpretation on every page by referring to vast amount of scholarly detail. The range of topics is exhaustive: music, musical instruments, *ars topiaria,* statuary, fountains, mosaics, intaglio and intarsio techniques, woven fabrics and cloth, geometry, the effects of distance on the perception of color, epitaphs, furniture, paintings, embroidery, herms, friezes, vases, tripods, trophies, candelabras, lapidary, perfume, food, wine, opera, choreography, ritual processions, and botany.

Many sources have been identified. For botany, the book relies on Theophrastus, Pliny the Elder, and Niccolò Boccadinello;[113] for astrology, alchemy, mineralogy, and hieroglyphics, on Pliny the Elder; for geography, on Aristotle and Ptolemy; and for herbal and medicinal matters, on Dioscurides. The terms related to topiarium and oluscarium derive from Pliny and Cicero; the knowledge of antique rituals from Varro, Paulinus Nolanus, and Maurus Servius Honoratus; and mythology rests on Nonnus, Virgil, and Ovid.[114] The book's use of mystical, Orphic, and Neoplatonic writings has been of special interest to scholars, who have found its sources to be Plato's *Timaeus,* Macrobius's *Saturnalia,* Servius's *In Aeneidem,* and Plutarch's *Moralia.*[115]

The *Hypnerotomachia,* in turn, had a profound influence on later artistic production. The artists whose works reveal their debt to the book include Dürer, Titian, Bernini, and Poussin.[116] We know that in the seventeenth century Fabio Chigi, Pope Alexander VII, owned the 1499 edition of the *Hypnerotomachia;* his copy is still among the books of the Chigiana in Rome and is described as "heavily annotated."[117] He was the patron of Bernini, and the book's elephant with obelisk influenced Bernini's elephant carrying an obelisk on the Piazza della Minerva in Rome.[118] The gigantomachia in the Plazzo del Tè in Mantua is based on the one described in the *Hypnerotomachia;* and, as Eugenio Battisti pointed out, many of the sculptures in Sacro Bosco at Bomarzo are directly copied from it.[119] The female figures in Giorgione's *Tempesta* recall one of the woodcuts of the *Poliphilo.* Other iconographic links have been found: Battisti sees a link between the Venus of Dresden and a nymph described in the *Hypnerotomachia.*[120] Its influence has even been tracked down in the representation of a pergola in an early-seventeenth-century Flemish tapestry.[121] Pinturicchio painted a fresco in the Libreria Piccolomini for Pope Pius II of a sleeping nymph, also thought to have been derived from the *Hypnerotomachia.*[122]

Of course, the *Hypnerotomachia* had an impact on architecture. Ernst Gombrich has suggested that it played a role in Bramante's design for the Cortile del Belvedere (begun in 1505). He relates Vasari's comment that Bramante was inspired to decorate the Cortile del Belvedere with hieroglyphs with the face of Julius Caesar and two arches—which was prevented at the insistence of the pope himself, for fear of appearing arrogant—by the hieroglyph in the *Hypnerotomachia* that reads "Divo Iulio Caesari semper Augusto." Gombrich also sees the influence of the *Hypnerotomachia* on Bramante's much more important project of turning the axis of St. Peter's to run south to north rather than west to east in order to have the church face the famous obelisk of the Vatican. Finally Gombrich notes that the garden Bramante designed just beyond the Cortile not only introduced a new mode of Roman gardening but also involved the revival of the ancient Roman nymphaeum as a feature of the garden, something he traced to the *Hypnerotomachia.* Indeed, among the sculptures in the garden beyond the Belvedere were a Cupid and Venus group and a nude nymph sleeping, the famous Vatican Ariadne, incorporated by Bramante into a fountain that so scandalized Gianfrancesco Pico della Mirandola when he came across it in the papal gardens because of its naked breasts—which figure in the book.[123] But in addition, if Gombrich is correct and Bramante was indeed influenced by the book, then its influence might have shaped one of the fundamental concepts underlying the section of the Cortile's design as a monumental, stepped exedra, first described by James Ackerman.[124] Indeed, this section could have been inspired, at least in addition to the garden hippodrome on the Palatine Hill that Ackerman sees as a source, by the amphitheater on the island of Cythera described in the *Hypnerotomachia* (y3–y7).

Another architect familiar with the *Hypnerotomachia* was Baldassare Peruzzi (1481–1536), who had numerous drawings in his *taccuino* (notebook) based on the woodcuts of the book.[125] Rudolf Wittkower claimed that the work's octagonal nymphaeum left a trace on the Venetian baroque architect Baldassare Longhena's octagonal S. Maria della Salute (begun in 1631).[126] Tommaso Temanza in the eighteenth century claimed he had based his design for S. Maria Maddalena in Venice on the temple of Venus in the book.[127] The French architectural historian Louis Hautecoeur has observed the book's impact on the first phase of the French Renaissance, and Anthony Blunt has established the important debt that seventeenth-century French architecture owes to it.[128] As late as the eighteenth century, Etienne-Louis Boullée may have drawn inspiration for the immense spherical chamber of his Cenotaph for Newton, and Claude-Nicolas Ledoux for that of the Shelter for Rural Guards in his ideal city of Chaux, from the description of the spherical chamber in the *Hypnerotomachia*.[129]

The admiration among scholars for the quantity of the learning in *Hypnerotomachia* is unanimous. As its prodigious display of knowledge has been universally acknowledged, the book has been characterized as an "encyclopedia of all artistic, archaeological and technological knowledge of the fifteenth century"; an "encyclopedia of the knowledge held at that time by a small group of people schooled in 'omnis scibili et quibusdam aliis' (all that could be known and more)"; and as "the most advanced voice of humanism at its most fanatic stage."[130] *Hypnerotomachia Poliphili:* An extraordinary display of architectural knowledge. A work of remarkable visual quality. A conventional *romanzo*. So the book has been read over the past five hundred years. Do these statements sum up what is interesting about it? Only partly, as we shall see

.

2

*

THE UNREAD *HYPNEROTOMACHIA*, OR DESIGN AS DREAMWORK AND THOUGHT EXPERIMENT

A LTHOUGH THE *HYPNEROTOMACHIA* DOES EXHIBIT A PROFOUND knowledge of all things antique, it is far from being a prosaic catalogue of facts. However staggering its degree of learning, the book is hardly weighed down by repetition of facts and obedience to authority. On the contrary, scholarship is used as a spring-board for leaps of the imagination. If the author does display a peerless mastery of antique precedents, it is all the better to take liberties with them.[1] The *Hypnerotomachia* is in line with antique tradition, but only up to a point. Moving beyond the simple knowledge base of precedents of antiquity, the book offers a new system of rules for designing with precedents. It provides not just a depository of architectural memories but a method for reusing memories creatively—a genetic method, or, to take some poetic license, an "algorithm."

The *Hypnerotomachia* unfolds in a dream world; that is, a world where new associations are born. The book is filled with extraordinary dream props. They are strange in relation to the real world and to the world of antiquity, but not in the hypnotic, oneiric world of the *Hypnerotomachia*. After all, the first part of the book's title, *hypnos,* means "sleep," and the kind of recombinant mixing that characterizes dreams is typical of the *Hypnerotomachia* at every level of composition. Like what Freud called "dream structures," these design objects tend to follow a logic of their own, "their own syntax." As products of the "dream-work," they are shaped by a combinatorial mathematics that negates the contradictions between elements that by definition are mutually exclusive in normal waking life; they are new, pre-viously unthinkable "composite structures" made up of elements that could not otherwise be brought together. In Freud's words, they "disregard 'No.'" Anything can be combined, in particular "contraries, especially elements which in our waking thoughts we should certainly have kept separate."[2] Dreams, of course, are privileged settings in which to carry out "thought experiments," to use a term of Thomas Kuhn's, offering a place within which mental leaps and wild thinking can take place.[3] Taking place in an imagined situation, dreams provide an environment that eliminates the condition of verisimilitude and thus permits the re-cognition of existing concepts.

According to Alexander Tzonis, this combinatorial logic is one of the ways archi-tectural creativity works. New design ideas are born not *ex nihilo* but out of the recombina-tion of precedents. By bringing together precedents in an unprecedented way, creative design uses memory and knowledge as a basis for innovatively combining elements.[4] What is inter-esting about the *Hypnerotomachia* is that here this mechanism is so dominant in its reiterations. Indeed, there is no structure that is not put together in this way. It almost seems that the author has isolated this genetic algorithm and put it to use in all his buildings. Moreover, it is as if he were conscious of this method and were using the book to theorize that creative design is precisely this process of rethinking and recategorizing precedent works.

Take the first recombinant architectural dream structure the reader encounters (fig. 17). It is a shocking aberration: part temple, part triumphal arch, part pyramid, part obelisk, part sphere, part labyrinth, part propylaeum, part cave, part mountain, and part some-

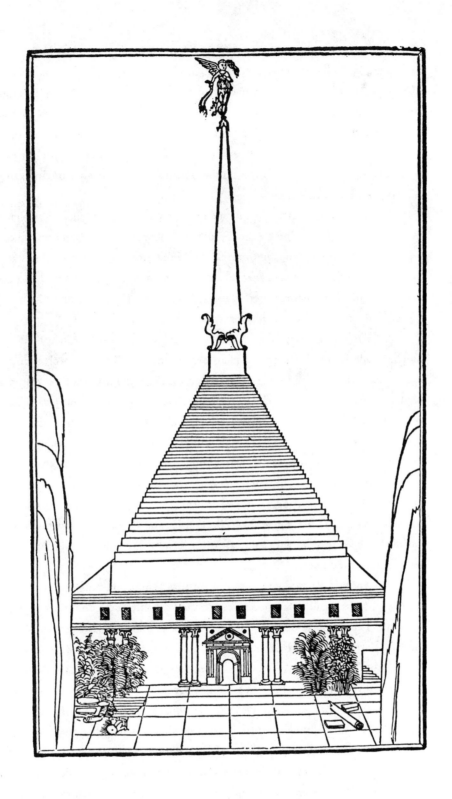

17. THE FIRST COMPOSITE BUILDING.

thing that could be a hippodrome. A baffled Poliphilo is at pains to identify the nature of the last building, which is in ruins. It could be, he conjectures, a palaestra, an *ambulatio* or *peridromos*, a *hypaethron*, a *xystus*, or a *euripus*. Not that it matters much. All are incongruous in this context: a palaestra, as we have seen, belongs to the gymnasium complex that was typical of Roman architecture, a *hypaethron* is a temple open to the sky and not roofed over, an *ambulatio* or *peridromos* is a colonnaded promenade, a *xystus* is a roofed colonnade for exercise in bad weather, and a *euripus* is a ditch around the arena of an amphitheater or circus to prevent wild animals from escaping.

Considered vertically, the building is an unlikely compilation of elements. On top of the temple is a plinth, and on the top of the plinth is a pyramid, and on top of the pyramid is an monolithic stone cube, and on the top of the monolithic stone cube is an obelisk, and on the top of the obelisk is a bronze statue of a nymph holding an inverted cornucopia. Poised on one leg with the other elevated in the arabesque, she pirouettes on a pivot with every shift of the wind, emitting a deafening shriek with every turn.

Down on the ground, things are no less out of the ordinary. The center of the temple facade is connected to the triumphal arch. The triumphal arch is connected to the unidentifiable building. Moving backward now, inside the ground level of the building, instead of forward in front of it, the triumphal arch serves, just as inappropriately, as the entrance to a narrow domed chamber. This chamber, in turn, leads to the labyrinth, and the labyrinth leads to the propylaeum. This is highly unusual for a number of reasons. First, rather than being used as the gate to a precinct containing many temples, as is customary, the propylaeum is connected to one single building element. Second, this element is not a temple but a labyrinth. Third, rather than being placed in front of a building in the manner of a gate, the propylaeum is placed in the rear, like a back door. Fourth, rather than being placed at a height (usually at the top of an acropolis, as in the case of the Acropolis of Athens), it is located under a huge mountain.

Inside, the building is also a surprise. Upon entering the pyramid through the snarling lips of a gigantic Medusa's head located directly above the triumphal arch, Poliphilo finds that it has been hollowed out to contain a perfectly spherical chamber. This is one of the most daring floutings of an established architectural "no" in the book, not only because the chamber is so immense—about one mile high—but beacuse of its utterly naked walls. This radical rejection of ornament is unique for the quattrocento. Moreover, the chamber is flooded with radiant light. With perfect, delusional dreamlike logic, the narrator explains that this is the result of slitlike light shafts, so thin they are invisible, cut into the flanks of the giant pyramid. He further specifies that so ingeniously calculated are the angles of these interstices that the lower part of the sphere is lit by light reflected from shafts placed at the top of the pyramid and, vice versa, the upper parts are lit by those at the lower part of the chamber. In fact, so perfectly located are the light shafts that no matter what the time of day, the luminosity is constant.

A typical tendency of dreamwork is to make things hypertrophic, and the *Hypne-rotomachia* is no exception. The building is dreamlike not only in its unexpected blending of familiar elements into a new whole but also in its enormous scale. The colonnade of the temple alone, which forms the base of the pyramid, is over two-thirds of a mile long and another two-thirds of a mile high. The gigantic pyramid, set atop a gigantic plinth—sculpted, incompatibly, with a gigantomachia on whose center is affixed a huge Medusa's head—is another two-thirds of a mile high; it is no less than six times the height of the great pyramid of Cheops at Giza.[5] The pyramid's freestanding, inclined, dry walls in turn support the obe-lisk, which is yet another two-thirds of a mile high. Having climbed the spiral staircase that rises up through the center of the immense spherical space inside the pyramid all the way to its summit, the hero exclaims, "My eyes could not make out the ground, so much did the objects that covered it seem erased by the distance" (a8-b3). Although all the narrator says about the height of the bronze statue above the obelisk is that it is "proportional" to the other elements in the building, she is big enough for him to be able to notice that her legs and breasts are bared by her billowing gown and that the back of her head is bald. Presumably this would make her extremely large herself. "This construction exceeds the immensity of the Egyptians," the author boasts understandably. "Be silent, works of Lemnos. Even the tomb of Mausoleus does not equal this building. Never before has such a building been seen or conceived." The complex is higher "by much" than "Mount Olympus, the Caucasus, and Mount Cylene" (a7v).

There do exist precedents in the "real" world of antiquity for each of the ex-tremely diverse pieces that make up the strange new hybrid. The triumphal arch with the single bay recalls the Arch of Titus; the pyramid, the pyramid of Cestius in Rome; the obelisk, the obelisk of the Vatican. There had been precedents for baths surmounted by a jingling *tintinnabulum* (tinkling or jingling bells), such as the baths of Hadrian, which were known to Renaissance scholars at the time the *Hypnerotomachia* was written.[6] There even exist prece-dents for the composition principle that brings such mutually exclusive architectural pieces together into one gigantic architectural whole. The Mausoleum in Halicarnassus, for ex-ample, is a pyramid resting on a peripteral temple, and the Domus Aurea in Rome is a com-mixture of different building types. In the world of fiction, Diodorus describes the tomb of Zarina, queen of the "Saces" and a woman of extraordinary courage and action. After her death, her grateful people erected a most magnificent tomb: a triangular pyramid with sides each measuring three-eighths of a mile long and one-eighth of a mile high. The top was surmounted by a colossal golden statue to whom honors equal to a hero were rendered.[7] Another classical author, Marcus Varro, describes the monument built by King Porsenna of Etruria close to the city of Clusium, in a place where he has left a square monument built of squared blocks of stone, each side being 300 feet long and 50 feet wide. Inside this square pedestal, there is a tangled, inextricable labyrinth which no one must enter without a ball of thread if he is to find his way out. On this square pedestal stand five pyramids, four at the

18.   THE BUILDING CONTAINING THE INDOOR SWIMMING POOL (FRENCH EDITION).

corners and one in the center, each of them being 75 feet broad at the base and 150 feet high. They taper in such a manner that on top of the whole group there rests a single bronze disk together with a conical cupola, from which hang bells fastened with chains: when these are set in motion by the wind, their sound carries to a great distance, as was formerly the case at Dodona. On this disk stand four more pyramids, each 100 feet high, and above these, on a single platform five more. The height of these last pyramids was a detail that Varro was ashamed to add to his account; but according to the Etruscan stories, it was equal to that of the whole work up to their level (about 600 feet high).[8] But heaped, packed, and interpenetrating as these buildings are, they form a new kind of disordered, chaotic architectural hybrid.

Another distinction dissolves in the *Hypnerotomachia:* that separating temples and baths, or thermae. Indeed, baths traditionaliy form a whole complex, involving at least three chambers that each have separate compartments: the *tepidarium,* a room heated with warm air; the *caldarium,* where the hot bath was taken in a tub; and the *frigidarium,* where the final cold bath was taken—not just one pool as is the case here (fig. 18). In addition, the pools were not octagonal like this one. One octagonal building that Alberti would have been familiar with was the Baptistery of S. Giovannni in Florence. The *Hypnerotomachia's* baths can be seen as a hypertrophic, desacralized version of the baptistery, constituting one of the book's

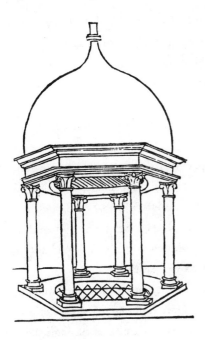 

19.   THE GROTTO IN THE CEILING OF THE "TRIBUNE."

most iconoclastic, and fetching, subversions of the architectural and institutional "no." The result is the first conception of what would eventually become the modern indoor heated swimming pool.

The building overturns yet another architectural "no." It is covered not by a normal roof but by the top of a jewel case blown out of proportion, again in a typical dreamlike manner. It is described as a lacy, frail, and intricate segmented vault formed by eight panels pierced "in a thousand places" with crystal laminae—unprecedented in antiquity and an imitation of openwork metal armature, a steel and glass structure constructed in order to create a maximum of light inside the building—hardly the standard covering for temple structures. The door of the building is similar to the roof, as is its effect upon the lighting conditions in the building. Made of a golden metal that is pierced, it casts light into the baths where all the walls are of a black marble so polished that they reflect like mirrors.

In a similar vein, the *Hypnerotomachia* combines a very small temple, referred to in the text as a tribune, with a grotto. Where is the grotto located? Following the purest kind of oneiric logic, in the ceiling. Although on a diminutive scale, especially compared to the pharaonic palace just described, the building holds its own among the book's other incongruous inventions (fig. 19).

Other structures are equally jarring in their combinatorics. Another highly unorthodox building represents the fusion of two round plan temples. It is made up of coupled twin *tholoi,* or circular plan temples. The two are joined at the vestibule, giving the single building the ground plan of a double circle, with two different centers. Both the temple and the sanctuary share the same *pronaos,* or entrance. The purely morphological innovation of the building is no less novel than the conception. We are very far here from traditional architectural forms in its ground plan.

Moreover, the small adjacent temple is transparent. Its walls are of a transparent stone that is called *phengite*—a stone found in the time of Nero in Cappadocia, according to Suetonius[9]—and its domed roof is of the same material. The effect is that "although the temple had no windows and its dome was unpierced, although its doors were solid gold, it never stopped being brightly illuminated" (o2): a building whose transparency would not be matched until nineteenth-century buildings such as Paxton's Crystal Palace.

In addition to being an odd combination of two round plan temples, the building, all too incongruously, is also part gigantic drain. The ten columns holding up the roof display a novel technical improvement: they are hollow, so that rainwater can pass through them directly into a cistern under the temple, thus preventing the exterior of the building from getting dirty, as the hero himself notes. These supporting columns are reinforced by pillars on either side, which are linked by arches. The walls are pierced with rectangular windows that take up almost the entire wall surface between the columns and are filled with a translucent stone sliced as thin as a blade. More arches link the inner ring of ten columns to an outer one of ten more; they serve as an ingenious system of flying buttresses that are strong enough to support the inner walls without blocking access to the light.

Perhaps the most appealing of the book's mental leaps is across the barrier that separates architecture and nature. Indeed, in the giant garden that provides the setting for all the buildings, there is almost total fusion between the two. Here architecture and nature form an integral, organic, inseparable whole. What is true on the level of the overall structure also holds for some particular buildings. For example, one composite is part citrus garden, part picturesque landscape, and part palazzo. Among the oneiric, improbable features of the citrus garden is its access through a cypress-lined path over half a mile long. Another is that it does not lie horizontally but tilts upward, on a vertical plane. Thanks to a "curious twisting of the branches and their green leaves so artificially twisted and grown together," one may enter the garden at any point and take a stroll up the inside of the fragrant, cool walls through lemon, lime, and orange trees smothered with bright, white blossoms and laden with fruit, "some ripe, others still green, some formed and some half-formed and yet others ready to pick" (e8v).

Forty-five feet high, the trees form a hedge surrounding an immense square court-yard on three sides; each segment is the same height, six feet thick, and about a mile long. Pruned in such a way as to have windows here and there, the walls of the hedge afford the strolling visitor a view either into the surrounding country landscape or down onto the court-yard framed by the fragrant walls. In the courtyard's center is a beautiful fountain made up of nymphs from whose breasts the water spurts (fig. 20). The fourth side of the perfectly equilat-eral enclosure is the facade of the palace of the queen. It comprises no less than two hundred columns, arranged in four rows of fifty apiece in a chromatic display of Numidian, Claudian, Simidian, and Tistean marble. The building is the first display of color in Western writings about architecture.

Other works bringing together architecture and nature are the amphitheater, which has a tiered garden inside in what would have been the seats for the public, and the labyrinth, whose aquatic paths make it partly a pond. As for the garden that covers the island of Cythera, it too is an incongruous blend of vegetation and sculpture. The box trees are sculpted according to *ars topiaria* into perfect circles and perfect spheres. Another tree is shaped in the form of a man wearing a hat. Each leg grows out of its own vase, and in each hand he holds a six-foot-high tower with a door and windows. From each one grows a stem surmounted by a round ball of foliage. From these balls spring other stems that join in the middle over the man's head in a semicircle, which serves as an archivolt whose height is equal to that of the towers. The center of the archivolt supports a conch that spans almost its entire width. From this support sprouts more foliage sculpted in the form of a lily with all its petals turned over. And from the center of the lily rises a small box sculpture, a corbeil of eight stalks whose ends taper at the top and are joined in the middle. Two other stems rise out of the towers, next to the ones forming the archivolt, which point straight upward and form miniature trees.

The dream structures in the *Hypnerotomachia* not only fuse diverse building types but also bring together architecture with the other arts. The reception hall of the palace of the queen, for example, is a *camera picta,* where the trompe l'oeil painting of a leafy hedge and a sky about it forms an indistinguishable whole with the surrounding walls. And another building transgresses the boundary between sculpture and architecture, using elements of the former to shape those of the latter. It is hard for readers today to realize how radical a mental act this was. No one else had such conceptions until the twentieth century (save briefly, around the time of the French Revolution, when architects in France imagined buildings in the shape of animals).[10] To look to other arts as a source of architectural form was unthinkable.

This hybrid sculpture/building is the colossus supine in the sands. (Lying next to it is a female counterpart, which Poliphilo refuses to enter.) He enters the male building

20. THE FOUNTAIN IN THE COURTYARD.

21. THE MOBILE FOUNTAINS.

through the mouth and finds within that it is formed exactly like the inside of a human body. All the internal viscera, nerves, bones, muscles, and flesh are there to be seen and visited. Above all the organs are listed their names and the different sicknesses generated in them. Each organ has a convenient entrance for visitors. Concealed light shafts brightly illuminate the interiors of the chambers. This anatomical theater is also meant to provide psychotherapy, for there is a chamber in the heart "where love is born" (b6v), along with its own list of cures. Unfortunately all the cures are written in Chaldean, and the hero does not divulge their contents. However, the more important innovation of this male colossus, like that of the architectural elephant, lies elswhere. They are the first architectural structures to be conceived organically: that is, to forsake the regular geometric outlines associated with the classical canon in favor of the irregularly curved forms of a living organism.

The "no" that existed between architecture and the advanced technology of the time also breaks down in the *Hypnerotomachia:* here, automatically opening doors employ an invention that was different from anything described up to that point.[11] There are magnetic panels on either side of the double door, which has iron strips on each interior edge. The powerful pull of the magnets draws the iron slowly. All that is needed for the two doors to part is to release the bolt of the double doors. Each of the two leaves of the door is furnished with a little cylinder turning on an axle fitted into the lower part of the panel, which, rolling on the ground, keeps the door from grating. There are also two automatically operating fountains on wheels (fig. 21), probably based on a precedent described by the great Hellenistic engineer, Hero of Alexandria, in his *Pneumatics.*[12] In addition, there are a number of wind-

22. THE TWIRLING TRUMPETER.

powered mechanical devices. One is a golden ball; on the top of this ball is a revolving pivot so perfectly calculated that the bronze wing resting on it swivels at every change of breeze. On top of this wing there is another ball, smaller than the first by a third, in which in turn is poised a child standing on his right foot and holding a trumpet to his mouth (fig. 22). Because the back of his head is hollowed copper that reaches to the trumpet, and the gyrations of the whole mechanism guarantee that the wind is always blowing from the back, the trumpet is constantly blaring. A similarly ingenious device is found inside the building, in the figure of a small boy urinating into the pool (fig. 23). Placing one's foot on the last of a series of steps leading up to it has the effect of tilting the child's "instrumento puerile" upward and releasing a stream of cold water, which squirts the beholder in the face.

Perhaps the most oneiric of all the book's features, the one that distances it most from normal waking life, is the illusionistic way the architecture embodies movement. The first case is the swimming pool. It is lined with a mosaic representing myriad brightly colored fish. Through the reflection of light on the shifting, glinting surface of the pool, they come alive and seem to be endowed with the ability to dart through the water. In the second instance, the temple of Venus, the hero describes a room whose walls are animated by moving pictures.[13] The mechanism is composed of a permanently ignited lightbulb, described as a small sphere placed in a circular hole in the partition between two halves of a transparent

23. THE FOUNTAIN IN THE SHAPE OF A SMALL BOY.   24. THE PROJECTOR OF MOVING PICTURES.

sphere of glass (fig. 24). One hemisphere is filled with water, probably in order to support the ball in the center, which sheds a light so bright that gazing at it directly is "as difficult as gazing at the sun." The lamp is of an admirably transparent and very thin material, and it reflects onto the walls of the chamber creating a perpetual and vacillating light "like a rainbow." The sun "after a rain storm cannot paint such a beautiful rainbow," the narrator cries. But the "greatest marvel of all" is the moving image that the ball, in turn, projects on the walls. Etched around the paunch of the sphere is an intaglio representing a skirmish among children on the backs of dolphins with spiral tails. The wavering light gives to the flickering scene animating the surrounding walls the semblance of a moving picture. In the third building, the amphitheater, the floor not only captures the images of nymphs dancing upon it, reflected "as in a mirror," but also "preserves their memory" (y4-y5).

*   *   *

Not surprisingly, given its overwhelming reliance on the dream device as narrative engine, the *Hypnerotomachia* also uses recombinant logic to structure the episodes of the plot. Like its architecture, the plot of the *Hypnerotomachia* has been dismissed as unoriginal. But rather than simply repeating standard love stories of its time, the *Hypnerotomachia* as a whole, like each one of the architectural constructions in the book, appears to be a startling recombination of preexisting narrative elements.

The word "extravagance" derives from *extra-vagare,* meaning to wander beyond the well-trodden path, to venture beyond the prescribed course of the conventional, predictable, and safe. Although it is anachronistic to use the term in the context of the fifteenth century,[14] "extravagant" precisely describes the *Hypnerotomachia.* The book "extravagates," in the tradition of Lucian's *True History.* It brings together in a highly original way the dominant literary stock of the time and gives a hyperbolic version of its most distinctive features. In Lucian's case, the dominant genre was the adventure story. For the *Hypnerotomachia,* it is the Renaissance *romanzo d'amore.* The book is mutated, individuated, so to speak, out of the gene pool of idyllic *romanzo d'amore* texts. But the plot is not business as usual—the lover's unrequited love, his quest to win the heart of the heroine, love's triumph. The plot divagates too much; to repeat, it is absurd even by the standards of the genre.

Like the embedded architectural treatise, the novel in the *Hypnerotomachia* displays a vast encyclopedic knowledge of its genre and constitutes a dazzling catalogue of topoi. There is no passage that does not reuse passages from Boccaccio or his predecessors—Ovid, Jean de Meung, Petrarch, Dante. The whole story of the *Hypnerotomachia,* one may claim, is a composite of citations that creates a highly artificial story line while displaying an astounding knowledge of literary history. Pozzi and Ciapponi, in their exacting and meticulous study of the classical and contemporary sources of the *Hypnerotomachia,* traced 13 of the passages of the book back to Diodorus Siculus's *Library of History;* 21 to Horace; 27 to Catullus; 28 to Columella; 35 to Martial; 48 to Homer; another 48 to Varro; 52 to Cicero; 55 to Gellius's *Attic Nights;* 123 to Virgil; 134 to Festus; 223 to Ovid; 445 to Apuleius; and over 500 to Pliny.[15] The opening paragraph of the narrative alone is a collage of words and phrases culled from Nonius, Ovid's *Metamorphoses,* Paulus Festus, Valerius Flaccus, Gellius, Plautus, Pliny, and, last but not least, Homer.[16]

The more obvious early Renaissance references with which the text is replete include the immediate precursors of the *Hypnerotomachia:* Petrarch, Dante, the *Roman de la rose,* and especially Boccaccio. Pozzi and Ciapponi find 19 allusions to Dante and 186 to Boccaccio.[17] Indeed, scholars have seen most of the episodes as referring to other literary works. Take, again, the opening lines of the narrative. They seem to echo the opening lines of Petrarch's *Trionfi:*

AL TEMPO CHE RINOVA I MIE' SOSPIRI
PER LA DOLCE MEMORIA DI QUEL GIORNO
CHE FU PRINCIPIO A SI LUNGHI MARTIRI,
GIA IL SOLE A TORO L'UNO E L'ALTRO CORNO

SCALDAVA, E LA FIANCIULLA DI TITONE

CORREA GELATA AL SUO USATO SOGGIORNO.

IN THE TYME OF THE RENEWINGE OF MY SUSPYRES,

BY THE SWETE REMEMBERAUNCE OF MY LOVELY DESYRES

THAT WAS THE BEGYNNYNGE OF SOO LONGE A PAYNE,

THE FAYRE PHEBUS THE BULL DYD ATTAYENE,

AND WARMYD HAD THE TONE AND THOTHER HORNE

WHERBY THE COLDE WYNTER STORMES WERE WORNE

AND TYTANS CHYLDE WITH HER FROSTYE FACE

RAN FROM THE HEATE TO HER AUNCIENTE PLACE.[18]

Another scholar has seen a parallel between the passage and the opening lines of Boccaccio's *Filocolo*.[19]

Similarly, the *Hypnerotomachia*'s device of the dream can be traced back to the precedent motif in the *Roman de la rose, Tesoretto, Fiore, Documenti d'amore,* the *Intelligenzia,* the *Amorosa visione,* and Petrarch's *Trionfi.* According to Ephrussi, the book takes from the *Roman de la rose* the idea of a story that begins in bed and constitutes a long dream lasting the length of a single day. In both works the hero is transported into an imaginary world located in a garden of love, where he sees such beautiful things that he cannot resist describing them to the reader.[20]

It is obvious that the *Hypnerotomachia* borrows from Dante's *Divina commedia:* here, too, the hero becomes lost in a dark forest, a savage place of cruel thorns, far from the straight and narrow path, and finds himself seized with an insurmountable fear.[21] Thus Dante's first canto begins:

NEL MEZZO DEL CAMMIN DI NOSTRA VITA

MI RITROVAI PER UNA SELVA OSCURA

CHE LA DIRITTA VIA ERA SMARRITA.

AH QUANTO A DIR QUAL ERA È COSA DURA

ESTA SELVA SELVAGGIA E ASPRA E FORTE

CHE NEL PENSIER RINOVA LA PAURA!

IN THE MIDDLE OF THE JOURNEY OF OUR LIFE I CAME TO MYSELF WITHIN A DARK WOOD WHERE THE STRAIGHT WAY WAS LOST. AH, HOW HARD A THING IT IS TO TELL OF THAT WOOD, SAVAGE AND HARSH AND DENSE, THE THOUGHT OF WHICH RENEWS MY FEAR![22]

25. THE WOLF.

Other parts of Dante's *Divina commedia* are replayed in the *Hypnerotomachia*. Poliphilo's encounter with ferocious animals appears to be another case of near plagiarism. Dante meets three beasts at the beginning of the *Inferno*—a leopard, a lion, and a she-wolf—that horrify him and keep him from attaining the hill he is trying to ascend. Poliphilo meets two, a wolf and a dragon (fig. 25). When "a famished and carnivorous wolf from the right with his mouth open wide appeared before me," Poliphilo exclaims, "my hair immediately stood on end, because of which I tried to scream but lacked the voice to do so" (a7v). The dragon is just as frightful. "Suddenly I saw on the threshold a terrible and horrifying dragon, with a triple-pronged and wriggling vibrating tongue with its gigantic jaws crammed with strong and pointed teeth," a sight that sends Poliphilo fleeing in the opposite direction (d3v).

There are many similar cases. Just as the *Divina commedia* goes through three phases—Inferno, Purgatory, and Paradise—so does the *Hypnerotomachia*. Poliphilo first goes through a world of horrendous surprises—the *boschetto,* the famished wolf, the dragon. His purgatory begins when he meets the Queen of Freedom in her palace; as Dante is initiated by Matilda. who describes the marvels of Eden and dispels the poet's theological doubts, so Poliphilo is initiated by two nymphs, who explain to him the great mysteries of love.[23] Again like Dante, Poliphilo does not spare the reader the account of his anguish and fright.[24] In his journey, Dante is always beset by worry; if he were not constantly reassured by Virgil and Beatrice, he would surely fall prey to the excesses of his emotions. The same is true of Poliphilo. If it were not for the nymphs, he would not reach his destination. In addition, it is necessary that Matilda serve as mediator for Beatrice, her dame, and thus have Dante wash his bodily filth in the rivers of Lethe and Annoe before appearing in her presence. So Poliphilo washes in the octagonal baths, before being led to the queen.

The story elements from Boccaccio are the most obvious borrowings of all. In Boccaccio's *Corbaccio,* we find the same beginning of the dream, in a valley full of flowers and wild animals. Pozzi and Ciapponi claim that the lengthy botanical descriptions in the *Hypnerotomachia* bear a striking resemblance to Boccaccio's *Ameto,* pointing especially to the garden of Cythera, a happy landscape in the land of Freedom described with extremely long lists of plants inserted here and there.[25]

Gnoli argues, furthermore, that the voyage to the island of Cythera on love's vessel is "stolen from Boccaccio." He goes on to locate the source for the doorway to a palazzo in the book in the seventh canto of *Teseide,* where in a similar way, a door is opened onto the world of "idea." He also points out that in *Amorosa visione* there is a Triumph of Love on the walls and a fabulous fountain that is like the fountain in the *Hypnerotomachia.*[26]

There are larger structural similarities with *Ameto,* whose story, like that of the *Hypnerotomachia,* is devoted to the events of a single, spring afternoon. The hunter Ameto and the nymph Lia go together to a woodland glade where they are joined by six nymphs; it is proposed that the nymphs tell the stories of their lives and loves, each following her narrative with a song. Ameto presides and the seven stories are told. There is an underlying allegory: Ameto's association with Lia and other nymphs typifies the refinement of nature's crudeness by love. Boccaccio gives us to understand that the seven nymphs represent the seven virtues.[27] But it is especially in the details, according to Popelin, that the parallels are apparent. Ameto quenches his thirst in a turbulent stream and is advised of the presence of nymphs nearby by the sound of beautiful music in the air.[28] Just before encountering his own share of musical nymphs, Poliphilo dips his mouth, which has become "rabid and panting" after the encounter with the wolf, into the waters of a river. "At that instant I heard a Doric chant," which, "entering my cavernous ears, penetrated my disquieted heart with its gentle and *concino* sweetness, like an unearthly voice, with so much harmony, and such incredible sonority and such lovely proportions" (a5).

Among the other similarities that Popelin identifies between *Ameto* and the *Hypnerotomachia* is the description of the garden of Pomona in the one and the island of Cythera in the other. Both have a concentric plan, trellises, and a fountain at the center. Ameto asks Lia if he dares to love a nymph who is probably the daughter of a god, and Poliphilo asks himself if he dares to love such a divine nymph as Polia. A nurse in *Ameto* tells of a nymph who, too headstrong in her youth, was forced to marry a wizened old man who "many times did not so much kiss as polluted [her] mouth with his own fetid one."[29] Similarly, a nurse describes to Polia an unhappy marriage of another woman who, because of her youthful rebelliousness against marriage, had been made to marry a lecherous old man. "The result was none other than having, to her great misfortune, her beautiful face and sweet red mouth given up to the spitting and drooling of the disgusting old man's slimy lips" (c1v).

Other works of Boccaccio also provide material for the *Hypnerotomachia*. In the *Decameron*, for example, there is a story entitled "The Torment of the Cruel Ladies" about the adventures of a wandering knight in a forest. He finds a girl, completely naked, whose stomach he pierces with his lance. Then he opens her back and rips out her heart and throws it to some wild dogs nearby. This violent scene is recalled here in the way Eros hacks to death two nymphs who have refused to be dominated by him.[30] And the last section of the story is very similar to *Fiammetta*. In the *Hypnerotomachia*, Polia recounts her illustrious birth in the same way as Boccaccio's heroine does. Like Fiammetta she dreams and is admonished by a prudent nurse. Prey to cruel suffering, Fiammetta wishes she had never been conceived. She cries, "O, cursed the day I was born, more detestable to me than any other! How much luckier I would have been if I had not been born or if I had been lead from that wretched birth to my tomb."[31] Let us listen to Polia echo these words: "O how happy I would be if the nourishing breast had never been pressed to my mouth! O horrible moment of my birth! Why was I not aborted?" (c4v).

Finally, it has been argued that out of Boccaccio comes even the preoccupation with architecture. In the *Amorosa visione* there is a great hall resplendent with gold.[32] More pertinent is the tower described in the sixth book of his *Filocolo*. It is so high that it touches the clouds; it is covered with marble of white, red, black, and other colors, the windows divided by columns not of marble but gold, the doors made not of gold but crystal. And in the tower is a great hall whose roof is held up by twenty porphyry columns with gold capitals.[33]

*   *   *

There is another feature unique to the *Hypnerotomachia:* it is as erotic as it is erudite. Eros shapes the narrative at every level of its composition. So intense and so exaggerated is the eroticism of the *Hypnerotomachia* that at a certain point it ceases to be just a piece of erotic writing and becomes writing about eroticism. It becomes an erotic manifesto, an erotomachic manifesto, a hypnerotomachic manifesto.

Let us begin at the level of construction of the hero. Poliphilo descends from the traditional, stereotypical protagonist of the novel. This means that, like the heroes of Jean de Meung, Petrarch, Dante, and Boccaccio, he breaks with the tradition of the chivalrous warrior of the epic and is instead a hero in the *dolce stil nuovo,* who by definition grapples with his amorous feelings rather than with an enemy army. But Poliphilo is more extreme than his colleagues in his opposition to the chivalric ideal. He is overemphatically a coward. When he sees a dragon, he refuses to confront it and he flees. When faced with the alternative of the *vita activa,* personified by a person in military armor, he refuses. Even the sight of nymphs scares him. He is polemically pacifistic, and repeatedly stresses his elation when he sees Eros trampling weapons under foot, Mars making love to Venus instead of making war, and banners bearing "amor vincit omnia" (love conquers all).[34]

Like the heroes of de Meung, Dante, and Boccaccio, Poliphilo loves his beloved for her virtuous and beautiful spirit. But while they are extraordinarily chaste,[35] he is hypererotic. For him Polia may be a "belissima psyche," but she occupies his soul "non senza concupiscientia" (r7) and above all else he is attracted to her "virginal and divine little body." His gaze is constantly drawn to it because her diaphanous garments flutter in breezes, as in a Botticelli painting. For instance, when they reach the island of Cythera, he follows behind her and notes that "I lowered my eyes now and then to see her feet" and "sometimes it would come to pass that the wind would make her clothes flutter and uncover her legs that seemed to be made of scarlet, milk, and music all mixed together" (x3). Again and again he describes her physical beauty with grandiloquent strings of superlatives extending over many paragraphs. The first time he catches sight of her, for example, so great is her "beautiful demeanor and attitude" that "never did the amorous Idalia appear so to Mars, nor Ganymede to Jupiter inflamed with love, nor the ardent Cupid to the beautiful Psyche" (x3). Poliphilo never tires of her body and mentions it whenever he can. In the end, these descriptions occupy fifty pages of the book's narrative with an insistence that is almost militant. Poliphilo's hypereroticism is not limited to Polia. His gaze is constantly drawn to the bodies of other nymphs also clad in garments that flutter in breezes. He kisses five of them, takes off his clothes and goes swimming in the nude with them, then has an orgy with them. Finally, in even greater opposition to all other heroes of the *romanzo d'amore,* Poliphilo is not blind to those of the same sex, and the illustrations of six erect phalluses in the book are one more expression of his inordinate, hyperbolic, Poliphilian eroticism (e1, m6, x8v, y2).

At the level of the construction of the heroine, too, there is a striking degree of eroticism. Whereas Petrarch's Laura and Dante's Beatrice were chaste, angelic objects of desire, Polia is a carnal creature. Like Laura and Beatrice, she is in love with the hero. But she is no angel. She interrupts Poliphilo's narrative, in which she is, curiously enough, almost totally silent, and recounts the story from her own point of view, taking the opportunity to launch into a tirade against the principle of chastity. At a time when chastity is a cornerstone

26. POLIA KISSING POLIPHILO, WATCHED BY OTHER NYMPHS.

in the construction of femininity,[36] she has at least as much, if not more, erotic *furore* as the hero, and her polemical defense of a woman's right to pursue erotic pleasure, *voluptas,* fills almost one-fifth of the book. Basically it is a negative version of Boccaccio's Fiammetta. Fiammetta is the tragic, passive victim of unrequited love, while Polia is the triumphant, active, even wild heroine of her own erotomachia (figs. 26, 27). In this regard, she also differs from the promiscuous ladies of Boccaccio's *Decameron.* Whereas they were simply indulging in the pleasures of the flesh, she makes a general case in support of female sexuality, lifting the topic from mere ribaldry onto the more daring plane of sexual politics.

In this barely veiled parody of the thirteenth- and fourteenth-century tradition of the love story, which makes up Poliphilo's part of the novel, the quest for hedonism and mutual seduction takes the hero and heroine through a series of mock-heroic predicaments as preposterous as they are pleasurable. One such trial occurs at a sumptuous feast, when Poliphilo is prevailed upon to convince his hostess, the Queen of Freedom, that he is genuinely devoted to the ideal of love. In the temple of Venus Physozoï (Venus of the natural life), he must undergo a solemn but also highly titillating purification rite before he can be joined with Polia. Some time later, Polia must revive her lover with a kiss after he has characteristically fallen into a swoon from momentarily unrequited love. In the end the lovers are rowed to the Island of Love; the boatswain is little Cupid, and six practically nude nymphs are at the oars.

27. POLIA KISSING POLIPHILO, SEATED IN HER LAP.

The name Poliphilo means "lover of many things." The name Polia, in turn, means "many things." And to be sure, Poliphilo does love many things besides Polia: diaphanous garments, precious stones and gems, gold, fine linen, food, chandeliers, sculptures, epigrams, sweet fragrances, ballet, triumphal processions, hieroglyphs, mosaics, antique vases, and, last but not least, women's shoes—all the objects that make up the "total design" or *Gesamtkunstwerk* of the quattrocento. But he loves architecture most: he loves it as much as he loves Polia, and in the same carnal way. One after the other, the buildings described in the book become objects of desire, metaphors for Polia's *solido corpo*.

Indeed, among the dreamlike features of the buildings is the inordinate feeling of happiness they impart to the beholder. Poliphilo characterizes the marble of the triumphal arch as "virginal" (c7v), the veinless marble of another surface as "flawless" (i5), which is the same term he uses to describe the skin of a certain nymph. Upon seeing the buildings, Poliphilo feels "extreme delight," "incredible joy," "frenetic pleasure and cupidinous frenzy" (h3, t8, dv). The buildings fill him with the "highest carnal pleasure" and with "burning lust" (c4). He loves them not just because they are beautiful to behold, but also because they are fragrant and agreeable to touch. He partakes of their pleasures with all his senses. In front of the frieze of a sleeping nymph, he cannot keep from placing his hand on her knees and "fondling and squeezing" them, nor can he resist pressing his lips to her breasts and sucking them (d8v).

28. THE SLEEPING NYMPH.

The sexuality of the buildings Poliphilo loves is polymorphic. He approvingly describes the columns of a certain temple as "hermaphroditic," because they combine male and female characteristics. The altar of Bacchus is made of a darkly veined marble especially selected to express the virility of that deity, and it is carved with a great phallus "rigidly rigorous" (fig. 29). Above the reclining nude body of a dreaming nymph leers a naked satyr with a watchful eye and an erect penis (fig. 28). This erotization of architecture comes to its logical conclusion. In three cases, Poliphilo manages to locate the appropriate orifice through which he can engage in sexual congress with particular buildings. His response, always described at length and in much detail, is sheer coital ecstasy. In one instance the effect on the building is mutual.

The unbridled eroticism of the *Hypnerotomachia* extends to the illustrations, many of which have been censored as pornographic (surely a reaction unique in the history of architectural publishing). Among the objectionable images observed by Lamberto Donati to have been either erased or inked over in the collection of the Vatican Library are the emblem of a priapic Hermes, the leg of an elephant mistaken for the genital organ of his neighbor, Bacchus's phallus, an anonymous phallus, the seduction of Leda by the swan, Polia kissing Poliphilo who sits in her lap, and a nymph's nudity (which is covered by a skirt)[37] (fig. 30).

29.   THE ALTAR OF BACCHUS.

30. Censored illustrations, with their originals.

HYEMI AEOLIAE.S.

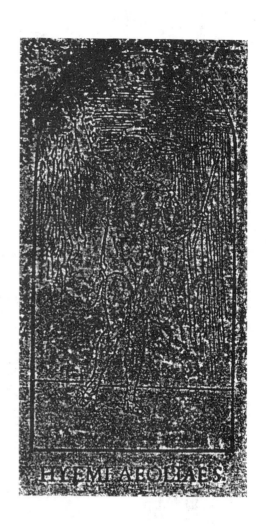

HYEMI AEOLIAE.S.

Closer reading of the *Hypnerotomachia* reveals that this hypereroticism is not only the raison d'être of the characters and the subject matter of the illustrations; it is the moving force of the plot. There are no other actions, actors, motivations, measures of suspense, fulfillments, or failures. Each episode illustrates the same principle, as almost all the actions are reduced to the repetition of one basic formula: a man desires an object. Most fundamentally it is bodies and buildings that he seeks, and his behavior makes no distinction between them. He experiences buildings in terms of desirable bodies and so do we, as readers; we apprehend buildings through Poliphilo's actions, through his viewing them, nearing them, coming into sensual contact with them, departing from them. Thus it is clear that the story is structured on the basic metaphor, "a building is a desirable body." The entire plot appears as nothing more than the instantiation of one "continued metaphor," to quote Quintilian.[38]

31. Amor vincit omnia.

More than a love story, then, the *Hypnerotomachia* is a string of situations that afford the author excuses to vent a militant, frenetic eroticism, very close in spirit, though in a dreamlike and hypertrophic way, to Lorenzo Valla's Epicurean manifesto *De voluptate,* which had scandalously in the early 1480s defended the principle of free love. Again and again, the topos "omnia vincit amor" is hammered home (fig. 31)—in the six processions the hero witnesses, not to mention the many idyllic scenes he describes between nymphs and youths, the orgiastic singing and dancing, the rape of Ganymede by Zeus, the love scenes between mothers and sons, and the many hermaphrodites, all celebrating the Triumph of Eros (and all derived from Petrarch's *Triumphi*). It is the theme of all the sculptures and bas-reliefs. It is the theme of innumerable epigrams the hero encounters: not just "omnia vincit amor," for example, but also that Eros is "Panton Tokadi" (the generator of all things). The words "Eros is the mother of everything" are carved onto the side of a mountain in three languages—Latin, Greek, and Hebrew. When faced with the choice between the *vita contemplativa,* the *vita activa,* and the *vita voluptuosa,* Poliphilo does not hesitate to choose the third. What could be more radically Epicurean than this? There is no episode in this story that does not make the same point. The very title of the book and the name of the hero reveal erotic *machia,* erotic *furore.*

How could such hyperbolic erotic *furore,*
particularly wild in relation to architecture, have eluded so many
scholars, with very few exceptions,[39] for almost
five hundred
years
?

3

* *
*

THE HARD *HYPNEROTOMACHIA*, OR
THE CODE OF RECOMBINATION

T HE *HYPNEROTOMACHIA POLIPHILI* IS ONE OF THE MOST UN-readable books ever published. The difficulty is apparent from the moment one picks up the volume and tries to utter its tongue-twisting, practically unpro-nounceable title. The difficulty only heightens as one flips through the pages and tries to decipher the strange, baffling, inscrutable prose, replete with recondite references, teeming with tortuous terminology, pulsating with prolix, plethoric passages. Now in Tuscan, now in Latin, now in Greek—elsewhere in arcane Hebrew, cryptic Arabic, imaginary Chaldean, and idiosyncratic hieroglyphics besides—the author has created a pandemonium of unruly sentences that demand the unrelenting skills as well as the unflagging vigilance of a prodi-giously endowed polyglot in order to be understood. One of the woodcuts the reader of the *Hypnerotomachia* comes across early in the book is of an equestrian statue: a wild, unbridled, winged steed is charging headlong at full gallop, ears drawn back, head twisted sideways, bucking the unlucky riders who try in vain to cling to its back and mane (fig. 32). The image might serve as an emblem for the whole work. At times even the most determined reader cannot help feeling bewildered when looking down upon this frenetic, fantastic specimen of whirling linguistic *furore,* hurling great semantic dust clouds into the air as it kicks and reels and pitches along on its impetuous course.

The *Hypnerotomachia* has never struck its readers as anything but hard to read. Its patron Leonardo Crasso wrote in his dedication to the first edition that its pages contain "so much science that one would search in vain through all the ancient books [for its meaning] as is the case for many occult things of nature." In order to understand the work, Crasso continues, "it is necessary to know Greek, Roman, Tuscan and the vernacular language," as the author, "an extremely wise man (*vir sapientissimus*), thought that this was the one way and reason to keep the ignorant from being able to impute his negligence." Thus, he writes, the author "devised his work so that only the wise may penetrate the sanctuary," for "these things are not for the populace, not to be recited on the streetcorners; they are drawn from the storehouses of philosophy and from the sources of the Muses, with the novelty of a language full of embellishments" (p. i). In the same vein, Jean Martin, credited with the first French translation of the book, declared in his preface, "You may believe, Gentlemen, that under this fiction there are many hidden things that it is not legitimate to reveal."[1]

If there is anything obvious about the *Hypnerotomachia,* it is its opacity, which results from the amount of erudition it displays. Other works belonging to the tradition of courtly love literature have presented their own difficulties, of course. Though it may strike the contemporary reader as an aberration, the combination of the erotic and the erudite is in strict accordance with the conventions of the courtly love literature established by the classics in the genre. Jean de Meung's *Roman de la rose,* Petrarch's *Triumphi,* Dante's *Divina comme-dia,* and Boccaccio's *Filocolo,* for example, display both aspects. Such works as a matter of principle always interweave learning, often in large amounts, into the plots otherwise fraught with romance.

32. THE UNBRIDLED STEED.

The *Roman de la rose* is well known for its digressions—on business and trade, friendship and justice, the goodness of Fortune, and even cosmetics and good table manners. The *Divina commedia* has often been studied as a comment on medieval scholasticism, as a philosophical system in its own right, and as a treatise on statesmanship.[2] The first cantos in particular were an attempt to concentrate an almost encyclopedic knowledge of Dante's time, bringing together a manual of orthodox Christian faith, a catechism, and a learned exposition of scholastic doctrine. And as the famous Renaissance literary scholar E. H. Wilkins noted of Boccaccio's *Filocolo* (the first Italian prose romance, 1337), the many references inserted in the book contain much material irrelevant to the love plot: geographical and astronomical lore, architectural descriptions, visions, fictitious classical deities, an infernal council, metamorphoses, battles, banquets, and an exposition of biblical history and of the Christian faith, along with parental instructions to a prospective ruler.[3] By the end of such works, the reader was expected not only to have been moved by the ups and downs of the plot but also to have gathered a great deal of learning along the way.

These works may have instructed, but beyond doubt they also aimed to please. A major means to this end was the use of the vernacular language. Classical Latin was reserved only for scholarly treatises. The works of Dante, Petrarch, and Boccaccio rely on Tuscan; those of Jean de Meung and Guillaume de Loris, French; and those of Chaucer, Middle English. Love literature found much of its raison d'être in the opposition of its authors to the Latin that dominated culture in the Middle Ages and in their desire to replace the classical language with that of the everyday life of the courts and cities.[4]

If anything characterizes the language of these love stories, besides their exquisite beauty, it is accessibility. Yet one would seek in vain to find any trace of accessibility in the *Hypnerotomachia*. Here, learning does not so much accompany the book's erotic content as interrupt it. This learning turns into a kind of opaqueness. The abstruse and recondite aspect of the *Hypnerotomachia* has drawn much comment from its readers. François Rabelais ridiculed the work by comparing it to the *Horoappollo*, the Renaissance occult book on Egyptian hieroglyphs (also published by Aldus Manutius) that was renowned, in this view, for its obscurity. Baldassare Castiglione, in the third book of *Il cortegiano* (1528), also mocked it: "I have known several men who, in writing or speaking to women, always use the language of Poliphilo. And so entrapped do they get in the subtleties of rhetoric that they defeat their own purpose, and they give the impression of being ignorant and they take a thousand years to finish their reasoning."[5] The book was attacked in satirical novels. Charles Sorel's *Le berger extravagant* (The extravagant shepherd) included the *Hypnerotomachia* among the *romans précieux* of his time, mocked for their nonsense. Antoine Furetière in 1666 mentions it in *Le roman bourgeois* (The bourgeois novel), in a long scene in which the author describes the books left after his death by a mystic-scoundrel famous for his nonsense. Here the *Hypnerotomachia* is classified among those "where it is shown by explication, in the moral, allegorical, anagogic, mythological, and enigmatic sense, that all things that ever were, are, and will be are contained therein: likewise . . . the secrets of the philosophical stone . . ." It is mentioned as a source of inspiration for a purported work that is dedicated to the keepers of the "petites maisons"—the "little houses" being the insane asylum of Paris.[6]

The book's defenders valued the same qualities. Jacques Gohorry was an alchemist whose master was the Parisian alchemist Nicolas Flammel (1330–1418); his own book *Le songe du verger* is an allegorical work whose meaning was intended to be "concealed to the profane but revealed to the initiated."[7] Gohorry, who was responsible for the French editions of the book that appeared in 1546, 1551, and 1554, praised the *Hypnerotomachia* for the way it too concealed alchemical teachings and characterized it as "stéganographique," a term coined from the Greek word meaning "tight," because it treated the subject of the book as something "so excellent that it should not be divulged, nor profaned to the populace for several reasons." He believed the author was "like many authors who have also dealt with similar subjects; they also affirm that there where they have spoken the most clearly is where in fact they have been the most obscure: so much that the ignorant louts who have followed their style have just wasted their oil and toil."[8] In 1600 Beroalde de Verville took Jean Martin's translation and published it under his own name, with the title *Le tableau de riches inventions couvertes du voile de feintes amoureuses, qui sont représentées dans le Songe de Poliphile, devoilées des ombres du Songe et subtilement exposées par Beroalde* (The picture of rich inventions, covered with the veil of amorous guises, that are represented in the Dream of Poliphilo, unveiled from the shadows of the Dream and subtly exposed by Beroalde). To him the author of the *Hypneroto-*

machia was a "speculative philosopher . . . , having as an aim the final point of the perfection of the Mercurialist wise men."[9]

More recently Edgar Wind saw in the *Hypnerotomachia* the union of love and death, a mystagogic initiation of the soul to its final fate, an expression of Neoplatonic mysticism, an orphic allegory with Poliphilo as a prince of darkness and despair. Maurizio Calvesi believed the book to be an alchemical allegory, with Poliphilo as a kind of mystical magus. Vladimiro Zabughin thought the work a Christian allegory, with Poliphilo as a soul in search of saintly salvation. Emanuela Kretsulesco-Quaranta suggested that the itinerary corresponded to a mystical spiritual allegory, a metaphysical parable, with Poliphilo representing the spirit and Polia representing wisdom. Linda Fierz-David was concerned with the Jungian symbolism of the book. In a wholly different vein, and more correctly in my view, the Italian literary scholar Salvatore Battaglia preferred to see it as a great linguistic experiment sui generis, a rejection of received patterns of literary acceptability; for him, the author was the James Joyce of the fifteenth century and the book a forerunner of *Finnegans Wake*.[10]

Indeed there is something Joycean about the polyglot recombinant associationism of the language.[11] It tests the reader even at the most basic level of lexicography. The text is so cryptic that Jean Martin felt obliged to accompany his French edition with marginal notes supplying definitions and clarifications. There is no page that is free of them. Pozzi and Ciapponi appended a glossary to their erudite and unsurpassed philological edition—which is the basis for most of the stylistic commentary that follows—containing translations into Italian of over 5,200 words. And from the first sentence of the book the reader faces an onslaught of esoteric terminology and references, setting the tone for the rest of the book.

PHOEBO IN QUEL'HORA MANANDO CHE LA FRONTE DI MATUTA LEUCOTHEA CANDIDAVA FORA GIA DALLE OCEANE UNDE, LE VOLUBILE ROTE SOSPESE NON DIMONSTRAVA, MA SEDULO CUM GLI SUI VOLUCRI CABALLI, PYROO PRIMO ET EOO, ALQUANTO APPARENDO, AD DIPINGERE LE LYCOPHE QUADRIGE DELLA FIGLIOLA DI VERMIGLINATE ROSE, VELOCISSIMO INSEQUENTILA NON DIMORAVA ET, CORRUSCANTE GIA SOPRA LE CERULEEE ET INQUIETE UNDULE, LE SUE IRRADIANTE COME CRISPULAVANO. (a2)

Here, word choice deliberately makes this sentence difficult for contemporary readers, most obviously by accumulating terms that are in Latin rather than in the vernacular. For instance, we find *caballi* instead of *cavalli* (horses), *cum* instead of *con* (with), *coma* instead of *capelli* (hair), *undule* instead of *onde* (waves), and *volucre* instead of *aligero* (winged). Throughout the text, the author uses the Latin *et* instead of the Italian *e* to mean "and." The examples culled by Pozzi and Ciapponi include *fiamma* changed to *flamma*, *giunto* to *gionto*, *sogno* to *somno*, *di sopra* to *de sopra*, *selva* to *silva*, *precedente* to *praecedente*, *verde* to *viridura*, *vittoria* to *victoria*, *frammenti* to *fragmentatione*, *allora* to *alhora*, *tedioso* to *taedioso*, and *bocca* to *bucca*.[12]

Casella and Pozzi have called the *Hypnerotomachia*'s approach to vocabulary "an obstinate chase after the most precious word taken from the most remote regions of Latin literature," and their search for the sources of the book's lexicographical peculiarities led to Òvid's *Metamorphoses* (*abactrice, affamine, allubescere, angulatamente, antelucio, anteventulo,* etc.), Aulus Gellius's *Noctes atticae* (*incantabulo, pensiculatamente, pudefacto, aerificio, collabellante,* etc.), Paulus Diaconus's excerpt from Paulus Festus's *De verborum significatione* (*accupedio, aegyptino, ambulaccro, antia arsineo, caprunculo, confugella, dapaticamente, edeatrice*), the only copy of which, they discovered in a triumph of philological detective work, was in the hands of Pomponio Leto; Pliny (*calciamine, comoso, cultrato, frugiperdo*); and many other authors.[13]

The Latin lexicon of the *Hypnerotomachia* derives not merely from classical antique sources. It is also the stuff of the author's febrile linguistic imagination, teeming with idiosyncratic quirks. Here again the recombinant logic of the rest of the book comes into play. Pozzi has described these coinages as "lexicographical centaurs and mermaids," bizarre hybrids of Tuscan prefixes with Latin suffixes. They consist of Latin or vulgar roots to which "tails" have been affixed: *-ale, -ario, -atile, -ato, -bile, -bondo, -bulo, -ceo, -culare, -culo, -eo, -ficare, -ifico, -ifero, -igero, -ivo, -izio, -mento, -mine, -oso, -ulare, -ura, -zione.* The result is a mass of thoroughly peculiar concoctions whose generating mechanism appears to be totally arbitrary but that, as Pozzi notes, are extraordinarily effective in yielding new words, especially adjectives.[14]

But what must have made the text especially impenetrable were the Greek terms.[15] During most of the fifteenth century, the readership familiar with Greek was confined to a small number of humanists. Greek scholars were in great demand and commanded huge honoraria and salaries; it is difficult to overestimate their importance. Local potentates vied for their services and plotted to steal them from one another. So rare was knowledge of Greek that Lorenzo Valla was paid a fortune by Pope Nicholas V to translate Thucydides into Latin. Bessarion, another Hellenist, bought himself a villa in Rome with the money he made from translations. Even in the late fifteenth century, Ficino was housed at the luxurious Academy in Florence by the Medicis to translate Plato and the pseudo-Dionysius.

The fashion of Hellenizing the language of romantic literature had started with Boccaccio's *Filostrato* and *Filocolo*. Two plays mentioned above, the *Batrachomyomachia* erroneously attributed to Homer and the satyrical play *Galeomyomachia* by Theodoros Prodromus, were highly popular at the time the *Hypnerotomachia* was published. We have seen that Aldus published the latter in 1494.[16] But such Hellenization tended to be limited to titles and names of heroes. Here it runs riot, driving the seventeenth-century Niccolò Villani to exclaim about "o idioma di idiomi! o ridicolo zibaldone, d'italo-greco-latini vocaboli!" (o idiom of idioms! o ridiculous scribblings made up of Italo-Greek-Latin words!) and Prosper Marchand, an eighteenth-century *homme de lettres,* to complain that the book is "a mixture of so many Greek and Latin words and certainly so much obscurity in mixing these languages, that we can say that it is written in none of them."[17] Tiraboschi, an Italian scholar of around the same time, remarks that "one finds in it . . . such an extremely strange jumbling of Greek, Latin, Lombard, Hebrew, and Chaldean voices . . . that one would be happy, if not to understand it, then just to be able to tell what language it is in!"[18] The *Hypnerotomachia* indeed is swarming with Greek words. They include not only proper names, starting with the hero's and heroine's, but also all the Greek nomenclature for plants, clothing, and gems. We have seen how correct the architectural terminology is. There are other terms whose meaning can be inferred only if the reader is familiar with Greek etymology.

Casella and Pozzi claim that the Greek words reflect the presence of the common Venetian dialect, influenced by its linguistic ties with its traditional trading partner, Constantinople. Pedraza concurs in her edition of the *Hypnerotomachia*.[19] But given the marked disdain for the populace expressed at the beginning of the book—the introduction by Crasso reads, let us recall, "these things are not for the populace, not to be recited on the street corners"— and the presence of highly specialized terminology related to the arts and architecture of antiquity, it is hard to see how these scholars could have found this hypothesis tenable, although they do point out that Crasso differentiates the vernacular, which might indeed be Venetian, from Tuscan.[20] But the Hellenized language of the book seems far more likely intended to make the language unfamiliar rather than familiar and appears closer in spirit to the higher learning of humanist circles than to even the most sophisticated Venetian merchants.

Here is a very small series out of the approximately 3,000 (*sic!*) rarefied, and also beautiful, examples gleaned by Pozzi and Ciapponi: *callitrichio*, "beautiful hair"; *calliplocamo*, "beautiful curls;" *callimo*, "beautiful"; *callotechnico*, "well crafted"; *chrysaoro*, "with a golden shield"; *chrysochari*, "golden hands"; *chrysocoma*, "golden haired"; *clepsiphoto*, "radiant"; *dorophora*, "gift giving"; *elicope*, "attracting attention"; *elioide*, "sunlike"; *epaphrodito*, "elegant"; *ergate*, "worker"; *euodio* and *euosmo*, "perfumed"; *eupathia*, "well-disposed"; *euplocamo*, "beautifully curled"; *euripio*, "ruins"; *eusebia*, "benediction"; *eutrapalio*, "urban"; *graphitura*, "design"; *graphiamento*, "writing"; *gyrulato*, "curved"; *hierophanta*, "priestess"; *hyalino,* "transparent"; *isochyrsso*, "golden"; *isotrichichryso*, "golden haired"; *lithographia*, "sculpture"; *lychno*, "lamp"; *micropsycho*, "timid"; *mnestorense*, "nuptial"; *myropolia*, "perfumed"; *mystagogia*, "liturgical act"; *phteretrio*, "triumphal"; *philesio*, "beloved"; *philoctetes*, "love"; *philotesia*, "banquet"; *phytonteo*, "in the form of a serpent"; *purrotricha*, "with radiant hair"; *pyrovolo*, "lightning"; *thalassio*, "color of the sea"; *thelithoro*, "that which penetrates right to the end"; *theophilio*, "dear to god"; *theophoriba*, "inspired by god"; *thereutica*, "huntress"; *thesphato*, "miraculous"; *thyaso*, "dance"; *uranothia*, "that which comes from the heavens"; *xanthothrico*, "with golden hair"; *xesturgia*, "delicate work"; *zygastrion*, "little box."[21] These terms, unlike the Latin ones, bore no relation to the familiar vernacular and were extremely hard to grasp.

It should come as no surprise that on the syntactic level too the text is crammed with *difficoltà*. The sentences are "made up of innumerable juxtapositions," again in Casella and Pozzi's words, which result from an "antidynamic conception of the language" that affects it not only semantically but rhythmically.[22] In order to illustrate the style for the reader of English I take Sir Robert Dallington's translation of 1592, which captures the original anacoluthic, spasmodic structure to perfection. Here are the *Hypnerotomachia's* opening lines cited above in the lovely, if flawed, original, followed by my own modern version:

WHAT HOURE AS PHOEBUS ISSUING FORTH, DID BEWTIFIE WITH BRIGHTNESSE THE FORE-HEAD OF LEUCOTHEA, AND APPEARING OUT OF THE OCEAN WAVES, NOT FULLY SHEWING HIS TURNING WHEELES, THAT HAD BENE HUNG UP, BUT SPEEDILY WITH HIS SWIFT HORSES PYROUS & ENOUS, HASTENING HIS COURSE, AND GIVING TINCTURE TO THE SPIDERS WEBBES, AMONG THE GREENE LEAVES AND TENDER PRICKLES OF VERMILION ROSES, IN THE PURSUIT THEREOF HE SHEWED HIMSELFE MOST SWIFT & GLISTENING, NOW UPON THE NEUER RESTING AND STILL MOOVING WAVES, HE CRYSPED UP HIS IRRADIANT HEYRES.[23]

PHOEBUS HAD JUST RISEN FROM THE OCEAN WAVES, BRIGHTENING THE CANDID BROW OF HIS DAUGHTER MATUTA LEUCOTHEA. THE SWIFT WHEELS OF HIS CHARIOT STILL HUNG IN THE BILLOWING SWELL. HIS WINGED HORSES, FIRST PYRO THEN EO, EMERGED. HE BRACED HIMSELF AND, WITH CARE, NOW READIED HIMSELF TO TINGE THE CHARIOT OF HIS DAUGHTER WITH THE HUE OF VERMILION ROSES. ALREADY THE RADIANT LOCKS OF HER HAIR GLITTERED AGAINST THE PURE DEEP BLUE AND RIPPLING SEA.

Jean Martin treated the passage with characteristic Gallic brevity, distilling the author's rapturous outpouring of three hundred words to a mere twelve: "Par un matin du mois d'Avril environs l'aube du jour . . ."[24]

Other techniques include various collages of direct and indirect phrases, the introduction of unexpected subjects, and the change sometimes in mid-sentence from one type of construction to another that is grammatically different, leading to an illogical, anacoluthic structure of periods. Such is the intricacy of the prose that Casella and Pozzi compare a typical sentence not to a series of logical ramifications but to a wall of intricate vines, developed into a "web" of propositions where "attributes, appositions, and secondary clauses are linked to a distant member, already closed logically, whose expressive efficiency has already been exhausted by the superagglomeration of other logical articles."[25]

To further complicate matters, the author often uses Latin syntax, as again Casella and Pozzi have observed. This means that the order of the sentences is not subject-verb-complement, which makes the text doubly difficult to understand: because these nouns and adjectives, unlike Latin, are not declined, they have no cases. As a result, the word order in many sentences is hopelessly jumbled. Its abundance of subjects that do not agree with their verbs, its relative or ablative phrases left dangling in the middle of sentences, and its sudden changes of narrative form make the syntax of the *Hypnerotomachia* another brake on understanding, further confusing and paralyzing the reader.[26]

Li errori del libro.facti ftampando,liquali corrige cofi.

Quaderno a Chartа.3.fazata pria.linea fecūdane fa nel,fazata fecōda linea.18.diffufo. fa diffifo ch.5.f.11.26. dilectione fa delectatione. Quaderno b ch.6.f.5.l.34.limata.fa liniata. Quaderno c ch.2.f.11.20.loquace. fa nō loquace.f.5.l.2.liberamēto,fa libramēto.l.19.præminētia fa prominetia.c. 3.f.11.l.11.laltra.fa laltro.f.5.l.5.edifinitio.fa ædificio.ch.4.f.11.l.23.in imo.fa i minimo.ch.5.f.11.l.25. nexuli fa Nextruli.f.5.l.28.decunati.fa decimati.ch.6.f.11.l.14.coniecturia.fa cōiecturai.l.15. prime fa pinne.ch. 7.f.11.l.5.inufitata.fa inuifitata.l.10.incinnato.fa uicinato. Quaderno. d. ch.11.f.11.l.12. Et quanta.fa Et di quanta.ch.11.f.5.l.13.hippotanii.fa.hippopotami.ch.3.f.11.l.31. trepente.fa repente.l.33. uerucofto. fa uerucofo.f.5.l.18.Solitamēte.fa folicitamente.ch.4.f.11.l.20.afmato. fa afinato.l.27.tera.fa ferra.f.5.l. 34.mortali fa mortui.ch.5.f.5.l.11.forma.fa ferma.l.5.aderia.fa adoria.l.16. Incitamente.fa incitatamen te.ch.6.f.5.l.25.& pofcia & quella antiqua.fa.poftica & quella antica.ch.7.f.11.l.14.cunto.fa cuneo.f.5.l. 21.certamente.fa certatamente.l.24.benigna patria di gente. fa benigna patria ma di gente.ch.8.f.5. l.2.le cofe.fa le coxe.l.4.ftrifti petali.fa ftricti petiolr.l.11.irricature.fa irriciature. Quaderno e ch.2.f.11.l.4.aretrorfo.fa antrorfo.ch.3.f.5.l.24.afede.fa affeole.ch.6.f.11.l.36.era.fa Hera.ch.8.f.5.l.7.aru rini.fa azurini. Quaderno f ch.11.f.11.l.11.preftamente.fa preftantemente.ch.7.f.11.ultima.angufta fa augufta.ch.8.f.11.l.33.politulatamente.fa politulamente.f.5.l.24.fuccedeterno.fa fuccedeteno. Quaderno g ch.11.f.11.l.7.fori. fa fora.ch.6.f.5.l.30.tuti recolecti & inde afportati manca & fa cofi tuti recollecti & tuti glī analecti 1de afportati.ch.7.f.5.l.21. Viretii.fa Vireti.ch.8.f.5.l.11.uifione.fa iuffione. Quaderno h. ch.3.f.11.l.17.Δοζα.fa.Δοξα.l.37.conduce.fa conducono.ch.4.f.5.l.36.Lamulatione.fa lamutilatione.ch.5.f.5.l.21. factiloquia.fa fatiloquia.ch.6.f.5.l.8. confabulamen.fa confabulamento. l.12. rnicrebbe fa rincrebbe.l.15.che e uno elephanto.fa che e uno. Quaderno. i ch.1.f.11.l.8.dixe ne.fa.di Sene.f.5.l.9.uoluprate pro uoluptate.c.4.f.5.l.4.teffute. p̃ texuto.ch.5.f.11.l.8.di feta.pro defo to.ch.7.f.11.l.7.mortali.pro mortale.f.5.l.33.fauilla. p̃ fcintilla. Quaderno K ch.11.f.5.l.carolette. pro parolette.ch.11.f.11.l.4.uditante. p̃ uolitante.f.5.l.1.fractura.pro factura.ch.3.f.11.l.fa cōgrumati ha ueano,cum exquifiti tormētuli tripharia infieme,& di uoluptica textura inodulati.Altre diffufamen te le inftabile .l.27.ferice. pro fericei.l.11.o ueru.pro o uero.f.5.l.13.uale fforza pro uale fe fforza.ch.6. f.11.l.7.longo.pro longe. QVaderno. 1 ch.3.f.11.l.11.di feta. p̃ defoto.l.15.laducitate pro laducitate. f.5.l.8.nū.p nō.l.19.eū.pro cū.ch.4.f.11.l.25.fi.pro.in.f.5.l.8.lune. p̃ lume.l.17.ornata.pro ornato.ch.6.f. 5.l.33.Colūmna. p̃ Colūba Quaderno. m ch.6.f.5.l.8.miratione.pro ruratiōe. Quaderno n ch.11.f.11.l.12.foforia adallo.pro fuforia dalo.ch.11.f.5.l.ultima rectitudine.pro reftitudine.ch.6.f.5.l.16. Di quelle.pro Di que,le.l.32. inuifta.pro iuifa. Quaderno o ch.4.f.11.l.di numere.pro di numero. ch.6.f.11.l.11.nelamino.pro nelanimo. Quaderno p ch.3.f.11.l.33.certamēte.pro certatame nte.ch.5 .f.5.l.4.& miarchitatrice.pro mia architatrice.ch.7.f.11.l.6.triumphale.manca Tropheo Quader no. q ch.11.f.5.l.19.laquale.pro lecile.ch.3.nel epitaphio.l.3.ella fa PVELLA.l.6.germinoe. p̃ germi naua.f.5.nello epitaphio.l.3,LAGVOREM.pro languorem.l.14.tamo.pro Tano.ch.4.f.11.l.2.Dē drocæfo.Dedrocyffo.f.5.l.26.laefure. p̃ le Sire.l.359.Area.pro Arca.c.5.f.5.nel epitaphio.NEDT. p̃ NEPT.ch.6.f.11.l.7.totque.pro torque.l.10.delinfino.pro delifimo.l.21.unoquali fuperfluo.ch.7.f.11.l. 6. riferuatl.manca.uidi.ch.8,nello epitaphio.l.41.culpa pro culpā.l.ultia.aethernū. p̃ eterno. Qua derno r ch.3.f.5.l.8.o uero.pro o oue.ch.5.l.16. fractici.pro fracticii.ch.7.f.5.l.14.confulamēto.pro con fabulamento.ch.8.f.5.l.12. & dapofcia.marica.La. Quaderno f ch.3.f.11.ultima.tinge.pro ti ge.ch.7.f.11.l.9.& il fuo.pro & dil fuo Quaderno t ch.11.f.5.l.8.pulluarie.pro pullarie.ch.6.f.11.l.7. limarii. pro lunarii.ch. 7.f.11.l.29.citrino.pro citimo.ch.8.f.5.l.35.cimiadeo. pro Cimiadon. Quaderno. u cb.11.f.11.l.29.pergutto.pro pergutato.charte.7.f.5.l.14.an hafta.pro in hafte. Quaderno. x. ch.11.f.11.l.35.depilo. p̃ depilo.ch.6.f.11.l.31. Tribaba.pro Tribada.ch.7.f.11.l.29. Cof modea.pro cofmoclea.ch.8.f.11.l.12.Syrimati. pro Syrmati. Quaderno. y ch.11.f.11.l.16. daedalifa cti. p̃ dædale facti.f.5.l.18.capo pro capto.ch.3.f.5.l.24.calice.pro calce.ch.6.f.11.l.ioui.pro Loui.ch.7. f.11.l.5.continiua.pro continua.f.5.l.20.Vrotiothia.pro Vranothia.ch.8.f.5.l.35.Cōexo.pro Cōuexo Quaderno. z. ch.11.f.5.l.11.mufcho.pro mofco.ch.3.f.11.l.19. ferimo.pro firmo.f.5.l.37.Carinatione. p̃ Cariuatione.ch.5.f.11.l.1. Ornate.pro ornato.l.11.Arfacis.pro Arfacida.l.ultima.uerna.pro uernea. f.5.l.3. excedente pro excedeuano.prope.io.uacat.l.17. aptiffima.pro aptiffime.l.35.mirando. pro ua rio.ch.6.f.11.l.32.cōpecto.pro comfpecto.l.ultima.diafpre.pro dediafprea.di.uacat.ch.8.f.5.l.17.fecuro fo.p̃ ficuriofo.l.37.picto.pro pecto.l.ultima.appropriauano. p̃ approbauano QVaderno. A ch. 11.f.5.l.22.Melinia.pro Melmia.l.25.perimorida.pro per iucunda.l.26.truncuto pro troncato.ch.5.f.5 l.14.manca dapo.Comente gli pectinaua.Dindi acafo paffando allhora Poliphilo.ch.5.f.11.l.7. Com moffa. p̃ comofa.ch.7.f.11.l.15.dfpumale.pro defpūa Lecanefcēte.l.16.petrace. p̃ petracce. Quader no. B ch.5.f.5.l.13.Saporofo.Pro Soporofo,l.36.fere. pro. fere. ch.8.f.11.l.9. iftinatione. proeftimatiōe QVaderno C ch.3.f.11.l.16.cōtemto. pro cōtempto.l.20.fufpicare.pro fufpicace. QVaderno. D ch.11.f.5.l.13.parare. p̃ parlare.ch.5.f.11.l.9. fa patturifce.ch.6.f.11.l.10. Gratis. p̃ Gracis. QVaderno. E. ch.11.f.5.l.ultima.feguitoe. p̃ feguiroe.ch.6.f.11.l.14.feruli pro ferali. QVaderno F ch.11.f.5.l.ultima amante.pro amātime.ch.3.f.5.l.2.Garo.pro Ciaro. Nō fe numera le linee delle maiufcule.

Venetiis Menfe decembri.M.ID.in ædibus Aldi Manutii,accuratiffime.

33. THE PAGE OF ERRATA.

Countless misspellings in the text can hardly have made reading the *Hypneroto-machia* any easier. Lamberto Donati notes that in spite of the list of errata at the back of the first edition of the book, exceptional not only in its great length but in its very appearance (fig. 33), the text still contains "thousands of errors."[27] It is possible that these corrections to the many typographical mistakes or inconsistencies indicate a particular lack of vigilance in the editing process. But given the extremely high Aldine standards, it is unthinkable that the "errors" were not intentional, though probably unbeknownst to the unsuspecting Aldus himself, who desperately tried to redeem the situation at the last moment, judging from his claim at the end of the errata list to have printed the book "most accurately." In the first sentence alone "fora" should have read the Latin *foras* (toward the outside of), "come" should have been *comae* (hair), and "undule" should have been *undulae* (waves).

The first of the book's misspellings and, thanks to an article by Philip Hofer,[28] one of the most famous, occurs on the second title page. Here the word *SANEQUAM* was misprinted "SANEQUE." In all paper copies the incorrect *E* has been replaced by *AM* (fig. 34). However, all copies on vellum, which as a rule were the last to be printed, have "SANEQUE" unaltered, probably, as Hofer speculates, either because Aldus just gave up and preferred not to disfigure the costly vellum or because the vellum copies were distributed before the error was noticed.[29] It is interesting to speculate that embarrassment over the number of errors might have led Aldus to forgo placing his imprint at the head of such a book, lacking as it was in exactitude.

Given the lexicographical, syntactic, and orthographical features that made the *Hypnerotomachia* so difficult to read,[30] what must it have been like to translate? One senses the frustration that the extreme artificiality and verbiage must have been caused Jean Martin, the humanist who is commonly credited with its French translation. In his 1546 introduction to the book, he characterized its style as endowed with "a more than Asiatic prolixity."[31] We have seen to what ends he was driven: he simply eliminated 288 of the first 300 words. Although Dallington, as we have also seen, attempted a diligent and thorough translation at the beginning of his English version of 1592, he succumbed to the rigors of the task, ultimately abridging the original by more than two-thirds. Moreover, inaccuracies abound. The first sentence wrongly attributes "heyres" (hairs) to Phoebus, instead of to his daughter Matuta Leucothea. More astonishingly, in the same sentence Dallington mistranslates "ad dipingere le lycophe quadrige della figliola di vermigliante rose" as "giving tincture to the Spiders webbes, among the greene leaves and tender prickles of Vermilion Roses" rather than as "tinging the chariot of his daughter with the hue of vermilion roses." Perhaps this reference to spiders was a natural slip for someone entangled in such a text.

As for Claudius Popelin, the French scholar who in 1883 provided the first scholarly translation, complete with learned commentary, he wrote that "to read it in the original language, that is so incorrect, written in a language so abstruse, is running a great risk, even

POLIPHILI HYPNEROTOMACHIA, VBI
HVMANA OMNIA NON NISI SO-
MNIVM ESSE OSTENDIT, AT
QVE OBITER PLVRIMA
SCITV SANEQVAM
DIGNA COM-
MEMO⸗
RAT.
✳✳✳
✳

34. ALTERATION OF THE WORD *SANEQUE*.

for an Italian, no matter how literate." [32] Pilar Pedraza, who recently produced a highly read-able and erudite translation of the work into Spanish, writes of the "obscurity of the prose, [which is] at times unintelligible." [33] This extreme linguistic difficulty explains the book's relative unpopularity in its native Italy, despite its wonderful merits.

Clearly, the *Hypnerotomachia* is not obscure by accident. If the text frustrates inter-pretation at every level, then the effect is undoubtedly intentional. The writing is nothing short of an exercise in cryptography. The author admits the inaccessibility of the book and suggests that it was a conscious tactic: "I am using words that are unknown to the vulgar," he warns (c4). And as the book continues, it exploits again and again, as if in a self-referential manner, the theme of hermeneutic impenetrability. For instance, there are eighty epigrams and inscriptions on walls, steles, podia, vases, banners, fountains, and the inside of the pyra-mid, on the colossus and the elephant, on obelisks and trophies. The hero spends thirty pages trying to decode them; they range from a single word to whole texts of over three hundred words. They are in Greek, Hebrew, Arabic, Egyptian hieroglyphics, and Chaldean as well as Latin (fig. 35). The hero always makes it a point to translate those inscriptions not already in Latin into that language while acknowledging the "novelty" of these "marvelous enigmas" (b8v). Thus their meaning remains unknown, except to readers familiar with Latin! This leaves the reader in the dark and keeps the opaqueness of the text intact. No key is provided for unlocking the meaning. In fact the meaning of the inscriptions is not always clear even to the hero. Sometimes he deciphers them with ease, sometimes with difficulty—and sometimes he cannot decipher them at all.

Along with incomprehensible epigrams and inscriptions, unknowable animals and humans, the *Hypnerotomachia* is full of obscure, dark, intractable places: forests, veiled entrances, labyrinths. Indeed, the labyrinth—a kind of emblem of hermetic difficulty, the symbol par excellence of search and the abstract model for most kinds of problem-solving activities—marks almost every step of the hero's wanderings as he makes his way through the story. As early as the first chapter, the reader follows the hero through a forest as he exclaims, "I had as my only recourse to implore the pity of the Cretan Ariadne, who gave the thread to Theseus to get out of the difficult labyrinth" (a3v). Readers are constantly finding themselves within labyrinths: one inside the viscera of the temple at the base of the pyramid; an aquatic one in the form of a circular, maze-like pool; the concentric-patterned garden on the

35. Epigrams in Hebrew, Greek, and Latin.

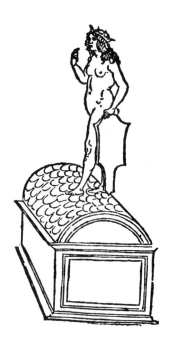

היה מי שתהיה קח בן האוצר הזה כאות נפשך
אבל אזהיר אותך הסר הראש ואל תיגע נגופו

ΟΣΤΙΣ ΕΙ. ΛΑΒΕ ΕΚ ΤΟΥΔΕ
ΤΟΥ ΘΗΣΑΥΡΟΥ, ΟΣΟΝ ΑΝ Α
ΡΕΣΚΟΙ. ΠΑΡΑΙΝΩ ΔΕ ΩΣ ΛΑ-
ΒΗΙΣ ΤΗΝ ΚΕΦΑΛΗΝ. ΜΗ Α
ΠΤΟΥ ΣΩΜΑΤΟΣ.

QVISQVIS ES, QVANTVN
CVNQVE LIBVERIT HV-
IVS THESAVRI SVME AT-
MONEO. AVFER CAPVT.
CORPVS NE TANGITO.

island of Cythera; and the subterranean meandering spaces under a landscape of ruins (d4–d5, t8, h8v, p8).

Polia herself is indecipherable. Poliphilo cannot identify her. He cannot read her. He is still wondering who she is when they meet for the fifth time. It is only three-quarters of the way through the story that he is finally certain Polia is Polia, explaining that "at first sight I had something like a certainty that is was Polia: but her unusual clothes, the strange place we met, dissuaded me." The hero is equally unknowable. When at one point Polia turns and addresses him, he confesses, "I remained stupefied and marveled greatly that she knew my name"(i6).

As if the text were not difficult enough, the accompanying illustrations themselves are cryptic and enigmatic. Take, for example, the first figure. It represents a young man in the midst of a thickly overgrown forest facing an obscure way forward. In the second, the same person is in a clearing, staring ahead in awe at the unknown. Two illustrations later, the enormous pyramid comes into view, set on a temple-like edifice supporting an obelisk that is in turn crowned by a nymph holding a reversed cornucopia. This is followed by the illustration of the children falling from the back of a bucking winged horse. The list of mysterious illustrations continues, including a series of dancing youths with faces on the back of their heads, creatures that are half-elephant and half-ant, a dolphin coiled around an anchor, a girl holding a tortoise in one hand and a bird in the other with one leg jutting straight out, an elephant carrying an obelisk on its back, and a three-faced head (part dog, part wolf, and part lion). For most people, even for the elite of humanist scholars, the meaning of these illustrations must have been very difficult to make out, since Cesare Ripa's book on iconology, which could have made a coherent description of such images possible, was not yet published.[34]

The *Hypnerotomachia* is a catalogue of every possible and imaginable foil to understanding. On every page one is confronted by words whose meaning must be deciphered, inscriptions that have to be interpreted, episodes whose conclusion is ambiguous, a hero and a heroine who embody ideas that have to be divined. Texts and images in code, symbolic images and their interpretation, are recurrent patterns in these cryptic tactics.

Thus, in a very obvious way, the book is self-consciously about the difficulty, if not the impossibility, of reading correctly—about hermeneutic inaccessibility, impenetrability, "steganography." It is not only obscure, it is a reflection on its own obscurity, an acknowledgment of its own hermeneutic *difficoltà,* foregrounding the hermeneutic stumbling blocks—indeed, brick walls—that the author places on the path to its own understanding. The book itself is a labyrinth, a series of veils, a cryptic epigram. Such vast hermeneutic impenetrability has concealed many of its remarkable features. This is all the more strange as deliberate obscurity is at the very heart of the book. Even translators have universally been blind to it. This seeming failure of the book, however, might in fact be its ultimate success.

Why write a text bursting with erotic passion and *furore,* then conceal it? The answer may simply be that the many residues of meaning in the text entice the reader. The book might be employing what George Steiner referred to as the "tactical obscurity" that mystery stories employ: giving a baffling account, patently incomplete, so that readers may be induced to figure out the concealed part for themselves.[35] The devices of prolixity, hyperbole, disjunction, and the use of distant or even invented languages in the *Hypnerotomachia* ensure that the meandering text yields its meaning only incrementally, extracted with great effort and difficulty. We are close here to the poetics of delayed gratification and discovery. The hero, in fact, enjoys the process of deciphering and decoding, as he acknowledges several times. The very plot of the book is about finding a lost heroine and, once she is found, about exploring with her an unknown world—neither of which occur without many peripeteias and postponements. "Semper festina tarde" means "always rush slowly" or "be patient"—always active but also always ready to accept inevitable delay. According to Edgar Wind, this is the theme of all the epigrams of the text (fig. 36).[36] As much as the book can be seen as a catalogue, then, it can also be read as a thesaurus of acts of recognition that are built into the episodes of the story: reticence and disclosure of meaning, search and discovery of places, disappearance and recovery.

Compounding the obscurity of this recombinant, encoded language, and of the self-reflectively hermetic plot, is the mystery of the author's identity. An acrostic concealed in the first letters of each of the book's thirty-nine chapters was discovered by a reader in seventeenth-century France, one hundred and fifty years after its publication. It reads "Poliam Frater Franciscus Columna Peramavit." This translates from Latin as "Brother Francesco Colonna loved Polia immensely." Ever since, it has been assumed that the author must have been Francesco Colonna.[37] But who was Francesco Colonna? Two possible Colonnas have been proposed: one, a debauched Dominican friar in the service of the convent of SS. Giovanni e Paolo in Venice, the other, a Renaissance patrician, the aristocratic scion of the powerful baronial Colonna dynasty of Rome.[38]

The almost total obscurity surrounding the *Hypnerotomachia* bristles with inscrutable riddles, mystifying perplexity, confounding intrigue. Why would someone produce a fascinatingly difficult and prodigious encyclopedia of humanist learning and ingenuity, then conceal his identity? Judging from their respective biographies, both the Venetian monk (1433–1527) and the Roman baron (1453–1538) were in the prime of life in 1499 when the book was published: sixty-six and forty-six years old, respectively. If either of them is the author, there are two possibilities. They were party to the secrecy, or they were not. The first makes little sense: why would either of the Francescos have produced one of the greatest examples of quattrocento humanist learning, indeed one of the most beautiful works of art of the period, only to step aside and disappear from view? The second is equally unlikely: how could anyone have produced such a manuscript and not notice that it had been pub-

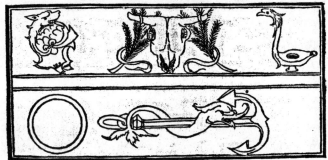

**PATIENTIA EST ORNAMENTVM CVSTO
DIA ET PROTECTIO VITAE.**

36. CALL TO PATIENCE.

lished? Both of these men lived on for decades after 1499, yet neither claimed his rightful
title as the author. Furthermore, neither proposal explains why the book ends with a reference
to Treviso in 1467, the calends of May, or why it includes a reference to the Lelli family,
which in fact originated from Treviso.

Apparently the authorship was also a mystery to those involved in its publication.
One of the editors, Andrea Marone, makes this quite explicit, in an introductory poem in
the original edition. So great and varied is the *Hypnerotomachia* in its learning that Marone
invents a fictional author, one who has perhaps taken lessons from the nine Muses and surpassed them:

CUIUS OPUS DIC, MUSA—MEUM EST OCTOQUE SORORUM—
    VESTRUM? CUR DATUS EST POLIPHILO TITULUS?
PLUS ETIAM A NOBIS MERUIT COMMUNIS ALUMNUS.
    SED, ROGO, QUIS VERO EST NOMINE POLIPHILUS?
NOLUMUS AGNOSCI. CUR? CERTUM EST ANTE VIDERE
    AN DIVINA ETIAM LIVOR EDAT RABIDUS.
SI PARCET, QUID ERIT? NOSCETUR. SIN MINUS? HAUD NOS
    DIGNAMUR VERO NOMINE POLIPHILI.

"MUSE, WHOSE WORK IS THIS?"
"MINE, ALONG WITH MY EIGHT SISTERS'."
"YOURS? WHY DOES THE TITLE ATTRIBUTE IT TO POLIPHILO THEN?"
"BECAUSE, AS OUR COMMON PUPIL, HE SURPASSED EACH OF US."
"BUT I BEG YOU NOW, WHO IS POLIPHILO, WHAT IS HIS REAL NAME?"
"WE DO NOT WISH FOR YOU TO KNOW."
"WHY?"

"IT IS BETTER TO BE CAUTIOUS, TO KEEP DIVINE THINGS FROM BEING
DEVOURED BY VENGEFUL JEALOUSY."
"BUT IF THIS JEALOUSY SPARES HIM, THEN WHAT WILL HAPPEN?"
"THEN IT WILL BE MADE KNOWN."
"AND WHAT IF THIS NEVER HAPPENS!"
"THEN WE ARE NOT WORTHY OF THE TRUE NAME POLIPHILO."

One can only assume that the author's identity was a mystery to others besides
Marone. Many prominent men were connected with the book. It is dedicated to Guidobaldo
da Montefeltro, patron of the great ducal court of Urbino, which was among the most cultivated of its day. Andrea Marone da Brescia was a protégé of the humanist cardinal Giovanni
de' Medici, the future Pope Leo X. Giovan Battista Scita, who wrote another introductory
poem in the same edition, was a well-known literary figure of the time. Leonardo Crasso,
the book's patron who underwrote its production at great cost, was a pronotary in the service
of the papacy, captain of the citadel of Verona, Superintendent of Fortifications at Padua, and
was connected to Guidobaldo da Montefeltro by one of his brothers who was working for
him; moreover, as a young man he had studied in Rome with one of the greatest scholars of
his day.[39] One cannot help wondering why so many cultivated people, obviously so fascinated
with this work, would have been party to stealing the manuscript from either Francesco
Colonna and publishing it anonymously. Aldus Manutius was the most distinguished and
prestigious publisher of the Italian Renaissance. As we have seen, his mission in life, to which
he was passionately devoted, was to produce the most scholarly edition yet of the works of
the classical Latin and Greek authors—Cicero, Aristotle, Caesar, Plato, Virgil—along with
those of only the most illustrious humanist scholars, such as Pope Pius II, Angelo Poliziano,
Niccolò Perotti, Cardinal Pietro Bembo, and Lorenzo Valla.[40] In carrying out this mission he
befriended many of the great Renaissance humanists of his day. Why would he have helped
conceal the identity of Francesco Colonna? This is all the more inexplicable as Aldus took
his own trademark—a dolphin twisted around an anchor—from a woodcut of the
Hypnerotomachia.
From the moment the *Hypnerotomachia Poliphili* first saw the light of day,
the book—with its unpronounceable title, unreadable text, and
unidentifiable author—has done nothing but raise un-
answerable questions. Who could have created
such an extraordinarily recombinant work,
so full of erudition, so full of
eros, so full of passionate
furore, so difficult to
decipher, and
why
?

4

* *
* *

IMPLAUSIBLE AUTHORS

A | CERTAIN FRANCESCO COLONNA WAS BORN IN 1433. OF HIS VENE-
tian childhood and family, nothing is known. The beginning of his Dominican
career also remains fairly obscure. Where he entered the order is once again a
mystery, and his biographers have discovered in the records only the most meager traces of
his existence. A novice called Francesco bought "ten cubits of bread" on 18 March 1455.
And a certain Francesco received eight *soldi* for saying mass. Finally, the name "Francesco da
Venezia" appears in the register of Treviso in 1465.[1]

That a monk could have been the author of a work of fiction such as the *Hypnerotomachia* is not as far-fetched as it might at first seem. As Francesco's biographers point
out, a pandemic of the plague had swept through Europe in the mid-fourteenth century and
decimated the Dominican order as a whole by the mid-fifteenth. In a desperate effort to
repopulate its convents, the community had been forced to employ "criteria of choice that
were other than rigorous and . . . ample dispensations of every kind."[2] As an indication of
how far the order had wandered from the path of the spiritual life, Vincenzo Bandello, the
captain of the convent of SS. Giovanni e Paolo under whom Francesco Colonna served, said
that among his *confratelli* in Lombardy were some who were "licentious, dissolute, rather
dishonest, and who lead a life that is scandalous and of the worst example, in whose hands a
roller or a shovel would be more appropriate than a breviary."[3]

Indeed, the convent under Bandello was itself hardly a model of monastic virtue.
The visiting Dominican Felice Fabbri was alarmed to find it overrun with what he described
as "nymphs of Venus sent by Satan." He reported to his superiors that during his stay in 1487,
"Venetian ladies decked out in all kinds of finery and pomp" had turned the entire convent
"inside out and upside down." In such company, he noted, every meal lasted well into the
night. The dining hall was cleared to the blare of tubas, trumpets, and organs. Celibacy,
chastity, and continence were not the only types of abstinence to be openly ignored in these
circumstances. The rule of asceticism was flouted in "every dormitory and cell and cunabula
and hall." The walls were covered with "incomparable decoration, including precious fabrics"
and "cloth of pure gold thread." It seems that the more customary liturgical activities of the
congregation were replaced by the celebration of banquets, consecrated with what Felice
described as "exquisite wines from Greece and Crete."[4] And when Pope Clement VII tried
in 1531 to get the community to reform and submit to a strict observance of the rule, the
indignant brethren invoked the protection of the doge, protesting that they "could under no
circumstance endure" such an idea and declaring that they would "sooner become Luther-
ans" than comply.[5]

In choosing the so-called conventual or unreformed convent of SS. Giovanni e
Paolo over S. Domenico in Castello—the other, officially reformed, Dominican convent of
Venice—Francesco Colonna must have found the uncouth spirit of the premises congenial
to his own natural inclinations, as described by Martin Lowry.[6] Remarkably, as Lowry points

out, Colonna managed to stretch the limits of tolerance even of that institution, and he was involved in frequent altercations with his superiors. On 29 May 1477 he was called before the highest authorities of his order under threat of jail and reprimanded on charges whose import remains unknown: they pertained to "many things." Whatever their nature, they were serious enough to cause him to be exiled from Venice to a small town, three days' travel away, from which he was recalled only in 1481.[7] In 1483 he once more brought ignominy upon himself, along with some of his fellows. Again there are no details as to the exact nature of their offense, but all of them were ordered to appear before the general of the order under the threat of being defrocked, the most severe form of punishment inflicted among the Dominicans. The extremity of this measure would suggest, in the words of his biographers, a "conduct that was less than edifying."[8] Nevertheless in 1493 he was given by his general the title of *predicator* in S. Marco and was recalled to the convent in 1496. In 1500 he received permission to live outside the cloister walls in order to pursue his callings there.

Although he was in his early eighties, the year of 1516 found him involved in a scandal that shook the community of SS. Giovanni e Paolo to its very foundations, involving both the Venetian Council of Ten and the general of the Dominican Order.[9] After accusing several of his superiors of "sodomy and other things," he retracted these claims, then was himself accused and convicted of rape, a charge he did not contest and for which he was exiled from Venice to Treviso for life. However, in 1520 the ban was revoked and he was allowed to return officially—perhaps, Lowry speculates, because of his advanced age of eighty-seven.[10] But four years later, he was at the center of yet another scandal, this time ignited by the unspecified accusations of a Venetian jeweler, Pietro Britti. Banished again from Venice, he still managed to return, apparently a somewhat legendary figure by then; for when he finally died in 1527—at the age of ninety-three—his memory was "enshrined," to use Lowry's image, in a novel by a fellow Dominican, Matteo Bandello. Recounting the adventures of a monk, it was entitled *Fra Francesco Veneziano ama a una donna che in un altro s'innamora e vuole far ammazzar il frate, il quale ammazza il rivale e la donna lascia per morta* (Brother Francesco the Venetian loves a lady who falls in love with another who wants to have the brother murdered, who in turns murders the lover and leaves the lady for dead).[11]

It is unclear how such a person would have found the time to amass the general philological and archaeological erudition necessary for the very conception, let alone the composition, of the *Hypnerotomachia Poliphili*. As Casella and Pozzi themselves observe, the typical *curriculum studiorum* of Dominican novitiates began after a period of three years during which the candidate, who had to acquire the rudiments of grammar, reading, and arithmetic, could apply himself to the study of logic, rhetoric, music, and astronomy, along with learning the duties of the religious life. The course, which lasted one year, was divided into levels. The first was the *studium artium,* that is, the study of Aristotelian logic or rational philosophy; the second was the *studium rerum naturalium,* or natural philosophy; and the third, the *studium theologiae,* consisted of commenting on the *Sententiae* of Peter Lombard (by the end of the fourteenth century, the writings of Thomas Aquinas were substituted). The theological instruction was imparted by each convent of each province, and the same had begun to be true of the rational and natural philosophy. The theological course was complemented at the beginning of the fourteenth century by the *studium Bibliae et sententiarum,* that is, by a more detailed discussion of the holy writings. This was surely a paltry curriculum, still in the medieval scholastic mold, dominated by the teaching of theology, and far short of the encyclopedic classical training necessary for the writing of the *Hypnerotomachia,* despite Pozzi and Casella's claim to the contrary.[12]

Even within this mediocre academic system, Colonna's performance was lackluster. He was not ordained until the age of thirty and not granted his bachelor's degree in theology at the University of Padua until forty—dubious beginnings for the author of the *Hypnerotomachia,* one of the most knowledgeable architectural, philosophical, literary, and artistic figures of the quattrocento, as well as being one of its foremost engineers. Indeed, this Dominican hardly seems to possess the literary, architectural, and technological background necessary to write one of the most learned compendia of humanist learning and one of the most creative displays of thought of the Renaissance.

* * *

In 1453, twenty years after the birth of the first Francesco Colonna, a second one was born, in Rome. About his lineage there is no shortage of information.[13] As his biographer, Maurizio Calvesi, demonstrates, he belonged to one of the most powerful families of that time, one of the baronial dynasties of Rome that had been battling for centuries to control the city. The Colonna, like the Orsini, the Catanei, and the Frangipani, were feudal landowners and soldiers. They had owned vast tracts of land east of Rome in the Tiburtine and Alban Hills and had commanded great feudal armies. Inside Rome itself, they occupied the key position of Augustus's tomb, from which they could control the northern part of the city and which they had transformed into a fortified enclave, or *rocca,* that was huge for the time, measuring 285 feet in diameter.[14] From at least the early fourteenth century, they had possessed gardens on the slopes bordering the Quirinal Hill, adjacent to the church of SS. Apostoli.[15] Francesco's great-uncle Oddone Colonna, Pope Martin V (1417–1431), had a palazzo built on the site and turned it into his papal residence. Both sites were not only strategically but also ideologically important, for both Augustus's tomb and Trajan's column, which stood in a piazza near the Palazzo Colonna, were symbols of the Roman Empire. The palazzo became, in turn, the residence of Francesco's uncle, Prospero Colonna.

At the height of their power, under Oddone Colonna's papacy, the family's feudal land holdings included the enclaves and strongholds of Zaragolo, Frascati, Rocca di Papa, La

Colonna, Capranica, Pietra Porzia, Gallicano, San Giovanni, and San Cesareo to the east of Rome in the Alban and Tiburtine Hills. Palestrina, the site of the ancient temple of Fortune, was the biggest—covering the side of an entire mountain which overlooked the distant city of Rome—and the most important of all.[16] Under Martin V, the family also acquired the Duchy of Amalfi and Ardea, then the Principate of Salerno. Prospero, the nephew of Martin, was a papal candidate in 1447. Through his marriage to Orsina Orsini, Francesco was related to the Medici dynasty: to Lorenzo de' Medici, who had married Clarice Orsini; to Giovanni de' Medici, the future Pope Leo X; and to Cardinal Giuliano de' Medici, the future Clement VIII.

Although they were probably of Tuscan descent, the Colonnas claimed their genealogy was Roman, stretching as far back as Augustus, Julius Caesar, and even Hercules. Through his aunt Caterina, the sister of Prospero Colonna, Francesco Colonna would have been related to the family of the powerful *condottiere* Guidobaldo da Montefeltro. The portrait of Guidobaldo's father, Federigo, hangs next to Prospero's in the Palazzo Colonna in Rome to this day.[17] Even in such company, Francesco Colonna cut no mean figure, occupying as he did the eminent position of heir to the title of signore of the dynastic seat at Palestrina.

As his biographer points out, Francesco Colonna belonged to a long line of prominent literary and cultural personalities. A great-uncle of his, Giovanni Colonna, wrote *Mare Historiarum,* a historical compilation of Rome,[18] and acted as guide to Petrarch when the poet visited Rome in the 1330s for the first time and introduced him to the Roman antiquities. So close was Petrarch to the Colonna family that he called Giovanni his "fratello amantissimo" and followed Jacopo Colonna to Gascony when he became bishop there. Petrarch was crowned in the Campidoglio through the initiative of another Francesco Colonna, whom he pronounced "il mio gran Colonnese, magnanimo, gentil, constante e largo." Furthermore, Oddone Colonna (Pope Martin V) was the first to take official action for the preservation of antique buildings, making their destruction a sacrilege. Caterina Colonna, wife of Guidantonio da Montefeltro and mother to his brother Federigo's illegitimate son and heir Guidobaldo, was a patroness of the arts and letters at the court in Urbino. Finally, Vittoria Colonna (1492–1547), another relative, was one of the greatest poets of the Renaissance.[19]

Closer to home, and of far greater and more immediate bearing on Francesco's education, was Cardinal Prospero Colonna, Francesco's uncle. He was a leading humanist of his times and, it has been suggested, Shakespeare's inspiration for Prospero, the very embodiment of humanist learning in *The Tempest.*[20] It was on a hunting trip in the Alban Hills with him that Flavio Biondo, gazing at the medieval towers that dominated the skyline of Rome in the distance, was moved to conceive the project of *Roma instaurata,* the Renaissance's first scientific archaeological reconstruction of ancient Rome. In a 1444 letter to Leonello d'Este, Marquis of Ferrara, Biondo recounts how Prospero had taken him to Albano to see what was left of the antique theater there.[21] Biondo visited the ruins of Antium with Prospero, and in his *Roma instaurata* he remembers the cardinal as the restorer of the Orti Neroniani, calling him "the Maecenas of our century, a most beloved man of the greatest humanity and liberality."[22] In that book, Biondo praises Prospero for bringing to the Palazzo Colonna on the Quirinal the cultivated and cultured humanistic ambiance that Horace had praised in the gardens of Maecenas in the ancient Roman Republic. Besides being a passionate amateur architect, Prospero must have been something of a collector of antique objects, as Fra Giocondo commented on the famous collection of marbles in the Casa Colonna in Rome, which included a torso of Hercules and perhaps the celebrated group of three Graces now at Siena.[23] Although there is no documentary evidence identifying Prospero's close associates during those years, we know that Lorenzo Valla was in his entourage and that Poggio Bracciolini dedicated his *De avaritia* to him[24]—a book, in spite of its title, expounding on the good of riches.

As a cardinal in the papal court, Prospero Colonna had firsthand contact with Roman humanism. Between 1447 and the end of the reign of Pope Nicholas V in 1455, Rome saw a flowering of Renaissance humanism second only to that in Florence. The city became a center of scholarship, particularly in ancient languages. Nicholas V, who as Tommaso Parentucelli had been head of the great Medici Library in Florence,[25] was himself one of the most learned humanist scholars of his day. He was a friend of Leonardo Bruni, Gianozzo Manetti, Poggio Bracciolini, and Carlo Marsuppini d'Arezzo,[26] and under him the greatest minds of the Renaissance were summoned to the papal court: Lorenzo Valla, Pier Candido Decembrio, Guarino Veronese, Theodoro Gaza, Giovanni Aurispa, Gregorio Tofernate, George of Trebizond, Niccolò Perotti, Orazio Romano (who translated the *Iliad* in Latin hexameters), and Iacopo Cremonese (who translated a work of Archimedes). Lorenzo Valla, one of the earliest arrivals, translated Herodotus and Thucydides into Latin and was the first to translate the *Horoappollo* (on hieroglyphs) into Latin.[27] Perotti translated works from the Greek for Nicholas V, but his major contribution was the *Cornucopia, sive Commentariorum Linguae Latinae*—a grand commentary on Martial's *Epigrams,* whose obscenity made him suspect among conservative clerics—a work carried out with Pomponio Leto. Other authors translated for the pope include Xenophon, Polybius, Diodorus, Appian, Philo, Theophrastus, and Ptolemy.[28] The pope also summoned Manetti, one of the first to read Hebrew, who also translated some of the early Christian fathers. Works in Arabic were translated by Nicholas of Cusa.[29] Through his uncle, Francesco could naturally have had privileged access to the current research being carried out at the papal court in all the languages included in the *Hypnerotomachia:* Latin, Greek, Hebrew, Arabic, Chaldean, and Egyptian hieroglyphs. This period represented what Calvesi calls the Renaissance cult of antiquity at its most fanatic. Of special relevance is that Rome under Nicholas became the locus of a revival of Roman culture expressed in particular by the fad of epigrams—with which the *Hypnerotomachia* abounds.[30] Fra Giocondo collected 2,000 of them.

Roman humanism had another center, and Prospero made his presence felt there too. This was the Colonna domain on the flanks of the Quirinal near the Fountain of Trevi, where Prospero resided in the Palazzo Colonna built by Oddone Colonna. Cardinal Bessarion, one of the great promulgators of Greek culture of the Renaissance, presided over the official Colonna church, SS. Apostoli. Bessarion lived in the Colonna compound, and the scholar Perotti was Bessarion's secretary. Among the people who frequented Bessarion's house were Ciriaco d'Ancona, Flavio Biondo, Bartolommeo Platina, Domizio Calderini, Francesco Filelfo, Poggio Bracciolini, and Lorenzo Valla. Bessarion's famous library formed the stock of today's famous Biblioteca Marciana in Venice. Prospero himself had an important library.[31]

But for our purposes, the most important of the prominent figures of Roman humanism with whom the young Francesco would, through his uncle, have had close ties was Leon Battista Alberti, whose mark, as we have seen in chapter 1, is so apparent in the *Hypnerotomachia*. Alberti's connection with the court of Nicholas V is well known; he dedicated his *De re aedificatoria* to the new pope in 1450. But his ties with the Colonnas were probably equally strong, if not stronger. In 1446 Prospero commissioned him to undertake the restoration of what he believed to be the gardens of the great patron of the arts in antiquity, Maecenas, and hired him to retrieve the boats of Lake Nemi, which had sunk centuries earlier.[32] Alberti was probably involved in the restoration of the church of SS. Apostoli, adjacent to the Palazzo Colonna.[33] Finally, it was possibly for Prospero that he undertook the immense public works project of restoring the Fountain of Trevi, located at the heart of the Colonna *rione* or district, involving the repair of the twenty-five-mile-long aqueduct of the Acqua Vergine, an undertaking that greatly enhanced the prestige of the Colonnas in Rome.[34]

Through such ties with the Colonna family, Alberti would have been introduced to Stefano Colonna, Francesco's father. Stefano hired Alberti as consultant for the reconstruction of the family holdings at Palestrina, of which he was the signore. As Ludwig Heydenreich has shown, the work was continued by Francesco. In 1447, with the election of Nicholas V, the fief of Palestrina had been returned to the Colonnas. Alberti was at Palestrina in 1450 in the years when Stefano had begun his reconstruction. Heydenreich claims that this reconstruction differs from that of the Orsini or Catanei compounds inside Rome because it is an archaeologically correct emulation of antiquity.[35] Although the actual reconstruction of the baronial palace was carried out between 1480 and 1500 at the same time as the work on the great Renaissance palazzi—Poggio Reale, the Villa della Duchessa in Naples, the Domus Nova in Mantua, and the Cortile del Belvedere—the initial plan was drawn up by Alberti in the 1450s. Thus it was the "primum exemplum" of the new typology. Heydenreich made the significance clear: Palestrina is the first Renaissance villa. According to Calvesi, this would explain the presence of references to Palestrina in the *Hypnerotomachia*.[36]

As a Colonna, Francesco would have come into contact with another remarkable humanist, Pomponio Leto (1424–1498), a bastard son of the house of the Neapolitan Sanseverini, princes of Salerno.[37] Born Giulio Pomponio, he assumed the name Leto, meaning "fortunate." He was Lorenzo Valla's student and succeeded him in the chair at the University of Rome, where he was an extremely popular and beloved teacher, as well as a friend of Alberti and Bessarion. He was self-made and fiercely proud. When his family finally, because he had made a reputation for himself, reversed its decision to disown him and invited him to live with them, he answered: "From Pomponio Leto, your relative and acquaintance, a salute. What you ask, I cannot do. Farewell." He was a fervent philhellene, philhebraist, and philarabist, and his library contained works in all three languages, along with those in Latin and Greek. Jacob Burckhardt has pictured him as the leading exponent of the worship of the ancient city, wandering throughout the city in blue buskins and purple tunic in imitation of the ancient Roman costume. According to Burckhardt, who portrays him in almost facetious terms, the remains of antiquity surrounding him touched him so deeply that he would "stand before them as if entranced, or would suddenly burst into tears at the sight of them."[38] In fact, Leto was a radical republican and a brilliant urban historian who exploited the ancient ruins and inscriptions of Rome in a more didactic way than previous generations of antiquarians had. He wrote a guide to Roman antiquities and would give walks around the old city using it as a vast memory theater, giving him a pretext for vividly eulogizing the ancient republican institutions that the ruins had housed and leaving blasphemous graffiti in the Catacombs.[39]

Leto's residence, which he shared with his fellow humanist, Bartolommeo dei Sacchi, Il Platina (1421–1481), was located directly behind the Colonnas' on the flanks of the Quirinal. The couple's villa opened onto a small, tended garden whose main feature was a large cage of chattering birds shaded by laurel trees; ducks and peacocks freely stalked the yard. He emulated the simple, rustic, and moral life of Republican Rome, and Cato the Censor, renowned in ancient Rome for his devotion to the old ideals of simplicity, honesty, and rusticity, was his particular hero. His friend Platina frequently commented on his austerity, noting the frugality of the meals Leto offered, which consisted only of vegetables. Leto seems to have been the first in Rome to gather a large collection of inscriptions for his suburban villa, as Poggio Bracciolini had done for his country residence of Terranova in Tuscany. Although Leto's house was destroyed in the early seventeenth century, contemporary accounts describe a modest house bought with his university salary or his pupils' fees. It would have been only natural for Francesco to have been acquainted with him. Indeed, it is conceivable that Leto could have been his tutor, or one of them, as was the case with the future Paul III Farnese, a relative of Francesco's through his mother.

Leto's Accademia Romana brought together the second generation of Roman humanists. Unlike the Florentine Academy under Marsilio Ficino, whose studies were primarily

Greek and philosophical, the circle of Leto was interested particularly in Roman histories and antiquities.[40] Most of the meetings of the Accademia were held in Pomponio Leto's *vigna* on the Quirinal Hill abutting the church of S. Salvatore, near the present Casino Rospigliosi. In the words of ecclesiastical historian Ludwig Pastor, he turned the group of humanist friends that he led into a "pagan republican confraternity." Membership in the Academy could explain, Calvesi claims, why Francesco Colonna was called "frater" in the acrostic of the *Hypnerotomachia*.[41] It was here that he introduced and directed the re-creations of ancient entertainments, mainly the satirical plays by the ancient Roman playwright Plautus. Every year it hosted two pagan festivals revived from ancient times: the Palilia, which fell on 21 April, the day of the "Natale di Roma" or birth of Rome, where the main activity was celebrating the ancient republic, and the Robigalia on 25 April, which was devoted to ridiculing the papacy by means of pasting satirical verses on an antique statue nicknamed Pasquino (near the Piazza Navona, on the route that the papal processions took, between the Lateran Palace and St. Peter's), a tradition that survives to this day.[42]

Because of its obvious support for the republican cause, with the advent of Paul II to the papal throne Roman humanism, which had flourished during the reign of Nicholas V, came to an abrupt end. In 1464, the very year of his election, he fired all of his court's abbreviators—whose task it was to abbreviate often lengthy papal pronouncements into a form suitable for official declarations. What the position lacked in distinction it gained in stability, and it was much sought after by humanists. This firing deprived them of their sole means of support. Cardinal Bessarion, the proponent of classical studies in Rome, withdrew to the Abbey of Grottaferrata after the election of Pope Paul II; the Roman humanists grouped around the Accademia Romana and turned to Pomponio Leto as their leader.[43]

In 1467, Paul's antihumanism entered a second, more decisive and forceful phase. He cracked down on the republican sympathizers with even greater force, dissolving Pomponio Leto's Accademia Romana, to which most of the humanists belonged, with a violent outburst against "questi studii di umanità." He believed such humanistic studies to be responsible for encouraging moral corruption, and he was particularly opposed to the teaching of the pagan poets to children. "Think of the vices that children of ten years of age would learn by reading Juvenal, Terence, Plautus, Ovid, and the rest," he declared. He also apparently tried vainly to prohibit the reading of poets in school. If God gave him "the necessary lease of life," he swore "to forbid these profligate studies, full as they were of heresy and malediction." Finally the academicians were denounced by one of his informers for leading "una vita achademica et epicurea."[44]

Pomponio did not escape punishment for his republican leanings. He decided to leave for Venice and from there to travel east, to learn Greek and Arabic. But his plans were thwarted by an accusation of homosexuality. With this excuse, he was repatriated to Rome, brought to court, and tortured. Many other academicians were also imprisoned and tortured, and one died from the treatment.[45]

Upon firing the abbreviators 1464, Paul had hired Rodrigo Borgia as prefect. This had the effect of providing Borgia with absolute power over all "research" activity of the church. The rise of the Borgias to power had begun. From then on, until Alexander Borgia assumed the papacy between 1497 and 1503, the city of Rome was theirs. The hideous cruelty of this family in exercising their new power goes beyond the pale even of the quattrocento, a period that Jacob Burckhardt saw as the bloodiest in the history of tyranny, atrocity, and abomination. One feels horror at Burckhardt's account of how one tyrant, Francesco Coppola of Naples, liked to have his opponents near him, dead and embalmed, dressed in the costume they were accustomed to wear before he had had them killed. He made no secret of his museum of mummies and would "chuckle upon regaling his listeners with how he had captured his victims, some while guests at his own dinners." Pandolfo Petrucci of Siena frightened the population of his town with occasional murder. His pastime during the summer was to roll "blocks of stone from the top of Mount Amiata, without caring what or whom they hit." The plotting was incessant. Ercole I d'Este is said to have poisoned his wife on discovering that she was going to poison him. [46]

There was no shortage of convenient assassinations during the Borgias' rise to the papacy, which was unabated between 1467 and 1492, as Burckhardt points out. The Venetian ambassador Paolo Capello wrote in 1500, "Every night four or five murdered men are discovered—bishops, prelates and others—so that all Rome is trembling for fear of being destroyed by the Duke [Cesare Borgia]." [47] It was Alexander Borgia who had Savonarola burned at the stake. Poison was favored by the Borgias. Onofrio Panvinio mentions three cardinals, Orsini, Ferrerio, and Michiel, who were among the victims, and hints at a fourth, Giovanni Borgia, one of the Borgias' own relatives. [48] According to Kretsulesco-Quaranta, many humanists suffered strange, violent, and identical deaths—all from the same disease, *podraga* (gout), which can be occasioned by poisoning: Prospero Colonna at sixty-three, Cardinal Nicholas of Cusa at the same age, and Pope Pius II at fifty-nine. Even Innocent VIII, supported by the Borgias, died of *podraga*. [49]

The main target of the Borgia faction was the Colonna family. [50] One of the most powerful of baronial dynasties, the Colonnas had also been the chief traditional rivals of the papacy in Rome. They had been the most important members of the Ghibelline faction, allies of the emperor, opposed to the Guelfs, allies of the pope. This rivalry harked back to the twelfth century; since that time, their land holdings had been attacked by the papacy. After Palestrina had been besieged in 1304 by Boniface VIII, the Colonnas claimed reparation for damages to their palace "inherited from the Emperor Julius Caesar." Palestrina was ransacked again under Pope Eugenius IV in 1437. According to Eugenius's decree allowing appropriation of all Colonna property, the purpose of the destruction was that "they remain always lacking and poor, squalid in their misery, and that death be their only relief and that their life be one of ordeals." [51] As we have seen, restoration was begun in the 1440s by Leon Battista Alberti, under the aegis of Francesco's father, Stefano Colonna.

The Colonnas had singled themselves out from the other baronial families by applying their own particular imperial idea of the Roman Republic to the group of merchants that drew their livelihood from trade, especially in the fourteenth century; this group is sometimes referred to as the civic nobility of Rome to distinguish them from the feudal nobility, and it was equally opposed to the papacy. In 1330 there was a popular uprising that pitted another Stefano Colonna against the pope. The Romans saw Stefano as the only one who could control the anarchy of the city. Some thought that the republic of Florence might serve as a model for a newly constituted Rome under him. In addition, the Colonnas had been the supporters of the archrepublican Cola di Rienzo, leader of a popular uprising in Rome in 1347 and self-styled Tribune of Rome. The family contained some diehard republicans. In 1511, mistakenly thinking that Pope Julius II was dead, Bishop Pompeo Colonna mounted the Campidoglio and harangued the people of Rome, invoking the past glories of the ancient republic that he had personally intended to revive. Apparently he never stopped his quest, for between 19 and 20 September 1526 he tried to lay siege to the Vatican, thus irreparably hampering the efforts of the city's papal leaders to fend off the Sack of Rome.[52]

These antipapal, republican leanings of the Colonnas did not keep them from entering into strategic alliances with the papacy when it suited their purposes, and even from entering into the papal curia themselves when they got the chance. As we have seen, Oddone Colonna succeeded in becoming pope. Prospero, his nephew and the uncle of Francesco, tried to regain the papacy—and Prospero was beaten by two voices in the conclave that brought Nicholas V to power.[53] Having failed, he supported Nicholas, an ally of the Colonnas. Under this new pope, all the family properties were restored, and it seemed that once again the fortunes of the Colonnas were in the ascendant.

The Colonnas' luck ran out quickly, however. Old conflicts reemerged in many bloody episodes during the rise of the Borgias, who were bent on supplanting the baronial powers throughout the peninsula. Thus Lorenzo Colonna was arrested in 1484. Imprisoned in Castel Sant'Angelo on 30 May, he was tortured and decapitated in the court of the castle; his body was brought to the church of the SS. Apostoli beside the Palazzo Colonna for the funeral service. During the ceremony the mother opened the top of the casket; seizing the head by the hair, she brandished it before the audience and cried: "Here is the head of my son, here is the faith of Pope Sixtus."[54]

The effect of this kind of ruthlessness was lasting, as it so often has been in history. By the time Alexander Borgia reached the papal throne, the Colonnas, along with all the other baronial families, had been permanently dislodged from the place of leadership they had one enjoyed.[55] Moreover, the attacks on the Accademia Romana effectively crushed any dissent from the humanists. The scholars assembled in Rome in the days of Nicholas V and Prospero Colonna had no intellectual heirs. Fifty years of obsequious and stifling conformity followed; their highlight was a book entitled *De cardinalatu,* a praise of good cardinalship by a certain member of the papal court called Paolo Cortesi, "clearly displaying his sympathies for the ruling powers."[56]

We have seen in chapter 1 how Roman the *Hypnerotomachia* was. In many ways, it·represents that area of the city between the Orti Salustiani and the Roman Forum. In this light, it is tempting to join Calvesi in looking on the *Hypnerotomachia* as an expression of the "fanatic cult of *romanità*" by Francesco Colonna, who was not only a *frater* of the Accademia Romana but a particularly prominent member of a powerful republican family.[57] Indeed, the *romanità* of the type the *Hypnerotomachia* espouses never fared well in Rome, as Anthony Grafton points out. This is because the city of Rome had always been highly charged with more than just archaeological value. When Romans admired ancient ruins, their reasons rarely were purely aesthetic. Antique stones had a "powerful and sentimental political edge."[58] Restoration had been linked with republican sentiments and passions since at least as early as the twelfth century, when the Roman Nicolaus Crescentii erected a palace for himself across the street from the ruins of the antique Roman Temple of Fortuna Virilis, using fragments of buildings of the ancient republic as a way of celebrating a victory of the republican faction over the papacy.[59]

The connection was even clearer in texts. The famous *Mirabilia urbis Romae* was more than a mere guide to ancient Rome. Compiled about the middle of the twelfth century, it obviously breathes the consciousness of the city's republican destiny.[60] It presents ancient Rome, which had been destroyed by Pope Gregory I in the sixth century, assailing the pope's implacable behavior and accusing him of destroying the sculpture of the Colossus, a powerful symbol of ancient Rome.[61] In his mid-fourteenth-century *Africa,* the republican Petrarch returned to the theme of Roman topography, inventing an imaginary tour of the Rome of the time of Scipio, who was always seen as the embodiment of republicanism as opposed to Caesar, the personification of the empire. His friend Cola di Rienzo, the most radical republican of all, spent every day sifting through the epigraphs, statues, and medals that were strewn about the city. When he finally discovered in the Lateran the so-called Lex de Imperio—the bronze tablet bearing the decree by which the Roman people formally transferred its power to the emperors (not the popes)—he used the text effectively to incite the city to civil uprising against the papacy in order to make the Roman people "imitate . . . the will, benignity, and liberality of the ancient rulers of Rome."[62]

In this context, we might again join his biographer in thinking of Francesco Colonna as attached to the generation of Roman humanists who were brought together by Nicholas V and were so closely associated with his family. Although Prospero died when he was just nine years old and Alberti when he was eighteen, Francesco would possibly have had the manuscripts of Alberti's work because of Alberti's close ties with the family—not only his *De re aedificatoria* but all his works, including novels. It is even conceivable that he could have been tutored by Alberti, perhaps becoming fascinated with Alberti's mind. He would have had every reason for embracing the ideals of the *Hypnerotomachia*: liberty, paganism, *ro-manità*.

However, there are three problems with Calvesi's scenario. The first is political. Prince Francesco Colonna, far from being opposed to the Borgias, in fact seems to have belonged to a part of the family that was in their good graces. His father, Stefano, was a *condottiere* in the service of Lodovico Sforza, an ally of the Borgias. Francesco himself fared sufficiently well under the new papal regime that he was granted a governorship of Tivoli.[63] When he did happen to be among those affected by the 1501 excommunication bull against the Colonnas by Alexander Borgia, Pope Alexander VI, which defined them as "sons of iniquity,"[64] his reaction was diplomatic to say the least. When he discovered that he was included among the excommunicates, he succeeded in establishing his innocence. So confident was he of his favorable standing with the Borgias that he did not budge from his castle in Palestrina, not believing he was in danger. But Alexander Borgia sent his army to take over the town and assigned the fief to Giovanni Borgia, his own nephew. Francesco surrendered without even unsheathing his sword and went to Rome, resigned to his misfortune. So much self-restraint for a Colonna was incredible for the time. In Rome he signed a title renouncing his fiefs; in return he was promised a pension for himself and for his descendants. He had, however, secretly written up a letter of protest beforehand. His patience payed off, for at the death of Alexander Borgia in 1503, Julius II restored all his property.[65]

The second, more serious problem is that for all the ties of his family to the humanists, Francesco Colonna seems not to have been a great humanist scholar or thinker himself. Prince Colonna was well placed socially and geographically for writing the book. However, the only literary traces we have of him are a couple of epigrams entitled "Francisco Columnae Antiquario" and thus addressed to him (at twenty) as an "antiquarius"—that is, a connoisseur of classical antiquity. They were written by a certain Raffaelle Zovenzoni, a courtier in the habit of writing unctuous Latin poems to powerful political figures, such as Cosimo de' Medici, Francesco Sforza, and Pope Sixtus IV.[66] As in the case of the first Francesco Colonna, we have slender evidence indeed of a mind capable of writing a book like the *Hypnero-tomachia*. Judging from the biographical evidence we do have, Colonna emerges more as a connoisseur of the arts than as a creative person in his own right.

Third, someone else had far more reason for writing a polemic manifesto in 1467 than did Francesco Colonna: this was Leon
Battista Alberti. Even more significantly, Alberti
possessed the knowledge and elsewhere
displayed the type of reasoning
that the contents of this
extraordinary
book re-
flect

108
—
109

5

THE REAL POLIPHILO

T HERE IS SOMETHING APPARENTLY IMPLAUSIBLE ABOUT THE IDEA of Leon Battista Alberti as the author of the *Hypnerotomachia*. Alberti has been a much-studied subject since Jacob Burckhardt first drew the attention of modern academic scholarship upon this first "universal man" of the Renaissance in his famous *Civilization of the Renaissance* in 1861. So has the *Hypnerotomachia*. Why has no one made the connection?

Two reasons: first, scholars have generally chosen to focus on just isolated aspects of Alberti's work instead of on its polymorphic wholeness.[1] Second, those who have looked at the work one way or the other have tended to see it as historicist and revivalist rather than as innovative. The two major exceptions have been Girolamo Mancini's biography of 1882[2] and Joan Gadol's study of 1968.[3] Without the kind of view informing these works, it is impossible to hypothesize the connection betwen Alberti and the *Hypnerotomachia*.

*   *   *

Among the many varied features that would be explained if Alberti were the author of the book is the *Hypnerotomachia*'s deep literary knowledge. Literature was Alberti's first love. In his autobiography—which is unusual in that he wrote about himself not in the first person but in the third—he claimed that he "enjoyed literature so much that it sometimes gave him the same pleasure as the buds of fragrant flowers, and then neither hunger nor sleep could make him leave his books. But so late did he stay up sometimes that his books assumed the aspects of scorpions, so that he could see nothing, let alone his books."[4] And as he wrote in his first book, *De commodis litterarum atque incommodis* (On the advantages and disadvantages of literary studies), where he considered the prospects of a life dedicated to literary pursuits,

FOR ME LITERATURE IS THE MOST JOYFUL THING THAT COULD EXIST. WHILE OTHERS WERE MAINTAINING THAT ONE SHOULD PLACE THE CULT OF LITERATURE AFTER ALL OTHER DISCIPLINES, I, BY CONTRAST, WAS CONVINCED THAT LITERATURE HAD TO BE PUT BEFORE ANYTHING ELSE. CONSEQUENTLY, I SET OUT TO ACQUIRE THE KNOWLEDGE OF LITERATURE WITH GREAT DILIGENCE, DESIRING WITH FEROCIOUS TENACITY EVERYTHING THAT WAS CONSIDERED ILLUSTRIOUS. THERE WAS NOTHING THAT WITH FATIGUE, ANGUISH, AND WATCHFULNESS I DID NOT TRY TO REACH AND LOOK FOR WITH INQUIRY THAT WAS AS CAREFUL AS POSSIBLE. I WAS REALLY CONVINCED THAT I HAD BEGUN THE MOST PRAISE-WORTHY OF ALL LABORS. IN FACT I CONSIDERED IT SUITABLE TO A LOFTY MIND TO BEAR WITH PATIENCE THE ANGUISH AND NIGHTLY STUDIES AND ALL THE OTHER PAINS AND DIFFICULTIES, OUT OF A DESIRE TO ACQUIRE NOT ONLY KNOWLEDGE, BUT ALSO THE FAME THROUGH LITERATURE I HOPED I WOULD BE ABLE TO REACH.[5]

Alberti did not just love literature. He went on to become one of the most productive and celebrated writers of fiction, nonfiction, and poetry of the Renaissance, a stylist obsessively preoccupied with language.[6] He was a defender of vernacular Italian, or "Tuscan" as it was called in the Renaissance, and his mastery of it was exemplary. He is credited with being the first, after Dante, to unite lofty themes with gracious form.[7] His ideal was "the naked, simple style, in which one can easily see that I wished to prove how well I could imitate the extremely gentle and sweet writer Xenophon."[8] Dante, Petrarch, and Boccaccio may deserve credit for transforming the vernacular into a literary language, as Cristoforo Landino wrote, but "in prose Battista surpassed the best."[9] Among his achievements is his *Grammatica della lingua toscana* of 1450, the first work to treat the vernacular on equal footing with the "rule-bound" classical languages and the first Italian grammar in history.[10] His *Della famiglia*—an acknowledged landmark of prose—was the first text written not in Latin but in the vernacular that was considered adequate for discussing humanist topics.[11] So exquisite was Alberti's prose style that one of his own earliest works in Italian, *Deifira,* was consistently attributed to Boccaccio until the end of the nineteenth century.[12] Moreover, he organized the first poetry competition in Italian in Florence in 1441, igniting a fierce debate concerning the possibility of creating great poetry in the vernacular.[13]

The attribution to Alberti would help explain why the *Hypnerotomachia* is a love story. Alberti wrote a number of pieces on the theme of love, in particular two pastoral eclogues, *Tirsis* and *Corimbus,* and two elegies, *Agilitta* and *Mirzia* (1429–1430). These were accompanied by a number of prose works, again on the theme of love, in the vernacular: *Ephoebia* or *Amator* (ca. 1429), a discourse on the nature of love; *Ecatonfilea* (1429), in which a woman talks about the virtues that the man she loves ought to possess; and *Deifira* (1429), which discusses how to escape from unhappy love affairs.

The immensely erudite linguistic knowledge in the *Hypnerotomachia* is also consistent with this attribution. To begin with, Alberti's authorship would explain the mastery of Latin—which Filarete and Francesco di Giorgio could not even read—in the *Hypnerotomachia.* Although he was a fervent defender of the vernacular, Alberti not only was educated at the famous school of classical studies of Master Gasparino Barzizza in Padua, where other great humanist scholars such as Francesco Filelfo and Francesco Barbaro were trained, but by all accounts he had been the most brilliant student of them all.[14] In fact, initially he knew Latin even better than the vernacular Tuscan, and he claimed that acquiring the latter took much effort. This was explained by his family's long exile from Florence; in his own words, he "had been educated in foreign countries and did not know his native tongue. Unfamiliar with it, he found it difficult to write it elegantly and concisely."[15]

His second written work, composed when he was barely twenty, is a comedy in Latin called *Philodoxeus* (1424). The *Intercenales* (1429) are in Latin, and his other works in that language are *Vita Sancti Potiti* (1433), *De commodis et incommodis litterarum* (1429), *Egloghe*

(1429), *Amator* (1429), *Uxoria* (1429), *De statua* (1434), *De pictura* (1435), *De iure* (1437), *Ponti-fex* (1437), *Apologi* (1437), *Mosca* and *Canis* (1441), *Descriptio urbis Romae* (ca. 1450), *Momus* (ca. 1450), *De Porcaria conjuratione* (1453), *De literis et ceteris principiis grammaticae* (1460), *Epistu-lae septem Epimenidis nomine Diogene inscriptae* (1462–1465), *Epistolae Leonis ad Cratem philoso-phum* (1462–1465), and *De componendis cifris* (1466). As for the Latin of the *De re aedificatoria*, it is universally acclaimed for its excellence and as representative of the new classicizing stan-dards of Renaissance humanism.

Alberti could easily have been responsible for the proficiency in Greek in the *Hypnerotomachia* as well. Lapo da Castiglioncho, in his letter dedicating his translation of the second-century Greek satirist Lucian to his friend Alberti, recalls the years during which, as students of the Bologna "studium," they attended Greek lessons together to perfect their knowledge of the language that had become so fashionable. Lapo writes that he had "started Greek to please you [Alberti] because you repeatedly recommended it, and also to take my mind off the troubles oppressing me. There was no greater solace for us, and no one had more influence over me than you. I made progress in those most liberal and complicated studies thanks not only to your friendship and help but to your stimulating example and encouragement."[16] Alberti's familiarity with Greek is apparent in his penchant for using Greek names for the characters in his literary works. In the individual pieces of his *Intercenales* we find Philargirus (cupidinous), Alochocratis (domineering), Zelotypus (jealous), Ethicomius (moderate), Perifronus (prudent), Asotus (slothful), Philoponius (work loving), Peniplusius (wealthy), Paleoterus (senior one), Polytropus (versatile), and Neophronus (young minded). Similarly in the *Hypnerotomachia,* we have Agrypnia (insomnia), Logistica (logic), Thelemia (desire), Aphea (touch), Offressia (smell), Achoe (sound), Geussia (taste), and Orassia (sight).

The *Hypnerotomachia* would have been one of several of Alberti's works with Greek titles. He particularly favored titles involving the root *philos-* (lover). For example, the title of his play, *Philodoxeus,* is Greek for "lover of glory"; and another of his titles, *Ecatonfilea,* means "a hundred loves." Alberti also tended to use Greek names to indicate the traits of their bearers. Two of his heroes have names containing the *philos-,* as in "Poliphilo." They are Philodoxos (lover of glory), in the play by almost the same name, and Philoponius (lover of hard work), in the *Intercenales.*

Alberti's authorship would also explain the remarkable coincidence that the Latin and Greek philological sources for the *De re aedificatoria* and the *Hypnerotomachia* are identical. Besides citing Vitruvius, both works contain references to Aristotle, Caesar, Celsus, Cicero, Claudianus, Diodorus Siculus, Demosthenes, Diogenes, Herodotus, Hesiod, Homer, Livy, Martial, Ovid, Pliny, Plato, Poliziano, Propertius, Sallust, Servius, Strabo, Suetonius, Tacitus, and Varro.[17] Moreover, only in these two architectural writings of the quattrocento do these sources coincide. Those in Filarete's *De architectura* (1450–1464) and Francesco di Giorgio's *Trattati d'architettura* are very different.[18]

Although there is no record indicating that Alberti knew Hebrew and Arabic, the appearance of inscriptions in both languages, brief but correct, in the polyglot concoction of *Hypnerotomachia* is consistent with Alberti being the author. Quattrocento humanists were on the whole discontented with the limitations of their own tradition and, at a time when the cultures of Africa, Asia, and the Americas were still unknown, they sought to expand their intellectual horizons by exploring all the cultures that were known at the time, particularly the Arabic one—a strategy that was to prove most favorable for the growth of the sciences.[19] As we saw in chapter 4, Rome under Nicholas V became a feverish center of translation: from Greek, of course, but also from other languages. The pope hired Manetti to translate from the Hebrew, and Nicholas of Cusa translated from the Arabic.[20] These were Alberti's associates. Even a second-generation humanist like Pomponio Leto had Arabic books in his library. The Vatican Library too contained them.[21] This was Alberti's world. It is obvious that even if he had no true mastery of these languages, he had privileged firsthand access to the greatest experts of his day, whose help he could have sought in composing the Hebrew and Arabic inscriptions of the *Hypnerotomachia*. While there is no mention of actual Chaldean texts in the papal library, the language itself was as highly regarded as the others.[22] And hieroglyphs would have been the province of Lorenzo Valla, who translated the *Horoappollo* into Latin for Nicholas V.

If Alberti were the author, the highly experimental, Joycean character of the prose—"Joysprickean," to borrow a term from Anthony Burgess[23]—would be explained. For all the famed clarity and purity of his prose style, Alberti had a long-standing tendency to innovate in his writing. He was known as an extremely versatile writer, renowned for his proficiency in a wide variety of styles. His friend Cristoforo Landino wrote: "I recall the style of Battista Alberti, who, like a chameleon, always takes the form of what he writes about."[24] His poetry, for example, consisted of not simply traditional sonnets and sestinas but also formally inventive unrhymed hexameters.[25] In his youthful *Intercenales,* a collection of dialogues and fables, composed in his twenties, his writing is highly unorthodox. Its style is both weighty and eclectic, admitting a wide range of expressions not only from classical but also pre- and postclassical Latin. In the words of one of his translators, Alberti was fond both of using rare words derived from "obscure authors and obscurer compilers" and of inventing his own words and names. With a technique similar to that used in the *Hypnerotomachia,* he formed new compounds with the prefixes *per-* or *sub-*. David Marsh lists among the examples *perstrenus, permaximus, perdissimilis, subimportunus,* and *subsinasnio.* Alberti also uses words not found in classical authors, such as *exhibitrix* and *insipiditas.*[26] In *Momus,* the writing is pushed to the limits of readability in certain passages where Alberti tries to forge a language of *furore* and passion, in particular when the hero, disguised as climbing ivy, succeeds in seducing Fame, whom he has caught in his tangled and entangling clutches.[27]

An additional aspect of the *Hypnerotomachia* might be explained by Alberti's authorship: the knowledge of engineering it displays. After graduating in 1428 from the University of Bologna at the age of twenty-four with a degree in law, a profession he loathed, he began to study engineering, eventually becoming one of the greatest engineers of the Renaissance. His *Ludi matematici,* or "mathematical games," a series of puzzles in the field of engineering, are a direct outgrowth of these studies. And so is *De re aedificatoria.* Its title, meaning "On building," is clearly at variance with Vitruvius's more general title, *De architectura.* It is foremost a technical manual, devoting just less than two-thirds of the book to functional matters, and the remainder to cultural ones.

De re aedificatoria is overwhelmingly, as the title suggests, about construction: about materials, foundations, soil, hydraulics, building management and building economics, functional analysis, and mechanics; only secondarily does it address issues of aesthetics. Alberti's major concern is proper construction techniques for vaults, plastering, roofing, shells, pavements, bridges, stairs, city walls, schools, hospitals, and infrastructure such as roads, sewers, pavements, artificial river banks, canals, locks, and bridges. One of his two sections on *concinnitas* is unsurprisingly placed in a chapter devoted to private houses, but the other is located in the midst of a chapter dealing with pins, wheels, pulleys, levers, and their parts, sizes, and figures; with screws and their circles and worms; with mortar incrustations on walls, different types of mortar, and stucco; with the manner in which lime has to be prepared; with methods of cutting marble; and with what cement to use in mosaics.[28] The book ends with a chapter that discusses hydraulics: how to find hidden water, the digging of wells and walling of wells and conduits, a method for transporting water, cisterns, passages by water, and artificial banks to rivers, canals, and sea walls. His last chapter ends with a section on such mundane construction matters as "by what methods to destroy or drive away serpents, gnats, bugs, flies, mice, fleas, moths and the like troublesome vermin," how to heat and cool rooms, and how to repair cracks (X.15–16, pp. 356–362). Clearly he enjoyed practicing the craft of building.

In particular, Alberti's authorship might explain the presence of ingenious mechanical devices in the *Hypnerotomachia.* Indeed, he is one of the most inventive mechanical engineers of the Renaissance. He designed an odometer, that is, an itinerary compass for measuring the distance covered by a vehicle; a mechanism to measure the speed of seaborne vessels; a method for measuring the depths of the sea; and a "fontana a termini," or perpetual fountain (described in his *Ludi matematici* of 1450–1451 and his architectural treatise).[29] His *De' pondi e leve di alcuna rota,* whose attribution is still dubious,[30] is a treatise on mechanical devices to convert water and wind into motive power based on the mechanical potential of the lever, the pulley, and the screw. This background would explain the *Hypnerotomachia*'s narrator's response to the devices he sees. Thus, when those who approach the sculpture of a urinating little boy receive a surprising squirt in the face, the narrator is no passive onlooker. He forms a hypothesis about the mechanism that makes this possible. He supposes that the stairs in front of the figure contain a movable step, under which there is a weight. Once the foot comes down on this step, a pipe behind it goes down like a lever and lifts another pipe through which the water streams. Similarly, when the narrator comes across a mobile fountain, he notes that "the water gathered all the time in the basin thanks to the air pressure that penetrated in the basin by passing through the axe of the vase" (g6–g6v). Again he attempts to deduce the mechanism and guesses that this is a result of a double articulated pipe, whose elbows are of different lengths, and that the water rises by the force of its own hydrostatic pressure, set into action by the rotation of the wheels carrying the fountain. It can hardly be a coincidence that in *De re aedificatoria,* Alberti writes that "hydraulic engineers can force water to leap high out of a vessel, by trapping an air pocket between two columns of water" (X.7, p. 341) and that chapter 9 of his *Ludi matematici* also includes a description of a similar device called a "fontana a termini," that is, a perpetual fountain of Heron, which fascinated Leonardo da Vinci.[31] As we know, Alberti was familiar with the writings of the Alexandrian engineers. This technical expertise would also explain the two figures—one a nymph holding a cornucopia on the top of the gigantic pyramid, the other a small child blowing a trumpet—set into a twirling motion by the wind and emitting a high-pitched sound. The device of the automatically opening door is also remarkable but more difficult to attribute to Alberti, because it is powered by magnets, and there is nothing like it in any of his other writings or even in the Hellenistic engineering treatises.[32]

Certainly, Alberti's authorship might explain why the narrator of the *Hypnerotomachia* marvels at the highly sophisticated construction devices he imagines were necessary for erecting the buildings in the book. From this point of view, the buildings are a direct outgrowth of the concerns of *De re aedificatoria,* where, as a construction engineer, Alberti described mechanisms for hoisting great weights (VI.6). A measure of his competence in this area was his previously mentioned attempt in 1446, at the behest of Prospero Colonna, to lift two Roman barges dating from the time of Caligula from the bed of Lake Nemi, on Prospero's property in the Alban Hills. They had been visible from the surface of the water for many centuries, and fishermen would pull up pieces of them in their nets.

They were the only ships known to have come down from antiquity, and in a period when Italians were exploring the world the information they contained was of great importance. In fact, one of them had the greatest beam of any known ancient ship. It was an enormous vessel: 240 feet long with a beam of 78 feet. The other was only slightly smaller (fig. 37). Many attempts were made to raise the immense vessels,[33] but Alberti was the only one to enjoy even partial success before the 1930s, when Italian archaeologists used an ancient Roman drainage tunnel to drain the lake. He proceeded by chaining together a row of empty barrels and stringing them across the lake as a sort of bridge. On the barrels he placed wind-

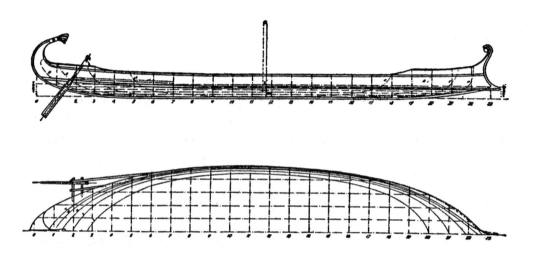

37. THE HULL OF A HELLENISTIC BARGE FROM LAKE NEMI. FROM L. SPRAGUE DE CAMP, *THE ANCIENT ENGINEERS* (CAMBRIDGE, MASS., 1960), P. 154.

lasses, which carried ropes with large grab hooks. Divers attached the hooks to the hull of the ship and the prow was lifted high enough for him to see it was a barge.[34] Submerged for a dozen centuries, it still bore lettering that proved it was a Roman state barge from the time of Caligula.[35] One ship had already been lifted out of the water when the rotten wood gave way, sending it back to the bottom. But the event, attended by the entire papal court, provided Biondo and Alberti with many details of how ships had been built in antiquity.[36]

Alberti clearly enjoyed resolving difficult problems concerning the lifting of great weights by investigating the mechanical potentials of hoisting devices. The same passionate love of ingenious inventions is obvious in a passage of the *Hypnerotomachia* in which the narrator, gazing at the pyramid, cannot help wondering, "With what virtue and human forces and order and incredible thinking, with what celestial emulation are such heavy weights transported so far in the air? With what workmen and what pulleys and other tractor machines

38. HOISTING DEVICES DESCRIBED BY ALBERTI IN *DE RE AEDIFICATORIA* VI.8. ILLUSTRATED IN THE MANUSCRIPT, C. 224 V., REGGIO EMILIA, BIBLIOTECA MUNICIPALE.

and carrying armature?"[37] He gives the correct antique terminology for the cranes—*polispasio, capre* (fig. 38). A *polispasio* is a crane with a pole set up and kept upright by means of cables stretched in four different directions. Where the cables meet at the top, two sockets are fixed; the block is attached to the sockets with ropes. Under the block is put a piece of timber. The block, with three sets of pulleys in its width, is fixed so that three guide ropes are inserted in the machine. And Alberti himself describes the *capre* in *De re aedificatoria* as "a machine consisting of three posts that are bracketed and tied together at the top, but whose feet splay out to form a triangle. Used together with pulleys and captans, this machine is very effective in lifting weights. Usually erected over the roof" (X.17, p. 362).

Drainage was another branch of engineering close to Alberti's heart. It is known that he renovated the aqueduct of the Acqua Vergine in Rome, thus restoring the flow of water to the Fountain of Trevi. He devoted most of the last book of his *De re aedificatoria* to "conveying water." In fact, he even waxes enthusiastic about the importance of drains, placing them on the same level as the great building types of Roman architecture and thus anticipating the famous claim of Francesco Milizia, the eighteenth-century functionalist theoretician of architecture, to prefer the engineering marvel of the Cloaca Maxima to all the temples of Rome. As Alberti writes in book VI of *De re aedificatoria:* "Need I mention the porticoes, temples, ports, theaters, and vast baths, which caused such amazement that experienced architects from abroad denied that some of those works could ever be built, although they saw them before their very eyes? Should I go on? They did not fail to have their drains beautifully built" (VI.3, p. 159). Furthermore, he observes:

As REGARDS DRAINAGE, I HAVE OBSERVED THAT THE BEST ARCHITECTS ENSURED THAT RAINWATER WAS EITHER DRAWN OFF BY DRAINPIPES, TO PREVENT IT FROM DRIPPING ON ANYONE ENTERING, OR COLLECTED IN IMPLUVIA TO BE EITHER STORED FOR HUMAN USE OR FORCED TO FLOW SOMEWHERE TO WASH AWAY HUMAN FILTH, MAKING IT LESS OFFENSIVE TO THE NOSES AND EYES OF MANKIND. IT SEEMS TO ME THAT ONE OF THE GREATEST CONCERNS WAS KEEPING RAINWATER OUT OF THE BUILDING, AND DRAINING IT OFF FAR AWAY, IN PARTICULAR TO AVOID THE GROUND ABOUT BECOMING DAMP. (V.3, p. 159)

In view of this attachment to hydraulic devices, it should be of little surprise that the round temple in the text of the *Hypnerotomachia,* to which I also referred in chapter 2, is conceived as a gigantic drain (fig. 39). It appears to reflect Alberti's concerns precisely: the ten columns holding up the roof of the round temple are hollow in order for rainwater to be able to pass through them directly into a cistern under the temple, thus preventing the exterior of the temple from getting dirty as well as visitors from being splashed.

By the same token, Alberti's authorship might explain why Poliphilo is no simple amateur with a passing fancy for geometry. Like all engineers, Alberti was enamored of Euclidean geometry. Prospero Colonna, his patron at Lake Nemi, called him "il nostro Leon Battista Alberti, geometra egregio" (our Leon Battista Alberti, distinguished geometer) in 1446.[38] The author of the *Hypnerotomachia,* who referred to an obelisk as the "three-sided column of Euclid" and enumerated the different geometrical figures in the mosaics as not only circles, triangles, and squares but also "conoid, almoid, hemial, and rhomboid figures,"[39] must have been someone as proficient as Alberti, for *almoid* was a highly technical term. In addition, the *Hypnerotomachia* gives a method for deriving a heptagon inside a circle. To that date, the problem had been solved by one person: the Arab geometer Abu'l Wafa. The narrator of the *Hypnerotomachia* was the second, and Leonardo da Vinci the third.[40] The construction of the decagon inside a circle is no simple matter either—except, apparently, for the narrator of the *Hypnerotomachia:*

39. THE GIANT DRAIN IN THE FORM OF A TEMPLE.

TO OBTAIN THESE SECTIONS, YOU DIVIDE IN TWO PARTS THE FIGURE. YOU WILL HAVE FORMED TWENTY VERY SIMPLY BY TRACING A CIRCLE, THE DIAMETER OF WHICH IS GIVEN BY THE INTERSECTION OF TWO DIAMETERS. YOU WILL MAKE A POINT OF YOUR CHOICE IN THE MIDDLE OF THE DIAMETER, THEN THROUGH THIS POINT YOU WILL TRACE AN OBLIQUE LINE THAT MEETS THE EXTREMITY OF THE OTHER DIAMETER. THIS LINE, PASSING THROUGH THE POINT JUST MENTIONED, GIVES THE QUARTER OF THE ENTIRE DIAMETER. IN PROLONGING IT TO THE INTERSECTION OF THE CIRCUMFERENCE, YOU WILL OBTAIN A TRIANGULAR SECTION, WHICH WILL BE THE TENTH OF THE CIRCLE. (s6v)

In addition to not being easy, this method is taken almost verbatim from *De re aedificatoria*.[41]

*   *   *

Yet another aspect of the *Hypnerotomachia* that would be explained by Alberti's authorship is the knowledge it displays of the rules of perspective. This obsessive emphasis on lines and their role in the construction of space is one of the most deeply Albertian features of the book. After all, Alberti did revolutionize our way of looking at the world in the literal sense:

he invented perspective.[42] As Erwin Panofsky and Joan Gadol showed, before Alberti expounded his rules of perspective in *De pictura* in 1435, there was no way of scientifically representing three-dimensional space on a two-dimensional plane. In pre-Albertian paintings foreshortened orthogonals converged, but never toward a single horizon and certainly not toward a single center. Of course magnitudes diminished and receded in these paintings, but again, this diminution was by no means constant.[43] Inventing perspective would not be surprising for someone like Alberti whose emblem, after all, was an eye. Did he not write in his *De re aedificatoria* that "the eye is by nature the organ most especially in love with beauty and *concinnitas*" (IX.8, p. 312)? In particular the attribution to Alberti would explain the omnipresence of what Joan Gadol calls a type of "geometric seeing." Everything is described in extraordinary detail in terms of lines. The account of the alignments of a single doorway takes up five pages (c1v–c3v).[44]

What to others may have seemed an unusual way of looking at the world was second nature to Alberti. Everywhere he looked, he saw lines. His statement at the beginning of *De pictura* that drawing was nothing but lines drawn between points obviously struck his contemporaries as highly idiosyncratic; otherwise, he would not have bothered to add that this was true even though these terms "seem closer to geometry than painting." Furthermore, he apologizes to his readers and reminds them that this is not a treatise on mathematics but one on painting.[45] As Gadol points out, he must have been sorely criticized for his claim, for he had to write two further works in which he clearly distinguished the geometric "point" from the painter's "point" to indicate that he knew what he was about very well indeed, and that it was nonsense to accuse him of trying to "see" mathematical concepts.[46] In the *De re aedificatoria,* he wrote, "We must . . . take great care to ensure that even the minutest elements are so arranged in their level, alignment, number, shape, and appearance, that right matches left, top matches bottom, adjacent matches adjacent, and equal matches equal, and that they are an ornament to that body of which they are to be part (IX.7, p. 171). And he conceived his *Ludi matematici* as a series of surveying "games," consisting in the construction of geometric pictures in order to determine magnitudes indirectly.[47]

As is well known, in this revolutionary new science of perspective that changed the way the world looked at itself, one of the main concepts Alberti incorporated was of the *velo,* the reticulated net, otherwise referred to as *quadrangulus.* The technique went back as far as ancient Egypt. The painter who used it according to Alberti's directions "saw" how three-dimensional objects appeared on its plane surface, and this appearance is what he transferred to his panel (or canvas) or wall by means of the parallels of the net and corresponding parallels drawn over the surface of the area to be painted (fig. 40). As Alberti writes in *De pictura,* "I trace a quadrangle," which "could be an open window where I look at what will be painted," in order "to trace with precision things seen."[48]

Alberti had canonized the use of the *quadrangulus* in his treatise on painting, and by 1499, when the *Hypnerotomachia* was published, Leonardo da Vinci was also discussing it.

lmearum ductionem ad singulas iacentis lineę di
usiones prosequor. Sed in succesiuis quantitatibus
transuersis hunc modum seruo

Ars Positionis plani peroptima

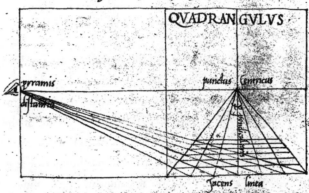

Habeo Areolam in qua describo lineam unam rectam hanc
diuido p eas partis in qua iacens linea quadranguli diuisa
est Dehinc pono sursu ab hac linea punctum unicu ad

quidem in linee demostrant queadmodum pene usqʒ
ad infimam distantiam qtitates transuersę succesiue
sub aspectu alterentur Hinc essent nam nulli qui una
ab diuisa eqdistantem lineam intra quadrangulum
ducerent spaciumqʒ qd̄ utrasqʒ lineas adsit in
tris ptes diuiderent tunc huic secundę eqdistanti
lineę aliam item eqdistantem hac lege adderent
ut spacium qd̄ inter primam diuisam et secundā
eqdistantem lineam est in tris partes diuisum una
parte sui excedat spacium id quod sit inter secundā
et tertiam lineam ac deinceps reliquas lineas adderet

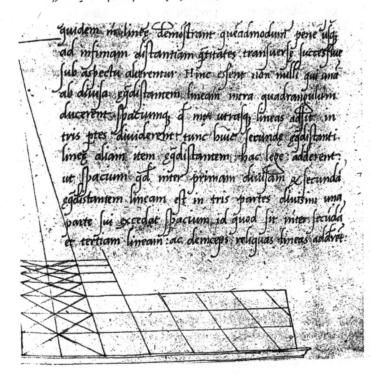

40. ALBERTIAN *QUADRANGULUS*, THE VISUAL PYRAMID, AND THE *PAVIMENTO*. FROM ALBERTI'S
DE PUNCTIS ET LINEIS APUD PICTORES, LUCCA, BIBLIOTECA STATALE (CAT. 15).

But at the time of the work's composition, the only writers besides Alberti who had mentioned it were Piero della Francesca and Filarete (who acknowledged his debt to Alberti in his treatise).[49] The author of the *Hypnerotomachia* is a striking exception. In that book, there is no building whose description is not mapped on a reticulated surface or a grid with a series of points and lines linking them. The narrator even defends his use of the "piano dil projecto quadrato" with the claim that "la invenzione la principale regula peculiare a l'architetto e la quadratura" (c3).

Quadrangulus was only one of the concepts basic to Alberti's science of perspective put forth in *De pictura*. A second, related idea is that the *quadrangulus* is an intersection of the three-dimensional structured space of the "pyramid" of vision, "intersezione della piramide visiva." Alberti was the first one to use the term "pyramid" of sight rather than the visual "cone" described by ancient optics—it was an interesting architectural analogy. When the model of a cone is used, the visual rays have to be thought of as extending from a circular base; but in Alberti's case the base was rectangular, an analogue of the window frame or picture frame.[50] According to Alberti's theory of perspective, the *quadrangulus* was simply a slice of the visual pyramid, whose apex started from the eye and ended in a rectangle, and was made of rays "like fine strings . . . all closely bound at one end within the eye where the sense of sight resides; and from there, almost like the trunk of all these rays, that knot extends its straight and fine shoots to the surface facing it."[51]

Alberti chose the lower side of the visual pyramid as the index for spatial values, that is, to determine the alignments and foreshortenings of the picture and the relative proportions of the figures. For practical reasons he suggested the use of the *pavimento*, the checkerboard floor. This idea was not new; as Erwin Panofsky points out, it goes back to the Lorenzetti brothers' painting of the Annunciation (1344) in the Pinacoteca of Siena.[52] In this space, structured by a *pavimento*, all visible perpendiculars or orthogonals are oriented toward the so-called vanishing point for the first time. Alberti's great innovation concerned the definition of the centric point, as Joan Gadol has remarked.[53] In the Lorenzettis' paintings, everything had been aligned according to a centric point, but that point had been placed at random. Thus the horizon was unrelated to the line of sight of the depicted figures and to the actual line of sight of the beholder, and the picture failed to be a systematic space that included the viewer as well as the scene viewed. Alberti made the centric point of the painting correspond to the centric ray in the pyramid of vision. In so doing, he made the actual space of the spectators seem like an extension of the space of the painting: the spectators have their feet on an extension of the same ground as the figures and objects in the painting. This construction of space gave substance to the bodies in the painting in a way no other did.

The *Hypnerotomachia* contains an accurate description of this device. The "sacred temple is constructed in a round manner by architectural art and within the quadrangular figure in the exactly measured area and when found the diametrical line so rendered of its height and in the circle of the area contained in a *quadratura*" (m6v). Moreover, this passage from the *Hypnerotomachia* is taken almost word for word from a similar exposition of the *pavimento* in *De pictura*.

CIRCLES ARE DRAWN FROM ANGLES. I DO IT IN THIS MANNER. IN A SPACE I MAKE A QUADRANGLE WITH RIGHT ANGLES, AND I DIVIDE THE SIDES OF THIS QUADRANGLE WITH RIGHT ANGLES, AND I DIVIDE THE SIDES OF THIS QUADRANGLE INTO PARTS SIMILAR TO THE PARTS OF THE BASE LINE OF THE FIRST QUADRANGLE IN THE PAINTING. FROM EACH POINT TO ITS OPPOSITE POINT I DRAW LINES AND THUS THE SPACE IS DIVIDED INTO MANY SMALL QUADRANGLES. HERE I DRAW A CIRCLE AS LARGE AS I WANT SO THE LINES OF THE SMALL QUADRANGLES AND THE LINES OF THE CIRCLE CUT EACH OTHER MUTUALLY. I NOTE ALL THE POINTS OF THIS CUTTING; THESE PLACES I MARK ON THE PARALLELS OF THE *PAVIMENTO* IN MY PAINTING.[54]

Not all the rays in the pyramid of vision were alike, according to Alberti. The so-called median rays, "that multitude in the pyramid which lie within the extrinsic rays," behave,

IN A MANNER OF SPEAKING, LIKE THE CHAMELEON, AN ANIMAL WHICH TAKES TO ITSELF THE COLOR OF THE THINGS NEAR IT. SINCE THESE RAYS CARRY BOTH THE COLORS AND LIGHTS ON THE PLANE FROM WHERE THEY TOUCH IT UP TO THE EYE, THEY SHOULD BE FOUND LIGHTED AND COLORED IN A DEFINITE WAY WHEREVER THEY ARE BROKEN. THE PROOF OF THIS IS THAT THROUGH A GREAT DISTANCE THEY BECOME WEAKENED. I THINK THE REASON MAY BE THAT WEIGHTED DOWN WITH LIGHT AND COLOR THEY PASS THROUGH THE AIR, WHICH, BEING HUMID WITH A CERTAIN HEAVINESS, TIRES THE LADEN RAYS. FROM THIS WE CAN DRAW A RULE: AS THE DISTANCE BECOMES GREATER, SO THE PLANE SEEN APPEARS MORE HAZY.[55]

Long before Leonardo, based on Alhazen's conviction that light rays carry color information, Alberti noted that colors and lights grow more dim and outlines hazy as the distance grows greater.

Alberti's authorship would certainly explain why we find this theory so clearly expressed in two passages of the *Hypnerotomachia*. In the first, the narrator admires how the artist knew how to locate "the lovely figures according to the right planes. And how the outlines of the buildings adhered to their proper shapes. And how to the eyes, some of the spots almost were lost. And the imperfect things were made perfect and the perfect things made imperfect, according to where they were placed in relation to the eye. . . . Water, fountains, mountains, hills, woods, animals were deprived of coloring when in the distance as if backlit."[56] In the second, which is even more explicit, he praises "the coloration and linear symmetry of perspective."[57]

Given the Albertian character of the visual thinking propounded in the *Hypneroto-machia,* one would expect the woodcuts to reveal perfect mastery of the perspective technique. But, paradoxically, perspectival visual thinking is more evident in the text than in the images. How can one explain so many erroneous executions of the foreshortenings and alignments associated with perspective? Even an untrained eye will notice that the technique is crude, particularly in the images of the temple of Venus and the inside of the grotto. The pergola structure on top of the fountain in the middle of the circular garden is another disaster of perspectival representation.

This lack of mastery is equally obvious in the representation of the bodies. While in the text they tend, as we have seen, to be extremely carnal, here the bodies seem to hover in preperspectival space. Furthermore bodies that are further away are sometimes bigger because they are more important, as in the depictions of Vertumnus and Pomona and of the introduction of Poliphilo to the queen. This flies in the face of everything we know about perspective since Panofsky wrote about it that, aside from being associated with rationality, it also expresses "three dimensionality and substantiality of bodies" and allows the representation of the markedly corporeal "Renaissance feeling for the body."[58]

Among the bodies hovering in preperspectival space is that of the spectator. This is especially clear in the illustration of the colossally big pyramid, two and a half miles high (fig. 41). It is a particularly Albertian choice. A colossus, according to *De pictura,* made extraordinary demands on the painter's mastery of the representational precepts of art; the outlining of the "most ample surfaces such as those in buildings and colossi . . . pertains in no small measure to composition." Since the most ample surfaces could not be circumscribed by means of tracing an image from a *velo,* they had to be constructed according to the principles of linear perspective. Consequently, colossal works tested more than any other the painter's representational ability: "in small images the greatest flaws are hidden to the greatest degree (*maxime*); in great (*magna*) effigies even the smallest errors are conspicuous."[59] Although in this woodcut from the *Hypnerotomachia* there is a checkerboard *pavimento,* the spectator is effectively floating about a mile high, somewhere in space. This means that the actual space of the spectator is not an extension of the virtual space of the painting: the viewer does not have his or her feet on the ground as Alberti demands in his treatise on painting.

It would seem that the author—Alberti—and the artist executing the woodcuts were at two different stages of visual thinking: one perspectival, the other preperspectival. As Arthur Hind has indicated, at the time the book was produced, cutters were still considered very backward, compared to the other visual artists.[60] Thus it is not surprising that the visual thinking expressed in the text of the *Hypnerotomachia* is more advanced than that in the illustrations. The pictorial rendering of the effects of perspective is flat, rough, far from equaling

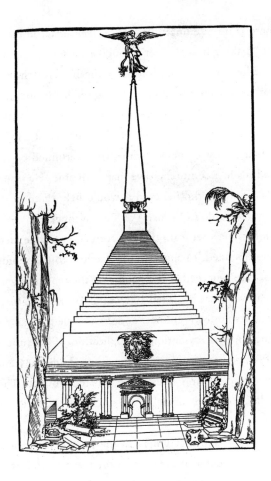

41. THE PYRAMID.

the verbal description. One can almost feel the wood cutter struggling to enter into perspectival space, in his attempts to imitate the foreshortenings—which here appear arbitrary—of the original Albertian drawing he must have had in his hands; he fails, because he does not have a true grasp of the rules behind them. This explains why in the *Hypnerotomachia* there is a sense of incorporeality, of what Panofsky called "aggregate" space rather than "systematic" space.[61] This situation is corrected in the French edition: fifty years later, woodcutting and printing had gained much prestige and themselves become elite Renaissance professions.

The precision in the *Hypnerotomachia* extends to all the measurements in the book; particularly noteworthy are the five pages of measurements of the great pyramid at the beginning. Alberti was a civil engineer in addition to a mechanical engineer. His *Ludi matematici* included methods of measuring the height of a tower, the depth of a well, and the surface area of a plane.[62] There is no building in the *Hypnerotomachia,* in fact, that is not seen as if through the device of "making triangles" or through *quadratura*—that is, as an intersection of a visual pyramid whose height can be derived scientifically through techniques of surveying. Moreover, Alberti was equally interested in surveying the landscape. In *Descriptio urbis Romae* (composed between 1431 and 1434), Alberti invented modern mapmaking and produced the first accurate map of a city ever made (figs. 42, 43). He arrived at a location of the perimeter of the Aurelian wall that almost coincides with that determined by modern scholars.[63] No one before Alberti had made a comprehensive map of Rome. He undertook the task at the urging of several of his friends, who believed it would help them in their studies; his technique was later used by Leonardo in his maps of Tuscan towns.[64]

Descriptio urbis Romae set forth the first correct, verifiable method of surveying and tabulating the sightings obtained. In applying this method to the monuments of Rome, Alberti "with scrupulous care" succeeded in "stabilizing the measurements with mathematical instruments."[65] His goal was what he called a "picture" of the city. Instead of relying on the older Ptolemaic technique of using rectilinear coordinates, he took an entirely new approach, employing an astrolabe. In this revolutionary application of a nautical instrument to land surveying, the map of Rome had an epicenter, the Campidoglio or Capitol. All the points of the map were plotted along "course lines" that radiated from it. The instrument itself is described as a bronze disk mounted parallel to the surface of the earth and divided into forty-eight degrees.[66]

The map of the island of Cythera in the *Hypnerotomachia* is based on the same method (fig. 44). There, the center of the circle is the theater, from which radiate a number of lines that serve to locate the various parts of the garden.

IN ORDER TO OBTAIN THESE SECTIONS, WE DIVIDE INTO TEN PARTS THE FIGURE. WE WILL FORM TWENTY OF THEM IF WE DRAW A LINE IN THE MIDDLE OF EACH OF THE DIVISIONS. THIS FIGURE IS MADE BY TRACING A CIRCLE OF WHICH THE CENTER IS GIVEN BY THE INTERSECTION OF TWO DIAMETERS. YOU WILL MARK THIS WITH A POINT IN THE CENTER OF THE HALF-DIAMETER, OF YOUR CHOICE, THEN BY THIS POINT YOU WILL LEAD AN OBLIQUE LINE RIGHT UP TO THE EXTREMITY OF ANOTHER DIAMETER. THIS LINE, BY PASSING BY THIS POINT, PROVIDES THE QUARTER OF AN ENTIRE DIAMETER. IN PROLONGING THIS UNTIL IT INTERSECTS WITH THE CIRCUMFERENCE, YOU WILL OBTAIN A TRIANGULAR SECTION THAT WILL CONSIST IN A TENTH OF THE CIRCLE. (t8)

Whether the subject is the invention of perspective in *De pictura,* the first method of correctly measuring the human body in *De statua,* or modern mapmaking in *Descriptio urbis Romae,* the work of Leon Battista Alberti reveals the blend of an exceptional talent for engineering and some of the most innovative visual thinking of the Renaissance. The emblem

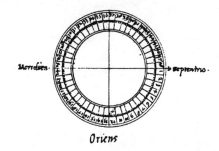

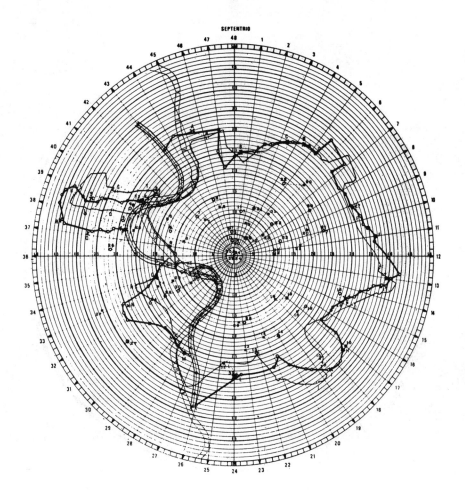

42. Diagram from the manuscript of Alberti's *Descriptio urbis Romae*. From Città del Vaticano, Biblioteca Apostolica Vaticana (cat. 22).

43. Reconstruction of Alberti's map of Rome (ca. 1450). From D. Vagnetti, "La 'descriptio urbis Romae' di L. B. Alberti," *Quaderni dell'Istituto di Elementi di Architettura e Rilievo de Monumenti di Genova* 1 (1968), p. 72.

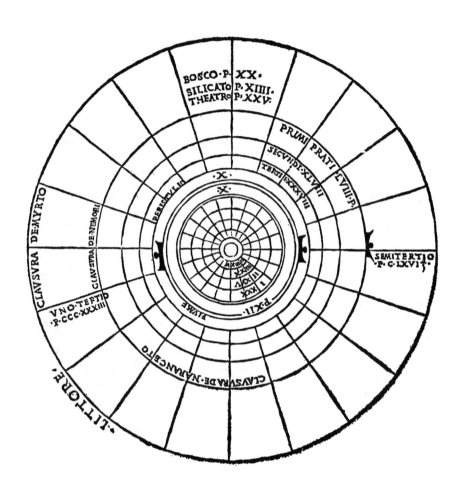

44.   ISLAND OF CYTHERA.

he conceived for himself at the age of twenty and he retained all his life, which Matteo de Pasti reproduced in his famous medallion of Alberti, was, as we have seen, the winged eye, indicating that vision was the predominant sense and that visual representation was of the highest importance for him.

Among the aspects of the *Hypnerotomachia* that therefore would be made intelligible by Alberti's authorship is its extraordinary visual character. In particular, this would explain the quality of the 172 woodcuts it contains. Scholars who have studied the *Hypnerotomachia* have assumed that the woodcuts were conceived in Aldus Manutius's workshop, at the time of its publication in 1499, by someone versed in the works of scholar painters—such as Sandro Botticelli, Andrea Mantegna, and Jacopo Bellini—if not by one of those very painters.[67] In other words, they have always taken for granted that the manuscript of the *Hypnerotomachia* arrived at its publisher without illustrations. They could not otherwise account for the extraordinary excellence of their design.

However, this scenario seems to me highly unlikely. It requires that the designer have sufficient knowledge of Latin and Greek to decipher the highly impenetrable prose descriptions of the *Hypnerotomachia* and thus coordinate the verbal and visual material in the astonishing graphic synthesis for which the book is famous. And he would have needed the leisure to translate no fewer than 172 passages in order to produce 172 images. This is an immense output of woodcuts by any standard, far surpassing even Mantegna's production of engravings. Neither Botticelli, Mantegna, nor Bellini had the necessary linguistic knowledge. It is unimaginable that any of them, by then highly sought after and successful professionals, would have invested the necessary effort and time and not taken credit for it. Moreover, the designer would have needed expertise in antique architecture to give these verbal descriptions accurate visual form. Only Mantegna had the required archaeological knowledge, but it is inconceivable that he would not have taken credit for so significant an achievement. By the time these woodcuts were executed, he was the leading artist of Italy and making a handsome income from his work.

It seems far more probable that the *Hypnerotomachia* manuscript reached the publisher's workshop already illustrated. After all, what else would explain the archaeological accuracy of both the visual representations and verbal descriptions of vases, bas-reliefs, clothes, sculpture, banners, and architecture, as well as the minute interdependence of word and image?

In addition, two passages of the book confirm that the publisher was simply copying a manuscript already illustrated. One is the description of an antique barge, which ends with the words "Cusi era," or "This is how it was" (s5), followed by the illustration of a barge (fig. 45). Who, besides the author, could have written "cusi era"? Where would the cutter have found the image of an antique barge but on the same manuscript? And who could the author have been but Alberti? Very few people in the quattrocento had observed an antique barge. The only examples known at the time were submerged at the bottom of Lake Nemi, and Alberti would have been among the handful of people who had seen one of them, thanks to his experience of retrieving it for Prospero Colonna.[68]

The second passage describes the richly woven and embroidered saddle of the sculpture of the elephant (fig. 46). After mentioning that the saddle bears an embroidered inscription in Greek and Arabic, it ends with the words "le quale cusi dicevano" (which said the following), followed, indeed, by the illustration of a saddle (b7). This instance is perhaps even more telling than the first, for it is difficult to imagine what outside source could have supplied the cutter with the Greek and Arabic phrases, which are not in the text. Obviously they must have been on the page of the original manuscript.

Illustrated manuscripts were more the rule than the exception in the quattrocento. We have the treatise by Filarete, for one, as well as Francesco di Giorgio's, both remarkable for the execution of the drawings. There is no reason to suppose that Alberti would have been a lesser draftsman. On the contrary: in his autobiography, he claimed to have "worked extremely hard at sculpture and painting, not to mention the rest, and neglected nothing in his effort to win the esteem of the best. His talent was of the highest order, and he may be said to have mastered all the arts." He would even "summon the friends he was accustomed to discussing literary matters with, and while dictating pamphlets to them, he would make sketches or make wax models of them."[69] In *De pictura,* which contains his theory explaining the variation of color under different lighting conditions, Alberti takes pains to distinguish himself from the mere theoreticians of painting, asserting that he is a practitioner: "It is enough for the painter to know what the colors are and how to use them in painting. I do not wish to contradict the experts, who, since they follow the philosophers, assert that there are only two colors in nature, white and black. Others however are created from a mixture of these two. As a painter I think thus about colors. From a mixture of colors almost infinite colors are created. I speak here as a painter." Later he adds, "Allow me to speak for myself

45. THE BARGE.

la gráde teſta cóiúcto,ambiua una maeſtreuole ligatura. Dallaquale uno ambitioſo ornato,ſúmaméte notabile di eramento traiectato per ſopra il ſuo ampliſſimo fronte pendeua,di dui quadrati cópoſito , cú liniamenti elegáte. Nella planitie dilquale(di foliatura undiculare circundata) uidi alcune littere Ionice,& Arabe,lequale cuſi diceuano .

Hora el ſuo uorace proboſcide,non ſi continiua cum il piano dil baſamento,ma ſubleuato,penſile ſi ſtaua,cóuerſo alquanto uerſo il fronte cum le ſulca te auricule largiſſime demiſſe,ouero cá cellate.Ilquale ſimulachro nella ſua ua ſtitate unquátulo meno móſtraua,che il naturale· Et nella oblonga circuitione dil baſamento erano cœlati hieragly phi,ouero characteri ægyptici. Depolito decentemente cum il debito Areoba to,cú il lataſtro,gula, thoro , & orbiculo , cú ſui Aſtragali,ouero nextruli , cú inuerſa Sima al pedamento.Et di ſopra non meno cum la proiecta Sima reſupinà,& torque trachili & déticuli cum gli Aſtragali. Secondo che alla craſſitu dine expediua eximie Symmetriati.La longitudine,latitudine,& altecia, paſſi, duodeci,cinque,&tre. Le extremitate

46. THE SADDLE.

here. Whenever I turn to painting for my recreation, which I frequently do when I am tired of more pressing affairs, I apply myself with so much pleasure that I am surprised that three or four hours have passed."[70]

That Alberti was more than just an amateur painter and draftsman is corroborated by others. Flavio Biondo mentions him before the painter Donatello in his guidebook *Italia illustrata* (completed around 1450), in a series of encomiums of Florentines who honored their city by being of "noble intelligence and versatile in many arts." We know from Manetti that Alberti was practicing "architecture, perspective, and painting."[71] Vasari mentions that Alberti made several drawings, in particular one that Vasari had in his possession of the Ponte Sant'Angelo and of its roof—Alberti designed the loggia as a shelter from the sun in summer and from the wind and rain in the winter.[72] We know that Alberti drew famous panoramas of Rome and of Venice, although both have disappeared. Other paintings Vasari mentions are a self-portrait and a portrait of another figure in the house of Palla Rucellai, a perspective of Venice and the church of S. Marco, and "three *storiette* and several perspectives" on an altar bench in the chapel of Our Lady on the Carraia bridge in Florence.[73]

The last Vasari rather disparagingly dismissed, claiming that "he has described better with the pen than the brush."[74] Indeed Vasari, who was writing about the works of Cimabue, Giotto, Botticelli, Ghirlandaio, Piero della Francesca, Mantegna, Leonardo, Raphael, Michelangelo, and the like, had a low opinion of Alberti's talents as a painter.[75] He wrote that "Leon Battista devoted himself to the study of Latin and the practice of architecture, perspective, and painting, and he left to posterity a number of books which he wrote himself," noting caustically "that none of our modern craftsmen has known how to write about these subjects, and so even though very many of them have done better work than Alberti, such has been the influence of his writings on the pens and speech of scholarly men that he is commonly believed to be superior to those who were, in fact, superior to him."[76]

But Vasari appears to be the exception; others seem to have held Alberti's skills as an artist in some esteem. Cristoforo Landino wrote, "Not only did he write about these arts [painting and sculpture] but he also practiced them, and I have in my possession highly prized works executed by him with the brush, with the chisel, with the graver, and by the casting of metal."[77] In his introduction to *De re aedificatoria*, Angelo Poliziano praised Alberti's skills as a draftsman thus:

YOU MIGHT HAVE ASKED YOURSELF WHETHER HE WAS MORE AN ORATOR OR A POET, WHETHER HIS STYLE WAS MORE MAJESTIC OR GRACEFUL. SO THOROUGH HAD BEEN HIS EXAMINATION OF THE REMAINS OF ANTIQUITY THAT HE WAS ABLE TO GRASP EVERY PRINCIPLE OF ANCIENT ARCHITECTURE, AND RENEW IT BY EXAMPLE; HIS INVENTION WAS NOT LIMITED TO MACHINERY, LIFTS, AND AUTOMATA, BUT ALSO INCLUDED THE WONDERFUL FORMS OF BUILDINGS. HE HAD MOREOVER THE HIGHEST REPUTATION AS BOTH PAINTER

AND SCULPTOR, AND SINCE HE ACHIEVED A GREATER MASTERY IN ALL THESE DIFFERENT ARTS THAN ONLY A FEW CAN MANAGE IN ANY SINGLE ONE, IT WOULD BE MORE TELLING, AS SALLUST SAID ABOUT CARTHAGE, TO BE SILENT ABOUT HIM THAN TO SAY LITTLE.[78]

Yet in the last analysis, Vasari was probably right. Alberti was no Leonardo, no Raphael, and no Michelangelo: if he had been, posterity would have treated his paintings with greater care. All the same, his skills did merit him a place in Vasari's *Lives of the Painters,* and the standards of ordinary competence at that time were extraordinarily high. The architectural treatises of Filarete and Francesco di Giorgio, though masterly manuscripts, drew no comment from Vasari—not even a negative one.[79]

If the author of the *Hypnerotomachia* were Alberti, another visual aspect of the book that would be explained is the stylistic similarities between woodcuts in the book and paintings by Mantegna, Bellini, and Botticelli. There was no one more familiar with these works than Alberti, author of the Renaissance's most respected treatise on painting. We know from his biographer, Girolamo Mancini, that from the court of the d'Este at Ferrara he knew Andrea Mantegna, Piero della Francesca, and Jacopo Bellini—the painters whose influence on the woodcuts has been noted by scholars. It would also explain the illustrations' likeness to the sketches of Ciriaco d'Ancona, whom Alberti would also have met at the court of Ferrara.[80] But if the images in the *Hypnerotomachia* are beholden to any source at all, it is Alberti's own 1434 treatise on painting, *De pictura.* The influence of that book on the paintings of Piero della Francesca has been noted by Eugenio Battisti, and H. W. Janson has shown how Alberti's *De pictura* prompted a radical shift in the construction of space between Donatello's first and second "feast of Herod" reliefs, between 1425 and 1435.[81] Indeed, it is not an exaggeration to say that Alberti more than anyone shaped the composition of quattrocento paintings.

Alberti hardly needed to be influenced by prominent painters in order to compose the images of the *Hypnerotomachia. De pictura* was written before he met Mantegna and Botticelli—before they even started painting. What influence there was went in the other direction. The key person responsible for transforming Mantegna into a scholar was in fact Alberti, and it is known that Mantegna was a student of *De re aedificatoria.*[82] The two men would have met in Ferrara or Mantua. It has been argued that Alberti is responsible for Mantegna's great change of style between the time he painted the Ovetari Chapel at the Church of the Eremitani in Padua and the Camera Picta at the Castello di S. Giorgio in Mantua; Alberti may even have acted as a consultant on the latter project.[83] Other scholars have shown the influence of Alberti's *De pictura* on Donatello, Ghiberti, Botticelli, and Ghirlandaio.[84]

The author of the *Hypnerotomachia* manuscript was also its designer; ascription to Alberti would explain the revolutionary graphic design of the book, its extraordinary typography and integration of text and image. Alberti loved typography and even invented a new script in the Tuscan style.[85] As is well known, he often incorporated lettering onto the facades and walls of his buildings, going so far as to integrate the proportions of epigrams into the structure's overall composition. Think of the lettering encircling the small temple in S. Pancrazio that he designed for the Rucellai, or that on his church of S. Martino. For Alberti, lettering had visual resonance beyond the meaning it literally expressed. In a manuscript, this propensity of his would have been accentuated by the very nature of the medium. He would naturally have been even more eager to exploit the relationship between text and image, to treat the letters as an unfurling and unfolding visual element, to integrate them into the page next to real images. Each page is considered a visual element of the same importance as the woodcuts, so they are integrated. It is amazing how the text twists around the images of the banners illustrated here (fig. 47). The entire section devoted to the epigrams that Poliphilo finds is a feast for the eyes; they are some of the finest pages that have ever been designed. The printed page becomes a malleable element, something beautiful to be looked at, not just a functional object to be read. The text is not static but moves. For instance, several daring double-page spreads give the idea of movement across the whole width of the book (see fig. 9).

Indeed, the book's visual obsession with representing movement, as well as exact appearances with the aid of scientific perspective, would be explained by Alberti's authorship. To be sure, there had been precedents before him among painters. Giotto a hundred years earlier had been the great innovator in this area, and his paintings had changed the quality and aims of pictorial representation from capturing a static *imago* to expressing a dynamic, fluid *istoria*.[86] But in *De pictura,* Alberti is the first to lay down a set of rules for representing movement: "We painters who wish to show the movements of the soul by movements of the body are concerned solely with the movement of change of place. Anything which moves its place can do it in seven ways: up, the first; down, the second; to the right, the third; to the left, the fourth; in depth moving closer and then away; and the seventh moving around. I desire all these movements in painting. Some bodies are placed towards us, others away from us, and in one body some parts appear to the observer, some drawn back, others high and others low."[87] The *Hypnerotomachia* provides superb illustrations of this precept (fig. 48). In another passage of *De pictura,* Alberti discusses the ancient Greek painter Parrhasio, whom Pliny described as able to portray all the states of the soul. "The movements of the soul are made known through the movements of the body. Care and thought weigh so heavily that a sad person stands with his forces and feelings as if dulled, holding himself feebly and tiredly on his pallid and poorly sustained members. In the melancholy the forehead is wrinkled, the head drooping, all members fall as if tired and neglected. In the angry, because anger incites the soul, the eyes are swollen."[88]

Alberti was obsessed with representing the movement not just of animate objects but of inanimate ones.

Subſequéte & una attolleua uno tropheo cũ
pcipua politura. In uno mucrone demigra
ua il ſupmo haſtile, ſubdeſcendédo uno co
ptorio ſopra una rotunditate ſemiſextante
craſſa, í modo platineo reſupinaua, nel me
diano inſculpta una formula circinata. La
quale uno pauculo di uaſeo pediculo ſuppri
meua. Poſcia una tabella cum tale ſcriptura
maiuſcula(QVIS EVADET?)ſubiaceua.
Aqueſta uno pomulo ſubigeua,& ſubſequé
te unaltra rotun
datione,quale la
ſuperna, ma mi
nore. Da uno a
lamento circũ
uallata & ad una
ſolida ouero ma
ſſicia ſcutella ſu
peraſſidéte. Dal
laquale cõtinua
to deſcendeua u
no longiuſculo
baluſto, & po
ſcia una pileta.

Similmente
portaua unaltra
nympha una ha
ſta. Nellacumi
nato era una figura ouola, cum orulo bul
lato in circinao,& nel meditullo uno rotun
damento ſaphyreo la figura imitante di craſ
ſitudine unciale,ſubacta una aſſula,tale cum
titulo.NEMO.Et in medio di due ale,la ha
ſta alquanto balluſticata intraiectaua. Infi
mamente una ſcutella ſequiua,quale ſopra e
recenſito.

Conſequéte

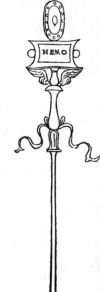

Conſequente era uno altro nobiliſſimo
trophæo baiulato. Nel ſublime haſtile una
pila ſopra uno pyrronio promineua tra uno
i flexo lunario di due pinne ſubtilmíte di bra
ctea doro foliate,uno ſolio paginataméte ſo
pra laltro ſoppſ
ſo.Il reſiduo dil
lequale in circi
naméto coacto
rendeua una co
rona cũ faſceo
la detenta, p me
dio la haſta exi
guaméte balau
ſtata traiectan
do perpendicu
larmte.Sotto la
corona una pi
leta, cum il fun
do di uno gut
turnio uaſo de
ſcendéte ſopra
il ſmigiodi due
coniuncte ale.
dapoſcia una fi
gura ouolata cũ
una bulla byſſi
na nel umbili
co corruſcante. Sotto queſta infixa era una
pila peponaceamte ſcindulata,cum uolan
te faſcicule opportunamte inſtricte.

Molti altri di plixo narrato gli ſtyraci de
liquali alcuni di Hebeno,altri di ſandalo ru
bente citrino & bianco, & di candidiſſimo Ebure,& aurati, & di argen
to contecti,& di altri pretioſi lignamini. Omni coſa fabre deformata di
tenuiſſimo oro,argento, & di leuigata materia,& di ſeta uirente formati &
di omni altra gratioſa coloratione,cum iucunda floratura.Cum gemme
multiplicemente ornati agli congruenti lochi omni coſa harmonicamé
te deſtinata & conſpicuamente applicata,cum præpendenti ſpondili, o-

x

47. EXAMPLES OF GRAPHIC DESIGN.

D
M

P.CORNELIA ANNIA.NE INDESOLATA ORBITATE
SVPER VIVEREM MISERA VIVAMME VLTRO IN
HANC ARCAM CVM VIRO DEF.INCOMPAR. AMO
REDIL.DAMNAT.DEDO.CVMQVOVIX ANN .XX
SINE VLLA DO. LIB.LIBERTAB.Q .NO. VT QVOT
ANN.SVP.ARCAM NO.PLOTONI ET OXORI PRO
SERPIN.M.OMNIBQ .. SACRVFICENT ROSISQ .
EXORNENT.DERELIQ. IBI EPVLENTVR DO.D.P.
.M.DA.EX.HSX.ATQ .T.FACIVNDVM DELEGA.
VALE VITA.

Sotto ancora (de q̃ partitomi) di una corymbifera & errante hedera
da uno deroſo alamento di muro propendula, molto di fronde denſa,
uno ſpectabile zygaſtrion aſſideua di una petra alleboro ſimigliante, fin
allhora nella maiore parte ancora terſa & luculea. Détro laq̃le curioſam
te riguardádo per una fixura, o uero rima dil cooptorio plano dui cada
ueri integri riſeruati. p laquale coſa dritaĩte arbitrai che di ſaxo chemi
tes era queſto ſepulchro. Nel frõte dilquale uidi queſti hieroglyphi ægy
ptici iſculpto,& ĩtro ancora molte ampulle di uitro & molte figuline
di terra,& alcune ſtatuicule archæo more agyptitio & una antiquaria lu
cerna di metallo artificioſamente facta ,& nel ſuffito dil tegumé
to pendice,quella una catenula illaqueata retinente ſuſpen
ſa ardeua,et proximo alla teſta degli ſepulti era
no due coronule. Lequale coſe auree iu
dicai,ma per il tempo,& per il lu
cernale fumo iſuſcate.tale
fue la interpreta
tione.

D. .M. S.
CADAVERIB. AMORE FVRENTIVM
MISERABVNDIS   POLYANDRION

Questo nobile & spectatissimo fragmento in uno solido frusto anco
ra & una portiucula dil suo fastigio, o uero frontispicio se retinea egregia
mête liniato·Nella triangulare planitie dilquale dui figmenti io uidi in-
scalpti,& non integri. Vno uolucre decapitato,arbitrai fusse di Bubone,
& una uetusta lucerna, tuto di perfecto alabastryte. Cusi io le interpretai.
VITAE LETHIFER NVNTIVS.

Peruenuto daposcia in la mediana parte dil tempio,alquanto imune
& disoccupata di fressidine la trouai. Oue ancora il cósumabile tempo,
ad una opera pclara di narrato,tuta di rubicundo porphyrite,solamente
hauea perdonato. Laquale era sexangula,cum le base sopra una solida pe
tra ophites dillamedesima figura nel pauimento ipacta,& sei columnelle
distâte una dalaltra pedi sei,cú lo epistilio.zophoro,& coronice,sencia al
cuno liniaméto & signo,ma simplicemente terso & puro·Gliquali erano
extrinseco la forma imitanti. Ma intersticii in figura circinata. Oue sopra
la piana dilla corona nasceua una cupula di unico & solido saxo ,mirabi
le artificio. Laquale graciliua nel acumine,quale uno peruio infu-
mibulo strisso &speculare copriua una subterranea uacui-
tate illuminata p una circulare aptione di egregia cancellatura impedita di metal
lina fusura. Ilquale spectando ci
borio di maxima pol·
litura cusi il tro
uai.

48.   IMAGES OF MOVING BODIES.

WE HAVE SAID ENOUGH ABOUT THE MOVEMENTS OF ANIMATE BEINGS; NOW, THEN, SINCE INANIMATE THINGS MOVE IN ALL THOSE MANNERS WHICH WE HAVE STATED ABOVE, LET US TREAT OF THEM. I AM DELIGHTED TO SEE SOME MOVEMENT IN HAIR, LOCKS OF HAIR, BRANCHES, FRONDS, AND ROBES. THE SEVEN MOVEMENTS ARE ESPECIALLY PLEASING IN HAIR WHERE PART OF IT TURNS IN SPIRALS AS IF WISHING TO KNOT ITSELF, WAVES IN THE AIR LIKE FLAMES, TWINES AROUND ITSELF LIKE A SERPENT, WHILE PART RISES HERE, PART THERE. IN THE SAME WAY BRANCHES TWIST THEMSELVES, NOW UP, NOW DOWN, NOW AWAY, NOW NEAR, THE PARTS CONTORTING THEMSELVES LIKE ROPES. FOLDS ACT IN THE SAME WAY, EMERGING LIKE THE BRANCHES FROM THE TRUNK OF A TREE. IN THIS THEY ADHERE TO THE SEVEN MOVEMENTS SO THAT NO PART OF THE CLOTH IS BARE OF MOVE-MENT. AS I HAVE NOTED, MOVEMENTS SHOULD BE MODERATE AND SWEET. THEY SHOULD APPEAR GRACEFUL TO THE OBSERVER RATHER THAN A MARVEL OF STUDY. HOWEVER, WHERE WE SHOULD LIKE TO FIND MOVEMENT IN THE DRAPERIES, CLOTH IS BY NATURE HEAVY AND FALLS TO THE EARTH. FOR THIS REASON IT WOULD BE WELL TO PLACE IN THE PICTURE THE FACE OF ZEPHYRUS OR AUSTRUS WHO BLOWS THE CLOUDS MAKING THE DRAPERIES BLOWN BY THE WIND FLY GRACEFULLY THROUGH THE AIR. IN THIS BLOWING IN THE WIND THE PAINTER SHOULD TAKE CARE NOT TO DISPLAY ANY DRAPE AGAINST THE WIND. ALL THAT I HAVE SAID ABOUT THE MOVEMENTS OF ANIMATE AND OF INANIMATE OBJECTS I HAVE OBSERVED. ONCE MORE YOU HAVE FOLLOWED WITH DILIGENCE WHAT I HAVE SAID ABOUT THE COMPOSITION OF PLANES, MEMBERS AND BODIES.[89]

Take the first image in the *Hypnerotomachia*. It is quite unlike any Renaissance painting, resembling none of the work of the painters generally mentioned in conjunction with the *Hypnerotomachia*—Mantegna, Bellini, Fra Giocondo, Botticelli—in its unconventional twisting lines. More than anything else, it is an excuse to illustrate Alberti's description of branches that go "now up, now down, now away, now near, the parts contorting themselves like rope." The woodcut is literally an exercise in drawing sinuous, gnarled curves for their own sake, where the arboreal element is in the forefront and the human subject in the background, rather than the more usual reverse (fig. 49). About 75 percent of the surface of the image is made up of the winding branches, making it almost an abstract composition, with the human figure reduced to relatively insignificant presence. To a lesser extent we find the same preoccupation in the second woodcut, with its sinuous rhythms of the rocky paths and river beds that wind into the arboreal setting of the dark, wooded background. A last example is the series of three woodcuts depicting the slaughter of the virgins.

So great was Alberti's passion for representing movement that it drove him beyond the surface of paintings to his experiments with boxes of his own design that he called his *dimostrazioni*. These may constitute one of the earliest prefigurings of cinema. Cinema, that is, not just in the sense of a projected still image—Giovanni Fontana had done this earlier in

49. THE SINUOUS LINES.

the century[90]—but in the sense of capturing *kinesis* (at the root of the word *cinema* is the Greek *kinēsis,* "movement"), the moving image. This, at least, is how the *dimostrazioni* struck Mancini, Alberti's late nineteenth-century biographer.[91]

The importance of this invention did not escape Giorgio Vasari. Begrudging as he was about Alberti's enviable talents, even he compares it to the invention of the printing press by Gutenberg. "In the year following, 1457, in which John Gutenberg, a German, discovered the most useful part of printing books," he wrote, and "Leone Battista likewise made a discovery for representing landscapes and for diminishing and enlarging figures by means of an instrument."[92] Quatremère de Quincy also suggested that Alberti's invention was as important as the printing press. According to him, this invention "multiplies the pleasures of the work of art and of nature and transports, one might say, whole regions, their inhabitants, their costumes, and the monuments of remote regions and establishes in the world a reciprocity and a mingling of knowledge that exercises the same power as a newspaper does on one's ideas."[93]

The exact workings of this invention have been a mystery to scholars. Alberti's own description is unclear and confusing. In his autobiography, he had talked about his *dimostrazioni* as "miracles of painting of my own making which several of my companions saw in Rome."[94] Again in the third person he writes of himself that

WITH HIS ART OF PAINTING ALBERTI PRODUCED THINGS UNHEARD OF AND UNBELIEVABLE TO THOSE WHO SAW THEM. THESE WORKS HE DISPLAYED IN A SMALL BOX THROUGH A TINY HOLE. YOU SAW THERE HIGH MOUNTAINS, VAST PROVINCES, THE BROAD MOVING SEA AND AT THE SAME TIME A VISTA OF SUCH DISTANT REGIONS THAT THEY WERE BARELY DISCERNIBLE. . . . BOTH LEARNED AND UNLEARNED ALIKE SWORE THAT THESE WERE THINGS OF NATURE, NOT PAINTED. THE *DIMOSTRAZIONI* WERE OF TWO KINDS, AND HE CALLED THE ONE SUNNY AND THE OTHER NOCTURNAL. THERE ONE COULD SEE ARCTURUS, THE PLEIADS, ORION, AND SIMILAR SPARKLING CONSTELLATIONS, AND THE MOON RISING FROM THE CRESTS, CRAGGY MOUNTAINS, AND THE MORNING STARS. IN THE SUNNY ONE THE ORB OF THE EARTH WAS RESPLENDANT AND AMPLY ILLUMINATED, WITH A SURFACE, TO QUOTE HOMER, THAT SHINES LIKE AURORA, THE MOTHER OF LIGHT. HE WOULD HAVE GREEK SAILORS LOOK AT IT, AND HAVING SHOWN THEM THIS IMAGINARY WORLD THROUGH THE LITTLE HOLE AND HAVING ASKED THEM WHAT THEY SAW, THEY WOULD ANSWER: "WE SEE A FLEET ON THE HIGH SEAS, PREPARING TO LAND, BUT HAIL, WINDS, AND VIOLENT STORMS ARE RISING FROM THE EAST AND PREVENTING IT FROM DOING SO. THE SEA IS ROUGH AND LOOKS THREATENING BECAUSE OF THE EXCESSIVE REFLECTIONS OF THE RAYS OF THE SUN." MOREOVER, HE PUT MORE INDUSTRY INTO INVESTIGATING SUCH THINGS THAN IN DIVULGING THEM, AND WAS MORE PREOCCUPIED WITH HOW TO EXCITE *INGEGNO* THAN TO SEEK FAME.[95]

Alberti perhaps got the idea of this box by combining at least two precedents. One would have been the box of the *camera obscura*. The second would have been Brunelleschi's illusionistic *dimostrazioni* which he would have placed inside the *camera obscura*.[96] Brunelleschi's device worked this way: he painted a small panel about twelve inches square of the Baptistery of Florence. The observer would look through a hole from the back of the panel, placed at what we now call the vanishing point, into a mirror held at arm's length. The mirror reflected the painting, and the results were illusionistically real. With his normal field of vision cut off by means of the eyehole and a funnel leading to it, the viewer saw only the painting as reflected in the mirror, his entire range of vision being taken up by the painted image of the baptistery and piazza as it appeared in reality. The upper half of Brunelleschi's panel was left coated with burnished silver, thus reflecting the clouds and sunlight of the real sky, which, in the mirror image, appeared to surround the painted baptistery, producing a picture more "real" than nature.[97]

Certainly, we know Alberti was fascinated with the same kind of illusory hyperreality of reflective surfaces like those supplied by the device described above or by mirrors more generally. He writes in *De pictura,* "I do not know why painted things have so much grace in the mirror. It is marvelous how every weakness in a painting is so manifestly deformed with a mirror. I have here truly recounted things which I have learned from nature."[98] There is an important difference between Alberti's *dimostrazioni* and Brunelleschi's, however. Alberti added the dimension of time. The scenes described are no longer static images, as in Brunelleschi's *dimostrazione* of the baptistery, but ones full of animation. In one case, stars are observed to be in the act of "rising," and in another, ships move on a choppy sea against a sky in which a storm is, again, "rising."

How was the illusion of movement achieved? Did Alberti use a sequence of two or more painted images to create it? One could conjecture that through the manipulation of light conditions inside the box, and the use of multiple mirrors reflecting different painted images at different times, this impression could indeed have been produced. How the light was introduced into the box, one can guess: from slits incised into the top and sides, just as in the great pyramid described in the *Hypnerotomachia*. Or did the animation simply result from Alberti's jiggling of the box and the resulting changes in lighting upon a single reflecting surface, such as a mirror painted so as to represent a dark starry sky or a seascape?

It is futile to try to answer this question in the absence of any evidence. Whatever the case, the *dimostrazioni* do place Alberti within the tradition of the early conceptors of cinema.

Although there is no indication of the impact upon Alberti's real architecture of his cinematic visions, in the architecture of the *Hypnerotomachia* there are two. In both cases the reflection of light is involved. First, we have the images projected onto the walls of the round temple of Venus Physozoï from the huge etched lightbulb in the center of the chamber, transforming the interior of the structure into a perfect 360-degree screen. And second, the floor of the amphitheater in the center of the island of Cythera captures images of nymphs dancing upon it and "remembers" them. This is a remarkable leap of the imagination for someone writing in the mid-fifteenth century, for the writer must have conceived of the possibility of preserving moving images on a photosensitive surface. One could say that the building is thought of as part of an immense video camera whose lens and screen are the floor.

But perhaps more important, the perception, representation, and conception of the buildings in the book are shaped by a cinematic *forma mentis*. The result is that the *Hypnerotomachia* contains the first description of architectural space—which by definition needs movement in order to be perceived—in history. It is not only the first illustrated architectural book. It is, cognitively at least, the first architectural film, and its integration of text and image is nothing short of cinematographic. Just look at the filmic sequence representing the punishment of the chaste nymphs by Eros (fig. 50). This is virtually a narration by a moving camera. The sequence of Poliphilo and Polia in the temple, which the reader will find in the last chapter of the present book, is an even more extreme case, with its sequence of eight images. This is the logic of animation, not just illustration.

The remarkably innovative visual character of the *Hypnerotomachia* is no doubt one of the many reasons it is so hard to read. It is a book written by a person who is using a visual rather than a narrative logic to structure the tale. This is also why descriptions of buildings take fourteen to fifty pages to complete. The author is writing in a verbal medium but thinking in a purely visual, kinetic one. It appears that by the time Alberti wrote the *Hypneroto-machia,* he believed perspective, although a necessary means for representing architecture, had to be supplemented: in order to give a sufficiently full account of the architectural experience, the movement of the human body through space had to be taken into account. The immobile eye through which Alberti had seen architecture when writing *De re aedificatoria* had begun to move, like the winged eye represented in Alberti's own emblem. It is possible that the idea came to him after he had begun planning S. Andrea in Mantua, the first major interior space he had been asked to design. Or perhaps it came after his commission for the city plan of Siena, which was not meant to be seen from one fixed point of view by a static eye but from many points, by a winged one.[99]

*　*　*

The realm of biography presents another reason for attributing the *Hypnerotomachia* to Alberti, helping to explain how such an important work of art could have been lost. Even under the best of circumstances, keeping track of manuscripts in the mid-fifteenth century was difficult; indeed, almost none of the manuscripts of that time are left. Bramante's treatises on architecture have been lost even though they still existed in manuscript form until the mid-sixteenth

50.   FILMIC SEQUENCE OF WOODCUTS DEPICTING THE PUNISHMENT OF THE CHASTE NYMPHS BY EROS.

century. Lomazzo mentions a whole book of Leonardo's on mills, now lost.[100] The same fate befell some writings of the sixteenth century. Palladio illustrated an edition of Polybius, but this work, which he dedicated to the Grand Duke of Tuscany, has disappeared, even though copies existed in print, according to Wittkower.[101]

Possessive book collectors, eager to hide away their treasures, are a nonnegligible factor. In his *Libreria* of 1551, Doni wrote of a drawing of Bramante's that he hoped "he who is keeping this treasure of Bramante's hidden away would bring it out." He described another book—one on antique scaffolding, which had been written "partly by the hand of Messer Filippo Brunelleschi," and in which was "drawn a great part of the scaffolding that he made for vaulting the dome of Florence": "had I been able to read it (since its owner merely allowed me to glance at it) truly I would tell of many beautiful things." Doni lamented in his introductory note "To those who do not read": "I believe few of the above [handwritten] books are to be printed since they are books and in the hands of persons who do not want to part with them, and would rather have them burnt." To which he adds: "If some gallant person would like to know where these works are, I am happy to let them know on condition of my only telling those who have given me full license to do so."[102]

One can hardly imagine less favorable circumstances for manuscript preservation than those faced by the *Hypnerotomachia*. Besides being one of the most prolific writers of his day, Alberti also had one of the most active architectural practices, with commissions in a number of Italian towns, including Florence, Ferrara, Mantua, Rimini, and Rome—other projects for which he never received any credit, incidentally. We know how tightly he controlled every aspect of the design of his buildings down to the most minute details not only of their mathematical proportions but also of site management.[103] In addition, at a time when no other means of locomotion was available, all of Alberti's travel was by horseback—a particularly slow and arduous way of covering long distances.

Alberti's professional activity was staggering, unsurpassed by other architects of his generation—and these were the most important buildings of their time. Apparently, he had already acquired quite a reputation by the mid-1440s, for between 1446 and 1451 he was given the commission to design the Palazzo Rucellai in Florence for the wealthy Florentine merchant and banker Giovanni Rucellai, and in 1448 he began the facade of S. Maria Novella, again for Rucellai. In 1450 he started the design of S. Francesco in Rimini, otherwise known as the Tempio Malatestiano, for Sigismondo Malatesta. In 1459 Gonzaga hired Alberti to build the church of S. Sebastiano in Mantua. When in 1447 Pope Eugenius IV died and was succeeded by the humanist Nicholas V, Alberti took on even more architectural work. Unlike his predecessor, the new pope had an ambitious building policy in Rome. Among the projects Alberti worked on during Nicholas's reign from 1447 to 1455 were the restoration of S. Stefano Rotondo, S. Teodoro, S. Prassede, and S. Maria Maggiore; the aqueduct of the Acqua Vergine; the design of a new Fountain of Trevi; and the restoration of the Ponte Elio, the bridge leading to the Vatican. He probably also made plans for a new St. Peter's and was probably involved in the design for the town of Pienza under Pius II.[104] As we have seen, he was hired by Francesco Colonna's father to restore Palestrina, and Benevolo claims that as Alberti was in Urbino very early on, Federigo da Montefeltro's palace in Urbino was probably designed by him. Benevolo notes both that Alberti was in that hill town as early as 1447 and that there are great similarities between the building and Alberti's description of the palace of a prince in book V of his *De re aedificatoria*.[105]

And by the time the *Hypnerotomachia* was completed, during the last years of Alberti's life, when he was in his sixties (1464 to 1472), his architectural career was more fevered than ever. He designed the Rucellai chapel in the church of S. Pancrazio in Florence in 1467 and, again in Florence in 1470 he completed the ornamentation of the facade of S. Maria Novella for Rucellai. In that same year, he designed the domed, circular tribune of SS. Annunziata for Lodovico Gonzaga in Florence. In 1471 Alberti sent plans from Rome for S. Andrea in Mantua, which were executed by the architect Luca Fancelli for Lodovico Gonzaga. He was dealing constantly not only with temperamental, egocentric clients but also with unruly construction teams in far-away places. He had to supervise two construction sites in Mantua and one in Florence. It is amazing that such an active architectural practitioner could at the same time have written so prolifically on such a variety of subjects. No wonder keeping track of his own manuscripts, once they were finished, was a low priority.

That his attention was demanded by his own self-promoting clients, some of the biggest egos of the time, did not help matters. One was the autocratic tycoon Giovanni Rucellai. In Florence, he was second in wealth only to the Medicis. "How much more pleasurable it is spending money than making it," he mused. Of all ways of spending money he preferred building because it honored God, the city, and, last but not least, "my own memory." His self-esteem knew no bounds. When he had the facade of S. Maria Novella renovated, a structure second in importance only to the Duomo of the city, he made sure it incorporated his own name inscribed in huge letters on the frieze under the pediment. Another band, placed halfway up the facade, was decorated with the Rucellai emblem (a puffed sail) as a sign of his personal sponsorship, the same band that he had placed onto the facade of his own palazzo. His own tomb was the climax of his architectural ambitions. Astonishingly he had it modeled, as he wrote to his mother, on "the Holy Sepulchre of our Lord Jesus Christ," and sent "two wood-carvers together with engineers and other men at my own expense" to the Holy Land in order to document it accurately. Although Alberti was the architect in charge of the facade of the church, the palazzo, and the tomb, Rucellai never acknowledged his role. Neither did he mention in his famous diary, the *Zibaldone quaresimale*,[106] that it was Alberti who introduced him to Rome during a tour on horseback when he had accompanied him in 1450. One would search in vain for any trace of Leon Battista's name in the records of the courts of his other patrons—the d'Este family of Ferrara, the tyrants Gonzaga of Mantua, and Sigismondo Malatesta, the tyrant of Rimini—for whom he built so much. Pope Nicholas V represents the opposite extreme. A fellow humanist, he was not one to credit anyone, not even himself, for the immense public works undertaken in Rome under his reign. Alberti is not mentioned in any papal records as collaborating with him. Characteristically, one would also look in vain in Alberti's own writings for any mention of these projects. Consequently, the most active and influential architect in Western culture since the Renaissance never received any official, written credit whatsoever for architectural works he carried out.

Professional rivalry and intellectual theft were other hurdles Alberti's works undoubtedly encountered. Although, as we have seen, Alberti was probably the inventor of perspective, Vasari, writing in the next century, referred to him only as a "student of perspective."[107] After his death in 1472, as Gadol points out, the next few generations of mathematicians, cartographers, surveyors, engineers, and cryptographers adopted from his works whatever was of value to them without ever acknowledging their debt. Leonardo da Vinci incorporated a number of passages from Alberti's *De pictura* in his own *Trattato* on painting. Cosimo Bartoli, who published a collection of Alberti's *Opuscoli* in 1568, wrote a book on mathematics which incorporated the surveying methods that Alberti had put forth in his *Ludi matematici*.[108]

It was not that he was falsely modest, nor that he eschewed *gloria*. On the contrary, he wanted nothing more. "Oh! How sweet is the glory that we gain through our efforts," he wrote. "What worthy efforts are ours, through which we may show to those who are not yet alive, that we lived with other values than those of our own times, and we have left something of our mind and name besides a mere inscribed and relegated funeral stone. As the poet Ennius said: do not cry for me, do not hold funeral rites for me, for I live in the words of learned men."[109]

Alberti was frankly enamored of himself. "In all by which praise is won, Leon Battista was from his childhood the first," he wrote in his autobiography.[110] Burckhardt was struck by this feature and captured the spirit of the autobiography in his paraphrase:

OF HIS VARIOUS GYMNASTIC FEATS AND EXERCISES WE READ WITH ASTONISHMENT HOW, WITH HIS FEET TOGETHER, HE COULD SPRING OVER A MAN'S HEAD; HOW, IN THE CATHEDRAL, HE THREW A COIN IN THE AIR TILL IT WAS HEARD TO RING AGAINST THE DISTANT ROOF; HOW THE WILDEST HORSES TREMBLED UNDER HIM. IN THREE THINGS HE DESIRED TO APPEAR FAULTLESS TO OTHERS, IN WALKING, RIDING, AND IN SPEAKING. HE LEARNED MUSIC WITHOUT A MASTER, AND YET HIS COMPOSITIONS WERE ADMIRED BY PROFESSIONAL JUDGES. UNDER THE PRESSURE OF POVERTY, HE STUDIED BOTH CIVIL AND CANONICAL LAW FOR MANY YEARS, TILL EXHAUSTION BROUGHT ON A SEVERE ILLNESS. IN HIS TWENTY-FOURTH YEAR, FINDING HIS MEMORY FOR WORDS WEAKENED, BUT HIS SENSE OF FACTS

UNIMPAIRED, HE SET TO WORK ON PHYSICS AND MATHEMATICS, AND ALL THE WHILE HE ACQUIRED EVERY SORT OF ACCOMPLISHMENT AND DEXTERITY, CROSS-EXAMINING ARTISTS, SCHOLARS, AND ARTISANS OF ALL DESCRIPTIONS, DOWN TO THE COBBLERS, ABOUT THE SECRETS AND PECULIARITIES OF THEIR CRAFT. PAINTING AND MODELLING HE PRACTICED BY THE WAY, AND ESPECIALLY EXCELLED IN ADMIRABLE LIKENESSES FROM MEMORY.[111]

But in spite of his high self-regard, Alberti was hopelessly bad at self-promotion. He tended to be overgenerous with people. As he wrote himself, he considered "all those who were famous for their studies as brothers, and willingly shared his knowledge with them. He gave every artist copies of his great, worthy treatises, and when a great and learned artist came to town he was quick to make friends with him."[112] This tendency could have disastrous consequences for his manuscripts. One case is notorious. His *Della tranquillità dell'animo*, otherwise known as *Profugiorum ab aerumna* [*sic*], would have been lost forever had his brother, who acted as his archivist and executor, not succeeded in retrieving it from the object of Alberti's generosity after Alberti's death. In the introduction to the book, addressed to a friend, Alberti's brother explained:

YOU HAVE ASKED ME MANY TIMES IN THE PAST FOR THESE BOOKS, *PROFUGIORUM AB AERUMNA*, WHICH WERE LOST TO US, AND WHICH OUT OF RESPECT I SHALL NOT SPECIFY HOW, BUT YOU WELL KNOW THE NATURE OF MASTER BATTISTA, MY BROTHER, IT IS IMPOSSIBLE FOR HIM TO DENY ANYONE WHATEVER THEY ASK OF HIM: I WILL NOT SAY MORE. A CERTAIN DOMESTIC OF HIS ASKED FOR THESE BOOKS AS SOON AS THEY WERE COMPLETED. THIRTY YEARS HAVE PASSED SINCE THEN. AND HE HAD THE FIRST ORIGINAL COPY. HE PRESENTED HIS APOLOGIES AND DENIED HAVING IT IN HIS POSSESSION, AND WE DID NOT KNOW HOW TO GET THEM BACK. WELL, WE HAVE THEM BACK AT LAST.[113]

Given these circumstances, it is a wonder the manuscript survived at all. In fact many of Alberti's writings have been lost. Although he dedicated *Philodoxeus* to Leonello d'Este when he first made his acquaintance and when his father died sent him *Teogenio*, about how to govern, this did not keep the third book of the latter from disappearing. In the codex in the d'Este collection, at the end of the second book is written "Deficit Liber Tertius" (the third book is missing). *De re aedificatoria* is another case in point. Although it was the most sought-after and copied manuscript of the fifteenth century—and thus was one of the first books printed—the original codex, on which was based the editio princeps published in Florence in 1485, has disappeared.[114] While there are extant codices of the treatise, each one is different: one now at the Vatican was copied in one consistent hand, and one at Eton College with the stemma of Bernardo Bembo is of the same hand except for one passage.[115] The Duke of Montefeltro, in order to reproduce the five-hundred-page manuscript, mobilized a staff of about twenty full-time copyists, in addition to people who passed through. Because the manuscript was copied out in this fragmented way, bits were easily lost. Only recently was one section discovered in Chicago.[116]

Thus even one of the most widely esteemed manuscripts of the fifteenth century did not survive intact. In the manuscript that Alberti presented to Nicholas V in 1450, a preface gives a description of the contents. Appended to the main text are *Navis* and *Economics, Arithmetic and Geometry, and the Service that the Architect Provides.* These too have been lost. Although there is no mention of the latter by others, we know that Leonardo had *Navis* in his possession, because he commented on it briefly in his own writings.[117] Some speculate that it helped inspire his design of a submarine. *De motibus ponderis,* which Leon Battista mentions in his *Della tranquillità dell'animo,* has never been found. The same is true of three other texts: *Commentaria rerum mathematicarum, Aeraria,* and *Historia numeri et linearum.* Leon Battista's last work, *De iciarchia,* was never known at all. Its single manuscript fortunately surfaced in the Laurentian Library in Florence at the end of the nineteenth century.[118]

Alberti's authorship of the *Hypnerotomachia* would explain why it is so arcane. Alberti loved the effect of playful associations and adored problems, puzzles, rebuses. His *Ludi matematici* are conceived as a series of problems to solve. His *Intercenales* are inspired by a passage from Macrobius's *Saturnalia* that features "gibes . . . couched in dissimulating or witty terms, that say one thing but mean another."[119] Many of the pieces it contains are purposefully recondite. Among them are "The Rings," which describes a series of twelve rings on which are engraved a hieroglyphic figure of Alberti's own invention, and "Veiled Sayings," where "noble and elegant principles" were uttered in "veiled fashion" in order for listeners to be struck with awe and listen more attentively.[120]

In this love of surprise, Alberti was a typical quattrocento humanist. It seems to have been a common mental quirk among many of his colleagues. Take Leonardo, for example: his notebooks were written in reversed handwriting, and we know he was fascinated with hieroglyphs and rebuses. In this way one may also explain Leonardo's "nonsense" rebus on a sheet at Windsor, which covers the plan of a large palace. This same plan is repeated in identical scale on a contemporaneous sheet (ca. 1487–1490) of the Codex Atlanticus.[121] So too the device of the thirty-nine letters of the initials of the chapters of the *Hypnerotomachia* has a well-known precedent. In *Amorosa visione,* the world's hugest acrostic, Boccaccio wrote three sonnets that together contained about 1,500 letters. Then he wrote his *Visione* in such a way that the initials of the successive tercets and of the final lines of his fifty "capitoli" correspond exactly to the letters of those three sonnets.[122] And Bramante devised a rebus for the Belvedere, though Julius II rejected it.[123] These games of memory jogging via hieroglyphics, through which the image of an object becomes associated to an idea, are simply one aspect of "artificial memory," a most ancient science; it in turn is a form of "perspective of memory," a means of manipulating a mental construction and therefore a useful tool in the service of study. The humanists loved these effects of surprise, probably because of their shared circumstance: they were highly creative minds who were violating whole world views. According to psychologist Jerome Bruner, surprise "provides a window on presupposition: surprise is a response to violated presupposition."[124]

The systematic crypticness of the *Hypnerotomachia* is typical of Alberti. In fact, at the time he would have completed the *Hypnerotomachia*, he would also have been completing his *De componendi cifris,* which contained the first known frequency table and, more important, the first polyalphabetic system of coding. Alberti set forth, in his words, "an extremely secret and convenient method of writing" that consisted in correlating the Latin alphabet with a scrambled alphabet by means of a cipher wheel, made out of two copper disks, one slightly larger than the other, with a pin serving as a central axis for both (fig. 51). He called the instrument a "formula," or "form of words."[125] A key correlates the two alphabets, so that the one letter is always replaced by the other. The device was still used at the time of the American Civil War by the U.S. Navy.[126]

Just as typical of Alberti is the book's anonymous publication. On top of everything else, Alberti was in the habit of concealing his identity. This peculiar feature extended even to his own autobiography, written anonymously in the third person. Similarly, Alberti's second book, *Philodoxeus,* written when he was twenty years of age, is signed only with his pen name, Lepidus, and he left it unclaimed for ten years. When he finally declared his authorship, he did so only in order to have something to present to his friend Leonello d'Este. Even the scrupulous, scholarly press of Aldus Manutius—the publishers of the *Hypnerotomachia*—found it hard to keep track of such an elusive author and published *Philodoxeus* as the work of "Lepidus" in 1588, well after Alberti had asserted his authorship.

This tendency to assume the identity of an "other" went hand in hand with a constant tendency to insert autobiographical allusions—what he referred to as "sprinklings"—into his works. In claiming the authorship to *Philodoxeus,* in his short *Commentarium Philodoxo fabulae,* he defended himself against his critics, explaining that he had inserted references to his identity deliberately into the play and the prologue. "So that my efforts would not be lost," he writes, "I added a prologue that I *sprinkled* with references to my studies, my age, and other important allusions to myself. My object was to claim, when I wished, the work as my own—and this I did."[127]

An abundance of this kind of autobiographical sprinkling appears throughout his oeuvre. His *Ecatonfilea* is narrated by a woman who gives advice on the best kind of man to love. The man whom Leon Battista describes through his narrator is, as the Italian scholar Bonucci notes in the introduction, none other than himself, depicted in almost the same terms as he uses in his own autobiography.[128] "Do not marry a rich man," he advises, but one who is "schooled in the good arts and possessed of many virtues," with "a beautiful appearance, gentlemanly," "delicate and full of marvelous humanity and ingenuity": one who is

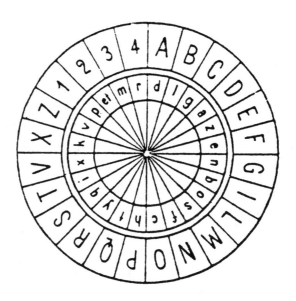

51. ALBERTI'S ENCRYPTION DEVICE. FROM J. GADOL, *LEON BATTISTA ALBETI: UNIVERSAL MAN OF THE EARLY RENAISSANCE* (CHICAGO, 1969), P. 208.

"discreet, modest, playful when appropriate; eloquent, erudite and liberal, loving, . . . astute, practical and above all faithful; . . . excelling in music, letters, painting, sculpture, and every good and noble art."[129] His *Canis,* a few years later, is written in the same partly self-revealing and partly self-concealing vein; Alberti, pretending to tell the story of his dog's life, makes many illusions to his own, in particular to the fact that he was a mongrel, or bastard. He also observed that he—the dog, that is—was "possessed of a most tenacious memory and retains things forever: in less than three years he mastered the Greek, Latin, and Tuscan language"[130]—like the author of the *Hypnerotomachia* himself.

His autobiographical sprinklings extended to his architecture, in particular to his design for the apse of the church of S. Martino di Gangalandi with a rounded arch. There, an epigram that he carved into the frieze on the entablature runs around the base of the calotte—"VIR POPULI D MARTINO D GANGALANDO FACIUNDUM CURAVIT" (a man of the people attended to that work for S. Martino di Gangalandi)—with the Alberti coat of arms on either end.[131] Moreover, generations of architectural historians have seen in Alberti's design for the facade of S. Maria Novella a reference to the facade of S. Miniato al Monte in Florence. Such a clearly personal architectural reference as this is an invocation of his family's traditionally strong ties to the church of S. Miniato; in the fourteenth century, they had patronized its paintings by Spinello Aretino on the massacre of the population of Antella, near Florence.[132]

If the references I have made so far to Alberti's own works were not convincing enough as "sprinklings," the *Hypnerotomachia* also contains five highly personal and revealing clues that identify the author as Alberti. First are the references to animals. Alberti loved all animals, which explains why he wrote so many things about them. He dedicated *Canis* to his beloved dog. He wrote on fleas, in *Musca*. He must have been particularly fascinated with elephants, for he placed two paired sculptures of them in the Tempio Malatestiano bearing the emblems of the patron. In the *Hypnerotomachia* there is the elephant-shaped memory palace, the elephant-drawn carriage, and the elephant-based hieroglyphs, including a very funny one—half ant, half elephant (fig. 52). But Alberti loved horses most of all, which might explain the equestrian statue at the beginning of the *Hypnerotomachia*. He was involved in organizing a competition for an equestrian statue for the d'Este family. He devoted an essay to horses, entitled *De equo animante* (On the living horse), describing their beauty, their nature, and their instincts; the best seasons for riding; and how to train them and detect their sicknesses. He was also a passionate horseman. In his autobiography, he wrote that "he could ride for hours without showing the slightest trace of fatigue, with one end of a rod placed against his foot and the other in his hand, without the slightest movement on the part of the rod. So fine and wonderful a horseman was he, that even the proudest and most mettlesome horses seemed to fear and tremble when he mounted them." [133] In fact, so attached was he to them that he compares what he considers the finest architecture in Italian history—the architecture of the early Romans—to a horse. The Italians' "inborn thrift prompted them to be the first who made their buildings like animals. Take the case of the horse: they realized that where the shape of each member looked suitable for a particular use, so the whole animal itself could work well in that use." [134]

The second personal clue linking the *Hypnerotomachia* with Alberti is its abundant musical musings. Alberti declares, "Battista was born of a music-loving father. And learned it without a master and composed songs that were admired by real musicians. He played several instruments and the organ and was admired by real musicians, and even had something to teach them in method. He loved song and exercised his voice, even in old age, between the walls of his house, in villas, or in the company of his brother or relatives. He had the spirit singularly predisposed to appreciate the sweetness of harmony." He made the same point again: "He was a self-taught musician and his compositions were highly esteemed by the music masters. All his life he was given to singing, but he did this when alone or in private, especially at home with his brother and relatives. He loved to play the organ and was one of the best organ players. Indeed his advice helped others become more proficient in music." Music affected him powerfully: "when a fierce attack of lumbago caused him to come out in a cold sweat, he summoned some musicians and forced himself to overcome the pain with a couple of hours of singing." [135]

52.   THE ANT-ELEPHANT HYBRID.

The third connection lies in names that Alberti used. As we have seen, he wrote *Philodoxeus* under a pen name, Lepidus. *Lepidus* is Latin for "the joker," or "laughing one." Apparently Alberti identified with the name, because Lepidus reappears, now as a protagonist who acts as one of Alberti's alter egos, in *Intercenales*.[136] The Greek equivalent of *lepidus* is *gelastos,* and Gelastos appears in *Momus,* again as Alberti's alter ego. Finally Gelastos resurfaces once more in the *Hypnerotomachia,* as Geloiastos (fig. 53).

Fourth, the eye, Alberti's emblem, is found in the illustrations of some of the hieroglyphs of the *Hypnerotomachia* (figs. 54, 55).

53. GELOIASTOS.

And fifth, and most revealing of all, there is a sartorial autobiographical allusion in the *Hypnerotomachia*. Look at Poliphilo's clothes: he is wearing a cassock and skullcap (fig. 56). In this respect he is not dressed in the normal attire of mid-quattrocento youths (as seen in the illustrations of b6), who wore tights and flared miniskirts. Alberti was a papal abbreviator and he has dressed himself, in the guise of Poliphilo, for the part (fig. 57).

The *Hypnerotomachia* would not have been the first book of Alberti's to be attributed to someone else. He often included among his characters people who really existed and placed in their mouths his own words and feelings. This occurs notably in *Della tranquillità*

54. ALBERTI'S EMBLEM, THE WINGED EYE. FROM HIS *DELLA FAMIGLIA* (1438), COD. II, IV, FLORENCE, BIBLIOTECA NAZIONALE.

55. THE EYE IN THE HIEROGLYPHS OF THE *HYPNEROTOMACHIA*.

dell'animo, a book in which the civic humanist and Florentine statesman Agnolo Pandolfini becomes the main spokesman for Alberti's own views, while Alberti himself is only a silent onlooker. At the end of the fifteenth century, a free adaptation of book 3 of Alberti's *Della famiglia* was attributed to Pandolfini, because, again, a character by that name presents Alberti's own views. Thus while the rest of the book sank into oblivion, this portion had a resounding success under the name of Agnolo Pandolfini and the title *Del governo della famiglia,* giving rise at the end of the nineteenth century to a controversy between the partisans of Pandolfini and those of Alberti.[137] The third book of the *Intercenales,* "Virtus," was published as the work of Lucian.[138] This attribution appeared in many editions, Latin and Italian; for example, *Luciani de veris narrationibus . . . Luciani Virtus dea . . . clarissimi Luciani philosophi* (1494). Alberti's *Efebie* was repeatedly ascribed to Alberti's brother and his *Deifira* to Boccaccio.[139]

If Alberti were the author of the *Hypnerotomachia,* it would explain the choice of Francesco Colonna as one of the author's alter egos. First, Alberti had many reasons to feel close to the Colonna family. Oddone Colonna, Pope Martin V, had been a protector of Alberti's. In 1428 he used his influence in the Florentine Signoria to obtain an annulment of the judgment passed against the Albertis at the beginning of the century. As a result they were

57. SELF-PORTRAIT OF ALBERTI, WEARING A CASSOCK. ROME, BIBLIOTECA NAZIONALE (CAT. 29).

56. POLIPHILO, WEARING A CASSOCK.

allowed back to Florence, and Leon Battista entered the beloved city of his forebears for the first time in his life. Alberti also had much in common with the Colonnas; as a civic humanist, he shared their republican sympathies. Not surprisingly, therefore, Prospero Colonna became Alberti's main patron.[140] It is possible that Alberti would have identified with Prospero's nephew, the young Francesco. Alberti could not have known what a conformist Francesco would turn out to be. At the time of the book's completion, he was only fourteen years old. What matters is that he would have been the scion of a powerful family with civic humanist leanings, which had just lost its high standing in society because of those leanings—as Agnolo Pandolfini and as Alberti himself had once been.

A final biographical connection to Alberti can be found in the claim at the end of the book that the author was in Treviso in 1467. Treviso is a town Alberti would have known through his close friend Donatello, who painted a series of triumphs that have been likened to the triumphs in the *Hypnerotomachia*. It would explain, although less convincingly, why the character Polia claims that she is a member of the Lelli family and a native of Treviso. The bishop of Treviso was Teodoro Lelli, a member of the papal curia like Alberti, and he had a niece named Lucrezia Lelli. She took her vows during an attack of plague, just as Polia does in the *Hypnerotomachia*.[141] Though Lelli was probably a friend of Alberti's, that does not explain the important role Lelli's young niece, identified with Polia, plays in the *Hypnerotomachia,* where she echoes Lorenzo Valla's defense of free love. Alberti's other works reveal his well-known misogyny.[142] This remains a mystery.

*   *   *

Obviously, Alberti being the author of the *Hypnerotomachia* would explain why architecture plays such an overwhelming role in the book, and particularly the great number of almost word-for-word quotations from *De re aedificatoria*. Not that the *Hypnerotomachia* had a monopoly on Albertian references: Alberti was the best-known architectural theoretician of the day and was frequently quoted in other works. Leonardo mentions him in his notebooks, as does Filarete in his treatise on architecture. Even Francesco di Giorgio, who was passionately jealous of Alberti, echoes passages from *De re aedificatoria*. For instance, like Alberti, he urges the installation of an adjustable fan to draw off the smoke from the chimney piece, and he too suggests that the master of a palace introduce apertures in the walls to listen to what is being said behind his back. His *Trattati* even contains a long attack on Alberti for not illustrating his treatise:

FOR A LONG TIME NOW MANY NOBLE AUTHORS HAVE WRITTEN ABOUT THE ART OF ARCHITECTURE, BUILDINGS, AND MACHINERY, AND HAVE WRITTEN DOWN THEIR IDEAS WITHOUT ILLUSTRATING THEM. AND THOUGH THESE WRITERS THINK THEY HAVE FULLY ELUCIDATED

THEIR IDEAS, YET I SEE THAT THERE ARE VERY FEW READERS WHO CAN UNDERSTAND THEM
WITHOUT THE HELP OF DRAWINGS. FOR THE READER HAS TO RELY ON HIS OWN IDEA OF
WHAT IS BEING DESCRIBED AND SOMETIMES IT IS AS DIFFERENT FROM THE AUTHOR'S AS
DAY IS FROM NIGHT. THUS THE READER IS LEFT IN SOME CONFUSION, FOR THERE ARE AS
MANY IDEAS OF WHAT THE AUTHOR IS TRYING TO DESCRIBE AS THERE ARE READERS.[143]

But whereas the works of Francesco and Filarete limit their Albertian references to a few lines in passing, the *Hypnerotomachia* incorporates no fewer than ninety-seven passages from that treatise, either verbatim or quasi-verbatim.[144]

Moreover, we have already remarked on the extraordinary archaeological knowledge displayed in the description of the buildings in the *Hypnerotomachia*. No one else would have had such a grasp of archaeological detail in 1467 as Alberti. For the purposes of composing his *De re aedificatoria* and his *Descriptio urbis Romae* (ca. 1450), he had been the first to undertake the systematic study of Rome's ancient monuments and thus would have been uniquely well placed to write a book of such architectural learning.[145] As he wrote himself in *De re aedificatoria*, "No building of the ancients that had attracted praise, wherever it might be, but I immediately examined it carefully, to see what I could learn from it. Therefore I never stopped exploring, considering, and measuring everything, and comparing the information through line drawings, until I had grasped and understood fully what each had to contribute in terms of ingenuity or skill" (VI.6, pp. 92–93). Concerning archaeological matters, there is a striking concordance between certain architectural elements mentioned in *De re aedificatoria* and in the *Hypnerotomachia*. For example, there is described in the former a "block of stone large beyond human belief, such as that quarried by Semiramis from the mountains of Arabia, measuring 20 cubits in height and breadth, and 150 in length" (VI.5, pp. 98–99), which reappears in the latter in the guise of a "shrine on the island of Chemnis in Egypt, remarkable not so much for the fact that the roof consists of a single stone as for the fact that such a huge stone could have been set on walls so high" (h2). The "rare and exquisite stone such as, for example, the marble of which the Emperor Nero reportedly built the temple of Fortune in the Golden House, pure, white, and translucent, so that even when all the doors were closed, light seemed to be trapped inside" in *De re aedificatoria* (VI.5, p. 166) reappears almost verbatim in the descriptions of the round temple in the *Hypnerotomachia*. Even more compelling evidence is supplied by the aquatic labyrinth in the *Hypnerotomachia*, which is derived almost verbatim from a part of Alberti's *Intercenales*, called "Anuli."[146]

Equally indicative of Alberti's authorship would be the strong character of *romanità* in the buildings in the *Hypnerotomachia*. Alberti was what we would today call a regionalist architect. Wherever he built, he did so in such a way as to incorporate local elements into his design. This is not to say he built in the traditional local style. Rather, in the fashion of the critical regionalists of the twentieth century, he incorporated local elements and recombined them in a way that was unfamiliar. In his facade for S. Maria Novella, as we have seen, he borrowed elements from S. Miniato al Monte nearby, and Richard Krautheimer contended that he conceived S. Andrea in Mantua in the Etruscan style of the region.[147] As we noted in the previous chapter, the buildings described in the *Hypnerotomachia* are based on the Roman buildings that are located in the area between the Orti Salustiani and the Via Appia.

The insistence on the olfactory, acoustic, tactile delight of the hero's description of architecture in the novel—the only such description in any architectural writing of the Renaissance—appears to be presaged in Alberti's early description of the interior of the cathedral of S. Maria del Fiore found in his *Della tranquillità dell'animo*.

AND CERTAINLY THIS TEMPLE IS ITSELF GRACE AND MAJESTY; AND, AS I HAVE OFTEN THOUGHT, I DELIGHT TO SEE JOINED HERE A CHARMING SLENDERNESS WITH A ROBUST AND FULL SOLIDITY SO THAT, ON THE ONE HAND, EACH OF ITS PARTS SEEMS DESIGNED FOR PLEASURE, WHILE ON THE OTHER, ONE UNDERSTANDS THAT IT HAS ALL BEEN BUILT FOR PERPETUITY. I WOULD ADD THAT THERE IS THE CONSTANT HOME OF TEMPERATENESS, AS OF SPRINGTIME: OUTSIDE, WIND, ICE, AND FROST; HERE INSIDE ONE IS PROTECTED FROM THE WIND, HERE MILD AND QUIET. OUTSIDE, THE HEAT OF SUMMER AND AUTUMN; INSIDE, COOLNESS. AND IF, AS THEY SAY, DELIGHT IS FELT WHEN OUR SENSES PERCEIVE WHAT, HOW MUCH, THEY REQUIRE BY NATURE, WHO COULD HESITATE TO CALL THIS TEMPLE THE NEST OF DELIGHTS? HERE, WHEREVER YOU LOOK, YOU SEE THE EXPRESSION OF HAPPINESS AND GAIETY; HERE IT IS ALWAYS FRAGRANT; AND, THAT WHICH I PRIZE ABOVE ALL, HERE YOU LISTEN TO VOICES DURING MASS, DURING THAT WHICH THE ANCIENTS CALLED THE MYSTERIES, WITH THEIR WONDERFUL SWEETNESS [*SOAVITÀ MARAVIGLIOSA*].[148]

Of course, echoes of Alberti's writings in the *Hypnerotomachia* are insufficient evidence of Alberti's authorship. As I have mentioned, other authors quoted him. More persuasive is the choice of details reused. The round temple described in the *Hypnerotomachia*—the first reconstruction of a round plan temple described in the Renaissance and a forerunner of Bramante's Tempietto at S. Pietro in Montorio (which is usually credited with being the first, in 1502)—echoes the round plan building that Alberti describes in *De re aedificatoria*.[149] It also bears some relation to the round plan church of S. Stefano Rotondo, which Alberti restored in Rome. In the process he repaired the columns of the inner ring: demolishing the outer wall and enclosing the building within the perimeter of the second ring of columns, walling up the spaces between them, and in effect transforming the church into a round-plan peripteral temple.[150] Similarly, the learned description of the orders in the book seems to mirror Alberti's interests; he was the first Renaissance architect to achieve a reasonably good understanding of the ancient orders.[151] If he were the author it would not be surprising that in the

Hypnerotomachia nearly as much knowledge is displayed and in terms so similar to those of *De re aedificatoria*. Moreover, the attribution would explain the presence of a rigorously correct classical building such as the book's round temple of Venus Physozoï, predating Bramante's Doric Tempietto at S. Pietro. Indeed, what has been regarded as a "mistake" in the *Hypnerotomachia,* particularly by Tommaso Temanza in the eighteenth century and Lamberto Donati in the twentieth[152]—the description of the columns of the peristyle on the island of Cythera where the Doric and the Corinthian are confused—would become an Albertian joke, probably another "sprinkling."

The *Hypnerotomachia* reads very much like a catalogue of Alberti's own building projects in Rome. It is an often overlooked fact about Alberti that he did not live to see even one of his many projects actually completed,[153] projects that were never finished anywhere but in the *Hypnerotomachia.* Obviously, as Alberti was commissioned by Francesco Colonna's father to restore the palazzo of Palestrina, he would use elements from Palestrina in the book. Alberti had also been commissioned to restore the Ponte Sant'Angelo, or Ponte Elio, as it was then called. Vasari claims to have had in his possession a sketch of Alberti's design for the bridge, with a roof having marble columns and covered with bronze and marvelous ornaments. Bernardo Rucellai refers to it as one of the great projects Alberti designed for Nicholas V.[154] This might explain the presence of the bridge in the *Hypnerotomachia* (d7-d8). The Alberti attribution might also explain the presence of so many fountains in the *Hypnerotomachia.* According to the eighteenth-century architectural theoretician Francesco Milizia, Nicholas V asked Alberti to direct the construction of a three-mouthed fountain of Trevi. Alberti is also credited with having designed an almost entirely subterranean conduit for water, over twelve miles long, leading to the Piazza di Trevi.[155] Perhaps his description of the bathhouse in the *Hypnerotomachia* alludes to his drawing for a bathhouse that was never built.[156]

The many hemispheric domed roof structures in the novel also suggest a link to Alberti. Brunelleschi's gigantic cupola on the cathedral of S. Maria del Fiore still betrayed a trace of the pointed Gothic form. In contrast, Alberti's project for the dome of S. Francesco di Rimini, unbuilt but represented on the reverse of the medallion made by Matteo di Pasti, is arched in the less spectacular but technically more difficult rounded Roman manner: it marks the creation of a new architecture totally different from the Gothic. Alberti's commission for SS. Annunziata in Florence for Gonzaga was also in this style. Although not considered a success, still the large-scale hemispheric cupola was a new kind of structure and an Albertian trademark.[157]

Other details of the buildings in the *Hypnerotomachia* are also important, particularly the emphasis on lighting effects. For instance, the pool is illuminated by means of chased glass within the openwork of the ceiling and doors. The round temple is illuminated by translucent panels that extend the full lengths of the walls, and its annex is completely made of translucent material. The chambers in the colossus all receive natural light. The most spectacular lighting is in the great spherical hall inside the pyramid, where the effects are achieved by reflected light. Alberti both understood the role of reflection and placed much emphasis on lighting in architecture more generally. In *De pictura,* he notes, "Shadow in which the rays of light are interrupted remains to be treated. The interrupted rays either return from whence they came or are directed elsewhere. They are directed elsewhere, when, touching the surface of the water, they strike the rafters of a house. More can be said about this reflection which has to do with these miracles of painting which many of my friends have seen done by me excellently in Rome." [158] In his later career, around the time he would have been writing the *Hypnerotomachia,* he was designing the church of S. Andrea in Mantua. Wittkower has described it—or rather has reconstructed its original state, for it has undergone devastating transformations—as a radical architectural experiment, eliminating the columns by incorporating them into the walls and thus creating an open space under its immense barrel-vaulted ceiling. Because barrel vaults cannot be pierced and they therefore cut off all sources of light from above, Alberti opened up circular or semicircular windows in each of the side chapels, which were also surmounted by barrel vaults perpendicular to the central one. This made them into great chambers of light, breaking up and lightening the effect of masonry and turning the immense central space of the nave into a vast reservoir of reverberating luminosity. [159]

Another distinctly Albertian feature of the *Hypnerotomachia* is the integration of architecture and nature. Few architects ever loved nature as much as Alberti. While most Renaissance writers saw nature as a realm of delights only, a symbol of innocence and seduction, as it had been for Petrarch's *Canzoniere* and Boccaccio's *Amorosa visione,* [160] Alberti's use of the topos was distinctive. Nature for him was the provider of rules for the governance of life at all levels. This is a theme that runs through many of his writings. He considered an organic screen as a garden wall in *De re aedificatoria* when he suggested columns in the form of tree trunks (X.1). As I have mentioned, garden design and botanical lore covers over sixty pages, or one-sixth, of the *Hypnerotomachia.* Unlike all other quattrocento architects except Leonardo da Vinci, Alberti was passionately attached to nature. In his autobiography he wrote that he "worshipped the beauties of nature, and that quadrupeds, birds, and other resplendent animals should be loved, for all nature granted her country was nature"; when ill, the mere sight of "flowers, or some pleasant natural scene" would often "cure" him. He loved villa life "where the air is crystal clear, the countryside cheerful and beautiful wherever the eye roams, fog rare, the winds moderate, the water good, and everything healthy and pure." [161] His *Teogenio* is one long paean to nature. It opens with a description:

HERE COLUMNS ERECTED BY NATURE ARE THE STEEP TREES THAT YOU CAN SEE. THERE, ABOVE US, ARE THE DELIGHTFUL BEECHES AND FIRS WHOSE SHADOWS COVER US FROM THE SUN. ALL AROUND WHEREVER YOU TURN YOUR EYE, YOU WILL SEE THOUSANDS OF RE-

FLECTED COLORS OF VARIOUS FLOWERS SHINING AMONG THE GREEN GRASS AND THE SHAD-
OWS, SURPASSING THE BRILLIANCE AND THE LIGHT OF THE SKY.. . . . AND HERE CLOSE BY
IS THIS SILVER AND PURE SPRING, WITNESS AND ARBITER IN PART OF MY STUDIES, WHICH
ALWAYS SMILES AT ME AND FLOWS AROUND ME, CARESSING AND HIDING AT TIMES AMONG
THE FOLIAGE OF THESE VERY FRESH AND CHARMING GRASSES, AND AT TIMES WITH ITS
EXUBERANT WAVES, IT RAISES ITSELF AND BABBLING SWEETLY AS IT BENDS TOWARD ME,
GREETS ME.[162]

He devoted much of his *Della famiglia* to agricultural matters and wrote *Villa* (ca.
1439), a pamphlet in the vernacular on agronomy.[163] Alberti not only was a theoretician of
landscape but also had a reputation as a practicing landscape architect. Flavio Biondo wrote
in 1446 that he "restored the gardens of Maecenas for Cardinal Colonna, and he did such a
good job that they surpassed any modern building existing in Italy."[164] There is no building
in the *Hypnerotomachia* that is not set in a landscape, and one finds the same integration of
architecture and nature in *De re aedificatoria*. In it, in the very heart of the city, he plans lakes
for swimming, groves, and a flowery meadow. He might have been influenced in this by his
own surroundings: Rome between the Orti Salustiani and the Via Appia was and still is a
greenbelt in which buildings are nestled.

Here we encounter an aspect of the *Hypnerotomachia* that cannot be readily connected with Alberti. This is the presence of the famed detailed descriptions of geometrical
layouts and *ars topiaria* in the book, which are generally recognized as the single most influential work in the design of European formal gardens for the coming three centuries.[165] There
are simply no precedents for these designs in Alberti's known works. Neither is there a precedent for something scholars have failed to notice—perhaps because it is too ahead of its time
and incongruous in the mid-fifteenth century—the "natural" garden. Here we have what in
the eighteenth century will come to be called a picturesque landscape garden: that is, a garden
that imitates *natura naturans* as opposed to *natura naturata*.[166] Indeed, the entire conceit of the
Hypnerotomachia—a natural setting in which the visitor is free to roam along a winding, irreg-
ular path, from which views of buildings and of natural settings are framed—is that of a
picturesque landscape. It is certainly possible that to all his other achievements, Alberti can
add being the first to describe a picturesque garden.

Ultimately, it is the book's passion for architecture—over half of its pages are taken
up with architectural descriptions—that most clearly points to Alberti as its author. There
were very few if any whose intellectual and professional lives were more taken up by architecture in mid-quattrocento Italy than his. His route to architecture was far from direct. After
studying law, a profession he found odious, and suffering a severe psychological breakdown,
mentioned in his *Della tranquillità dell'animo*, he briefly attempted to make a living from literature. Perhaps out of extreme poverty, he was compelled to enter the orders—an unhappy

solution, in view of his contempt for the church, but one that at least provided him with enough free time to write. He became a secretary in the service of Cardinal Aleman and later of Cardinal Albergati, whom he accompanied on a long journey across the Alps to Germany in 1430. In 1432 he settled in Rome, then no more than a provincial outpost compared to the cultural centers such as Florence, Bologna, Ferrara, and Mantua, and obtained the position of abbreviator in the papal chancery under Pope Eugenius IV.

The job was neither particularly prestigious nor well-paid. There were 102 papal abbreviators, including Alberti. Alberti expresses his intense loathing for his life as a civil servant in his *Della famiglia,* where he complains that he "lived subject to others." He goes on:

I HAVE ALWAYS PREFERRED EVERY OTHER KIND OF LIFE TO THAT OF WHAT WE CALL THE CIVIL SERVANT. AND WHO COULD POSSIBLY LIKE IT? A MOST TROUBLESOME LIFE, FULL OF SUSPICION, FATIGUE, AND EVERY KIND OF SERVITUDE. WHAT DIFFERENCE CAN YOU SEE BETWEEN THESE MEN WHO WORK AWAY AT STATE AFFAIRS LIKE SLAVES? ONE RUSHES ABOUT HERE AND THERE, BOWING BEFORE THIS MAN, COMPETING WITH THAT, INSULTING ANOTHER. ONE IS SUSPECTED BY MANY AND ENVIED BY ALL. ONE HAS COUNTLESS ENEMIES BUT NO LOYAL FRIENDSHIPS, ANY NUMBER OF PROMISES AND OFFERS EVEN THOUGH ONE IS SURROUNDED BY PRETENSE, VANITY, AND LIES. AND WHAT YOU NEED MOST YOU CAN-NOT FIND—A SINGLE LOYAL, TRUSTWORTHY PERSON. AND SO EVERYTHING YOU STRIVE AND HOPE FOR IS SUDDENLY SWEPT AWAY, TO YOUR DAMAGE, SORROW, AND NOT A LITTLE TO YOUR UNDOING TOO. AND IF, AFTER COUNTLESS APPLICATIONS, YOU SUCCEED IN OBTAINING SOME FAVOR, WHAT HAVE YOU ACHIEVED? THERE YOU ARE, SEATED IN AN OFFICE, AND WHAT ADVANTAGES HAVE YOU BESIDES BEING ABLE TO STEAL AND COMMAND WITH GREATER FREEDOM? YOU WILL HEAR COMPLAINTS, ENDLESS ACCUSATIONS, GREAT UPROARS, AND YOU WILL BE SURROUNDED BY GREEDY, QUARRELSOME, WICKED MEN, FILL-ING YOUR EARS WITH SUSPICION, YOUR HEART WITH GREED, AND YOUR MIND WITH FEAR AND WORRY. IS IT WORTHWHILE LEAVING YOUR OWN AFFAIRS IN ORDER TO DEAL WITH THE STUPIDITY OF OTHERS?[167]

Alberti seemed destined to the stifling life of a bureaucrat with literary inclinations when in 1434 the course of his life changed dramatically. He was forced to flee Rome with the rest of the papal curia because of the civil unrest directed against the papacy. As a result, for the next ten years, Alberti lived in Florence, with extended stays in Bologna and Ferrara, and thus came into contact with the works of the greatest artists, sculptors, and architects of his day—Donatello, Luca della Robbia, Filippo Brunelleschi, Lorenzo Ghiberti, Masaccio.[168] So exhilarated did he become in this company that he soon wrote two treatises, one on sculpture and one on painting (*De statua* in 1434 and *De pictura* in 1435), which established him as the leading theoretician in both fields.

But it was the contact with architecture through the work and person of Brunelleschi that affected Alberti most.[169] Although he pursued other activities—artistic, literary, and philosophical—from that time on, architecture dominated his life. In the early 1440s he started *De re aedificatoria,* which was probably at least mostly completed by 1450. From that book, all his architectural commissions followed, and his new career as an architect was launched. By 1467, the year the *Hypnerotomachia* was finished, he had become the leading architect of his day. He was universally acclaimed, respected, and revered. Roberto Rucellai called him "amatore dell'antichità e peritissimo nell'architettura" (lover of antiquity and expert in architecture).[170] In 1439, at the age of thirty-five, he was referred to by Girolamo Aliotti, a colleague of the papal court, as "dottissimo, eloquentissimo, per natura ingenuo e liberale, decoro di Firenze e d'Italia, il cui ingegno maraviglioso, divino, omnipotente, e giudizio di molti dev'essere lodato ed ammirato" (extremely learned, eloquent, by nature ingenuous and liberal, an honor to Florence and Italy, in whom a marvelous, divine, and omnipotent genius and a sound judgment about many things ought to be praised and admired). He was called "autore d'elegantissimi libri sull'arte d'edificare."[171] He was at the height of his reputation. No architect was more successful professionally, except perhaps Francesco di Giorgio.[172] He had managed to amass enough wealth to buy a house in Rome, and he had attained true "gloria," what the hero of his first literary work, *Philodoxeus,* had prized so much. His services were in demand in the most powerful courts of his day, those of Sigismondo Malatesta, Pope Nicholas V, Lodovico Gonzaga, and the Florentine merchants Giovanni Rucellai and Leonello, Niccolò, and Meliaduso d'Este. When Lorenzo de' Medici came to Rome, he visited Alberti. He spent every fall at the court of Federigo da Montefeltro.

It is possible that Alberti's passion for architecture would have increased along with his professional practice. To experience a beautiful building is pleasurable. To create a design for a building is even more so. In the Italian Renaissance this pleasure was felt in the keenest terms. Antonio Averlino, the architect known as Filarete, a disciple of Alberti's, went so far as to describe it as analogous to the erotic pleasure involved in the act of procreation. "Building is nothing more than a voluptuous pleasure," he writes, "like that of a man in love. Anyone who has experienced it knows that there is so much pleasure and desire in building that however much a man does, he wants to do more." Like "a man in love" is "he who builds": he "goes gladly to see his building, and as often as he sees it the more he wants to see it and the more his heart swells. Time passes and he is never reluctant to look at it or to talk about it exactly as a man in love [would] do."[173] The dispassionate *De re aedificatoria* launched Alberti's design career. The *Hypnerotomachia,* crowning seventeen years of practice, can be seen as the legacy of an architect passionately enamored of his work.

*   *   *

So far we have examined the knowledge in the *Hypnerotomachia* and found it to be particularly Albertian in content. Now we will look at the method of reasoning that the book displays.

Here too there are great similarities. The extraordinary mental leaps in the design of the buildings in the book are strikingly similar to those in the buildings Alberti designed in real life. It is hard to imagine what could have been more disconcerting in the mid-quattrocento than the facade of S. Maria Novella. To begin with, it piles a classical temple on top of an older Gothic church facade, the two elements being totally at odds with each other. Compounding the incongruity, irregularities abound in the facade. The triangular pediment of the temple, for example, seems to be resting on the gigantic circular window below instead of on a colonnade. Then, the devices that serve to attach the temple facade to the Gothic facade are two bizarre and immense curvaceously serpentine volutes never before used in any other building.[174] The Tempio Malatestiano is another unprecedented combination of precedents that Wittkower called a "daring experiment in joining incompatible motifs."[175] The sides of the building emulate a Roman aqueduct and the facade mimics a triumphal arch. This strange amalgam is surmounted by something resembling the dome of the Pantheon. In the same highly unconventional spirit, the church of S. Andrea in Mantua is based on a combination of the Basilica of Maxentius-Constantine and the baths of Diocletian, and the church of S. Sebastiano makes bedfellows of a triumphal arch and the temple of Theodoric in Ravenna.[176] As for the Rucellai sepulchre in the church of S. Pancrazio, it juxtaposes elements of "oriental" architecture from the Holy Land with regional Tuscan forms. The piazza of Pienza, with its eccentric combination of classical and Gothic elements, is a similar case.[177] On a much smaller scale, Alberti personally designed a base for an equestrian statue in Ferrara for Leonello d'Este in the surprising form of a triumphal arch.[178] Wittkower was correct in noting that in such projects "the purist approach to classical architecture gave way to a deliberate and free combination of its elements" and that classical architecture became a "storehouse which supplied him with the material for a free and subjective planning of wall architecture."[179]

No wonder Cardinal Gonzaga qualified Alberti's style as "fantastic" and Luca Fancelli, his fellow architect and collaborator, as "wonderful."[180] It is through such daring leaps of the architectural imagination that he became one of the most influential architects of all time. Indeed, he is responsible for adapting the antique classical architecture to the new building types of the Renaissance. There is no classicizing facade of the last five hundred years that does not owe a debt to these projects of Alberti's.

This recombinant tendency is everywhere evident in Alberti's vast output, which reflects his tendency to make new, composite structures out of different, often widely divergent, and even mutually exclusive elements. His subjects varied widely, as we have seen, from mechanics and engineering, to an essay on horses and a biography of his dog, to works on how to govern wisely. Not only was Alberti's output composite as a whole, but even individual works tended to be material put together in unprecedented ways. *Intercenales* (late 1420s and 1430s), for example, a collection of forty-three extremely heterogeneous pieces of varying lengths, comprises dialogues, dreams, fables, allegories, apologias, and short stories; it is divided into eleven books. It is dedicated in part to Leonardo Bruni and Poggio Bracciolini, purely literary figures, and in part to Paolo Toscanelli, the greatest mathematician of his day and the teacher of Brunelleschi. *De pictura,* where Alberti expounds for the first time his theory of perspective, is a similarly mixed treatise, partly on painting and partly on mathematics, as Alberti himself warns the reader in his introductory remarks.[181] In this context, the exceptionally hybrid nature of the *Hypnerotomachia,* part fiction, part learned exposition, appears to be more the rule than an exception in the Albertian corpus.

This combinatorial character of Alberti's vast output is not a matter of chance. It derived from a thought-out formula. As Joan Gadol points out, did he not fruitfully reuse a navigational instrument, the astrolabe, in applying it to land surveying? Did he not reuse the same instrument to measure the human body in *De statua?* Did he not reuse it once again in his cipher wheel?[182] And isn't his model for the box of his *dimostrazioni* a combination of the *camera obscura* and Brunelleschi's experiment with the mirror image of the Baptistery of Florence, as we have seen?

Recombinant thinking would have been second nature to Alberti, who had, we should remember, first been trained in the law, the field in which precedent-based reasoning is most dominant. The *Hypnerotomachia* makes clear that Alberti thought of previously accumulated knowledge as a thesaurus from which to construct the present, unprecedented case. Rather than regarding past accomplishments as an inviolate authority from which to forge imitations, he, like a lawyer, considered them as a knowledge base from which to assemble new constructs. In other words, he saw them as potentially creative rather than constraining.

Alberti would not have been the first artist to consider creativity, or *ingegno* as he called it, as resulting from the recombination of preexisting elements. Cicero was, as Alberti himself remarked. In the third book of *De pictura,* Alberti praises diligence and study as a means of achieving perfection. He advises young painters to study from nature. But nature itself cannot provide directly for beauty "because complete beauties are never found in a single body, but are rare and dispersed in many bodies." He gives the well-known example of Zeuxis, who was asked to make a painting for the temple of Lucina near Croton. Alberti relies, in the story that follows, on Cicero's *De inventione* (2.1.1–6). Instead of inventing a beautiful form *ex nihilo,* or mimicking the form of one person, Zeuxis asked the citizens of Croton to provide him with the most beautiful women of the town; this they did, after a public decree. From them Zeuxis selected five, because, and here Alberti paraphrases Cicero, "he did not think all the qualities he was after to combine within a portrait of beauty could be found in one person." Cicero in fact proceeds to explain that when he decided to write a textbook of rhetoric he did not adopt a single model but proceeded in a similar fashion, "and so culled the flower of many minds," an idea he recommends to any artist or writer.[183]

One of Alberti's innovations is to have made this method into a general principle applicable to all areas of creative thinking, including engineering. The *Hypnerotomachia* is interesting because it sheds light on the mechanisms and self-reflections of a highly creative mind. "Laymen" have always wondered greatly, as Freud wrote, "like the cardinal who put the question to Ariosto," how "that strange thing, the poet, comes by his material," and have wished to gain insight into the creative powers of imaginative writers.[184] But with very few exceptions, creative people themselves have rarely been forthcoming on the matter.[185]

It makes sense that Alberti would be one of these exceptions, given his obvious propensity for discovering the laws that made things work. He wrote the first Italian grammar, set down the rules of perspective, codified the use of color in painting, formalized the first technique of modern mapmaking, used his knowledge of forces to invent mechanical devices, devised an ingenious encrypting device, and created the theoretical framework from which all subsequent architectural practice and urban planning derived. It would have been natural for him to have taken the same approach to his own mind and regarded it as a thinking machine. After all, he seems to have been quite conscious of his own *ingegno*. It can be argued that his own flattering if anonymous autobiography constitutes the first formulation of the polymath persona of the genius that has been dominant in Western culture ever since.

Alberti's concern with the laws of creativity or *ingegno* begins early. In *Della tranquillità dell'animo,* he uses two metaphors to describe its workings, as Christine Smith has pointed out. One is the mosaic. He describes the process by which the pavement of the temple of Artemis at Ephesus was designed. Although it is assembled from the remains of the expensive materials that had served for the building itself, the mosaic patterns of these arrangements are as pleasing as the rest, he states.[186] The other is the dream, as again Smith points out. For Alberti, its recombinant, associative mechanisms are the very source of creativity, as he writes:

I AM ACCUSTOMED, MOST OF ALL AT NIGHT, WHEN THE AGITATION OF MY SOUL FILLS ME WITH CARES AND I SEEK RELIEF FROM THESE BITTER WORRIES AND SAD THOUGHTS, TO INVESTIGATE AND CONSTRUCT IN MY MIND SOME UNHEARD-OF MACHINE FOR MOVING AND CARRYING WEIGHTS TO REINFORCE AND CONSTRUCT EXTREMELY BIG AND INVALU-ABLE THINGS. AND SOMETIMES IT HAS HAPPENED THAT NOT ONLY HAVE I GROWN CALM IN MY RESTLESSNESS OF SPIRIT, BUT I HAVE THOUGHT OF THINGS MOST RARE AND MEMO-RABLE. SOMETIMES I HAVE DESIGNED AND BUILT WONDERFULLY COMPOSED BUILDINGS IN MY MIND, COMBINING DIFFERENT ORDERS AND MANY COLUMNS WITH DIVERSE CAPITALS AND UNUSUAL BASES, AND ADDING THESE TO CORNICES AND ENTABLATURES, CONFERRING UPON THE WHOLE A HARMONIOUS AND NEW GRACE.[187]

Obviously, Alberti thought of dreams as laboratories for his controlled thought experiments, which depended on the algorithm of recombining preexisting precedents. Dreams do offer ideal conditions: imaginary worlds where transpositions are permitted in a way unconstrained by any demand for verisimilitude. It is in such environments, according to Thomas Kuhn, that the greatest historical reformulations of physics have occurred, from Aristotle to Galileo, Einstein, and Bohr. This is because a "thought experiment is one of the essential analytical tools which are deployed during crises and which help to promote basic conceptual reform."[188] From this perspective, the *Hypnerotomachia* was not only a compendium of everything Alberti knew but also a kind of treatise on the laws of the creative process, which he saw in essence as associative, all-embracing—in a word, "Poliphilian." Here he identified the recombinant thinking characteristic of dreamwork as an algorithm. The *Hypnerotomachia* is a complement to *De re aedificatoria*.

This celebration of creativity and *ingegno* is nowhere more explicitly and systematically put forth than in *De re aedificatoria*. Here, Alberti begins by praising the knowledge of the ancients. "We shall relate the advice handed down to us by the learned men of the past, in particular Theophrastus, Aristotle, Cato, Varro, Pliny and Vitruvius," he writes, because "such knowledge is better gained through long experience than through any artifice of invention; it should be sought therefore from those who have made the most diligent observations on the matter. We shall proceed, then, to gather this information from the many, varied passages in which the best authors have dealt with the question" (II.4, p. 38). However, he is not prepared to accept the authority of the ancients blindly, as Vitruvius had. Vitruvius, in fact, is the first whom Alberti submits to the process of rational and critical inquiry: "What he handed down was in any case not refined, and his speech such that the Latins might think that he wanted to appear Greek, while the Greeks would think that he babbled Latin. However, his very text is evidence that he wrote neither Latin nor Greek, so that as far as we are concerned he might just as well not have written at all, rather than write something that we cannot understand" (VI.1, p. 154).

As Vitruvius is found wanting, Alberti turns to other authority figures of antiquity. They too are subjected to critical inquiry: they too are found deficient. How can they be seen as authorities if there is no agreement among them, Alberti asks. "Some maintain that man first lived in caves, and that master and herd were sheltered under a common roof: they accept the account given by Pliny, that it was Taxius, a Gelian, who was the first to imitate nature and build a house of mud. Diodorus states that the Goddess Vesta, daughter of Saturn, was the first to invent the house. Eusebius Pamphilius, a respected scholar in matters of the antique, maintains, on the basis of ancient manuscripts, that the descendants of Protogenes devised the first dwelling place for man from screens platted of reed and papyrus" (II.4, p. 39).

Contradictions between the writings of different antique authorities abound, particularly concerning what the best construction materials are. Theophrastus recommended the fir, the pitch tree, and the pine, felled as soon as they germinate, while others recommended maple, elm, ash, and linden, cut down after vintage. Vitruvius prefers timber felled in the beginning of autumn, while Hesiod prefers that cut in the summer and Cato the winter (II.4). Alberti finds the same lack of agreement among ancient authorities when it comes to the more cultural aspects of architecture, such as ascribing the origins of temples. Some maintain that the first one was dedicated to Janus. But "others maintain that the first temple was dedicated to Jupiter in Crete. . . . Then again, in Phoenicia, a certain Uso is said to have been the first to set up statues to the Fire and Wind, and to construct a temple. Others record that before any cities existed, Dionysius gave a temple to every town he founded" (VII.2, p. 193).

The unsoundness of the philological authority of ancient writers leads him to turn to the empirical archaeological evidence embodied in the antique buildings themselves; he states that "examples of ancient temples and theaters have survived that may teach us as much as any professor" (VI.1, p. 154). But even here the authority of antiquity is found to be dubious. He notes that "we have discovered, by measuring the works ourselves, that the Latins did not always follow these rules exactly" (VII.6, p. 202). As an example, he cites the lack of consistency displayed in the method for designing scotias and rings: "The method for the scotias and rings was as follows: the space between the tori was divided into sevenths, one of which was taken up by each of the rings, and the five remaining divided equally between the two scotias. The tori had the same projections as in the Doric, and, when channeling out the scotias, they did not cut beyond the vertical of whatever was built on top. . . . Some did it another way" (VII.7, p. 203).

In the face of such arbitrariness, Alberti came up with a solution unprecedented in the history of Western architectural theory: not to reject the precedents altogether, but strip them of their absolute authority, to conceive of them as elements of a thesaurus that can be recombined to create modern structures. Greece becomes his example of successfully using this kind of reasoning. In this country "where upright and noble minds flourished," builders "began by examining the works of the Assyrians and the Egyptians" and decided to "surpass through ingenuity those whose wealth they could not rival, in whatever work they undertook." As a result "with building, they sought it in, and drew it out from, the very bosom of Nature, and began to discuss it thoroughly, studying and weighing it up with great incisiveness and subtlety." Alberti sums up the Greek method that he will adopt as his own recombinant genetic algorithm in architectural design:

THEY INQUIRED INTO THE DIFFERENCES BETWEEN BUILDINGS THAT WERE ADMIRED AND THOSE THAT WERE NOT, OVERLOOKING NOTHING. THEY PERFORMED ALL MANNER OF EXPERIMENT, SURVEYING AND RETRACING THE STEPS OF NATURE. MIXING EQUAL WITH EQUAL, STRAIGHT WITH CURVED, LIGHT WITH SHADE, THEY CONSIDERED WHETHER A THIRD COMBINATION MIGHT ARISE, AS FROM THE UNION OF MALE AND FEMALE, WHICH

WOULD HELP THEM TO ACHIEVE THEIR ORIGINAL AIM. . . . THEY ADDED, TOOK AWAY, AND ADJUSTED GREATER TO SMALLER, LIKE TO UNLIKE, FIRST TO LAST, UNTIL THEY ESTABLISHED THE DIFFERENT QUALITIES DESIRABLE IN THOSE BUILDINGS INTENDED TO ENDURE FOR AGES, AND THOSE ERECTED FOR NO GOOD REASON AS MUCH AS THEIR GOOD LOOKS. THIS WAS THEIR ACHIEVEMENT. (VI.2, pp. 157–158)

The radicalness of this view cannot be overestimated. It constitutes a major epistemic break with the thinking of the past and initiated a new type of reasoning in Western architectural culture. Alberti had early on been interested in forging a new kind of thinking, different from that of all previous generations. In the prologue to *De pictura* he argued that contemporary *ingegno* should be prized over the imitation of antiquity:

OUR FAME OUGHT TO BE MUCH GREATER [BECAUSE] WE DISCOVER UNHEARD-OF AND NEVER-BEFORE-SEEN ARTS AND SCIENCES WITHOUT TEACHERS AND WITHOUT ANY MODEL WHATSOEVER. WHO COULD EVER BE HARD OR ENVIOUS ENOUGH TO FAIL TO PRAISE PIPPO [FILIPPO BRUNELLESCHI], THE ARCHITECT, ON SEEING HERE SUCH A LARGE STRUCTURE, RISING ABOVE THE SKIES, AMPLE ENOUGH TO COVER WITH ITS SHADOW ALL THE TUSCAN PEOPLE, AND CONSTRUCTED WITHOUT THE AID OF CENTERING OR GREAT QUANTITY OF WOOD? SINCE THIS WORK SEEMS IMPOSSIBLE OF EXECUTION IN OUR TIME, IF I JUDGE RIGHTLY, IT WAS PROBABLY UNKNOWN AND UNTHOUGHT OF AMONG THE ANCIENTS. . . . AS YOU WORK FROM DAY TO DAY, YOU PERSEVERE IN DISCOVERING THINGS THROUGH WHICH YOUR EXTRAORDINARY *INGEGNO* ACQUIRES PERPETUAL FAME.[189]

Later he had written in *Della tranquillità dell'animo* (1441–1442) that a similar mode of thinking served both the Asians and the Greeks in inventing all the arts and disciplines, as Smith has noted.[190] The moderns should follow their example, he had argued, adding that the needs of the moderns were new and that their solution was aesthetically valid.

Alberti's greatest innovation in *De re aedificatoria* was to have elevated the new way of reasoning associated with his formula for creativity into a theory of modernity. Alberti broke the Vitruvian model of reasoning, based on the acceptance of the authority of precedents as the ultimate backing in a reasoning process. For the first time, architectural thinking was freed of the arbitrary weight of authority of antique precedent and open to critical inquiry.[191]

Leon Battista Alberti is, historically speaking, the first modern. To borrow a notion from Alexander Tzonis, modern architectural reasoning began at the moment when reasoning based on authority was replaced by reasoning based on rational and critical inquiry. Both types of reasoning are defined by their approach to precedent. In the first case, precedent is seen as a rule or exemplar whose authority dictates that it be strictly emulated. In the second, the authority of the precedent is open to question. The approach of the first is imitative; that of the second, creative.[192]

All cultures have an urge to innovate and experiment. As Ernst Robert Curtius points out, the opposition between ancient and modern already existed in Latin culture.[193] In fact there is no culture that is not Janus-faced, in which the old is not juxtaposed to the new, in which tradition and rule making are not set in opposition to experimentation and rule breaking. The difference introduced by Alberti is that the balance tips totally in favor of the modern, of change, of the new, of progress. For the first time a kind of architectural reasoning comes into being that rejected the very idea of authority. For the first time in Western thinking, the relative authority of precedents gave way to absolute relativity.

Quid tum? "What next?" This was Alberti's motto. It could have been the motto of no architect prior to him, but it could be the motto of any since. With Alberti, architecture is a dilemma, an ever-present problem constantly outpacing its solutions, infinitely open to recategorizations and reevaluations of its relation to everything else: painting, sculpture, drawing, the sciences, engineering, new technologies, language, music, political power, divine experience, gender, nature, civic society, urbanity, regional identity, universal culture, domesticity, morality, reason, and last but not least passions. As a result, he opened up an age of relativism that has affected Western architectural thinking ever since.

*   *   *

Alberti, however, did more than set the terms of this dilemma of total relativism inherent to modernism. He also, in his usual fashion, invented a solution. This solution was as novel as the problem it solved. It did not aim at denying relativity but at constraining it. In order to save recombinant design logic from total arbitrariness, he subjected the endless possibilities engendered by it to a higher-level, conciliatory imperative: and this was *concinnitas*. The concept was central to Alberti's whole *forma mentis,* and it is what makes him a humanist first and a modernist second, in my view.

The term *concinnitas,* again, Alberti no doubt found in the writings of Cicero— *Brutus* (38, 287, 352, 327), *De oratore* (38, 81, 149, 202), *De natura deorum* (2.19), and *De inventione* (1.25), and the tradition of commentators and adaptors that followed, where it became associated with the verb *cum-canere,* "to sing together," probably a translation into Latin of the Greek *sumphōnai (sun,* "together"; *phōnai,* "voices"): the bringing together of heterogeneous elements into a harmonious whole.

There is much dispute over the exact school of thought Albertian *concinnitas* belongs to. Many scholars have sought to attach its meaning to Platonic sources, specifically to Plato's theory of musical analogies linking the macrocosm and the microcosm put forth in his *Laws*. More recently, it has been linked to Aristotle's radically sensualist, antimetaphysical theory that beauty is what pleases the senses.[194] But in keeping with Alberti's propensity to creating composite wholes out of different precedents, it is more likely that the concept of *concinnitas* is itself a composite structure, based on a number of schools of thought. However contradictory, there are undeniably elements of a Platonic theory of proportions, of Aristotelian sensualism and organicism, and of Ciceronian oratory, in addition to Renaissance polyphonicism. There is, finally, an element no scholar has mentioned, to my knowledge: Epicureanism, the belief that nature is the source of all good, the ultimate example to follow. Alberti would have become familiar with this philosophy in Rome, from his acquaintance with the leading Epicurean thinker of the Renaissance, Lorenzo Valla. Whatever the intellectual debts involved in Alberti's use of the term *concinnitas,* no one else during the Renaissance used it in his sense or gave it the same importance.

That Alberti was a humanist hardly needs to be noted. It is well known that his family's mansion had been one of the birthplaces of Florentine civic humanism at the end of the fourteenth century. As Hans Baron points out, passages of the *Paradiso degli Alberti* recount, in a fictional way, discussions about civic humanism that used to occur in the Alberti household among "fellow citizens in this illustrious patria, . . . who devote all their time and attention to the affairs of our sacred Republic, in order to . . . maintain her in her sweet liberty."[195] Alberti dedicated his second book to Leonardo Bruni, a senior figure and the best-known upholder of Florentine civic humanism of his day. Agnolo Pandolfini, the main spokesman of Alberti's *Profugiorum ab aerumna* and of *Della famiglia,* was also a representative of this tradition.

As James Hankins notes, quattrocento humanists could be "idealistic to the point of fatuity" and genuinely believed that society could be reformed if exposed for long enough to humanist teachings. Advancing knowledge would transform life by its stimulating power: the humanities would "make men wise and good, refine and elevate their tastes, dulcify the harsher notes of public discourse." Alberti too believed in the possibility of establishing a civic society on the basis of reasoned discourse, a republic where individuals are motivated to be "useful to others,"[196] where the example and eloquence of the humanistically educated might even spread their virtues down through society as a whole. Philosophically speaking, this stance is grounded not only in optimism, but also in an anti-materialist view of history, where words have a "worldmaking" function, to borrow a term from Nelson Goodman.[197]

Such strong support for civic humanism abounds throughout Alberti's writings. In *Teogenio,* subtitled *De republica, de vita civile e rusticana, e la fortuna e la tranquillità,* he insists that the well-being of a society depends on knowing how to rule itself with reason, to adapt itself to the order of nature. In this work, Alberti makes clear his preference for the Greek definition of the state over the Roman, the democratic over the authoritarian. His ideal was an association of citizens united for the common good, with leaders devoted to the individual well-being of citizens. In this perfect state, the citizens were considered links in a human chain, forming a society aimed at the perfection of the whole.[198] Alberti's lifelong devotion to an ethical notion of serving in a civic society is plain: in *Della famiglia,* in *De iciarchia,* and in his biography of St. Potitus, he supports being useful to the others and oneself. The map of Rome he draws up in his *Descriptio urbis Romae* is revealing of his sympathies. At the center he places not the Vatican but the Campidoglio, the seat of the ancient senate and a powerful symbol for Rome's republicans.

There is however a most significant difference between Alberti and most of the civic humanists up to that time, a difference that explains why Alberti might wish to write the *Hypnerotomachia.* Unlike them, Alberti came to follow a profession—architecture—and thus had the opportunity to put his ideas into practice. As he explains in *De re aedificatoria,* a humanist architecture ought to be functional and serve society through technological progress:

NEED I STRESS HOW, BY CUTTING THROUGH ROCK, BY TUNNELING THROUGH MOUNTAINS OR FILLING IN VALLEYS, BY RESTRAINING THE WATERS OF THE SEA AND LAKES, AND BY DRAINING MARSHES, THROUGH THE BUILDING OF SHIPS, BY ALTERING THE COURSE AND DREDGING THE MOUTHS OF RIVERS AND THROUGH THE CONSTRUCTION OF HARBORS AND BRIDGES, THE ARCHITECT HAS NOT ONLY MET THE TEMPORARY NEEDS OF MAN, BUT ALSO OPENED UP NEW GATEWAYS TO ALL THE PROVINCES OF THE WORLD? AS A RESULT, NATIONS HAVE BEEN ABLE TO SERVE EACH OTHER BY EXCHANGING FRUIT, SPICES, JEWELS, EXPERIENCE AND IDEAS, INDEED EVERYTHING THAT MIGHT IMPROVE HEALTH AND OUR STANDARD OF LIVING. (prologue, p. 3)

But above all Alberti believed in the power of architecture. He saw beautiful architecture as having the power to shape civic behavior in its image:

LET IT BE SAID THAT THE SECURITY, DIGNITY, AND HONOR OF THE REPUBLIC DEPEND GREATLY ON THE ARCHITECT: IT IS HE WHO IS RESPONSIBLE FOR OUR DELIGHT, ENTERTAINMENT, AND HEALTH WHILE AT LEISURE AND OUR PROFIT AND ADVANTAGE WHILE AT WORK, AND IN SHORT THAT WE LIVE IN A DIGNIFIED MANNER FREE FROM ANY DANGER. IN VIEW OF THE DELIGHT AND WONDERFUL GRACE OF HIS WORKS, AND OF HOW INDISPENSABLE THEY HAVE BEEN PROVED, AND IN VIEW OF THE BENEFIT AND CONVENIENCE OF HIS INVENTIONS, AND THEIR SERVICE TO POSTERITY, HE SHOULD NO DOUBT BE ACCORDED PRAISE AND RESPECT, AND BE COUNTED AMONG THOSE MOST DESERVING OF MANKIND'S HONOR AND RECOGNITION. (prologue, p. 5)

As an indication of the strength of his belief in the civilizing power of architectural *concinnitas,*[199] he was convinced that architecture was the originator and guarantor of human civilization:

SOME HAVE SAID IT WAS FIRE AND WATER WHICH WERE INITIALLY RESPONSIBLE FOR BRINGING PEOPLE TOGETHER INTO COMMUNITIES, BUT WE, CONSIDERING HOW USEFUL, EVEN INDISPENSABLE, A ROOF AND WALLS ARE FOR THEM, ARE CONVINCED THAT IT WAS THEY WHO BROUGHT PEOPLE TOGETHER. WE ARE INDEBTED TO THE ARCHITECT NOT ONLY FOR PROVIDING THAT SAFE AND WELCOME REFUGE FROM THE HEAT OF THE SUN AND THE FROSTS OF WINTER (THAT OF ITSELF IS NO SMALL BENEFIT), BUT ALSO FOR HIS MANY OTHER INNOVATIONS, USEFUL TO BOTH INDIVIDUALS AND THE PUBLIC, WHICH TIME AND TIME AGAIN HAVE SO HAPPILY SATISFIED DAILY NEEDS. (prologue, p. 3)

He even argued that architectural *concinnitas* could serve to disarm and overcome anarchy, civil strife, and war: "Those besieged would consider no protection better than the ingenuity and skill of the architect . . . and that the enemy were more often overcome by the ingenuity of the first without the other's weapons, than by the latter's sword without the former's good counsel. And what is more important, the architect achieves his victory with but a handful of men and without loss of life. So much for the use of architecture" (prologue, p. 4).

Besides Alberti's *De re aedificatoria, De pictura, Della tranquillità dell'animo,* and *Pontifex,*[200] the only work in which *concinnitas* appears in this Albertian sense is the *Hypnerotomachia,* where it is used, for example, to describe the proportions the narrator finds in the doorway to a temple. He mentions that they were derived *concinnatamente* (c3). Indeed, it is used repeatedly in the novel. The ceiling of the chamber under the great pyramid is covered "concinnamente" with aquatic animals (c8v); the palazzo of the queen forms a perfect square "cum concinnissima dimensione et correspondentia distincte" (f3v), has "concinna distributione," and is laid out "cum regulata correspondentia et harmonia" (f4). The temple of Venus is "cum debito illigamento dagli pili circunferito sopra il muso per tutto bellamente concincto" (m7v), leading to "congruentia della structura opportuna e la integritate della harmonia, imperoche omni cingibile ligamento intraneo expostula el concincto extraneo" (m8v). The amphitheater is an "incredibile, invisitata et inaudita structura, imperoche il pedamento elegante et gli emusicati concincti overo illigamenti et il symmetriato columnio in gyro, trabi, zoophori et coronice, tutto exclusive era di conflatura aenea, enchausticamente obaurata di fulgurante oro" (y2). "Ultra questo," the author continues about the same building, the overall effect of the proportioning is "concinctura," the effect being that "omni proportione harmonica circumligava" (y3).

Even more revealing is the way *concinnitas* is described and achieved. In both the *Hypnerotomachia* (m7) and *De re aedificatoria* (IX.5), the term "sexquialtera" is used of a certain harmonious relationship between elements in the circular temple. In *De re aedificatoria,* Alberti had urged, "We must therefore take great care to ensure that even the minutest elements are so arranged in their level, alignment, number, shape, and appearance, that right matches left, top matches bottom, adjacent matches adjacent, and equal matches equal, and that they are an ornament to that body of which they are to be part" (X.7, p. 171). In the *Hypnerotomachia,* too, *concinnitas* is carried out by means of alignments and correspondences.

Moreover, the human body is important in both works. In Alberti's *De re aedificatoria, concinnitas* in architecture had been modeled on bodily *concinnitas.* "Beauty is that reasoned harmony of all the parts within a body, so that nothing may be added, taken away, or altered, but for the worse. It is a great and holy matter; all our resources and skill of ingenuity will be taxed in achieving it; rarely is it granted, even to Nature herself, to produce anything that is entirely complete and perfect in every respect," a famous passage states (VI.2, pp. 93–94). In the *Hypnerotomachia,* the proportions of the entrance to the great pyramid are so *concinnamente* conceived that Poliphilo refers to them as the proportions of a *solido corpo* (c4).

Finally, in the *De re aedificatoria, concinnitas* is something "instantly recognized" by means of "sight or sound," and "it is in our nature to desire the best, and to cling to it with pleasure" (IX.5, p. 302). It goes virtually without saying that no work could be in more concordance on this final point than the *Hypnerotomachia.*

*   *   *

The question remains, why did Alberti write this book? Why did he put together a compendium of his entire literary, artistic, technical, and architectural knowledge and *ingegno,* then cast it in the form of such an astonishing hypererotic fantasy? It was important to him. Of all his writings it is the longest. From the emphasis placed on the date at the end of the book, 1467, it was obviously intended to be the legacy of a highly creative individual enamored of his life's work. But why the passion that one feels pulsating throughout it?

After all, in 1467, Alberti would have been looking back at a particularly gratifying period in his career in Rome, starting in 1447 with the ascension to the papal throne of Nicholas V. During that period he would have come closest to seeing his humanist vision of *concinnitas,* in the fullest political and aesthetic sense of the word, fulfilled. If Rome is featured so predominantly in the book, it could be because it stood out against the other cities in which he had worked. In Rimini, Mantua, and Florence, his designs had served to glorify patrons such as Sigismondo Malatesta, who was the *condottiere* of Nicholas V, and the tyrannical Gonzaga family, or ambitious individuals, such as Giovanni Rucellai. It would have been only natural for Alberti to be attached to the figure of Nicholas, a fellow civic humanist. Alberti was by no means short of patrons, but it was to Nicholas that he had presented his manuscript of the *De re aedificatoria* in 1450. Nicholas's purpose was, in Alberti's own words, to "reconcile people of every condition with benevolence and humanity,"[201] and to pacify a city that had been torn by a bloody civil war in which the papacy and the traditionally republican population were opposed.

As an indication of how far Nicholas had been prepared to go in the direction of reconciliation with the Roman republicans, among the scholars he hired to carry out his massive program of translating the ancient Latin and Greek classics was Lorenzo Valla, with whom Alberti would have become acquainted at that time. The last person one would have expected a pontiff to embrace was Valla. Not only was he the author of the notoriously pagan *De voluptate, de vero bono,* arguing for free love, but he had also written a tract proving that the text upon which the papacy founded its authority over Rome, the *Donatio Constantini,* was an eighth-century forgery. This, along with his villification of the popes as "tyrants," "robbers," and "murderers," had earned him sixteen years of forced exile from Rome.[202]

In Nicholine Rome, the search for a new *modus vivendi,* based on compromise and mutual accommodation between the papacy and the city, had its most ambitious expression in the papal projects for the design of the city and its architecture. Although the exact extent of Alberti's role in these policies still remains to be determined, with one much-respected architectural historian arguing that it was almost nil, they would have been germane to his civic humanist values, for each one is an expression of the pope's attempted reconciliation with republicanism.[203]

Nicholas's projects included the restoration of the basilica of St. Peter's, located in the papal enclave called the Borgo across the Tiber from the city of Rome proper. Alberti mentions the project five times in *De re aedificatoria.*[204] It would have meant reinforcing a symbol of papal presence but also opening up the papal fortress to the republican Roman population. This project never did get off the ground. The restoration of the church of S. Stefano, on the other hand, did. The work consisted in demolishing a wall that had been added by Christians to the inner ring of columns of the original circular plan of what Alberti and his contemporaries believed was a pagan temple, thus forming an ambulatory.[205] Demolishing the ambulatory meant, in effect, returning the temple to its original state, that is, making it again a vestige of ancient Rome and a symbol of Roman republicanism.

Other grand architectural and urbanistic gestures of Nicholas would have appealed to Alberti's well-known deeply rooted republican sentiments. One of these was the reconstruction of the twelve-mile-long Acqua Vergine leading to the Fountain of Trevi, making it the only ancient Roman aqueduct to carry water to Rome.[206] Another was the rebuilding of a bridge linking the Borgo and the city, with the addition of a roof for protecting its users from sun and rain. But the most politically daring of Nicholas's gestures of compromise was the planned creation of three arcaded commercial streets in the Borgo, extending from the foot of the renovated bridge to St. Peter's. This would have meant transforming the traditionally fortified enclave of the papacy into an urban theater for the free enactment of civic humanism.

However, in the year 1467, Alberti would have been looking back at the more recent past. Here he would have found much cause for distress, what he had called, in an earlier work, *aerumna*. Nicholas had died twelve years earlier. He left his architectural and urbanistic projects uncompleted and his vision of reconciliation in shambles. Alberti would also have been contemplating the more recent past, when just three years earlier he had, along with Pomponio Leto and all his fellow humanists, been fired by a new pope, Paul II, on account of their republican sympathies. From the vantage point of 1467, Alberti might also have been looking ahead, at the future. What he saw there would have inspired even more distress: the end of humanism and republicanism in Rome, the destruction of the Colonna family, and the assured rise of the Borgias.[207]

Passionate outbursts were alien to the cool, restrained, reasoned persona Alberti projected in most of his writings. In *Della famiglia*, he writes of resolving to "bear with adversities, know oneself, avoid anger and revenge, not be overtalkative, be calm in one's judgments; first in the midst of inevitable trials never yield to despair and keep one's mind occupied with mental exercises."[208] In *De pictura*, he condemned "un ingegno troppo fervente e furioso."[209] In *Teogenio*, he rejected all forms of excess, holding nature up as the source and model of all *concinnitas*, and he remained true to this principle. But, as Manfredo Tafuri pointed out, early in his career his dissenting spirit earned him the reputation of an anticonformist and a polemicist, and he targeted magistrates, priests, philosophers, writers, and merchants, denouncing abuses of power at every level of contemporary society.[210] In *Pontifex*, he attacks the corruption of priests, lamenting their crass ignorance and disregard for education as they condone violence, nepotism, and the behavior of the slothful parasites they surround themselves with. In his *Commodis et incommodis litterarum*, he writes about the difficulties of the civic humanist in a society rapidly slipping toward autocracy. In his encomium to his dog, *Canis*, he compares himself to a pet dog, controlled by masters before whom he is powerless and doomed to silence; and in his encomium to a flea, *Musca*, modeled on the ancient Greek satirist Lucian's work by the same title, he inveighs against the bombastic style of many contemporary authors. In his *Life of St. Potitus*, a satire on the canonical genre of the lives of saints, he creates an "extremely beautiful" devil to persuade a saint to abandon the life of asceticism and *contemptus mundi* and devote himself instead to being useful to himself and others in civic society. His play *Philodoxeus*, modeled on Plautus and Terence, denounces the opportunism of many of his contemporary intellectuals.

This machic element in Alberti's work is associated with a markedly anacoluthic, emphatic, almost dithyrambic style of writing. Twice he had, earlier in his career, written works imparted with what one scholar has called "rhetorical energeia," bringing to the surface a "labyrinthine world" bristling with "ferment, solicitation, strength, rebellion."[211] Thus in "Dream," written in the 1420s and published in his *Intercenales*, stones jump from the river bank in order to join their companions and swim with them, but they are overwhelmed with mire, mud, and dung, a metaphor for a world hopelessly corrupt. *Momus* too abounds with disturbing images of violence. Written in the mid-1440s in Alberti's boldest critical act, it is a direct attack against the sanguinary ferocity, rapaciousness, iniquity, and mercenary behavior of no less than his own employer at the time, Pope Eugenius IV; in it, the hero is castrated and chained to the ocean's floor after having been guilty of rape and destruction.[212]

Like these two works, the *Hypnerotomachia* is a deeply flawed, almost incoherent composition made up of incompatible elements. Shaped both by fantastic exuberance and extreme rage, the product both of passionate attachment to a vision of reconciliation and of desperation at the spectacle of the upcoming collapse of the political conditions that were necessary for that vision's flowering, this ecstatically erotic and profoundly wrathful book must be seen not only as the legacy of a humanist enamored of his life's work but also as a polemic manifesto in defense of civic humanism and republicanism in the face of an increasingly aggressive absolutist, papal order.

It is not certain that Alberti himself knew what to make of the *Hypnerotomachia* once he had finished it. There is an indication that even he was surprised by its excess. It proved not to be his last work after all: he had time for one more, *De iciarchia,* a dramatically different work. In it he made a long, sustained, logically argued exposition of the benefits of *mediocritas,* measure in all things.

There is one final reason for attributing the *Hypnerotomachia* to Alberti: the role in it of *istoria.* He had been the first to introduce the concept to painting and had devoted part of the second chapter and almost the entire third of *De pictura* to it, saying it was "the greatest work of the painter."[213] He had used it to argue for the use of painting not merely to represent reality but to vent the "movements of the soul," to express feelings. With the *Hypnerotomachia,* it would appear that he transferred the idea to architecture, using it as a means to vent his emotions. The implications of associating the expressive potential of *istoria* with architecture were enormous. With the *Hypnerotomachia Poliphili,* Alberti threw open the gates for a new architecture to come, conceived as a means for expressing the feelings of the subjective self of the architect and triggering the same in the onlooker. In this sense, the *Hypnerotomachia* is the invention of the romantic sensibility in architecture.

*   *   *

Yet something about the *Hypnerotomachia* is more difficult to explain: the nature of the passion, at once erotic and architectural. For the source of this element we must search outside the world of Alberti's preoccupations. An individual mind can never be understood in isolation. Consciously or not, it is inescapably engaged with a greater, collective mind, a mentality, in an immense dialogue, to use a phrase of Mikhail Bakhtin's.[214] Thinking is always bound up with a heritage of preconceived categories, values, intermeshed into tenacious patterns of thought. The *forma mentis* of each culture or society, like that of each individual, has a logic of its own, and within the constraints of this logic, change unfolds in a manner and at a pace all its own.

What is true of individual minds also holds for individual works. The *Hypneroto-machia* took shape in the relatively narrow but highly charged microhistorical context of humanist culture of mid-quattrocento Rome as a militant defense of humanism and particularly of Alberti's own life's work, which had met with real adversity in Rome in 1464. But works do not draw their meaning only from their immediate content. They are part of a much broader horizon. The *Hypnerotomachia* is hardly an exception. The horizon in which we now place it extends no less than seven hundred years. The process in which the *Hypnerotomachia* is caught up here is the slow rise of Western humanism—as it concerns architectural thinking, that is—with its succession of what Erwin Panofsky called "renascences" preceding the Renaissance, from the time of Charlemagne to the quattrocento.[215]

This world we now step back from and look at. Here, the *Hypnerotomachia,* with its questing, struggling dream-work, its erotic *furore,* far from being the exception, is the rule

.

6

✻ ✻ ✻
✻ ✻ ✻

RECONFIGURING THE ARCHITECTURAL BODY,
CHANGING THE ARCHITECTURAL MIND

I MAGINE A WORLD WHERE IT IS FORBIDDEN TO LOVE ARCHITEC-
ture. This is a world where architectural ornaments, color, craftsmanship, construction feats, and cities inspire intense hate and loathing, revulsion and revilement and contempt. Architectural abnegation and abstinence reign. The cult of asceticism
and the denial of pleasure prevail. A mentality dominated by a *contemptus mundi* has the mind
in its grip. This is western Europe from the fall of the Roman Empire to about the eighth
century. This is a world where change is constricted, inhibited, straitjacketed by what, adapting a phrase of Claude Lévi-Strauss's, we might call "cold" thinking.[1]

Now think of the *Hypnerotomachia,* a world where architecture is, on the contrary,
an object of intense attachment, a world where architectural ornamentation, materials, colors,
light, space, engineering, construction, and workmanship give rise to a general celebration in
writings, in the visual arts, in paintings, sculptures, townscapes, and, last but not least, in the
design of buildings and cities themselves.[2] This is the mid-fifteenth century, the world of
early Renaissance Italian civic humanism. This is a world where the militant incitement of a
generalized *amor mundi* translates into an equally militant *libido aedificandi.* It is a world characterized by "hot" thinking,[3] that is, thinking that is committed to change, to creative rethinking, or, to use the term of the time, *ingenio.* These changes involve not just the content of
thought but the act of thinking itself, the framework for thinking about thinking.

In between these two times a cognitive revolution, or immense process of re-
cognition, took place. The world of architectural thinking got "turned upside down," to use
an expression of Mikhail Bakhtin.[4] And the human body was the main lever in this process.
The radical transition from "cold," or sterile, to modern, "hot" or "creative" architectural
thinking between the eighth and fifteenth centuries is part of a generalized larger shift in
mentality. Lewis Mumford called this rethinking an immense "change of mind," which involved "the reorientation of wishes, habits, ideals and goals" of the entire Western civilization.[5] On one side of the divide, we have a mindset of the early Middle Ages that prizes
ignorance, fatalism, abnegation, and poverty.[6] On the other, we have early Renaissance humanism with a commitment to the cult of knowledge and a belief in unlimited progress—
aesthetic, scientific, and social.

This highly complex re-cognition process entailed a restructuring of paradigms,
the myriad patterns of reasoning that make up categories of thought and beliefs. It brought
about a massive recategorization of all constructs related to human experience, from the most
mundane to the most monumental. Of the studies devoted to this change, most have focused
on the growth and evolution of scientific thinking: Lewis Mumford's study of the importance
of the growth of "technics" or technical knowledge, E. J. Dijksterhuis on the mechanization
of the world picture, Pierre Duhem on the birth of physics, Thomas Kuhn on the birth of
modern scientific thinking.[7]

But there was another dimension to this paradigm shift, one that might have been even more crucial to the overall change of mind. This was the battle for beauty: for the aestheticizing, hedonizing, and, as we shall see, eroticizing of thinking. Indeed, among the elements of culture to undergo a revolutionary transformation at that time are sexual desire and the body. These are highly charged concepts by definition. As Michel Foucault wrote in his *History of Sexuality,* they are the first elements a social order controls in order to control its members. Sexual activity is the one aspect of private life that is at the very heart of every society's existence, of its reproduction.[8] Yet eros is also an irrepressible instinct, as Freud pointed out, particularly in the passages devoted to Eros and Ananke in *Civilization and Its Discontents.*[9] Plutarch, a philosopher whose works Alberti knew very well and was influenced by, wrote of "the longing for being" as "the oldest and greatest forms of eros."[10] Desire is never easy to tame, and that is why the history of sexuality is such a fascinating subject. And indeed, what we observe during the period from the eighth to the fifteenth century is a gradual lessening of the older social order's grip over sexuality, accompanied by a growing affirmation of desire and eroticization of the body.

When the period opens sexual desire and its object, the body, are seen as dangerous things. They are considered repugnant, loathsome, and despicable, no less than the root of all evil—the *radix omnium malorum.* Condemned as perverse and disgusting, they are hated and reviled, or at least mistrusted, as many historians have shown.[11] By the time humanist culture begins to flourish in the Italian city-states, however, they come on the contrary to be identified, in the most extreme, even militant terms conceivable, as the supreme good—the *verum bonum,* in Lorenzo Valla's phrase. In fact the whole epoch comes under the sway of what Eugenio Garin called the "soave giocondità del corpo."[12]

This change was crucial for the shift in architectural thinking, from backward looking to creative, from cold to hot, from archaic to modern. Indeed, as I hope to show, a seemingly isolated shift in cognitive operation, the recategorization of body from something "contemptible" to something "good," had immense consequences for the way people viewed, conceived, and used buildings. It was necessary to the rise of Renaissance humanist architectural thinking and its offspring: the uniquely human buildings and cities of the early Italian Renaissance.

One reason the eroticization of the body was so crucial for architecture is the role of the body metaphor in the Renaissance. It is a commonplace to say that it is omnipresent in the architecture of the period. But scholars have tended to see it in a limited way, as something that gives to buildings their proportions, geometry, and symmetry.[13] This limited view, and the concomitant overemphasis on the body metaphor as a unique characteristic of Renaissance architectural thinking, is a result of seriously underestimating the role of anthropomorphy in general. Actually, it is at the heart of every culture. It would appear that there is no part of human culture that has not been steeped in the body metaphor. In this universal capacity, the human body has been the basis for representing or mapping gender, power relations in society, race, and the universe; experiencing the afterlife; communing with the divine. This has been shown most famously by Richard Broxton Onians in his *Origins of European Thought,* most recently by the anthology edited by Michel Feher, *Fragments for a History of the Body.*[14] The body is one of the instruments for what Lévi-Strauss in *La pensée sauvage* calls "the science of the concrete." It acts as "a conceptual tool with multiple possibilities for detotalizing or retotalizing any domain." It serves as a "matrix, a genuine system by means of a creature" that "constitutes the object of thought and furnishes the conceptual tool." According to him, this is because it lets us recognize in all kinds of not-yet-structured phenomena an organization, an order projected out of the body.[15]

In making these claims, Lévi-Strauss has in mind such cultures as those of the peoples of the Tyukyu Archipelago, the pygmies of the Philippines, the Coahuila Indians of southern California, and the Montagnais, Naskapi, and Micmacs of Canada. The essays in Feher's collection range over the Presocratic philosophers, medieval theoreticians of royalty, the *Upanishads,* the Aztecs, the Piegan Indians of Canada, Melanesian tribesmen, thirteenth-century China, the courts of fourteenth-century France, ancient Rome, and seventeenth-century Holland; Onians discusses Greek, Roman, Jewish, and Christian beliefs. In all these cultures the body serves to project an image of a unified organic whole or congruity on the world. The anthropomorphic metaphor is no less pervasive in our own society. What has changed, as Barbara Stafford has recently claimed, is that the body (as it has been represented in twentieth-century art) no longer serves to represent wholeness and coherence but rather the chaos and fragmentation at loose in our world.[16]

Perhaps the reason the body is so "entrenched" in culture, particularly in architectural culture, is that it is "prewired" or, as Leon Battista Alberti would have said, "inborn" in the mind.[17] Marc Johnson, in his *Body in the Mind: The Bodily Basis of Meaning, Imagination, and Reason,* goes so far as to claim that the body is the basis for the other forms of cognition. All knowledge in his view is "embodied," meaning that thinking is fundamentally founded upon the anthropomorphic metaphor. For him the body is a basic category of the mind, a phenomenon; it shapes reality.[18] Close to this radically "innatist" position is that held by "realists," who see the most basic level of cognition as a reflection of the "world as it is": thus people view the world through concepts that originate out of reality. This is the position put forth by Francisco Varela, Evan Thompson, and Eleanor Rosch in their *Embodied Mind,* as they use the research of cognitive scientists on semantics in arguing that the grounding level of all concepts is experiences.[19] For them the body is an epiphenomenon of reality; it emerges from experience.

Which of the two positions—the innatist or the realist—is correct does not concern us here. What matters is that the anthropomorphic metaphor takes us to the very fundamentals of cognition. This explains why it is so universal in human culture, particularly in relation to architecture, and why the cognitive substratum of the body is the soil out of which an enormous tree of architectural metaphors has grown.

The roots of this tree are very deep; they are possibly neural, possibly experiential. Without doubt, however, they are entangled with and constrained by social institutions and literary traditions. This idea is owed to another philosophical school, that of the "constructivists" who belong to the Wittgensteinian tradition.[20] In "Meaning, Other People, and the World," Hilary Putnam has argued that categories are primarily social artifacts or constructs, "a form of cooperative activity, not an essentially individualistic activity."[21] Viewing the anthropomorphic metaphor as a group-constructed entity makes understandable the many differences in the anthropomorphic metaphor from culture to culture. Indeed, there is no one body that characterizes all cultures, in spite of the metaphor's universality, as Feher's anthology has most cogently shown. The body appears in an incredible number of guises and roles: as gendered, ungendered, healed, mechanical, divine, transparent, coprophilic, homoerotic, maternal. From the *Upanishads,* part of the *Veda* composed in India around 900 B.C.E., we learn that women produce semen; from the writings of medieval European monarchical theory, that kings had two bodies; from the Presocratics, that the body of God is a transparent sphere; from Incan societies, that bodies are made in order to be sacrificed; from nineteenth-century European doctors writing on female anatomy, that women have penises turned upside down; from French sixteenth-century lore, that some men have wolves' bodies.[22]

In my examination of this metaphor, I use a combination of these three independent approaches. Metaphor has traditionally been the domain of scholars of literature. They have tended to see it as a privileged species of figurative language that is particular to literature, a kind of anomaly that must be treated separately from all the other types of mental activity. Aristotle, however, saw it as part of basic reasoning, what he called "enthymemic."[23] But more recently, others have explored the role metaphors play in diverse areas of mental activity, including science and engineering. Thus works by Donald Schön and by George Lakoff and Mark Johnson present metaphor as a much more typical form of thought, key to the very way we think about things and make sense of reality.[24]

Of particular relevance here is that Lakoff and Johnson take into account the way metaphors affect not only isolated categories but whole "category structures," whole "conceptual systems." They look at metaphor, in other words, "as a means of structuring our categorical frameworks and the kinds of everyday activities they perform." Among the many things a metaphor can do is "encapsulate" a whole conceptual system, a large and coherent network of entailments. There may be many "instantiations" of the metaphor in this sense. Metaphorical transfer involves changes not only from one category to another, but one conceptual system to another. What we experience with such metaphors, in their words, is a kind of "reverberation down through the network of entailments that awakens and connects our memories of past experience and serves as a possible guide for future ones."[25] These

Lakoff and Johnson call "basic" metaphors. Alexander Tzonis, in an earlier analysis of design and engineering metaphors, referred to them as "epiphoric objects": that is, objects used as sources applied to design targets to generate or justify design interventions.[26] The difference between simple metaphors and basic metaphors or epiphoric objects is the extent of their influence: the latter reverberate more. They represent in a condensed way a whole paradigm, a whole mentality.

During the period under study—that is, from the late eighth century to the second half of the fifteenth—the body is not just a metaphor: it is a basic metaphor, encapsulating a whole paradigm, a whole conceptual system, as it categorizes and entails. Furthermore, it instantiates an infinite number of metaphors. We will find numerous such subsidiary metaphors dispersed in the texts, produced over almost five centuries, that are analyzed in the following chapters. And we will also find them in the text of the *Hypnerotomachia*. Every act in which the heroes of the story engage that relates them to the body of buildings is, in fact, one of these instantiations.

One of the reasons metaphors are so pervasive in our thinking is that they are so effective at "cutting up our world into clusters, so we can deal with clusters instead of elements."[27] As Lakoff and Johnson point out, basic metaphors represent a "ready-made" mentality that includes an inventory of structures, of which patterns of reasoning are established parts. Once we learn a pattern of reasoning or a schema, we do not have to create it from scratch or relearn it each time we use it. It provides an economical cognitive shortcut to a whole flow of reasoning. It eventually becomes conventionalized and is used automatically, effortlessly, and even unconsciously. Metaphors and metaphorical entailments can evoke a coherent system of metaphorical concepts and a corresponding coherent system of metaphorical expressions for those concepts. Metaphorical definitions can "give us a handle on things and experiences we have already categorized."[28] As in the life of an individual, so in the life of a culture. Epiphoric objects can serve to instantiate what Kuhn in *The Structure of Scientific Revolutions* calls a scientific "paradigm," shaping the development of vast areas of knowledge over a long period of time.[29] Similarly they influence the whole culture of an era, its value system, and its way of life. Mumford has written in a masterful way about how the clock became a basic metaphor in the early Renaissance, regimenting and disciplining the minds of an entire civilization.[30] Closer to our present concern, Tzonis and his collaborators examine those periods of history when epiphors in architecture and city planning change, such as the replacement of the divine body metaphor by the metaphor of the mechanical body in the seventeenth and eighteenth centuries, and later by the metaphor of natural living objects, such as the forest.[31]

For the same reasons that basic metaphors give us power to conceptualize and reason, so they, conversely, have power over us, as Lakoff and Johnson put it. They cannot be easily resisted, in large measure because they are barely noticed. To the extent that we use any metaphor, we accept its validity. Consequently, when someone else uses it, we are predisposed to accept its validity. Once we learn a metaphor, they write, "it is just there, conventionalized, a ready and powerful conceptual tool—automatic, effortless, and largely unconscious. The things most alive in our conceptual system are those things that we use constantly, unconsciously, and automatically."[32]

But just as established metaphors can condense, encapsulate, or freeze patterns of thinking, so new basic metaphors can work critically on them. In this capacity, they "put pressure" on patterns of thinking—bend, crack, and break them. In philosopher Donald Davidson's terms, they can be used like "sticks" to deal "a bump on the head" of the user.[33] Turner has written that any analogical categorical connection "makes a bid to establish or influence category structures," for "category structures are dynamic and subject to transformation under the pressure of analogy." The fragments are "products of a process of breaking up and destroying." Thus metaphors can be deeply disruptive of established category structures, and just as established metaphors can structure experiences we have already categorized, so new ones can lead to recategorization. In such cases metaphors serve to "unmask, capture, or invent connections absent from or upstaged by one's category structure."[34]

New metaphors, besides filling a critical role, can also fill a creative one by making novel patterns of reasoning possible: in other words, they can free the mind to consider what would otherwise have been unthinkable. They permit broad change.[35] New epiphors enable an organization of important experiences that our conventional conceptual system had not made available, striking a blow against older thinking patterns, dislodging old categories or the connections between them, turning old truths into new fallacies, bad into good, and old prohibitions into new imperatives. To borrow another image from Lévi-Strauss, a new epiphor can act as a "kaleidoscope" in which new thinking patterns are created out of the fragments of the old.[36] As Lakoff and Johnson point out, much of cultural change arises from the introduction of new epiphors, categories, or concepts and the loss of old ones. For example, the Westernization of cultures throughout the world is partly a matter of introducing the "time is money" epiphor into those cultures, as we have seen above.[37]

It is cognitive economy that makes metaphorical thinking so effective at pulling mentalities together and breaking them apart. As Aristotle first observed, metaphors lead to plausible rather than truthful conclusions, and the reasoning they display is more flexible than that offered by apodeictic syllogisms. While with apodeixis, explicitness and precision of terms are the rule, in metaphor the opposite holds: implicitness and ambiguity reign. But what metaphorical inferences lose in truth value they gain in suggestiveness.[38]

Take two examples, one of a classic syllogism and one of a now classic metaphor. The first is Aristotle's: "Socrates is a man; all men are mortals; therefore, Socrates is a mortal." Here we are guaranteed a truthful conclusion, given sound premises. From the metaphorical statement that "Sally is a block of ice," however, we can draw no conclusions with absolute certainty.[39] But undeniably it does permit the mind the freedom to explore a potentially endless field of plausible inferences: that Sally is emotionless, that a lack of emotion is like ice, that emotions are like fire, that fire can be stronger than ice, that Sally is perhaps capable of melting. It is easy to see why the creation of new mentalities probably has more to do with enthymemic thinking fueled by metaphors than with truth-based reasoning.[40]

Why is it that we prefer jumping to conclusions to taking small steps of solid reasoning in logical sequence? The answer is that people tend to operate within limits that do not permit such ideal cognition, which advances through cumbersome and intractable details that immobilize mental activity. So they proceed instead by "highlighting" parts of the world picture "at the expense of hiding" other parts of it.[41] As Aristotle long ago stated, metaphorical language has the power of quick solutions: it provides mental shortcuts, which very well suit the reality of the time limits of human life.

For Jerome Bruner, "fictional thinking" represents a separate kind of "cognitive functioning," a different "mode of thought" that provides a distinctive way of ordering experience, of constructing reality.[42] It has its own criteria of well-formedness that are quite different from those of scientific thinking. This is what makes metaphors especially well-suited to affect the bastions of "mentality"—fundamental ways of understanding, describing, explaining, envisaging, and acting upon the world—and to transform them. To stress the universality of such a use of storytelling, Bruner quotes the philosopher Michael Rorty on the creation of hypotheses: in order to study the phenomenon, "we must study how we come to endow experience with meaning." He also quotes an economist's admission "that when forecasts based on economic theory fail, he and his colleagues take to telling stories." From such cases, Bruner concludes that this is "perhaps . . . why tyrants," who resist change above all, "hate and fear poets and novelists even more than they fear and hate scientists." He quotes Aristotle's *Poetics* approvingly: the poet's function is to describe "not the thing that has happened, but a kind of thing that might happen," and metaphor can do this with unique evocativeness and force.[43]

As we will see in the *Hypnerotomachia* as well as in the medieval texts, metaphors are an effective way of communicating, of achieving cultural change, of learning. They are more persuasive than a logical "proof." Their potential affect on worldviews explains why fiction is probably even more destabilizing than science. It is also why much of the shift from the "cold" mentality to the "hot" thinking of humanism occurs through metaphor rather than through scientific demonstration.

In reading the *Hypnerotomachia,* one extracts out of the text the fusion between building and body. The parts of each building are perceived as if they were parts of a body. Persons and buildings are perceived as relating to each other as if they were equivalent entities. The attitudes toward buildings are identical with those expressed toward a body. However strange, this fusion is made acceptable.

This is typical of how metaphors work. They enable us to relate to something previously unfamiliar through something else which we know well, without self-consciousness or reliance on any complicated reasoning. They permit "mental leaps," to use Holyoak and Thagard's phrase.[44] Moreover, behind this accidental and casual appearance of metaphor, there is a system, as current research in literature and linguistics has shown. While the phenomenon of metaphor was traditionally seen as something piecemeal and paradoxical, investigations now show that the use of metaphors within a family of texts of a period or of a culture appears highly systematic; they are interlinked in a fundamental way.

During the period under review, the body metaphor was used in order to reinforce and conserve a mentality. But it was also used as a means of breaking up a way of looking at the world. The *Hypnerotomachia* must be seen as part of this process, which says something about the role of the somatic metaphor in our culture in structuring knowledge. The body serves to map knowledge, to bring disparate pieces together in ways that otherwise would have been unthinkable. The more basic the metaphor, the more it pulls elements together.

What historians like Mumford, Dijksterhuis, Kuhn, and Duhem have all emphasized is the role of mechanistic basic metaphors in the development of modern civilization, especially in the shaping of higher norms and values. Mumford, in particular, has stressed that for the modern world to be born, "men had to become mechanical."[45] But I would argue that equally important for the modernization of thinking was the radical recategorization of the metaphor of the body. To be clear, although it was not a sufficient condition, it was a necessary one. Without the long conceptual change that accompanied the rise of the erotic body as a newly effective basic metaphor, the systematization of knowledge and the recombinant, creative thinking exemplified in the *Hypnerotomachia* would have been unthinkable. The body was a wedge that turned the cognitive world upside down.

As we shall see, the *Hypnerotomachia* is merely the most extreme statement in this long, drawn-out battle to recategorize architecture through its aestheticization, which was part of a greater movement toward the aestheticization of life. In the following chapters, we will examine a very large number of texts that keep hammering home the same idea: the building is a desired body. In each, it will be the implicit basic metaphor that permits the coming together of a new *forma mentis,* a new set of "wishes, habits, ideals and goals."

The transformation of the anthropomorphic metaphor in architecture between the eighth and the fifteenth century does not follow a straight and narrow path. The old does not give way easily to the new. Radical rethinking is not so easy. Alternately referred to by historians as "late medieval" and "early modern," the period in fact contains elements of both worlds, locked together in an intense struggle. The Dutch historian Johan Huizinga's remarks about the last part of this period, the fourteenth and fifteenth centuries, could probably be generalized to the whole: the period would indeed appear to be one long transitional period when "two layers of civilization," the archaic and the modern, are "superimposed, coexisting through contradictory . . . now blend[ing], now collid[ing]."[46]

This mixed image of blending and colliding is an apt one to describe the struggle that occurs in relation to architectural thinking during this period. This battle is not altogether out in the open. It is waged largely underground and left undeclared. Some assaults will be headlong, but, at least in the beginning, most are couched in subterfuge. There is tension, friction, confrontation, resistance. There is indeterminacy, experimentation, trial and error. There is, most remarkably, a polemical, questing spirit that finally erupts in the *Hypnerotomachia*.

All writings are inevitably marked by their relations to others, whether this relation is one of harmony or cacophony, agreement or dissent. Intentionally or not, each discourse on architecture comes into dialogue with others on the same object: what is a building? How should one relate to it? As Mikhail Bakhtin observes, "Discourse (as in general all signs) is interindividual." The mechanism of metaphor and storytelling has therefore to be related to a social mechanism, in a fashion that Bakhtin calls "dialogical."[47] Thus the meaning of a text lies equally within it and in other texts outside it.

In *Discourse in the Novel,* Bakhtin discusses "authoritative discourse," which he sees as being, for example, "religious, political, moral; the word of a father, of adults and of teachers, etc." and typified in the "the authority of religious dogma, or of acknowledged scientific truth or of a currently fashionable book." In his words, the authoritative discourse "demands that we acknowledge it, that we make it our own; it binds us, quite independent of any power it might have to persuade us internally; we encounter it with its authority already fused to it. The authoritative word is located in a distanced zone, organically connected with a past that is felt to be hierarchically higher. It is, so to speak, the word of the fathers."[48]

The image of the father is an ironically apt one in the present context. The "other," against which the emerging strategies for thinking are aimed, is the bulk of the ascetic writings of the Christian church fathers and of the continuing patristic tradition. Among the more striking characteristics of these writings, as we shall see later on, is that its prohibitions are very clearly spelled out. What we may call the ascetic prohibition—"do not love architecture"—is relentlessly and explicitly hammered home. In addition, this particular deontic is woven interdependently into an explicit network of other equally dogmatically stated prohibitions.

Although the dialogue with this "cold" thinking serves to structure the formation of the new Poliphilian thinking, the opposition is not clearly expressed. It is muted. In the beginning the oppositional relation to the old thinking stays "masked." This is because, as Bakhtin argues, however powerful the dialogical relation, it cannot always be seen or heard. It may be clearly apparent, but only in a concealing subtext. The idea of the unuttered is an important component of the dialogical principle. Bakhtin refers to what occurs in this type of elliptical interaction as communication through "passwords."[49]

In the context of this study, it is the anthropomorphic epiphor in storytelling that serves as such a password. This is the framework in which the *Hypnerotomachia* and the new erotic imperative it propounds with regard to architecture must be understood. As we will have many occasions to see in what follows, the body metaphor is often left unuttered and is communicated only in elliptical fashion. Thus its adversarial nature remains concealed and the patristic strictures are never openly denied. The subtle opposition is achieved by using parts of the overall patristic dogma as a kind of "ur-text," elements of which are used to weave new counterarguments with new strategies of thinking.

Each of these strategies is a particular negation of "cold thinking," and as the negations differ, so do their particular rules. There are three of them and each one represents a step toward assertiveness and overt adversariness. One will be almost recklessly wayward. Another will seem to recant and relinquish its openly aggressive traits. The third will launch a frontal attack. The body that runs through this cognitive battlefield from beginning to end is not always explicitly present. In the first instance, the body of the building is equated with its luxurious accoutrements, glinting gold, sparkling gems; it is the "marvelous body," as portrayed mostly in the *mirabilia* literature from the tenth century on. In the second strategy, the body is an incorporeal body of virtue, of divine light, of pure geometrical relations. This is what I will call the "divine body," and it is to be found in the writings of figures like Suger or Hugh of Lincoln or Abelard from the twelfth century on. The building-body metaphor becomes asserted as a real living thing and an object of passion in Leon Battista Alberti's *Hypnerotomachia,* which represents the third strategy, the "desired body."

The order in which the strategies will be presented here, one per chapter, is more logical than chronological. As we have noted, the configuration of change during the period under investigation is not a neat and orderly one. It is a process occurring not only on several levels but also at different speeds. This is not to say that there is no chronological progression. The earliest texts in which the first strategy appears antedate the earliest text in which the second does. But texts that enact the first strategy continue to be written well over two centuries later; the argument is reechoed, its appeal lingering on, long after its innovative character has faded.

Where did the battle for beauty take place? Who were the soldiers? the actors? the historians? the storytellers? the listeners? Where did they come from? Its first stirrings are in the court of the Carolingians, of the House of Aquitaine, of the Capetians. Its flowering is in the court of the Medicis and the Montefeltri. From the courts, the centers of the cult of learning that serves as the cradle of the Renaissance humanist thinking, the new hedonism migrates to the new centers of what Hans Baron called "civic humanism": [50] the prosperous, republican city-states of Italy, most notably Florence. The readers of Petrarch were urban (and Florentine, and Roman); the readers of Dante were urban (and Florentine); the readers of Boccaccio were urban (and Florentine).

This process of re-cognition took the form of dreamwork and fiction. In the life of an individual, dreams often say what in normal circumstances would be censored. It is remarkable how commonly shared these dream thoughts are. The particularity of Western culture between the tenth and the fifteenth centuries is just beginning to be noted. During this period, dreamwork arguably was the main vehicle of change.

To a surprising extent, the slow formation of the humanist paradigm of architecture can be charted in a great variety of writings: the *Hypnerotomachia,* a fragment of the *Alexander Romance,* Abbot Suger's administrative reports of the progress of the construction of the church of Saint-Denis, a travel guide for pilgrims visiting Rome, Boccaccio's *Filocolo,* Guillaume de Lorris and Jean de Meung's *Roman de la rose,* Francesco di Giorgio's treatises on architecture, a passage from the epic cycle of *Der jüngere Titurel,* Robert of Clari's description of the Fourth Crusade, the founding charter of one of the Carthusian communities in France, the deed by which the chapter house of the abbey of Saint-Ouen decided to continue construction of their chapel, Honorius of Autun's theological tract on the symbolism of church construction, Chaucer's *House of Fame.* There is nothing anomalous about this apparently hybrid corpus of writings, which combines the literary and nonliterary. They are seen here as making up one system of utterances—sometimes discordant, sometimes harmonious, but always interrelated and interacting. That is how they were perceived in their own time: as part of the same dialogue. What they have in common is that they put together a world to which the love of beauty in architecture is integral; and all are written by and for the same social groups, the emergent and upwardly mobile in the court and city.

Almost all of the authors are in the employ of a court. Rabanus Maurus worked at the court of Charlemagne, Leon Battista Alberti was an employee of the pope, Suger was an administrator in the service of Charles VII and Eleanor of Aquitaine, and Gervaise of Canterbury was in the service of Henry II and again Eleanor, after she divorced her first husband. The *Hypnerotomachia* was dedicated to Federigo d'Urbino. One author was himself a pope, Pius II. Robert of Clari was a soldier who recounted his tale upon his return from the Fourth Crusade in Constantinople. Others were poets and troubadours, such as Albrecht, the author of *Der jüngere Titurel.* The tales of the Round Table were intended for new monarchs of small countries. The tales of Marco Polo (1254–1324), however, were intended for the urban bourgeois as well as the courtly reader interested in the market routes to supply luxury goods such as silks to an urban clientele. The *Mirabilia urbis Romae* purported to be a handbook for pilgrims visiting Rome, but it was no doubt read by its contemporaries as expressing the views of the republican merchant population of Rome. Cavalcanti's history of Florence was intended for its citizens, and the many encomia included on the delights of its new church buildings were directed at the population at large.

The aestheticization of life has been categorized by Werner Sombart in *Luxury and Capitalism* as nothing more than the expression of the appetite among the feudal suzerains and their vassals for extravagance, and particularly for lavish, luxurious buildings, in the wake of the despoiling of the East in the Crusades.[51] While Sombart's insights are undeniably useful, and the new acquisitive values do accompany the eroticization of life (as we shall have many occasions to note throughout chapters 7 and 8), the growing attachment to the things of this world that took place between the eighth and the fifteenth centuries cannot be reduced to consumerism. It is also the mark of a culture trying to escape a repressive mentality that denied the pleasure principle, to free itself from the constraints of the past, to rethink its relation to reality and life. By the time this aestheticization is espoused by early Renaissance humanists—Alberti, Francesco di Giorgio, Leonardo, Filarete—it is above all a rejection of *contemptus mundi* and an affirmation of *amor mundi*. It played a role in forming Renaissance humanism, in clearing the way to innovative thinking about architecture and freeing the forces of creativity and invention.

The recategorization of the body, carried out through centuries of dreamwork, freed thinking from the confines of an older conceptual framework. It allowed the humanists to think about the world, particularly about architecture, in a new way. For in addition to being a physical reality, the "body" was also a cognitive system, a paradigm, a mentality. As the new category of the body overturned the former one, it supported the new humanist *forma mentis* that overturned its more archaic predecessor. It permitted a "re-cognition" of architecture, a restructuring of architectural cognition.

Perhaps what we respond to and what moves us so instinctively when we contemplate
portrayals of architecture in the writings, paintings, and drawings of the early
Italian Renaissance of the fifteenth century, as well as the buildings and
towns of the period themselves, is the new vision of an all-
embracing humanism. This vision, of what Freud called the
"civilizing" force of Eros, for one brief period in the
history of Western culture held the architecture
of the physical world under its sway.[52]
But before we can begin to appreciate that world, we must go
back to a time when
the prospect was
quite the
oppo-
site

.

7

✳✳✳✳
✳✳✳

THE DANGEROUS BODY

B ACK IN THE WORLD BEFORE HUMANISM, IT IS FORBIDDEN TO love architecture. Because humankind has been condemned to an unhappy existence in a debased world where all is fleeting and transitory, all material pursuits are futile. "Nothing is stable," warns Gregory the Great at the end of the sixth century. To Peter Damian, writing at the end of the eleventh, the world is still the same: unsure, shifting, treacherous, and horrifying, "like the sea."[1]

This paranoid view, which prevailed among the literate population of Europe for approximately ten centuries, also held for architecture. At the end of the twelfth century, Petrus Cantor writes that because the temporal world is transient, because any earthly undertaking is by definition hopeless, there is no point in building anything. He particularly condemns the habit of imitating the sumptuous buildings of ancient Rome.[2] At about the same time, Hildebert of Lavardin expounds much the same sentiments on the futility of architecture. He too attacks Rome as the symbol of fleeting earthly attachments, invoking its present state of ruin and the destruction that has befallen the castles of the Caesars and the temples of the gods, which are now "buried in a swamp."[3] In the thirteenth century, Alexander Neckam takes aim against height in buildings. He condemns those who confuse the elevation of the spirit toward the heavens with the elevation of towers on churches: "The towers rise up threatening the stars, exceeding the height of Mount Parnassus. Even the summit of Mount Nisa is astonished that he cannot equal the tops of these products of human labor. . . . Are the builders trying to take over these places from demons, whose dwelling is this gloomy air?"[4]

Other writers have even harsher views of architecture, castigating it as not only futile but sinful. Alexander Neckam, beholding the excessive spending on church buildings, exclaims: "O curiosity! o vanity! o vain curiosity! o curious vanity! Making suffering with the illness of inconsistency."[5] Bernard sees it as an example of vanity and insanity—"O vanity of vanities, but not more vain than insane"—and associates sumptuous construction with avarice.[6] Petrus Cantor, too, links architecture to the sins of *vanitas* and *curiositas,* to profligacy, superfluity, and lethargy: "Many are profligate, both in building and superfluous expenses, . . . they forgo everyday necessities out of greed, lethargy, and somnolescense" (*P.L.* 205, col. 255). As for Hildebert of Lavardin, he denounces ancient Rome for having been built on money, *lucra.*[7] Architecture is condemned as belonging to the category of things "mercenary"; it is connected with private means of making a fortune in money, "ultra privatum pecuniae modum fortunae," which are incompatible with the ideal of poverty.[8]

In fact the most forceful attack on building as mercenary appears quite late—in 1483—and is made by Girolamo Savonarola himself. He accuses "prelates and teachers" of feeding "upon vanity" and "rejoicing in pomp" by filling their churches with "gold." The "cure of souls" is no longer their concern; they have forsaken the "real church of God . . . made of the living rock of Christians living steadfast in the living faith and mole of charity," in order to devote themselves to "the mercantile world" and "the receipt of revenue." In the old times, Savonarola claims, the church had redistributed whatever it received in order to "relieve the needs of the poor." Now it only "robs the poor as [its] only means of support."[9]

Throughout this period, it is necessary for those intending to build at all to somehow accede to the condemnation of worldly architecture. The only acceptable approach was to build poorly. The *Minorite Statute* of 1260 warns that "Because these curiosities and superfluities go directly against the ideal of poverty, we order that the curiosities of buildings in pictures, in windows, and columns and such, or superfluities in length, breadth, and height be avoided."[10] And indeed poverty is praised as the greatest possible joy:

THE POVERTY THAT YOU BLAME IS JOYFUL RUIN.
O HAPPY THE POOR! SAYS THE DIVINE VOICE,
POOR PEOPLE LIVE SOBERLY,
THE RICH FROM ROBBERY.[11]

The consequences of the cult of poverty for architecture are obvious. The buildings should "non superflua sint, sed humilia" (not be superfluous but humble), declares Hugue de Fouilloi. Abelard's first chapel is a hut humbly constructed out of "calamis et culmo" (reeds and thatch).[12] For Petrus Cantor, the ideal is to return to the simplicity of traditional buildings—the "simplicitate antiquorum in construendis domibus." His model is Abraham, who, not sedentary but a traveling pilgrim, lived "under a thatched roof." Petrus admires Lot and Noah because they lived in tents, as well as some other "ancients" who inhabited stone caverns and even the trunks of trees. Likewise, Elijah is worthy of emulation for he too spurned a "real house," choosing instead a little chamber under another's roof. Paul is another exemplar because he was the first hermit, lived either in basements or underground, and was often taken for a wild beast of a wolf. Christ teaches that we "must be content with humble huts to live in" rather than "ostentatious" buildings (*P.L.* 205, col. 256).

The restrictions are severe: "Let those who show care for their interior, and contempt and neglect for everything external, build for themselves the form of poverty, the beauty of simplicity and the forms of paternal frugality. Let no industry be applied to creating artifice unless by oversight."[13] We might with justice question how well the imperative of poverty went down with the poor themselves. A cleric complains about their lack of enthusiasm:

PEOPLE WHO ARE POOR IN SPIRIT ARE SAID TO BE HAPPY
BUT OUR POOR ARE TOO PROUD.
AND ACCORDING TO THE LAWS OF THE WORLD,
THEY YIELD TO INGRATITUDE AND WHEN SOMEONE

KNOCKS AT THEIR DOOR,
THEY CRY, AS IF THEY WERE BEING PUT TO DEATH.

TODAY, THE POOR MAN WANTS TO GO AROUND IN THE WORLD
MORE THAN TO TAKE CARE OF THE FLOCK.
IT NO LONGER MAKES SENSE TO GIVE HIM ALMS
BECAUSE HE WOULD SOONER DIE OF HUNGER
THAN SERVE THE LORD.[14]

The demand for poverty is not limited to the material realm. It also extends to the spirit, and ignorance also becomes an imperative. As the historian John Taylor observes, since the time of Augustine it was thought that the only true knowledge worthy of men's mind was that contained in the Scriptures; whatever men learned outside the Scriptures was harmful and condemnable.[15] When William of St. Thierry, a friend of Bernard's, declared that "debauchery is as bad as learning" (*P.L.* 134, col. 381), he illustrated how closely identified learning was with sin. Apparently some clerics, however, were not convinced that their happiness rested in being poor in spirit as well as body:

I AM A LONELY CLERIC BORN TO LABOR
I AM TROUBLED OFTEN BY BEING GIVEN UP TO POVERTY
I WOULD LIKE TO SWEAT OVER LITERARY STUDIES
BUT POVERTY KEEPS ME FROM IT.[16]

Vanity, excess, avarice, and curiosity, of course, are damning vices, and threats of social opprobrium could effectively control behavior. They must have played a role in strengthening the prohibitions against building and enforcing the imperatives of passivity, ignorance, and poverty. But there is another world-structuring idea that would have been particularly important: the metaphor of the building as a dangerous body.

Historians who have looked at the so-called medieval mentality have been struck by the strength of what Jacques Le Goff has called "the horror of the body" that dominated it and by the fury with which the sin of bodily lust was attacked.[17] Perhaps nothing gives a clearer idea of the magnitude of this paranoid horror than the pages of Migne's *Patrologia Latina,* a monumental compendium in over two hundred volumes of the writings of the European Middle Ages. Well-known among its remarkable features is the univocal nature of the views that it contains. Whether an author writes in the fourth century or the twelfth, one observes the same strict adherence to dogma. The chronology of the writings is irrelevant: there is no change over time. And one of the things that obsessed these medieval writers was sexuality.

Migne's own "Index of Special Vices and Errors" provides overwhelming evidence of ten centuries of fixation on *libido* and *cupiditas*. They receive more attention than *vanitas*, *superfluitas*, and *avaritia*. Under the upholders of the idea that *cupiditas* is the *radix omnium malorum*, Migne lists no fewer than forty-three authors (*P.L.* 220, cols. 895–896). For Gregory the Great, for example, "voluptuousness" is the "great detractor" of "perfection" in this earthly world and the cause of every failing of mankind. That is why God teaches men to avoid "voluptuous flesh" and "the lust of the flesh": all good acts are offset by acts that follow fleshly promptings, from which only "innumerable evils" can arise. Ambrose, for his part, claims that "the commotions of lust, only the devil can find exciting" and that "lust alone suffices to exclude us from paradise." For Augustine the opposition between the City of God and the city of man can be reduced to the opposition that exists between life "according to the spirit" and life "according to the flesh." To live according to the flesh is the quintessential characteristic of evil that marks the human condition as by definition sinful. As Augustine never tires of repeating, "to move among men is carnal; and whatever concerns flesh has to do with men." He asserts that love as practiced by "lubricious lovers" is "depraved." This love, extended to "the love of all earthly things," is a form of "diabolical insidiousness." Anselm Laudunensis claims that "*voluptas* or concupiscence of the flesh is the evil above all other evils." No hyperbole, it would seem, is too extreme for him: "In the mire of human feces," he asks, "is there anything more fetid than the lust of the flesh?" Surely, he concludes, it is "better to be defiled by death than by lust" (220, col. 896).

Condemnations of love of the body are heaped up with unflagging ardor. Rabanus Maurus condemns lust as the original sin. For Elogius lust is associated with the "filthiness" and "impurity" of "the Mahomettans." For Haymo Halberstad, the duty of those who are chosen as custodians of the soul—that is, priests—is to "spend their whole life extinguishing the fires of lust." It is their obligation "to instruct the faithful to resist these passions by any means and live a life of chastity and continence in order to avoid hell." Hincmarus Rhenensis, in equally menacing terms, claims that those who yield to the perverse desires originating in the "fetid flesh" will "perish in the fire and sulfur of hell." For Ratherius Veronensis, mankind must combat "earthly lusts" in order to avoid burning in hell. That is why it is necessary to "extinguish carnal desires through abstinence." He warns against the "ruin of lust" and the "prostitution of lust." For Fulbertus lust is "a servitude that keeps one in captivity." Balduin of Cambridge defines any form of "amor mundi" as "cupiditas." Gigue condemns the "voluptuous" and "vile" delectations of the five senses. Guibertus warns that no one who is "inflamed with carnal desire" may enter heaven and that the indulgence of the flesh "corrupts not only externally but internally." Anselm Laudunensis confirms that "many on the road to truth get detracted by earthly lust," and on a more positive note, Bruno Astensis writes that happy are those who "combat every vice, every lust of the flesh in themselves." Hildebert of

Lavardin, on the other hand, says that whoever "fails to brake his lusts" incurs "eternal damnation." Bernard, not one to be outdone, pronounces lust to be "the original vice and evil" and condemns the "perverse and filthy thoughts of lust" that "separate us from God," categorizing "lustful passions" as "living death." In the same spirit, Helinandus says that "delectation in carnal lust leads to death." Summing it all up, Maximus concludes that lust is "a scorpion." Indeed, to succumb to the pleasures of the flesh is to descend to the level of animals. According to Anselmus Laudunensis a man "infected" by sensuality becomes "an animal and a brute"; Petrus Cantor likens a man in a state of lustful transport to "a pig," as does Rabanus Maurus (200, col. 893).

Lust debases man to the level of a woman and, of course, given the misogyny that characterized medieval writings of this type,[18] this is even worse than becoming an animal. Indeed, the long anti-*libidines* tradition in the patristic theology is intimately associated with an equally passionate misogynous tradition in which women are equated with lust and pictured as purely sexual beings: perverse, filthy, dangerous, the very embodiment of evil. Alanus of Insulis sees lust as something that "effeminates" the state of mind. For Alcuin, fornication is the greatest of all the sins because it gives birth to "blindness of the soul, lack of consideration, inconstance, inattention, and love of oneself." Lust is what "empties purses, inebriates the soul, effeminates the state of the mind, and filthies the soul." Tertullian says that women are "the gateway of the devil," Ambrose that woman are "nothing but lascivious creatures." Jerome compares virgins and widows to "the pest," saying that "all evil comes from their heads" and that "for Samson the damage caused by a woman was far greater than that caused by lions." Augustine claims that women are good for "nothing but lust and that there is nothing worse for virile souls than the temptations of women." Fornication with a woman is a "great evil" and "corrupts the image of God and the temple in man's soul." Petrus Chrysologus, referring to Helen of Troy, complains that "the lasciviousness of women causes war" and that "they are to be avoided." Salvianus claims that "women make men renounce God" and that "one whore makes many fornicators." For Eutropius, fornication with a woman conjures up the image of "being swallowed whole by a horrible stomach" (200, col. 900). In the *Vita Patrum* we read that woman is a "dragon, that is, a subspecies of demon." She is again regarded as a "demon whose only purpose is to dominate men" by Gregory the Great. The invectives go on, equating womankind with the evils of lust. Atto Vercelliis points out that the devil seduced not a man but a woman and it is by woman that man was deceived. Martinus compares "woman's seduction by a serpent to man's seduction by woman." For Absolo, "Eve was the first sinner." Ratherius of Verona says that the mind of a woman is "full of vices and lust" and that "even the Virgin Mary was a sinner for having ignited divine love," that first was lustful. Clearly all this points to one conclusion: to quote Augustine, "women were made to be dominated by men" (ibid.).

Disgust with the body and lust goes hand in hand with the exaltation of self-mortification, which also has roots in the earliest writings in the patristic tradition. Jerome writes that mortification is a "great virtue." Augustine writes that "the love of things is pernicious and must be eliminated by punishing the body." Cassian, Adalgerus, and Alanus of Insulis all wrote treatises entitled *De mortificatione,* praising its virtues. Cassian even calls mortification the "instrument of perfection." Benedict writes that internal mortification leads to grace and Cassiodorus claims that God visits the mortified. By mortifying the flesh one reaches a state of "great joy," according to Odo. Peter Damian shuns the company of those whose flesh has not been mortified, because such flesh is "horrendous"; indeed, according to Hildebert, to be truly Christian one's flesh must be mortified. Consequently, Bernard describes how he assiduously mortified himself. Godfried sees in mortification a way of "enlivening the spirit," which "thus becomes a sweet delicacy for God to ingest." For Bernard, again, mortification of the flesh does the flesh itself "a lot of good." Many authors—including Ambrose, Jerome, Augustine, Cassian, Cassiodorus, the Venerable Bede, Alcuin, Rabanus Maurus, Peter Damian, and Bernard—take relish in individual cases of "stupendous" mortification, which they describe in detail. There is a general consensus that, as Godefricus says, the body is "the symbol of corruption" and that, as Hilarius says, "our flesh is the sister of Babylon and confusion" (220, col. 555 ff.).

Given the evidence put forth by Freudian writers of the twentieth century concerning the symbolism of clothes—by de Clérambault in particular[19]—it should come as no surprise that the scope of invective should be extended from the body itself to the clothes that cover it. Indeed, in the writings of these medieval authors, clothes very clearly symbolize the body. They become its representation in the eyes of the desiring onlooker and thus become invested symbolically with the dangerous, evil attributes of the body. They take its place as an object of *libido, concupiscentia,* and *fornicatio.* In the words of Godefricus, clothes are "the symbols of the human body." Sicardus echoes this idea when he observes that "Cleopatra used her precious clothes as well as her beauty in order to seduce Octavius and provoke lust in his heart" (220, col. 906).

It therefore follows that the cult of clothing is condemned as a form of *libido.* Love of clothes becomes as bad as the lust for the body they adorn. To delight in beautiful clothes is to live not according to God but according to the flesh, yielding to every fleshly desire (40, col. 1053). Again clothes are associated with women and seen as something feminine. Tertullian says women sin against God when "they wear gold, put creams on their skins, paint their cheeks, and put black makeup on their eyes" (1, cols. 304, 1325). Cyprian condemns the cult of precious clothes, saying that "to decorate oneself" with "gold and gems and pearls" is "perverted" and that "virgins who wear gold and pearls are doomed"; therefore a virgin should wear "proper" rather than "ornamental" clothing (4, cols. 489, 462). For Hilarius, clothes that are luxurious are "demonic," and therefore he recommends dressing with modesty (9, col. 980; 10, col. 612). Jerome claims that they sin against God when they color their faces with "purple and cherry" (32, cols. 957, 891). Augustine says ornamentations are nothing but "invitations to sin" and that whoever wears superb clothes only corrupts others (33, col. 1080; 38, col. 205). Alcuin says that the pomp of clothing is "inane" and "neither helps the temporal world nor serves God." Because of the *vanitas* and insanity of clothing, he recommends modesty and lauds the example of St. Agnes, who "shed the beautiful and precious clothing of her youth and remained a virgin all her life" (100, col. 166; 123, col. 197). Guericus also carries over the negative qualities belonging to the body to dress. He compares those who don rich clothes to "lepers" who are "superb but miserable" (185, col. 61). Anselmus Laudunensis says that John the Baptist taught that those who pay too much attention to clothes are "dominated by the flesh" and that "Babylon the whore is described as adorned in superb clothes" (162, col. 1263).

But the most important transposition of negative values from the body of the woman to the world that surrounds it is the transferral of the negative qualities of the libidinal body to the libidinal building. It is here that the references in the texts assume their highly metaphorical language, instantiating the basic metaphor of "a building is a body." To begin with, as the beginning of this chapter made clear, to indulge in the admiration of beautiful buildings is wrong because it is similar to the admiration of beautiful bodies. "O mira, sed perversa delectatio" (O what a marvelous but perverse delectation) Hugue de Fouilloi cries out against those who indulge in the pleasures of beholding buildings.[20] Petrus Cantor goes even further. He condemns the palaces of princes as the fruits of lust for building, or *libido aedificandi,* which he qualifies as *detestabile.* To live in luxurious surroundings is to indulge in lust, he continues, in *concupiscentia.* He condemns basilicas that are built to resemble private palaces, because they are the "receptacles where vile bodies of men circulate" (205, cols. 257, 260, 259).[21] Peter Damian says that whoever wishes to build the divine atrium with stones of virtue must first cleanse himself of the thorns of carnal delectation (144, col. 129). Alexander Neckam condemns glorious buildings as "voluptuous."[22] Petrus Cantor goes so far as to counsel his brethren to live "humilibus habitaculis" (in small and humble cells), without so much as a place to recline their heads (205, col. 257).

By this point, it should come as no surprise that the invective is extended still further, from the architectural body to the architectural clothes, so to speak, that cover the building and represent it symbolically. We have seen that the imperative of probity of the human body goes hand in hand with the condemnation of pleasing clothing; so too, love for architectural adornments, by analogy with love for the clothing of the body, becomes the target of strictures.

The importance of equating architectural clothes with the architectural body cannot be overstressed here, for it informs so much of the architectural writings we shall be studying in the rest of this book. A building must be "non voluptuosa, sed honesta" (not voluptuous but honest), Hugue de Fouilloi asserts, condemning ornamentation. *Honestae*, again, is what buildings must be according to Gigue. "Like the bodies of Adam and Eve," buildings must be kept nude. This is because adornment affords pleasure to the senses.[23] For Hildebert of Lavardin, to indulge in architectural pleasure is to succumb to a "rerum temporalium amore" and to submit the eyes to the "culpa concupiscentiae." To the faithful, he suggests that in order to preserve their innocence, they keep their eyes closed. A room therefore should be free of *delicatoria* (delights). It should be like a "cellam de virgis" (a cell of twigs and branches), consistent with the way of life that is *decentissima* (171, col. 745). Petrus Cantor's urging that one should inhabit surroundings that are pristine "causulis pristinis" subliminally evokes the same image of architecture as an undefiled body. Hugues de Sylvanès in the same vein directs his fellows to live in buildings characterized by "shame" and "honesty."[24]

Bernard, for his part, denounces architectural ornament as made to appeal to the "carnalis populus" (the carnal folk). Architectural adornments are sinful because they are like the adornments of a body, like clothes: cladding, accoutrements, and ornaments made to excite the beholder sensually.[25] Architectural adornments come to be condemned as symbols of the evil body. Bernard sees the "immense heights, immoderate lengths, incredible widths, sumptuous polishings, and curious depictions" in buildings as belonging to the category of the pleasures of the flesh, together with all kinds of "fine bright things, melodious caresses, sweet fragrances, sweet tastes and pleasant touchings." He prohibits the sensual pleasures that arise from buildings along with those that come from *vestis*. "An honorable person," he writes, "should be decorated not by the beauty of clothes, nor by the pomp of horses, nor by great buildings."[26]

Petrus Cantor too makes the association between clothing and architecture when he equates bodily and architectural *vestis*, placing the *superfluitas* and *sumptuositas* involved in architectural ornaments among the vices of the flesh: "Just as the superfluity and curiosity of clothes and food cover the work of nature in guilt and make it fall into vice, so it is with superfluity and sumptuousness in buildings."[27] Indeed, according to the *Analecta Divionensia*, architectural *vestis* such as stained-glass windows and patterned floor coverings are subject to the same prohibitions as meat. Abbots who tolerate such adornments of the architectural flesh or, worse, who order them to be carried out are subjected to a diet of bread and water, the same mortification imposed upon those who indulge in other pleasures of the flesh, of *caro*.[28]

For Gigue, buildings, like bodies, should avoid being covered not only with sensually pleasing clothes but with any element that is sensual. In his words, buildings should be *eremeticas*, "hermitlike," and not *aromaticas*, "perfumed." The carnal, sensual aspects of architectural cladding make those who behold them descend to the level of animals.[29] According to Petrus Cantor, to indulge in the pleasure of admiring architectural coverings is to be a "pig" (*P.L.* 205, col. 260). Equally bad if not worse, it makes their inhabitants lose their "virility": "These beauties enervate the virile tendencies and feminize the masculine spirit."[30] Too much pleasure from architectural bodies is wrong because, in the words of Petrus Cantor, "one lives longer with the worms in one's grave than in a house of this world" (*P.L.* 205, col. 258).

A prohibitive, paranoid mentality encapsulated in and reinforced by the metaphor
of the building as a dangerous body, clad in equally dangerous "clothes"—
a metaphor that·a formidable yet sterile group of people hammered
home relentlessly—provides the background against which the
revolution in thought that culminated in Renaissance
humanism took place. This is the metaphor that
all the writings subsequently discussed,
including the *Hypnerotomachia,*
will in individual ways be
attempting to thwart,
overturn, recon-
figure

.

8
****
****

THE MARVELOUS BODY

W̅ E NOW LEAVE WHAT JACQUES LE GOFF CALLS "THAT WORLD
which had become a nightmare," where "the repression and manipulation of
dreams" prevailed. We enter a completely different world of representations, "a
moment when dreams undergo the first big wave of liberation."[1] A new "imaginary," a new
paradigm of the body, is just beginning to take shape, as new counterrepresentations, imperatives, and values are starting to coalesce into new ways of thinking. This is a mental world in
the making, in flux; one part under threat and the other, the world of dreams, on the offensive. The present chapter examines a greatly changed mental world. Unlike the patristic tradition, this mentality is undogmatic. The authors are engaged in entertaining courtly society
or the newly formed urban population. Here, as in dreamwork, the "no" does not exist, and
anything is possible. This way of thinking responds to the prohibitions of earlier writers. It
replaces cold thinking with hot, fictional thinking. Buildings are no longer objects of ignominy, reviled as badges of vanity and superfluity, but objects of sheer, unabashed wonder. To
be more precise, they are objects of marvel. Rather than directly confront the older prohibitions against the aestheticizing of architecture, this new mentality simply ignores them.

The first stage in "turning upside down" the older mentality into the humanist
one, then, occurs in the register of the *mirabilia*. In the process, this register becomes fantastic
and dreamlike, characterized by metaphorical thinking and, in general, what I have called
fictional thinking: a mode in which all things are possible—the more incredible, the better.
Besides the *Travels of Marco Polo*, this chapter considers passages from the *Alexander Romance,
Fimerodia*, Giovanni Boccaccio's *Filocolo* and *Amorosa visione*, the *Mirabilia urbis Romae*, Arthur-
ian legend, *Le pélerinage de Charlemagne*, Albrecht's description of the temple of the Holy Grail
from his *Der jüngere Titurel*, Robert of Clari's *Conquest of Constantinople*, Odon of Deuil's
description of the marvels of Constantinople, William of Tyre's description of the palace of
the Khalif of Cairo, and Chaucer's *House of Fame*. The buildings they describe are all typical
settings for *mirabilia*: palaces, castles, and whole cities, both imagined and seen.[2]

Nowhere in this material will the reader find the metaphor of the building as a
body explicitly spelled out. Here, to transpose again the Freudian term, the architectural
body is "displaced" by the architectural clothes that cover it.[3] The difference is that now the
architectural clothes are not objects of loathing. Indeed, this one feature in particular is crucial
in overturning the older mentality. The clothes of the building take the literal form of cloths
draped over parts of the building, but also are the accoutrements, the precious and dazzling
materials—gold, gems, marbles, artworks—that serve to attract attention to particular areas
of the building.

No longer hated, these symbolic representations of the body become the focus of
fascination and attraction. For example, at a time when, in the words of Einhard (770–840),
Vitruvius's *De architectura* is still considered "verba et nomina obscura" (obscure language and
words), Rabanus Maurus, a German scholar employed at the court of Charlemagne and one

of the most learned figures in ninth-century Europe, writes his *De universo*, an encyclopedia. In it we find, brief as it may be, what is probably the first mention of architecture in a learned text since antiquity. It is presented in terms of garments that don the body of the structure. Indeed architecture is "all the things that are added to the buildings as ornament and decoration, such as the elegant paneling of the roofs decorated with gold and mosaic works of precious marbles and colored pictures."[4]

A ninth-century text from the *Codex Carolingianus* contains a letter, purportedly from Pope Hadrian I (772–795) to Charlemagne, that describes the palace at Ravenna. The emphasis, again, is on the architectural clothing, which consists of marble and mosaic: "We have received a letter of your majesty's from Duke Aruinus. In this letter is related that we have given you the marbles and the mosaic from the palace of the city of Ravenna placed on the floor and on the walls. . . . [This is to make official that] we give you the permission to remove the marbles, the mosaic, and other pictures from this palace."[5]

In an account that has survived from the year 870, what catches the eye of the anonymous observer one day in St. Peter's in Rome are real clothes covering a part of a chapel: "he sent a garment for the altar of St. Peter composed of his golden vestments ornamented with two golden crowns and ornamental gems."[6] Imad-ad-Din, an Arab historian of the Crusades, was shocked to see crusaders drape holy places like the Dome of the Rock with "veils covered with images."[7] Notker, known as the Stammering Monk of Saint Gall (a Benedictine monastery), wrote a biography of Charlemagne in about 884. It describes a bishop's palace as "adorned with carpets of every color and tapestries of every kind."[8] William of Malmesbury, visiting Canterbury Cathedral, notes the "cloths and sacred vestments" that are used as the "ornaments" of the building;[9] an anonymous monk of Malmesbury praises another building for "its golden ceilings," "metallic shell," and "gemmed fabric."[10] In the encyclopedic *Didascalicon*, written in the late 1120s by Hugh of St. Victor, who was Saxon born and an abbot of the School of St. Victor in Paris, architecture—or what he refers to as the "building arts"—is placed in the category of "armament," which in turn falls under "those things under which we take cover," which in turn is classified as a type of "external cover."[11]

Leo of Naples's tenth-century version of the *Alexander Romance*, one of the most popular literary accounts written during the period we are studying, recounts Alexander's dramatic expedition to what he calls "India," a region that includes present-day Pakistan. Among the wonders of this strange and marvelous land he describes are an elephant, a hippopotamus, a flying device with which to "climb to heaven and see if this heaven is that which we see," a submarine device for examining the bottom of the sea, and the palace of King Porus. But the amount of detail concerning the covering of the palace is staggering. The building is totally bedecked in gold and gems. The "golden columns" of the palace are topped with "golden capitals" and overhung with "vines, also out of gold," which sprout "golden leaves." The hall in which these columns are located is itself covered with a "vest" of gold.

Of the twelve different elements that are featured in the description of the palace, in fact, nine are similarly dressed with gold. The other architectural objects are hardly less extravagantly laden. The walls are covered with "gems that are called pearls, and with even bigger pearls and carbuncles." [12]

The emphasis on the clothing of buildings grows. The *Mirabilia urbis Romae* (ca. 1143) is a catalogue of the buildings of antique Rome that had been considered pagan in the eyes of the church. In 1143 Rome underwent an internal crisis caused by the temporary overthrow of the aristocratic and papal regime. The new popular government, the Senate, sought to revive the antique republican institutions. It seems quite possible that this famous pamphlet was composed during these events as a means of disseminating the Senate's ideas. [13] It was one of three books published under the title of *Graphia aurea urbis Romae*.

Here the temple of Emperor Hadrian is also described in terms of its radiant cladding. It is "all covered with stones and . . . fenced in with brazen railings all about, with golden peacocks and a bull. At the four sides of the temple were four horses of gilded brass, and on every face were brazen gates. The Colosseum is depicted as being "of amazing size and beauty and with diverse vaults and it is said that the whole was covered with heaven of bronze and gold." Ancient Rome is to a great extent perceived in terms of its "beauties of gold and silver, bronze and ivory and precious stones." The Needle, which holds the ashes of Caesar, was "adorned in the lower part with tables of gilded brass, and lined in a lovely way with Latin letters; and above the wall, where he rests, it is decked with gold and precious stones. The "basilica called the Vatican" is admired because it is "adorned with a marvelous mosaic," which "glitters when covered with water." Finally the Capitol is depicted as "covered with walls high and strong, rising over the top of the hill, and covered all over with glass and gold and marvelous carved work." And inside the Capitol, the author adds, "were molten images of all the Trojan kings and emperors. Within the fortress was a palace adorned with marvelous works in gold and silver and brass and costly stones." [14]

The equation of Roman architecture with its clothing is echoed interestingly in Fazio degli Uberti's *Dittamondo* (composed mid-quattrocento). It is a description of visionary travels, in which the author is accompanied by the old geographer Solinus, as Dante was by Virgil. Together they encounter a "venerable matron in torn garments"—Rome herself. She tells them of her glorious past and gives them a minute description of old triumphs. [15] But Rome is not the only city to be described in terms of what it is wearing. Constantinople is another subject of real and fictional descriptions of architectural clothing in the twelfth and thirteenth centuries, as chroniclers praise its palaces and other monuments. The palace of the legendary King Hugo of Constantinople, for example, is described in *Le voyage de Charlemagne* (anonymous, ca. 1150), the story of the fictional crusade of Charlemagne to the Holy Land and Constantinople in search of relics and of the presentation of these relics to the abbey of

Saint-Denis. In Hugo's palace, the columns are of "marble" and "fine gold," the staircase of "marble."[16]

In *Chanson de geste* (early thirteenth century), Aymeri de Narbonne dwells on the ostentatious brightness of the materials on the outside of a fictitious palace. The gold and gems are as bright as the rising sun, or so bright one has to shield one's eyes with a hand. One building is wearing a gigantic pearl:

ON THE FLOORS OF THE PRINCE'S PALACE,

DECORATED WITH FINE GOLD FROM BEYOND THE SEA,

[WAS] A GIGANTIC PEARL THAT WOULD HAVE MADE A PERSON TREMBLE

SO MUCH WAS IT RADIANT AND BRIGHTLY RESPLENDENT

LIKE THE SUN THAT RISES IN THE MORNING.[17]

Robert of Clari's account (1216) of the capture of Constantinople by his fellow chevaliers of the Fourth Crusade is full of real buildings similarly bedecked. "The pavements of the chapel were of such a smooth white marble that it seemed to be made of crystal," he observes. There was no column in the church of Hagia Sophia that was not "jasper or porphyry of rich stones," he adds. In addition he notices the "silver columns" in Hagia Sophia, and the door that bears copper carvings; in this church there had never been "hinge pins" or any other members usually made of iron that were not "completely made of silver."[18] Benjamin of Tudela, who visited Constantinople some years later, expressed the same admiration: "In addition to the Palace inherited by Manuel from his ancestors, he has had built, beside the sea, another called Blachernae, whose walls, and whose pillars too, are covered with gold and silver." Odon of Deuil, a crusader and chaplain to Louis VII of France, described Constantinople in similar terms in 1147.[19] The other cities encountered by the crusaders—Antioch and Tyre—are also mentioned in this respect by travelers. Of particular interest is the description by William of Tyre of the palace of the Cascer of Cairo. Here, "they [Hugh of Caesarea and his brother Fouchez] were introduced into a vaster place which the sun penetrated into, and which was uncovered: there were galleries with marble columns."[20]

No matter how remote the buildings described, they always seem to be wearing the same clothes, so to speak. The same series of topoi reaches even deep inside China. Marco Polo's description of "a city called Shang-tu, which was built by the Great Kahn now reigning, whose name [is] Kubilai," includes a palace "of marble and other ornamental stones. Its halls and chambers are all guilded, and the whole building is marvelously embellished and richly adorned." In the midst of this enclosed park, where there is a beautiful grove, "the Great Kahn has built another large palace, constructed entirely of cane, but with the interior all gilt and decorated with beasts and birds of very skillful workmanship. It is reared on gilt and varnished pillars, on each of which stands a dragon, entwining the pillar with its tail and supporting the roof on his outstretched limbs."[21] His other palaces are equally opulent.

YOU MUST KNOW THAT FOR THREE MONTHS IN THE YEAR, . . . THE GREAT KAHN LIVES IN THE CAPITAL CITY OF CATHAY, WHOSE NAME IS KHAN-BALIK. INSIDE THE WALLS OF THE HALLS AND CHAMBERS ARE ALL COVERED WITH GOLD AND SILVER AND DECORATED WITH PICTURES OF DRAGONS AND BIRDS AND HORSEMEN AND VARIOUS BREEDS OF BEASTS AND SCENES OF BATTLES. THE CEILING IS SIMILARLY ADORNED, SO THAT THERE IS NOTHING TO BE SEEN ANYWHERE BUT GOLD AND PICTURES. . . . THE ROOF IS ABLAZE WITH SCARLET AND GREEN AND BLUE AND YELLOW AND ALL THE COLORS THAT ARE, SO BRILLIANTLY VARNISHED THAT IT GLITTERS LIKE CRYSTAL AND THE SPARKLE OF IT CAN BE SEEN FROM FAR AWAY.[22]

Finally, in the city of Manzi "is the most beautiful and splendid palace in the world that has roofs supported by columns painted and wrought in fine gold and azure. . . . [T]he walls are adorned with paintings and with gilded columns, and the ceiling gorgeously embellished with gold. On the inner walls are pictures of beasts and birds, knights and ladies, and scenes from the history of past kings, portrayed with consummate artistry. On every wall and every ceiling nothing meets the eye but a blaze of gold and brilliant color."[23]

In Albrecht's description of even more fantastic architectural clothing featured in his *Der jüngere Titurel* (1270), the same marvelous, precious details are equally pervasive. The vault of one structure, for example, "schein uz rotem golde" (shines with red gold), the roof is "von rotem gold," the clock is golden, the main tower "gleams with reddish gold," the statues of the evangelists are golden, and the cross-tower "is so golden one would have thought marvels (*wunderwerkes*) had occurred."[24] All the chapels in the temple are "rich with gold"; the ceilings are painted with ornamental reliefs that are "ornamented with gold," intertwined with decorative vines that are "stiff with gold," and covered with marine monsters that "twinkle with gold." Also rich with lustrous reddish gold are "the grilled doors," and "of reddish gold" is the organ.[25] The clothes are made not only of gold but of countless sparkling gems and color pigments. The keystone is a sapphire, the roof crowned by a "big ruby piece" and "painted blue." Sapphires also stud the vault along with carbuncles, or large pearls. The whole is of beryl and decorated coral. The chapel walls "shine with carbuncles," and one "is largely made of emeralds." The windows are made of beryl and crystal.[26]

From one piece of fiction to another, the same elements of architectural bedecking inevitably reappear. In *Perceval le Gallois*, in one castle even "the hinges and screws are of fine gold; one of the leaves of the door is of finely chiseled ivory, the other of finely and beautifully worked ebony wood, and both are illuminated with gold and precious stones." In addition, "the flooring of the hall was of a well-polished mosaic and decorated with the most varied colors, where the most striking were green, vermilion, indigo, and purple."[27] And in *Gauvain,* "in the great hall, in front of the tower, burned a very beautiful fire and all around were sumptuous chairs, covered with a rich silk cloth of purple. The palace is before it. The walls are made of marble and draped with rich silk cloths. Above the windows are so clear that whoever cared to could make out everyone entering the palace. . . . The glass was tinted in the most beautiful and most pleasant colors one could have imagined. And I am very far from telling you everything. In the palace four hundred windows were open, and one hundred were closed."[28]

The world of Islam is a great source of inspiration for these descriptions of brightly, even luminously dressed bodies of buildings. In the *Ladder of Mohammed*—originally written in Arabic, whose translation, extremely popular in Europe in the thirteenth century, influenced Dante—the first heaven is of steel, the second bronze, the third silver, the fourth gold, the fifth a single pearl, the sixth a single emerald, the seventh a single ruby, and the eighth a single topaz. The seventh heaven is the highest, and from it like a citadel one can see the rest. There are two columns there, one of emeralds and the other of rubies, and they are at the door of paradise. Inside, there are a great number of towns and castles that are made of light, and also palaces, dwellings, halls, and rooms; and in all the other places the insides of these towns and castles are made of light.[29] According to Marco Polo, the city of Alaodin has "in a valley between two mountains the biggest and beautiful garden that was ever seen, planted with all the finest fruits in the world and containing the most splendid mansions and palaces that were ever seen, ornamented with gold."[30] And in *Floire et Blancheflor,* imitated from a tale of the *Thousand and One Nights,* there are "high citadels decorated with carbuncles illuminating the night twenty miles round."[31]

Closer to home, in England, Chaucer (1383) describes an imaginary structure equally resplendent with bright materials, the House of Fame:

ME METTE I WAS
WITHIN A TEMPLE Y-MAD OF GLAS;
IN WHICHE THER WERE MO IMAGES
OF GOLD, STONDINGE IN SONDRY STAGES,

. . . .

AND QUEYNTE MANER OF FIGURES
OF OLDE WERKE, THEN I SAW EVER.

. . . .

AL WAS OF STONE OF BERYLE,
BOTHE CASTEL AND THE TOUR,
AND ECK THE HALLE.[32]

Entering the temple in Boccaccio's *Amorosa visione* (1375), one finds a great hall that was "bright and beautiful and resplendent with gold" (chiara era e bella e rispendente d'oro).[33] Moreover, a tower described in the sixth book of his *Filocolo,* so high that it touches the clouds, is covered with marble of white, red, black, and other colors, with windows divided by columns not of marble but of gold and doors not of wood but crystal. And in the tower is a great hall whose roof is held up by twenty porphyry columns with gold capitals; in it are tables and plates, all of gold. "Lastly, the pavement itself is of gold and of precious stones."[34]

Finally, Florence becomes just like these distant and fictional places. The "Terze rime" (1459), which is a description of Cosimo de Medici's palace in Florence, sounds no different from these accounts. It contains as much if not more gold, silver, expensive stones, and bright silk.

AND THE WALLS COMPLETELY COVERED . . .
WITH RICH CLOTHS OF GOLD, SILVER, AND SILK,

·   ·   ·   ·   ·   ·   ·   ·   ·   ·   ·   ·

ON THE BED, ALEXANDRIAN VELVET
ENRICHED WITH FINE SILVER AND GOLD.

·   ·   ·   ·   ·   ·   ·   ·   ·   ·   ·   ·   ·

A GREAT NUMBER [OF ROOMS] WERE ORNAMENTED WITH MANY BOOKS
AND WITH ALABASTER AND BRONZE VASES
OUTLINED WITH FINE GOLD AND SILVER.[35]

Another description of Cosimo's palace, by Niccolò de' Carissimi da Parma, stresses that it is "decorated with . . . gold and fine marble."[36]

Marvelous architectural clothes such as these are not found exclusively in private buildings such as Cosimo's palace. In the choir of Lincoln Cathedral, "the ample surfaces of the two walls were resplendent with gold heightening the effect of the majestic gold of the entrance to the choir." Furthermore in Canterbury Cathedral, two columns are "suitably decorated with gold and silver."[37] Etienne de Tournai declares that he bought "elegant stones that are effulgent on the outside" for the cathedral of Tournai.[38] Dazzling architectural clothing is also prominently featured in Suger's design (1144) for the abbey of Saint-Denis. He refers to the central west portal as having "golden doors." The presence of gold and of gems in the new abbey church is overwhelming, if we are to believe him. He states that the new addition to the building would be "illustrious" thanks to the "elegant craftsmanship of the goldsmith's art and to the wealth of gold and precious stones." He continues: "We made it noble in this way and with such decoration. The outside of the building we adorned with gold-plated copper panels, although not as richly as the occasion demanded, to cover up the cheapness of the stones that would have been visible otherwise . . . namely with refined gold and a profusion of amethysts, emeralds and other precious stones."[39]

In one interesting variation of the theme of architectural clothing, human bodies are themselves used to decorate the architectural body of the building. They are described in exactly the same terms as the other architectural cladding; that is, in terms of their materials. In the section of *Perceval le Gallois* (Perceval the Welshman) entitled "Gauvain chez le Nauto-nier" (Gawain at the Mariner's), we read that "on the other side of the river . . . in a palace of grey marble on the cliff, six hundred windows displayed a multitude of ladies and maidens that were looking at the meadows and the flowering orchards; some were dressed in silk brocade, others in . . . multicolored capes and silk dresses interwoven with gold. From the outside, one noticed from the windows their beautiful bodies from the waists to the gold of their hair."[40]

The architectural clothes described so far stand out not only in their materials but also in their craftsmanship. Boccaccio mentions a fountain so perfectly carved that he "did not know if from a natural source or an artificial one."[41] The author of the "Terze rime" marvels at the "ingenuity" embodied in the "carving, metal work," and "architecture" in Cosimo's palace, done as if by an *uom divino*.[42] For Suger the chased relief work in the abbey church of Saint-Denis is "equally admirable for its form as for its material," so that "certain people might be able to say: the workmanship surpassed the material."[43] Similarly, in Lincoln Cathedral the "craftsmanship fits very well to the price of the material." The skill of the craftsman who constructed the vault is eulogized:

ALMOST LIKE A FLYING BIRD, THE ROOF SPREADS ITS BROAD WINGS
AND, SIMILAR TO A BIRD, IT SOARS TO THE CLOUDS STANDING ON
SOLID COLUMNS. A VISCOUS LIQUID GLUES THE WHITE STONES
THAT THE HAND OF A CRAFTSMAN CHISELED PERFECTLY.
AND THE WALL BUILT FROM THE MASS OF THEM
REFUSES, ALMOST CONTEMPTUOUSLY, TO ACKNOWLEDGE THE PRESENCE
OF SEPARATE PARTS; IT SEEMS TO BE SO,
NOT BY ART BUT BY NATURE. NOT UNIFIED, BUT ONE.[44]

The same author points out the special skill by which the black stones of Purbeck marble have been made to "shine with a high polish": "the surface is ground down by mani-fold rubbing of sand," then "the solid marble is permeated with strong vinegar." As a result of this process, the outer surface of the shafts of the columns are "more polished than the growing fingernail, or a shining star[,] . . . almost as in nature."[45] Gervase of Canterbury, speaking of his own cathedral, draws special attention to the construction skill necessary for the replacement of load-bearing walls by the new gothic vault. Albrecht considers the vaults of the temple of the Holy Grail "precious because of the materials and because of the art." [46] Chaucer admires the craftsmanship in the House of Fame whose masonry is so skillful that the building seems to be "withouten peces or joininges," giving the impression of "many subtil compassinges." [47] In one instance, a building described by Odoric of Pordenone in 1321—the palace of the Mongolian Kubla Khan—is wearing perfume. Here "all the walls were covered with red leather," from an animal that is "very sweet smelling," and they release a "sweet odor." [48]

* * *

So far we have looked at writings describing the coverings that swathe architectural bodies. But there is another group of *mirabilia* writings, in which that architectural body begins, surprisingly, to stir beneath its coverings. It begins to express itself, so to speak, in ways that suggest a core of vitality deep beneath the sartorial surface. The buildings so described are powered by automata, of course. Like other automata, they rely on the metaphor of the body as a machine. [49] But overlaying this metaphor is that of the body as a building. Indeed, there is something undeniably anthropomorphic about the way some of these buildings move, or parts of them move, as if they were living human beings. And as they move, architectural anthropomorphism takes on a more animated aspect.

Marco Polo describes an architectural body whose actions are loyal. A church in Samarkand triumphs over matter and defies the very laws of gravity in support of the cause of its builders. The stone at the base of a column supporting the roof of the church had been stolen by the Christians from the Saracens. When the nephew of the Great Khan ordered it to be removed and handed back to its rightful owners, the column that had been resting on the stone rose up "to a height fully three palms and stayed there as firmly supported as if the stone had still been underneath. And from that day onwards the column has remained in this position, and there it still is." [50]

Buildings can act in a benevolent way. Thus, the stones in the temple of the Holy Grail in Albrecht's *Der jüngere Titurel* are endowed with healing properties; the palace of the Great Kahn, according to Marco Polo, keeps rainy and cloudy weather at bay and the sun shining above it constantly. [51]

But other buildings can be sadistic and cruel. When Gauvain sits on the "Marvelous Bed" in one castle, it triggers a mechanism that instantly launches a hail of arrows at him from the walls, then sends in a famished lion to attack him. In another case, a sword suspended from the ceiling swoops down and slices off a thin piece of his flesh every time he tries to make love to the damsel lying next to him. [52]

Some are crazy and dangerous, such as the "Twirling Castle" in *Le chateau tournoyant,* which swirled faster than the wind and had in its crenellations archers of copper that no arms in the world could protect against. Beside these automata were men of flesh and bones who blew their horns and trumpets "so loud that it seemed the earth would collapse." Lions and bears chained to the walls growled so loud that the whole valley echoed. Perlesvaus "headed at great speed on his horse toward the twirling castle. He hit the door so hard that it sunk three fingers deep into a marble pillar." At that, the lions and the bears go back to their cages and the castle comes to a stop. Yet another castle has before it a "perilous bridge" with a twirling blade that cuts the tail off the Knight of the Parrot's horse as he charges to enter it.[53]

Some are obnoxious. Liutprand, bishop of Cremona, reporting on a visit to Constantinople in 969, describes a palace where he was received by Emperor Constantine. It contained an amazing throne surrounded by mechanical lions covered with gold that beat the ground with their tails and gave dreadful roars with open mouths and quivering tongues. Then when he had three times made obeisance to the emperor with his face to the ground, he lifted his head, "and behold! the man whom just before I had seen sitting on a moderately elevated seat had now changed his raiment and was sitting on the level of the ceiling," thus cutting short any discussion between the two as the wide distance between them rendered conversation "unseemly."[54]

Other buildings are hyperactive. In the anonymous eleventh-century *Le voyage de Charlemagne,* for instance, the Great Hall in the palace of the legendary Hugo of Constantinople is one gigantic mechanical *mirabilium* that "turns with the wind," to the great delight of his guests.[55] And, finally, one talks back. In the Castle of Hesdin there is a window "in which there is a box suspended in the air." The window "answers all questions that are asked of it," and one can really "hear the voice coming from that box."[56]

*   *   *

All these buildings are described in the same terms used by the patristic writers, insofar as the emphasis is on the clothes that cover their bodies and on giving the buildings human characteristics. But the attitudes expressed toward the buildings are vastly different. The nucleus of feelings is associated not with revilement and ignominy but with the "marvelous."[57] The main characteristic of the marvelous is, as Le Goff points out, disbelief. The author often accompanies such descriptions with "I really did see this." This reveals strangeness and novelty that the experience of these unfamiliar metaphorical architectural bodies produces.

And indeed many writers even admit to being at a loss for words. "I saw so many other admirable things that I am unable to recite them," Alexander the Great is made to exclaim to his mother in his fictional letter recounting the wonders of India. "To describe such magnificence would be a task beyond my capabilities," confesses Albrecht.[58] "One would never be able to relate to you the great nobility of this chapel," Robert of Clari exclaims about the chapel of the Blachernae in Constantinople. Repeatedly he laments his inability to describe to his readers the buildings he has seen there: "One could never ever tell or say the truth."[59]

Similarly, as William of Tyre is writing about a mission with which he has been charged in Antioch, he interjects in the middle of his account, as if he can't control himself, an encomium of Constantinople:

IF I WANTED TO UNDERTAKE THE ACCOUNT IN THIS WRITING OF THE GAMES OF THE CIRCUS [OF CONSTANTINE] THAT THE INHABITANTS OF THIS CITY CALL THE HIPPODROME, AND THE IMPACT OF THE DIFFERENT SPECTACLES THAT WERE OFFERED TO THE PEOPLE DURING THESE SOLEMN DAYS, AND TO DESCRIBE THE IMPERIAL MAGNIFICENCE WITH REGARD TO THE GARMENTS AND ALL THE JEWELRY OF PRECIOUS STONES AND PEARLS OF AN INCALCULABLE WEIGHT AND NUMBER; IF I HAD TO SPEAK OF THE INFINITE RICHES IN PURE GOLD AND SILVER, OF THE SUPERB CURTAINS SUSPENDED ON ALL SIDES TO DECORATE THE APARTMENTS, AND ENUMERATE ALL THE SERVANTS AND ALL THE PEOPLE OF THE COURT; IF I WANTED TO RECOUNT IN EVERY DETAIL THE POMP AND MAGNIFICENCE OF THE WEDDING CELEBRATIONS AND ALL THE ACTS OF LIBERALITY THROUGH WHICH THE EMPEROR WIELDED HIS GREATNESS BEFORE ALL THE PEOPLE . . . THEN I WOULD SUCCUMB UNDER THE IMMENSITY OF SUCH A TASK, IF I HAD TO MAKE OF THESE THINGS A PARTICULAR ACCOUNT. THIS IS WHY I GO BACK TO THE REST OF MY STORY.[60]

Again, describing a palace in Cairo, William remarks that "the elegance of the materials and of the works retained the gaze of all that passed, and the avid eye, attracted by the novelty of this spectacle, had great difficulty in disengaging itself from it, and could not get its fill of this vision."[61]

To those who do not directly experience them, these sights are unbelievable. Gervase of Canterbury avows that his verbal account of Canterbury Cathedral is "less clear and less delectable than would be a direct experience of the forms."[62] The same is true of the author of *Gauvain chez le nautonier.* "On the other side of the river, on the cliff, rises a castle so strong, so well set out, and so rich that never has the eye of a man seen anything similar," the author writes. "Never had Gawain in his whole life seen such opulent ones." But he insists, "I will have you know that I am not telling you fables."[63]

In the "Terze rime," the palace of Cosimo de' Medici is similarly described as almost unbelievably novel:

SO MARVELOUS AND SO SMOOTH

THAT IT IS LIKE NO OTHER

. . . .

NO ONE DEAD OR ALIVE

EVER SAW SUCH A BEAUTIFUL BUILDING ON EARTH

AS THE ONE THAT HAS BEEN BUILT BY THIS ILLUSTRIOUS CITIZEN.

About the same building, Niccolò de' Carissimi too expresses amazement and disbelief: "These things I do not say distinctly, which would not be possible, because these are things that are not only inexpressible but also unimaginable, and that whoever sees them believes them to be divine rather than earthly. And everyone believes this house to be the most elegant and ornamented that ever existed, and beyond compare."[64]

For Hugh of Lincoln's biographer, the experience of such amazing architecture is so unfamiliar that he apologizes for his descriptions as being "quasi pueriliter" (almost as if by a child).[65] Gervase of Canterbury ends his description of Canterbury Cathedral by admitting that he lacks the words to faithfully render the object and by urging that his readers see the building for themselves, since it "may be more clearly and pleasantly seen by the eye than taught in writing."[66] Albrecht predicts that his description of the beauty of the temple of the Holy Grail will be received with incredulity because so seldom are such sights witnessed. Should one think him a liar, he admonishes, it can only be because one so rarely gets the opportunity to behold art and magnificence.[67]

There was probably no one readier with minute descriptions than Marco Polo. His book is one long catalogue of things encountered. Most of the time he can describe them without much difficulty. For example, he discusses geography: "In the heart of greater Armenia is a very high mountain, shaped like a cube, on which Noah's Ark is said to have rested. . . . It is so broad and long that it takes two days to go around it. On the summit the snow lies so deep all year round that no one can ever climb it; this snow never entirely melts." Elsewhere, he notes odd details of natural history: "At the end of the three day's journey lies a city called Ishkashan, which is ruled by a count. His other cities and towns are in the mountains. Through the midst of this city flows a river of considerable size. In this district are a lot of porcupines. When hunters set their dogs on them in hopes to kill, the porcupines curl up and then shoot out their quills." Near the Georgian border he comes upon "a spring from which gushes a stream of oil, in such abundance that a hundred ships may be loaded there at once. This oil is not good to eat; but it is good for burning and as a salve for men and camels affected with itch or scab." But before the Palace of Manzi, he is dumb with amazement. "No words of mine could describe its superlative magnificence," he writes, "but I will briefly relate some of its main features."[68]

For all the strangeness of these buildings emerging out of those metaphors, the main feeling they evoke in the beholders is another component of marvel: unabashed delight. "Gaude mi, carissima mater" (rejoice for me, dearest mother), exclaims the fictive Alexander the Great about the ingenious wonders he has encountered in the course of his military campaign.[69] For Rabanus Maurus, the cladding of a building is tantamount to *venustas,* that is, something associated with seduction and the cult of Venus. When it comes to describing the pleasure of beholding these architectural clothes, the authors pay no attention to the patristic strictures discussed in chapter 7. Albrecht, for his part, is quite exuberant. "If only I could gaze on them again," he exclaims about the bright windows of the temple of the Holy Grail. "It was a beautiful spectacle," he continues, "its charms were infinite."[70] Robert of Clari writes about the exhilarating effect of Constantinople on his fellow crusaders: "The pilgrims gazed upon . . . the great marvels that were in the city; and they marveled mightily."[71] This sense of marvel and exhilaration with the bedecked, and at times animated, architectural bodies of the *mirabilia* is the first step in the humanist rethinking of architecture and in a fundamental change in architectural thinking itself

.

9

✳✳✳✳
✳✳✳✳

THE DIVINE BODY

T HERE WAS SOMETHING NAIVE AND UNGUARDED ABOUT THE pursuit of *libido aedificandi* exhibited by the writers in the last chapter. The second strategy in the battle for beauty in architecture is different. Full of sophistry, its underlying intention is to blur its distinctions from the older doctrine. This strategy borrows many of the features of the old and thus begins to subvert orthodoxy from within. Through an adept kind of double-talk, the new strategy conceals its nonconformity and in fact appears to comply with accepted values. By intentionally cultivating ambiguity, it attempts to destroy the old without a trace of a struggle.

The architectural bodies described here, unlike those of chapter 8, are all real, not fictional, though now the metaphorical bodies are not human but divine. Moreover, instead of being indirectly symbolized through architectural clothes, the buildings are naked. And the feelings they inspire are even more pleasurable than those that accompanied the marvelous body. We have traveled very far from the admonitions against architectural *voluptas* that we looked at in chapter 7. Far from being condemned, the desire for architectural bodies is in fact often vented in an ecstatic—sometimes even erotic, albeit exalted—register.

The body is now that of a divine being: the apostles, Christ, the Virgin, the Holy Spirit, or God himself.[1] Reference to elements of the church as metaphorical representations of either the apostles or the church fathers is quite common. Honorius of Autun writes that the columns that support the house of God are the bishops who "keep the organization of the church in a high rectitude of life." The stained glass windows are the wise men: "The transparent windows that keep out the storms and introduce the light are the teachers that resist the storm of heresies and spread the light of the doctrine to the church. The glass of the windows through which the rays pierce is the mind of the teachers that contemplates the heavenly things almost like in a mirror and in an enigma."[2] Similarly, the church towers of the Milan cathedral are made in a "square form according to the order of geometry," because around the throne of God in his celestial abode there are the four evangelists.[3]

The Virgin is another source of the bodily metaphor in architecture. Hugh of Lincoln, for example, sees in the hewn white stone of his own cathedral something of her "whiteness" and "well-formedness." Its whiteness stands for her *pudor* and its well-formedness for her *dogma*. The marble, which is "smooth, gleaming, and snow white" is an embodiment of the "bride" who is simple, gentle, hard working. The smoothness of the marble "truly exemplifies" the "simplicity" of the Virgin; its polish, her *mores;* its darkness, her *labor.*[4] The deed by which the abbey of Saint-Ouen decides to enlarge its church contains the claim that "the church represents our mother, made by hand and with building material."[5]

In the anonymous *Cursor mundi,* the description of the body of the Virgin is inspired by Grosseteste's *Le château d'amour:*

A CASTLE OF HELP AND COMFORT STANDS HIGH ON A ROCK, SO POLISHED THAT NO WEAPON CAN TOUCH IT: IT IS ENCLOSED BY FOUR STONE WALLS AND A DEEP DITCH, FORTIFIED WITH BATTLEMENTS AND BARBICANS, WITH GATE AND TOWER. EVERY FUGITIVE CAN TAKE REFUGE THERE. IT IS PAINTED WITH THREE COLOURS, THE FOUNDATIONS GREEN, THE MIDDLE BLUE, THE BATTLEMENTS RED. A CLEAR WELL, FROM WHICH RUN FOUR ALL-HEALING STREAMS, SPRINGS FROM THE TOWER. WITHIN THE TOWER IS A THRONE, WITH THE BRILLIANT LIGHT OF WHICH THE BRIGHT COLOURS MINGLE. THE CASTLE IS A SHIELD AGAINST OUR ENEMIES. THE POLISHED ROCK IS MARY'S HEART, THE GREEN COLOUR BETO-KENS HER END, THE BLUE IS HER LOVE AND TRUTH, THE RED HER HOLY CHARITY. THE FOUR TOWERS ARE THE FOUR CARDINAL VIRTUES; THE SEVEN BARBICANS REPRESENT THE SEVEN OTHER VIRTUES WHICH QUELL THE SEVEN SINS. THE WELL IS MARY'S MERCY, WHICH CAN NEVER BE EXHAUSTED, THE BRILLIANT THRONE IS CHRIST, WHO MADE HIS SEAT IN MARY'S SOUL."[6]

The architectural body of the Virgin is sometimes described in erotic terms. Jo-annes de Janduno justifies the pleasure he feels while entering the Chapel of the Virgin in Notre Dame cathedral in this way: upon crossing the threshold, he writes, "one feels as if ravished to heaven." Using a related metaphor, Godfrey Admonensis describes the manner in which Christ "entered" and "departed" the Castle of the Body of the Virgin in such a way as not to "violate" but rather to "decorate" and "glorify" it.[7]

Buildings can be the embodiment of God himself. In Honorius, the ring at the base of the dome in a church is *Deus*.[8] Roger Bacon (1267) sanctions the imitation in *opera artificialia* (earthly buildings) of biblical prototypes—the temple of Solomon in Ezekiel, Noah's ark in Esdras—that so far are immaterial, only described *in scriptura,* on the grounds that they would induce in the onlooker a state of divine transport and exaltation. "If only the materialization of such prototypes could be placed before our eyes!" he writes:

WE WOULD BE ELATED IN THE HEREAFTER WITH NOAH, HIS SONS, AND ALL THE LIVING BEINGS WHO HAVE ACCEPTED THEIR OWN PLACES AND RANKS, AND WITH THE ARMY OF THE LORD, WE WOULD KEEP GUARD IN THE DESERT AROUND THE TABERNACLE OF GOD, THE TABLE OF THE COMMANDMENTS AND THE ALTAR, AND THE HOLY OF HOLIES, GIVING A PLACE TO THE CHERUBIM, AND WE WOULD SEE THE OTHER SIGNS OF THAT ANCIENT PEOPLE AS BEING PRESENT. AFTER THIS, THE INSTABILITY OF THE IMPERMANENT TABERNA-CLE WILL BE ELIMINATED AND THEN WE WOULD ENTER THE STABLE TEMPLE OF THE LORD MADE BY THE WISDOM OF SOLOMON. AND WITH EZEKIEL WE WOULD CONTEMPLATE IN THE SPIRIT OF EXULTATION THAT WHICH HE HAS UNDERSTOOD ONLY SPIRITUALLY, SO THAT AFTER THE REPAIRING OF THE NEW JERUSALEM WE AT LAST WOULD ENTER WITH ESDRA AND NEHEMIAH THE GREAT HOUSE THAT HAD TO BE DECORATED WITH EVEN MORE GLORY.[9]

In fact, for Roger Bacon, the essence of transport caused by the divine bodies made architectural flesh is the tantalizing of the senses at their sight: "If we contemplated the spiritual and the literal sense of the Scriptures, we would be excited by the visible instruments and we would be glad that we know that all things have been completed in the church of God, which show their corporeal bodies themselves to our eyes." All this, he claims, rests on the authority of the Scriptures: "Just as the Father teaches us from his own scriptures, so all the ancient wise men have dealt with the Scriptures."[10]

Such writings serve to thwart the *contemptus mundi* tenets of patristic authors by providing an excuse for earthly architectural pursuits. But there is another approach that serves the same end. Based on the fourth-century writings of the Hellenistic philosopher known as the pseudo-Dionysius, its most prominent spokesman is Suger. It displays a number of features that might explain its quick rise to prominence once it makes its appearance in the twelfth century.[11] First, it is a grand unifying theory, founded not on a point-by-point denial or subversion of the elements of the patristic tradition but on an alternative, systematic theology. Second, it is intentionally obscure, and therefore difficult for upholders of the patristic tradition to refute. Third, it has an aura of prestige, for its source is the most prominent center of learning of the times, Constantinople. Fourth, and most significant for our concerns, is that in this theology, which is often referred to as the theology of light, the divine presence is manifested through light. This means that potentially everything that shines is a metaphor for the divine.

Because God's body is a divine body of light, the church too becomes one. Indeed Suger's Saint-Denis is a showcase of gleaming gems and, above all, gleaming gold: "We hastened to adorn the main Altar of the Blessed Denis where there was only one beautiful and precious frontal panel from Charles the Bald, the third Emperor; . . . we had it all encased, putting up golden panels on either side and adding a fourth, even more precious one; so that the whole altar would appear golden all the way round."[12] And thus contemplation of the church is a means of contemplating God, of being elevated to a state of mystical exaltation and elevation toward God, through "anagogy" with the divine:

THUS, WHEN—OUT OF MY DELIGHT IN THE BEAUTY OF THE HOUSE OF GOD—THE LOVELINESS OF THE MANY-COLORED GEMS HAS CALLED ME AWAY FROM EXTERNAL CARES, AND WORTHY MEDITATION HAS INDUCED ME TO REFLECT, TRANSFERRING THAT WHICH IS MATERIAL TO THAT WHICH IS IMMATERIAL, ON THE DIVERSITY OF THE SACRED VIRTUES: THEN IT SEEMS TO ME THAT I SEE MYSELF DWELLING, AS IT WERE, IN SOME STRANGE REGION OF THE UNIVERSE WHICH NEITHER EXISTS ENTIRELY IN THE SLIME OF THE EARTH NOR ENTIRELY IN THE PURITY OF HEAVEN; AND THAT, BY THE GRACE OF GOD, I CAN BE TRANSPORTED FROM THIS INFERIOR TO THAT SUPERIOR WORLD IN AN ANAGOGICAL MANNER.[13]

The same metaphor of the building as a divine, radiant body of light is expressed in the writings of another of the great patrons of ecclesiastical buildings, Hugh of Lincoln, in briefer form but in no less ecstatic a register. In his eyes, the stained-glass windows of his cathedral shine with a "divine light" through which he himself, as a member of the "radiant army of the clergy," helped "illuminate the world."[14]

Less purely spiritual is Robert Grosseteste's image of the architectural experience of God. For his *Templum Domini,* he claims there should be two temples: the "ghostly" temple in which to receive the godhead and the bodily temple in which to receive God's manhood.[15] But all pretense of metaphysical elevation and virtue behind this *libido aedificandi* would disappear, as we shall see in the next chapter
.

10
*****
*****

THE HUMANIST BODY

T HE PRECEDING TWO CHAPTERS PRESENTED STAGES IN THE transformation of the metaphor of the building as a body. It first served to recategorize architecture from something evil to something marvelous, then from something marvelous to something divine. Now, in the third and final stage, the body of the building becomes humanist.

We are no longer in the realm of fabulation and fantasy, or that of mystical metaphysics. We are now in the world of Renaissance architectural treatises and drawings. Whereas the authors of the documents previously examined were nonarchitects, here they are directly involved in building. The writing becomes bound up with the thinking of practicing architects: professionals and insiders, people used to conceiving architectural forms for clients, concerned with functional, visual, and engineering innovations. This means that the anthropomorphic metaphor reverberates with more force. In this final strategy, the tone of caution that has characterized the argumentation up until now is abandoned. Restraint gives way to assertiveness and an uninhibited eroticism in the use of the anthropomorphic architectural metaphor.

Due to a strange cultural oversight, scholars have tended to overlook the obvious eroticism of the anthropomorphic architectural metaphor of the early Italian Renaissance and see in it purely the expression of Platonic geometry and proportion.[1] Yet, if there is a prevalent topos in the representation of architecture at this time, it is its unabashed eroticism. This is why Filarete likens a building to the child of the union between architect and patron, and the act of designing to the sexual act; there is no chapter of Francesco di Giorgio's treatise that does not open with an invocation of the bodily metaphor, and his Corinthian column is a slender young body of a girl, his ideal fortified city a nude youth; Leonardo's and Cesariano's Vitruvian figure is emphatically virile. Alberti opens his discussion in *De re aedificatoria* about beauty and ornament with the body: "The great experts of antiquity, as we mentioned earlier, have instructed us that a building is very like an animal, and that Nature must be imitated when we delineate it. Let us investigate, then, why some bodies that Nature produces may be called beautiful, others less beautiful, and even ugly." As an example, he compares a building to the figure of a young girl: "one man might prefer the tenderness of a slender girl; yet a character in a comedy preferred one girl over all others because she was plumper and more buxom; and you perhaps might prefer a wife neither so slender of figure as to appear sickly nor so stout of limb as to resemble a village bully." Similarly, he likens the entrance of a house to its "bosom" and columns to bodies with a "neck," "belly," and a "navel."[2]

From this point of view, the *Hypnerotomachia* is clearly representative of the thinking that characterized Renaissance humanist architecture. It is simply its most oneiric, struggling, questing expression.

* * *

Poliphilo loves architecture. He describes his "senses" becoming "captivated with excessive pleasure" before the pyramid (b3v). At the sight of the triumphal arch, he is filled with "excessive pleasure." The ruins of an archaeological site, which he is "exquisitely exploring," transport him with "tacit joy" (p4) and with "the greatest delectation and pleasure" (q6v). In some baths, he finds himself in a state of "extreme delight and pleasure" (e6) and becomes "totally immersed in joy and contentment" (e6v). Before the pyramid, again, he is "all confused with inconceivable pleasure" (a7v). "Oh, with what festivity and with what delight of my exhilarated heart did I look upon it, . . . with what unbridled delight and lust did I see it" (d5), he sighs before the palace of Queen Eleutherillida. "Oh how happy I was to be in such a place," he exclaims before another building, his delectation "being so extreme that to express it is inconceivable" (h2). He wanders through a peristyle in a garden that affords him "incredible joyfulness in viewing it" (t7). "Gratifying to the eyes" (b5) is how he qualifies a mausoleum. The ruins provide him with the "most delightful solace" (r4v) and again he is "delighted with incredible solace" before them (q6). Full of "pleasure and solace and such delectable feelings," he contemplates the amphitheater (v5v). Later the same amphitheater fills him with "distraction and excessive and happy solace" (y6v). Among the few utterances the mostly silent Polia addresses to him is that she knows that antique buildings are "extremely pleasing for you to look at" (p5v).

Poliphilo, of course, experiences his love with his mind. Love is intellectually and spiritually elevating. An orange grove next to some baths is pleasing because it is "worthy of the estimation of the intellect" (e8v). The goodness of architecture springs from the intellect of the artist: good architecture, he affirms, "corrects our confused ignorance and detestable presumptuousness and damnable errors." It is a "clear light," and, at its contemplation, our "obscured eyes" are "uncovered." He admires the "sharp prescient investigations" of the "perspicacious" architect and what he calls the excess of the *subtiligiencia* "the architect displays, along with his "incredible power of thinking and his great and extremely exquisite investigation." Poliphilo is struck with admiration by the pyramid, because it is a "pure product of the intellect" (d1).

But, as he relentlessly attests, one word sums up Poliphilo's appreciation of architecture, and that is *voluptas*. "How voluptuous was the pleasure I felt," he exclaims upon seeing a temple (m6v). "Voluptuously" he contemplates some antique ruins; "with extreme voluptuousness," he is overcome by them (p4v). He is "inflamed with voluptuousness" at the sight of the temple door (c1v); he is filled "with extreme voluptuousness" (f7) as he comes upon the "voluptuous" palace of Queen Eleutherillida (g7), whose "voluptuous delightfulness" he admires (g7v). The amphitheater fills him with "happy and voluptuous" solace (y6v).

This response only increases once he has entered the building. As Poliphilo says: "I cannot say whether I was insensate and stupidly in love or overtaken with extreme voluptuousness" (g8). Over the fountain in the amphitheater, which he contemplates with "so much voluptuousness" (v5v) in the center of the "voluptuous" (s8) island of Cythera, he becomes "exhilarated with voluptuousness and burn[s] with a sweet flame," which runs all through him "delightfully and indefensibly" (z5v). "Voluptuously inviting, attracting, provoking" (ibid.): so he and Polia find the fountain. The mere thought of the ruins of an antique city fills him "with voluptuousness" (p5v). He feels that the pleasure of conceiving and constructing such places in antiquity must have been equal. "With what voluptuousness," he wonders, must the architect have conceived the pyramid (b3).

So intense is Poliphilo's feeling of architectural *voluptas* that he becomes totally "enraptured and captured" by it, so entirely "conquered and occupied" by it that he can "think of nothing else." He beholds a pyramid in "a stupor" that he feels "sharply and obstinately" (a7v). He experiences such "pleasure and delight" before a temple that he "loses his senses" (d6). Before a palace, which is "such a delightful place," he is rendered "not a little stupefied and separated from his soul" (d7v). The obelisk contains "such a great amount of marvels" that he is driven "insensate with stupor at its contemplation" (a8). The garden of a queen he finds to be such an "excessively delectable artifice" that it cannot but "exhaust any human intuition and sense" (u2v). In addition, it leaves him "hallucinating and equally oppressed in all his senses, distracted by the lovely variety of excessive contemplation," "completely hallucinating and excessively engaged in the delight of looking" (g7, h3v). He finds himself "perplexed in the mind" (*circonfulto nella mente,* d1) before a pyramid, and "seduced to such a degree" before a small temple in a graveyard that he becomes "deprived of any other capacity to think" (p8). In the baths, he becomes "full of hallucinations in all his senses and stupefied" (f2v). So strongly does the pyramid affect him that he enters a "trancelike state" (h2). At the sight of a fountain he finds himself "filled with stupor," so "delectable was it to my senses" (ev). In fact, Poliphilo's voluptuous love is so intense that it totally overpowers his purely intellectual appreciation of architecture. Before the pyramid he stresses that "the delight of contemplating it exceeded my great admiration" (d4).

The buildings Poliphilo loves are voluptuous themselves. They include many unclad bodies, in the form of sculptures adorning them. The palace of Queen Eleutherillida contains a fountain in the shape of three nymphs whose breasts serve as water spouts (e1v–e2). On the wall of a palace, part of a wall is taken up by the frieze of a sleeping nymph. Her naked hips and legs are so realistically carved, according to Poliphilo, that they seem to be made of living flesh. "The legs were still those of a young girl," he observes, "with the rounded knees slightly bent toward her in such a way as to show her fine feet" (d8v). In the *pastophores,* or nymphs that presided over weddings, carved in cameos on either side of the arch of the door, there are "milk-white and candid figures, with virginal little bodies revealing parts of their lovely chests and with their hair disheveled" (c6).

The bodies adorning the buildings do not only belong to nymphs. Over this same nymph the satyr looms, in a state of "lascivious prurience and excitement" (d8). Similarly, from the altar of Bacchus extends a protrusion, "rigidly rigorous" (mv). The sexes are mingled hermaphroditically in this architecture. In antiquity every temple "to one sex or the other had to be dedicated ritually, whether it be to a god or a goddess, to a father or a mother, or a mother and son" (c4v). This is why the columns on either side of the door to the pyramid, dedicated to the Venus and Eros, are bisexual. The bottom third of the two columns, left rough and unfluted are male. The flutings of the top are more smooth and lascivious, he states, "because the feminine one exceeded the virile one in lasciviousness" (c4v). There is also an invocation of homoerotic ardor in one building, where the figure of Ganymede being carried off by the eagle is embossed on the keystone of the triumphal arch (c4v, c6).

Bodies serve not merely as adornment but provide the very stuff of which the buildings are made. References to the corporeality of buildings abound in the book. Poliphilo praises "the most wise master Vitruvius," who compared buildings "to the well-proportioned and decorously dressed human body" (c6v). He himself observes that the ornamentation on the door to the pyramid gives a definite "corpulence to the door" (d1). "True corpulence" is also what he sees as a result of the entasis in the temple of Venus Physozoi (m7). Poliphilo refers to both the veinless marble of a portico and the skin of a nude nymph in the baths as "flawless" (i1v, e6). He points to the "virginal makeup" of the marble of the entrance to the temple (b3). In contrast, the darkly veined marble of the altar of Bacchus has been specially selected to express the virility of that deity.

Poliphilo loves architecture more than he loves Polia. Although he is waiting to be taken to the island of love by Cupid so that he may seduce his beloved Polia there, he is irresistably drawn away from the appointed meeting place, to "wander licentiously in this deserted building collapsed by age and consumed by fire" (p5v). He becomes "extremely confused with unthinkable pleasure" and is filled with "multiplying desire" (a7).

The buildings fill the narrator with strong feelings of *voluptas*. When he writes that certain buildings are "delectable" to his senses and that the amphitheater provided "so many delights to the human senses" (y5v), he means it. His eyes get excited at the sight of buildings. He becomes "almost captivated" (*quasi rapto*): "[I] lifted my eyes and saw before me an artificial pergola that was of the highest visual pleasure" (e8v); "with what great pleasure I gazed at it," he exclaims upon encountering another garden (f4). Involved also is his sense of touch. Before the frieze of the sleeping nymph, he cannot refrain from "placing his hand and stroking and fondling" it (b8). In the baths where he disrobes and swims, his pleasure is above all olfactory. "Ecstatically" he enters the pool, which has "so many fragrances that never in

Arabia could they have grown them," and the structure itself filled with delicious fragrances coming from the "redolent resins and woods" (e6, e5v). Kneeling before the fountain of Venus he "avidly" smells "its wonderful fresh fragrance" (y7v). In the amphitheater he is so "distracted with so many pleasures" that he "forgets to control" himself. He is reduced to "avidly" inhaling the fragrance also emanating from that building, which is "virginal" like the body of Polia (y6v).

He finds the acoustic side of architecture no less seductive, taking pleasure in the sounds that buildings make. In many, there is a "tinkling sound of falling water." A *locus amoenus* he comes upon in a garden he admires because it "resounds everywhere with sweet warblings" (d7v). At the fountain of Venus again, in the "pleasant and incredibly delicious site" decorated "with springtime ornamentation, with the air full of the sweet songs of birds flying through the lush greenery and the senses ecstatic and with the most lovely nymphs singing melodies together, their enchanting tones accompanied with divine and modest movements moved me to extreme voluptuousness" (y7).

What is it about these buildings that drives the narrator to such extremes? It is, their mechanical, construction, and hydraulic engineering; their display of architectural knowledge; their formal innovations; their integration with nature; their perfect proportions carried out according to *concinnitas*—all the features that, as we have seen, characterize the architectural treatise in the *Hypnerotomachia* as Albertian.

The *voluptas* derived from architecture heightens until it becomes an insatiable appetite. Poliphilo's walk through his beloved ancient ruins excites these longings. He compares his state to that of a "rapacious animal," as he gazed "with the greatest delectation and pleasure, admiring and ever more avid to find even more. I was like an animal searching for a prey getting ever more desirable. This is how I wandered through the ruins, some with broken columns, some with whole ones" (q6v). The more architectural *voluptas* Poliphilo gets, the more he wants—or, in his own words, the more "ardently invaded" (q8) and the more "lustfully attracted to investigate other novelties" (q6) he becomes. He finds himself filled "with a curious, lustful desire to look upon other new things" (r4v). Before the ruins he finds himself "inflamed with a curious cupidinousness" (p7v). He becomes "obsessed with unthinkable and exquisite elevation" in front of an obelisk (p5). "Nothing absolutely could satisfy my avid eyes and inexplicable appetite to gaze and gaze again," he explains as he looks over the pyramid (d1). His love of architecture is an "appetite" that is "insatiable," and the distress of wanting and not getting fills him with "a keen and noble commotion" (d2, c4). In a graveyard, his desire is such that "even more without doubt it excited his soul insatiably to investigate yet other things" (q7v). "Without tiring with the present things nor with enough of them," he contemplates the palace of Queen Eleutherillida, "still more avid" (h2). Just as "avidly," he beholds an obelisk, only to discover once more that "his desire is only multiplied in doing so" (a7v).

58. THE TRIUMPHAL ARCH (FRENCH EDITION).

Poliphilo's architectural *voluptas* becomes so great that it becomes intolerable and he loses control. "So suddenly excited" by the sight of a temple, he begins to sigh "hotly" (b3). At times he becomes so aroused that he finds himself "looking with instability and indeterminacy" (d1). He finds it difficult to control his body. As his breathing becomes spasmodic, he begins to pant and to "gasp with his mouth open" (d1). He sighs, and then is taken by surprise by the echo of his sigh that returns to him amplified through the ruins. "I was excited to tears" by them (q7v). He loses his power of speech upon entering the pyramid. "It happened that I looked upon it again most intensively, with open mouth," he explains, "to such a point that I was rendered speechless." Thus "robbed of my soul, it was as if I had nothing left inside me" (d2v).

Poliphilo has just set off on his *erotomachia,* his amorous quest. He is all alone, wandering through the ruins. He pines for Polia and, in his despair of ever finding her, so weeps and sobs that the sound reverberates loudly against the buildings that surround him. Startled, he raises his eyes, and suddenly, through his tears, from afar, he notices the triumphal arch that serves as the entrance to the pyramid (fig. 58). He finds it architecturally interesting and admires its "incredible artifice and elegant outline" (c1–c3v). It "brings to mind the loving and celestial Idea of his divine and immeasurably desirable Polia." Aroused by the "noble commotion" arising from the "pleasing love that he feels for the solid body of the building," Poliphilo is passionately drawn to it; he advances toward it, "extremely confused with a pleasure that he had never imagined possible" (a7v).

This first experience will be frustrating. In front of the arch is a horse, and written across the horse's forehead are the letters *GENEA,* meaning "origin" in Greek and, by extension, "first time." Poliphilo notes that the pedestal bearing the horse refers to the "stallion of unhappiness" (*equus infoelicitatis*). In fact he is rearing in such panic that he has bucked all the little cupids who are trying to ride him into the entrance of the triumphal arch (b4). And some bas-reliefs on the pedestal bespeak the same pessimism. The right panel of the pedestal is sculpted with fourteen dancing figures, seven men and seven women. They are dancing in one big circle, one sex alternating with the other, but there is no contact between the sexes (fig. 59). The men hold hands with men, women with women, and the arms of the former

59. THE DANCE OF THE SEVEN COUPLES.

pass under those of the latter. Each of the figures wears two masks, one in front that bears a laughing face and another on the back that cries, in such a way that as they advance, an unhappy face is always turned toward a happy one. The other panel of the pedestal hardly gives a happier picture of the relation between the sexes. It represents a number of young men plucking flowers in a field, surrounded by nymphs who appear nervous and agitated as if being robbed of something. Under the first panel we read "Waste" (*Amissio*); under the second, "Time" (*Tempus*).

A similar message of futility is expressed by the next omen, the building in the shape of the elephant (fig. 60)—a symbol of modesty and chastity in the iconological tradition.[3] Inside it Poliphilo finds a sculpture of a naked man and woman facing one another (fig. 61). An epigram beneath the man ends with the words "Let me be" repeated three times— once in Latin, once in Greek, once in Hebrew—while an epigram beneath the woman finishes with the words, likewise three times and in the same three languages, "Do not touch my body."

60. THE ELEPHANT.

Poliphilo begins his approach to the building and heads for its second entrance, the triumphal arch. While he is gazing "insaturabilmente" at the "wonderful beauty" (d1v) of the arch, he begins to muse: what would "knowledge of its wholeness" be? In the same thought, he wonders if by penetrating into the inner sanctum of Venus he will find the object of his desires (d1v). Once inside the vaulted temple (*fornicato templo*), he discovers its walls awash with "tiny aquatic monsters." He is impressed when he notices a mosaic panel covered with more erotic scenes: Europa being ravished by the bull and Pasiphae in "lascivious congress" with yet another "robusto tauro" (d2v), the Minotaur. This entrance into the building

61. THE NAKED MAN INSIDE THE ELEPHANT, WITH EPIGRAMS.

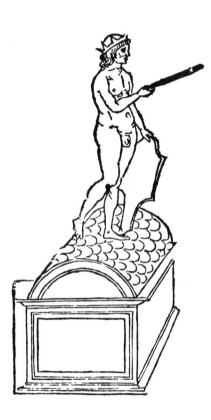

אם לא כי הבהבה   כסתה את בשרי
אזי הייתי ערום חפש ותמצא הניחני

ΓΥΜΝΟΣ ΗΝ ,ΕΙ ΜΗ ΑΝ ΘΗΡΙ-
ΟΝ ΕΜΕΚΑΛΥΨΕΝ. ΖΗΤΕΙ.ΕΥ-
ΡΗΣΗΔΕ.ΕΑΣΟΝ ΜΕ.

NVDVS ESSEM, BESTIA NI ME
TEXISSET, QVAERE, ET INVE
NIES.ME SINITO.

brings about "nothing less than an unimaginable pleasure" (d1v). Initially he finds "full of fecund delectation" and "pleasure and delight" in which he "loses his senses" (d2v). Poliphilo's pleasure is short-lived, however, for he meets a hissing "terrifying and horrifying" dragon (fig. 62) with great, sharp, jagged teeth and a heavy, lashing tail standing in the doorway and ready to enter the chamber (d2v). He flees.

The hero's second attempt to locate the appropriate orifice through which he can enter a building, the temple of Venus Physozoï (Venus of the natural life), is more successful. Polia has finally met Polia, and in their wanderings they have come upon the temple. In-

62. THE DRAGON AT THE THRESHOLD (FRENCH EDITION).

63.   FILMIC SEQUENCE OF EIGHT WOODCUTS. FIRST, THE HIGH PRIESTESS GIVES POLIA THE TORCH.

wardly he is desperately lamenting that while Polia has ignited in him a love that is like "a flame of Cupid that burns me all over," she herself remains "frigid" (m2). Once within the sacred precinct they are received by a high priestess. Before admitting them to the temple, she and her retinue of nymphs halt at the opening. There they pray to the gods and goddesses that preside at thresholds. Then she presses Poliphilo and Polia to enter after her and partake in the rites of Venus. Obediently they follow her to the center of the temple where a cistern is located (n2v).

The rites begin. The high priestess lights a torch and gives it to Polia (fig. 63). The high priestess asks her: "What do you desire, my daughter?" to which Polia replies, "I pray that we may be allowed to arrive at the domain of the divine mother [Venus] and to drink at the sacred source." Then the high priestess turns to Poliphilo and hands him the torch, commanding him to plunge it into the center of the fountain (n7v) and to "make the ardent flame rotate around the middle of the opening" while reciting the following phrase: "As water extinguishes this flame, in the reverse will this flame revive the frozen heart" (n8v).

64. SECOND, POLIPHILO PLUNGES THE TORCH INTO THE FOUNTAIN.

Poliphilo obliges (fig. 64). And then, as a result of the gyrations of his incandescent staff inside the cistern, Polia, who is standing nearby, turns to him and, "with a sigh as if emerging from the depths of her inflamed heart," tells him she feels as though it is she who had been penetrated by the torch (fig. 65): "I felt the ignited fire of fervent love run through me and sparkle." Now that she has felt his "ardent and excessive desire," his "cordial fire," she becomes "placid and overtaken with a sudden sweetness." Overcome with "tears and sweet small sighs," she gives him a kiss, declaring that her love for him is also like "a flame." As for Poliphilo, the result is a "remedy to the serious and unpleasant pains" that have been plaguing him throughout the story. "Overcome" by "such a sweet flame in every part of his body" and "inflamed from his head to his feet, he is reduced to sweet and loving tears and overcome with a sense of being lost." He enters a state close to epilepsy (o1–o2).

The rites continue (fig. 65). The high priestess signals to Polia that she must proceed to another part of the temple for the "complementorio de gli penetrarli sacrificii" (o1v). They enter the *adyton,* or smaller shrine connected to the main temple. Again, there is an

65.   THIRD, POLIA TURNS TO POLIPHILO.

66. FOURTH, PREPARING FOR THE NEXT STAGE OF THE RITES.

67. FIFTH, PURSUING "TENDER UNIONS."

artifact at the center of the chamber, this time an ornate "altar" in the form of a large chalice-like bowl. This element becomes the focus of the next series of erotic rites, rites whose intoxicating enthusiasm, according to Poliphilo, make those carried out by the ancient "Clodones, Edonites, and Mimallones"—different types of bacchantes famed for their lascivious practices—pale in comparison.

"Let us proceed," says the high priestess, inviting Polia to follow, in pursuit of "tender unions" (fig. 67). First a conch-shaped basin is filled with a concoction of "whale sperm, odorous musk, crystal clear and runny camphor oil, some mastic, almond oil, and other substances" (o4v). The viscuous mixture is put on the altar and set aflame, and two doves are sacrificed while the nymphs of the retinue dance around the altar to a Lydian tune. Then the priestess gathers the ashes, encloses them in a box, and symbolically throws it into the cistern next door. Next, praying to Venus, mother "of burning and sacred loves, and of the fires of love and of the sweet conjugations," the high priestess begins to lightly tap the chalice-altar with her wand (fig. 68). She places roses and conches, symbols of Venus, on the

68. Sixth, the high priestess taps the chalice.

top of the altar and splashes it with seawater (fig. 69). In the final stage of the rite, Polia is ordered to rub the floor at the base of the stem of the chalice (o8).

The effect of these rites upon the building is no less than cataclysmic. In response to the final part of the rite, the entire structure immediately begins to heave. The floor starts to "move and quake under his knees." A groaning sound comes from the depths of the structure, "with an incredible rumbling" like "thunder," which Poliphilo likens to the roar that accompanies the "cracking of ice when it melts, no different than if a huge mountain had fallen into the sea" (o8). The tremors cause the hinges of the doors to shudder.

For the hero, who is kneeling before the chalice of the altar, "avidly" absorbed by its "fragrance so unexpected" (yv), the temple serves for a second time as a source of vicarious pleasure. When he raises his head from the ground where he has momentarily crouched in fear in the trembling building, he is amazed to find that the chalice has borne fruit. And upon sampling one of these (fig. 70), he feels "renovated in his rough and crass intellect, no more and no less that if he had just emerged from the depths of the sea" (p1v).

69. SEVENTH, THE HIGH PRIESTESS SPLASHES THE ALTAR WITH SEAWATER.

*   *   *

A whole cognitive world has been turned upside down. The slow revolution that began with the dreamworld of the *mirabilia* is achieved. With the *Hypnerotomachia,* the process of replacing an older way of reasoning and conceiving architecture with a new one is complete. *Libido,* the most abject of all prohibitions, is now elevated to the status of one of the highest imperatives.

The radical recategorization of the body, from "dangerous" to "marvelous" and from "marvelous" to "divine" and finally "humanist," made this change possible. Humanism represented a transformation not only of the content but also of the form of architectural thinking. It constituted a rethinking of architectural thinking itself. The metaphor of the humanist architectural body was used as a means of sanctioning what I have called the "hot" thinking, creative and open to change, to the detriment of "cold" thinking, dogmatic and resistant.

This phenomenon says much about the power of metaphor, and in particular the somatic metaphor, in effecting a paradigm shift on the level of a whole culture. The old metaphor of the architectural body had acted as a brake on innovation. The new, redefined one

70. Eighth, Poliphilo samples the fruit brought forth from the chalice.

brought together knowledge that would otherwise have been separate and inassociable. It offered a cognitive shortcut, making possible the mental leaps that in turn made possible humanist architecture. It opened the way to a restructuring of a specific domain of knowl-edge—quattrocento architecture—and changed the very architecture of architectural knowl-edge. The body served as a map of architectural thinking, as a representation of the world, and one that also carried within it a new set of prohibitions and impera-tives. Its transformation from something dangerous to something positive led to a cognitive revolution that otherwise would not have been possible. It made certain things thinkable that would not have been before. It allowed architects to conceive their role in the world in innovative and creative humanist ways. In the last analysis, the recognition of the architectural body was essential in turning "no" into "yes."

NOTES

*

INTRODUCTION: METAPHORS AND MENTAL LEAPS

1. I am referring to the work carried out in the cognitive history of architecture by the Design Knowledge Systems Group directed by Alexander Tzonis at the Technical University of Delft. Among the publications of the group are: P. Scriver, *Rationalization, Standardization and Control in Design: A Cognitive Historical Study of Architectural Design and Planning in the Public Works Department of British India, 1855–1901* (Ph.D. diss., Delft, 1994); D. Bilodeau, *Precedents and Design Thinking in an Age of Relativization: The Transformations of the Normative Discourse on the Orders of Architecture in France between 1650 and 1793* (Ph.D. diss., Delft, 1997); and L. Molinari, *Precedent and Innovation in Post-War Italian Architecture* (Ph.D. diss., Delft, forthcoming). In a similar vein is D. W. Fokkema, "The Concept of Convention in Literary Theory and Empirical Research," in *Convention and Innovation in Literature,* ed. T. D'haen, R. Grubel, and H. Lethen (Amsterdam, 1989), pp. 1–16.

2. J. Burckhardt, *The Civilization of the Renaissance,* trans. S. G. Middlemore (New York, 1944; German ed. 1860), p. 1.

3. This definition of modern design reasoning is taken from A. Tzonis et al., *Les systèmes conceptuels de l'architecture de 1650 à 1800* (Cambridge, Mass., 1975).

4. See A. Tzonis, *Creative Design* (Cambridge, Mass., forthcoming).

5. M. Boden, *The Creative Mind: Myths and Mechanisms* (New York, 1990). She mentions Friedrich von Kekule, dozing by the fire, whose dream suggested that the benzene molecule might be a ring, and Jacques Hadamard, who found more than once that a long-sought solution came "at the very moment of sudden awakeness" (p. 15). See S. Freud, *The Interpretation of Dreams,* trans. J. Strachey (New York, 1965), and T. Kuhn, "A Function for Thought Experiments," in *Essential Tension* (Cambridge, Mass., 1977), pp. 240–265, and K. J. Holyoak and P. Thagart, *Mental Leaps: Analogy in Creative Thought* (Cambridge, Mass., 1995).

1. THE READ *HYPNEROTOMACHIA,* OR THE *HYPNEROTOMACHIA* AS KNOWLEDGE

1. The edition quoted in the present study is the Garland fascimile (New York, 1976) edition of the editio princeps *Hypnerotomachia Poliphili* published at the press of Aldus Manutius (Venice, 1499), hereafter cited throughout by page number only. Other editions mentioned here are by G. Pozzi and L. Ciapponi, 2 vols. (Padua, 1980) hereafter cited as Pozzi and Ciapponi. The French edition is *Le songe de Poliphile* by Jacques Kerver (Paris, 1546; rpt. Paris, 1963). The English edition is *The Strife of Love in a Dreame* published by Simon Waterson (London, 1592; rpt. New York, 1976). The pages of the *Hypnerotomachia Poliphili* are paginated not in numerical but alphabetical order. This makes referencing very complex. Every sixteen pages, corresponding to the folded folio, we pass on to the next the letter of the alphabet. The "v" that often appears stands for "verso." Thus "b3v" means the reverse side of the third page of the group of pages labeled *b.* This is the system adopted throughout this book for quotations from the facsimile edition.

2. For more reading on the *romanzo* genre, see E. H. Wilkins, *A History of Italian Literature* (Cambridge, Mass., 1954). See also F. de Sanctis, *Storia della letteratura italiana,* vol. 1 (Milan, 1946); V. Branca, *Tradizione delle opere di Giovanni Boccaccio* (Rome, 1958); E. Bréhier, *The Middle Ages and the Renaissance* (Chicago, 1965); A. Givens, *La dottrina d'amore nel Boccaccio* (Florence, 1968); A. D. Scaglione, *Nature and Love in the Middle Ages* (Berkeley, 1963).

3. Translated from the Greek: *hypnos* means "dream," *erōs* means "love," *machia* means "struggle," or "quest." For a schematization of the plot, see O. Pelosi, *Il sogno di Polifilo: Una quête dell'umanesimo* (Salerno, 1988).

4. T. Temanza, *Vite dei più celebri architetti e scultori veneziani che fiorirono nel secolo decimosesto* (Venice, 1778); and L. Cicognara, *Catalogo ragionato dei libri d'arte* (Pisa, 1821).

5. The *Hypnerotomachia* subsequently became the object of many studies, mainly in two scholarly journals: *La Bibliofilia,* published in Rome, and then the *Journal of the Warburg and Courtauld Institutes,* published in London. Most of the articles cited here appeared in these two journals.

6. "Die Hypnerotomachia is der erste Kunstroman im modernen Sinne, das einzige Beispiel, dass die Kunstbegeisterung der Renaissance ihre Anschauungen und formalen Prinzipien durch einen in sich selber wieder künstlerischen Vorgang darlegte" (A. Ilg, *Ueber den kunsthistorischen Werth der Hypnerotomachia Poliphili: Ein Beitrag zur Geschichte der Kunstliteratur in der Renaissance,* Eingereicht zur Erlangung des philosophischen Doctorgrades an der philosophischen Faculteit der Universität Tübingen [Vienna, 1872], p. 26). This is the first study of the *Hypnerotomachia* in the framework of academic art history.

7. See B. Croce, "La Hypnerotomachia Poliphili," *Quaderni della Critica* 6 (1950), pp. 46–54, quote from p. 46; M. Ivins, "The Aldine Hypnerotomachia Poliphili of 1499," *Bulletin of the Metropolitan Museum of Art* 18 (1923), pp. 249–252, quote from p. 250; R. Weiss, "A New Francesco Colonna," *Italian Studies* 16 (1961), pp. 78–83, quote from p. 78; F. Fabbrini, "Indagini sul Poliphilo," *Giornale Storico della Letteratura Italiana* 35 (1900), pp. 1–33, quote from p. 25.

8. D. Gnoli, "Il sogno di Poliphilo," *La Bibliofilia* 1 (1899–1900), pp. 189–212, 266–283; C. Popelin's introduction to his French translation and philological edition of *Le songe de Poliphile ou Hypnerotomachia,* by F. Colonna (1883; rpt. Geneva, 1982), hereafter cited as Popelin; C. Ephrussi, *Étude sur le Songe de Poliphile* (Paris, 1888).

9. Fabbrini, "Indagini sul Poliphilo," pp. 5, 29.

10. Ibid., pp. 25–26.

11. V. Zabughin, "Una fonte ignota dell'Hypnerotomachia Poliphili," *Giornale Storico della Letteratura Italiana* 74 (1919), pp. 41–49.

12. Alberti's *De re aedificatoria* was written in the 1440s; Antonio Averlino, il Filarete, *Trattato di architettura* in the 1450s and early 1460s; Francesco di Giorgio Martini's *Trattati* between 1480 and 1495. See L. Lefaivre and A. Tzonis, *De Oorsprung van de moderne Architectuur: Een Geschiedenis in Documenten* (The origins of modern architecture) (1984; rpt. Nijmegen, 1990).

13. Alberti's *De re aedificatoria* was published, with an introduction by Angelo Poliziano, in Florence in 1485.

14. Fra Giocondo was the first to publish the Latin text of Vitruvius with illustrations in 1511, preceding by ten years Cesare Cesariano's (Como, 1521).

15. According to Ambroise Firmin-Didot in *Alde Manuce et l'hellènisme à Venise* (Paris, 1875), Aldus studied in Rome with Gasparo da Verona and Calderino. Then he went on to Ferrara, where the professor of Greek was Battista Guarini. He was a friend of the philhellenes Pico, Poliziano, and Emmanuel Adramytheos. He used the title "philhellene" and even "Greek" to refer to himself in his books. For example, he signed the second volume of his epoch-making Aristotle of 1497 in Greek, εγραφε ἐν Βενετιας . . . ᾿Αλδου τοῦ Μανούτιου ῥωμαῖου και φιλελλήνοε (p. 7): "Aldus Manutius, Greek [under the Ottoman Empire, Greeks were referred to as *Romei*] and philhellene, wrote this in Venice." For more details concerning Aldus's philhellenism, see M. Lowry, *The World of Aldus Manutius* (Ithaca, 1979).

16. Lowry, *The World of Aldus,* pp. 112–113, 144–145, 150–151, 162–163.

17. See N. G. Wilson, *From Byzantium to Italy: Greek Studies in the Italian Renaissance* (London, 1992).

18. A. Grafton, "Texts as Treasures," in *Rome Reborn,* ed. A. Grafton (Washington, D.C., New Haven, and Vatican City, 1993), p. 15.

19. S. Morison, *A Tally of Types,* 2nd ed. (Cambridge, 1973), p. 6.

20. Aldus seems to have been enthusiastic about his work in general. Perhaps the most vivid of his introductions, because it is at once so warm and so frantic, is the one he wrote to his friend Marino, published in the preface to Ovid's *Heroides, Arte amatoria* (1502): "io vorrei poter sempre stare con te, vivere con te. Ma poiche cio non e possibile a cause degli impegni che ci trattengono ambidue—i mei nella repubblica delle lettere, i tuoi in questa illustre Veneta . . . —, poiche dunque stare con te non e possibile, mi consolo della sua assenza inviadoti queste epistole, di modo che con questi volumetti io possa essere in tua compagnia, essere nelle tue mani. Addio" (in G. Orlandi, *Aldo Manuzio, editore* [Milan, 1976], 2:8). Translated, it reads: "I would have wanted to be with you always, to live with you always. But as this is not possible because of the duties that detain us both—mine in the republic of letters, and yours in this illustrious one of Venice— . . . as, then, to be with you is not possible, I console myself for your absence by sending you these letters, so that with these small volumes, I may somehow once more be in your company, and in your hands. Farewell."

21. See A. A. Renouart, *Annales de l'imprimerie des Aldes*, 2nd ed. 3 vols., (Paris, 1925), and Firmin-Didot, *Alde Manuce*, for the complete catalogue raisonné of Aldus's publications.

22. Lowry, *The World of Aldus*, p. 113–114.

23. Ibid., p. 142.

24. Nicolas Jenson or Janson (died ca. 1480), as he is variously referred to, was a Venetian printer, born in France, who studied with Gutenberg in Mainz for three years. His design for the roman type was perhaps the most influential of the Renaissance. He published under his own name with his own type in Venice in 1470; after his death, his type was adopted by the Aldine press.

25. See S. Morison, "Early Humanistic Script and the First Roman Type," *The Library* 26 (1943), pp. 1–30; "Towards an Ideal Type," *The Fleuron* 2 (1924), pp. 57–75; and especially "The Type of the Hypnerotomachia Poliphili," in *Gutenberg Festschrift* (Mainz, 1925), pp. 254–258. See also his *Typographic Book* (London, 1963), pp. 32–33. See the excellent B. Ullmann, *The Origin and Development of Humanistic Script* (Rome, 1960), and also L. Febvre and H. -J. Martin, *The Coming of the Book: The Impact of Printing, 1450–1800*, trans. D. Gerard (London, 1990; French ed. 1958).

26. Morison, "The Type of the Hypnerotomachia Poliphili," pp. 254–258; *Tally of Types*, p. 30.

27. See G. Painter, *The Hypnerotomachia Poliphili of 1499: An Introduction to the Dream, the Dreamer, the Artist, and the Printer* (London, 1963), p. 18.

28. Lowry, *The World of Aldus*, p. 137.

29. Painter, *The Hypnerotomachia*, p. 18. He notes the capitals *P, O, L, R, T,* and *V*.

30. It is remarkable that a book bought by such a huge public as Rabelais's *Gargantua* was printed in "black letter" or gothic type font, as Febvre and Martin remark; see *The Coming of the Book*, p. 83.

31. Painter, *The Hypnerotomachia*, pp. 17–18. The other hugely influential font to come out of the Aldine press was the italic. See N. Barker, *Aldus Manutius and the Development of Greek Script Type in the Fifteenth Century* (Sandy Hook, Conn., 1985). Although ostensibly concerned with Greek type, it provides a good overview of Aldus's production, e.g., pointing out that the italic type was introduced in the octavo editions of Virgil of 1501, perhaps influenced by Pomponio Leto. For the history of the roman and italic type and their beginnings, see S. Morison, "Towards an Ideal Type," pp. 57–75; "On Script Types," *The Fleuron* 3 (1925), pp. 1–25; "The Chancery Types of Italy and France," *The Fleuron* 3 (1925), pp. 23–51.

32. Aldus's Greek font is considered inferior to his roman font. Based on the handwriting of the Byzantine scholar Musurus, it lacks the simplicity essential for a readable type, such as cut previously by Jenson. See C. Clair, *A History of European Printing* (London, 1976), pp. 143–144. See also Barker, *Aldus Manutius*; R. Proctor, *The Printing of Greek in the Fifteenth Century* (Oxford, 1900); Painter's introduction to his edition of the *Hypnerotomachia*; and Lowry, *The World of Aldus*, pp. 126–134.

Lowry, *The World of Aldus*, claims the first use of Hebrew type appears in the *Opera* of Poliziano, published by the Aldine press in 1498 (p. 118). Another candidate is the *Hebrew Bible* of Naples (ca. 1490–1491), mentioned by A. M. Hind, *An Introduction to a History of Woodcut, with a Detailed Study of Work Done in the Fifteenth Century*, (1935; rpt. New York, 1963), 2:409. Actually, the first two Hebrew passages of the *Hypnerotomachia*, on bviii and bviii v, are in movable type. The third, on hviii, is part of a larger woodcut.

The Arabic passages here are parts of larger woodcuts, not set in movable type. The first Arabic type in Europe appeared in a translation of *Le livre de la prière des heures* in 1514, in Fano (near Venice). See J. Balagna, *L'imprimerie arabe en occident* (Paris, 1984). I would like to thank Dr. Vrolijk, of the Arabic Collection of the Library of the University of Leiden, for directing me to this title.

33. In particular see J. Poppelreuter, *Der anonyme Meister des Poliphilo,* (Strassburg, 1904). See also Ilg, *Ueber den kunsthistorischen Werth*, and Duc de Rivoli, *Bibliographie des livres à figures venitiens: L'arte de la stampa nel rinascimento italiano* (Venice, 1894).

34. However, two other books each contain two rather mediocre engravings apiece: *Musaeus* (1494) and a life of St. Catherine (1500).

35. Hind believes that only cutters signed their works, not designers; see *A History of Woodcut*, 2:471. According to the Duc de Rivoli, the ".b." on the engraving of a6v is the sign of a simple engraver's shop in Venice. See his "Notes supplémentaires sur quelques livres à figures vénitiens de la fin du XVe siècle," *Gazette des Beaux-Arts* 31 (1889). However, other authors have taken the *b* to designate the designer. Ambroise Firmin-Didot, in his *Essai bibliographique et typographique sur l'histoire de la gravure sur bois* (Paris, 1863), argues that the cutter must have been Benedetto Montagna, as Hind also believes. Ilg, *Ueber den kunsthistorischen Werth*, shares this opinion. Montagna is one of five engravers to whom the woodcuts of the *Hypnerotomachia* are usually attributed. Eugene Piot has a second, whom

he names the Master of the Dolphin and from whose hand the emblem of Aldus Manutius comes, the dolphin wound around an anchor. See Piot's "Le maître aux dauphins," *Le Cabinet de l'Amateur* (1861-1862), pp. 253, 365. Third, G. Pozzi proposed Benedetto Bordone as the cutter in *Francesco Colonna et Alde Manuce* (Bern, 1962). Fourth, R. Weiss suggested Cima de Conegliano in "A New Francesco Colonna," *Italian Studies* 16 (1961), pp. 78-83. George Painter has, for his part, assigned the cutting to a follower of Bellini and Mantegna who "died in his twenties" (*The Hypnerotomachia*, p. 16).

36. See M. Sander, *Le livre à figures italien depuis 1476 jusqu'à 1530*, 6 vols. (New York, 1941). See also E. C. Rava, *Arte dell'illustrazione nel libro italiano del rinascimento* (Milan, 1945).

37. Popelin, in his introduction to 1:lxxxii, states that Federigo's holdings included all the Latin authors known in his day, all the commentators of Aristotle, all the lexicographers, everything written by the men of letters who were his contemporaries, all their translations, and all the books in existence on the Christian writings, medicine, and philosophy. Vespasiano da Bisticci, the famous fifteenth-century book dealer, wrote about Federigo as a collector of manuscripts in his *Renaissance Princes, Popes, and Prelates*, trans. W. George and E. Waters (New York, 1963), claiming that Federigo even possessed a complete edition of Menander, whose works exist only in fragments today (see also Alatri, *Federigo da Montefeltro*). If Vespasiano is correct, then it is likely that this unique copy was destroyed when Cesare Borgia captured Urbino. Federigo had in his service at all times a group of thirty to forty calligraphers who worked at producing these manuscripts, all on parchment, richly bound in gold brocade and crushed velvet with silver locks. Many of them contain superb miniatures that one can admire today at the Vatican Library.

38. Hind, *A History of Woodcut*, 2:493.

39. See L. V. Gerulaitis, *Printing and Publishing in Fifteenth-Century Venice* (Chicago, 1976), p. 17. The Malermi Bible of 1490 is considered by Hind to be in the "popular" style. In its 1493 edition, new plates were introduced, this time in the "classicizing" style. See Hind, *A History of Woodcut*, 2:470-473.

40. The term is Poppelreuter's, *Der anonyme Meister*, p. 49.

41. See Firmin-Didot, *Essai bibliographique* (Paris, 1863).

42. See Hind, *A History of Woodcut*, 2:492. Mantegna was, of course, also the most influential in shaping the new style of painting, in particular in his *Parnas-sus* (1497) and in his *Triumphs* (produced in Rome, 1488-1490). See also G. Romano, *Verso la maniera moderna: da Mantegna a Rafaello* (Turin, 1976), pp. 1-16. See also P. Kristeller, *Andrea Mantegna* (London, 1901), and the exhibition catalogue *Andrea Mantegna* (Milan, 1992).

43. Fra Giocòndo is mentioned by Gnoli; see "Il sogno di Poliphilo." There is a marked resemblance between Carpaccio's Dream of Saint Ursula and the engraving of Polia in her bedroom, down to the bed, the window, and the little dog; this was first noted by M. T. Casella and G. Pozzi, *Francesco Colonna: Biografia e opere* (Padua, 1959), 2:74, hereafter cited as Casella and Pozzi. On Gentili Bellini, see Hind, *A History of Woodcut*, 2:492.

44. See J. W. Appel, *The Dream of Poliphilus: Fac-similes of 168 Woodcuts in "Poliphili Hypnerotomachia,"* (London, 1888).

45. Hind, *A History of Woodcut*, 2:492.

46. See E. Gombrich, *Aby Warburg: An Intellectual Biography* (London, 1970), p. 61. The reference is taken from Warburg's dissertation, *Sandro Botticellis "Geburt der Venus" und "Frühling": Eine Versuchung über die Vorstellung von der Antike in der italienischen Frührenaissance* (Hamburg and Leipzig, 1893).

47. See Poppelreuter, *Der anonyme Meister*, pp. 50, 55.

48. In fact Ivins contends that isolated from the text, the engravings do not bear comparison with pictures in a number of volumes published in Florence and several of the northern Italian towns ("The Aldine Hypnerotomachia," p. 252).

49. See L. Donati "Studio esegetico sul Poliphilo," *La Bibliofilia* 52 (1950), pp. 128-162, where he refers specifically to pages g2v, q4, s1v, t4, x1v, y2v. As Casella and Pozzi point out, this is derived from the *technopaegnia* used in the Greek tradition, such as in Theocritus's *Siringa;* Simmiade's *Pelexus, Pteriges,* and *Oion;* and Diosade's *Bomos* (2:148).

50. So Donati, "Studio esegetico," p. 140.

51. For a list of holdings, see Pozzi and Ciapponi, 2:36-37. Among its owners were John Ruskin. "Mine during my work in Oxford," his copy of the second Aldine edition of 1545, now at the Houghton Library at Harvard University, reads, "Brantwood, 3rd April, 1880." Albrecht Dürer also owned a copy, now in the Staatsbibliothek of Munich, as reported by G. Leidinger, "Albrecht Dürer und die Hypnerotomachia Polyphili," *Philobiblion*, no. 4, (1931), pp. 146-180.

52. Ivins, "The Aldine Hypnerotomachia," p. 252.

53. Archivio del Veneto Collegio, fol. 38, recto of the notorial registry no. 4 for the years 1507-1511 (qtd. by Popelin in his introduction, p. XCV).

54. Lowry, *The World of Aldus,* p. 115.

55. For a detailed description of the ill-timed fiasco, see ibid. Lowry provides the best discussion of the book's financial history (pp. 124–125).

56. Ivins, "The Aldine of Hypnerotomachia," p. 252.

57. Sir Robert Dallington (1561–1637) was translator and commentator on Guicciardi, traveler, author of guidebooks and epigrams in Latin and English, secretary to the earl of Rutland, and Gentleman of the Privy Chamber to both Prince Henry and Prince Charles. The book amounts to nothing more than a summary of the original Aldine edition.

58. On the difficulties of translating the *Hypnerotomachia,* and for an example of this version's errors, see chapter 3.

59. The manuscript, Fr. 12 247 at the Bibliothèque Nationale, was first mentioned by L. Dorez, "Les origines et la diffusion du Songe de Poliphile," *Revue des Bibliothèques* 4 (1896), pp. 239 ff. It was then republished by A.-M. Lecoq and J. Roubaud in "Les hieroglyphes du songe," *FMR,* May–June 1988, pp. 15–42. The manuscript is by the French illuminist François Desmoulins. Among the rebuses studied in the article by these two French scholars is the one referring to the incestuous love of Francis I for his sister, Marguerite d'Angoulème (p. 22). On his copy of the original, see Dorez, pp. 239 ff. The copy, bearing the arms of Francis I, is to be found in the Bibliothèque Nationale in Paris.

60. Popelin, introduction, 1:ccvi.

61. The subsequent French editions include one in 1772, entitled *Les amours de Polia ou le Songe de Polyphile traduit de l'italien,* and another in 1804, entitled *Le songe de Poliphile: Traduction de l'italien par F. Legrand,* 2 vols. (Paris, 1804). The work also seems to have been more popular than Alberti's treatise, which waited forty-five years for translation (vs. only about thirty for the *Songe*).

62. For Cousin, see Ambroise Firmin-Didot in his *Étude sur Jean Cousin* (Paris, 1872), who supports his claim by pointing to the "contained force and elegance" of the figures and the "accentuated caryatids of the title page, the long statues, the elegant forms, the tapering extremities of the figures, the lovely children. . . ." In addition, the "accessories, such as the bushes piercing the rocks, also demonstrate analogies with the vignettes in Cousin's *Traité de perspective*" (p. 33). That the attribution is still accepted was confirmed to me orally by Madame Geneviève Monnier, former curator of drawings of the Louvre, whose help I gratefully acknowledge.

   Febvre and Martin assign the engravings to Goujon; see *The Coming of the Book,* p. 96.

63. These include the geometrical schema of the arch of triumph described in the text, two depictions of the baths (one exterior and one interior), one depiction of the temple of Venus from the outside, and seven representations of gardens. In the Kerver edition of 1546, these are on pp. 26, 27, 41v, 43, 43v, 74, 106, 107, 111v, 112v, 113, 113v.

64. See Blondel's note to the second edition of Savot's *Architecture française* (1685), p. 351; qtd. in A. Blunt, "The Hypnerotomachia Poliphili in Seventeenth-Century France," *Journal of the Warburg Institute* 1 (1937–1938), p. 121.

65. Felibien is quoted in Blunt, "The Hypnerotomachia Poliphili," p. 126: "Il faut se contenter ici de marquer combien le songe de Poliphile, quand il a paru, pouvoit élever l'esprit des architectes de ce temps, et de les engager à la perfectionner l'art et la science qu'ils professoient. Car quelque idée avantageuse que Vitruve ait donnée de l'architecture ancienne, Poliphile semble encore la representer avec plus de majesté et de grandeur: il l'a fait envisager comme la seule science qui régit tous les Arts et qui embrasse elle-mesme les notions les plus sublimes. Il rapporte a cette science non seulement l'ordonnance et la construction de toutes sortes d'edifices, mais encore l'intelligence parfaite de ce qui doit décorer et accompagner ces grands ouvrages."

   [Suffice it to remark how much the *Songe de Poliphile,* when it appeared, was capable of elevating the spirit of the architects of the time, and to commit them to perfecting the art and science they professed. For whatever advantageous idea Vitruvius gave of ancient architecture, Poliphile seems to present it with even greater majesty and grandeur: he pictured it as the only science that reigns over all the arts and that embraces itself the most sublime notions. He brings to that science not only the ordonnance and the construction of all kinds of buildings, but also a perfect understanding of that which should decorate and accompany these great works.]

66. Temanza was Engineer of the Serene Republic of Venice, member of the Accademia Clementina of Bologna and of the Olympica of Verona, and associate of the Académie royale in Paris and that of Toulouse. See Popelin, introduction, p. lxxxvii. Milizia was a Venetian theoretician of architecture and disciple of the rigorist Carlo Lodoli. See Lefaivre and Tzonis, *De Oorsprong van de moderne Architectuur,* pp. 360–370. For his change of opinion, see Temanza, *Vite;* cited in Popelin, introduction, p. lxxxvii.

67. J. M. Schlosser, "Sulle tesi teorico artistiche del primo rinascimento," chap. 4 of *La letteratura artistica* (1924; rpt. Florence, 1979), pp. 134–136. For him, the *Hypnerotomachia* is comparable to the work of Leon Battista Alberti, *De re aedificatoria* (Florence, 1485), edited by Bernardo Alberti (cousin of Leon Battista), with a dedication to Lorenzo Medici and a preface by Angelo Poliziano (trans. J. Rykwert, N. Leach, and R. Tavernor, *On the Art of Building in Ten Books* [Cambridge, Mass., 1991], hereafter cited parenthetically in the text); Antonio Averlino, Il Filarete, *Trattato* (1461–1464, composed in Milan), ed. and trans. J. R. Spencer, 2 vols. (New Haven, 1965); and Francesco di Giorgio, *Trattati d'architettura civile e militare*, ed. C. Maltese, 2 vols. (Milan, 1966).

68. G. Folena, "Noterelle lessicale albertiane," *Lingua Nostra* 18 (1957), pp. 6–10. But see especially Casella and Pozzi, 2:35.

69. Respectively: b3v, b2, a8v, b2v, f3, y3v, z1, f3.

70. Popelin, *Le songe de Poliphile*, 2:223.

71. See ibid., 2: 223, n. 2, and Pozzi and Ciapponi's critical edition of the book with an extensive introduction. See also Pozzi and Casella, which contains a study of the sources of the architectural culture of the *Hypnerotomachia* (2:31–60).

72. C. Huelsen, "Le illustrazioni della Hypnerotomachia Poliphili e le antichità di Roma," *La Bibliofilia* 12 (1910), pp. 161–176; Pozzi and Ciapponi, 2:58, n. 2.

73. Pozzi and Ciapponi 2:91–92; Popelin, 1:126, n. 1 (see also Vitruvius, *De architectura* 1.6.4, also referred to by Casella and Pozzi, 2:63).

74. E. Kretsulesco-Quaranta, *Les jardins du songe: Poliphile et la mystique de la renaissance* (Paris, 1976), p. 365; Pozzi and Ciapponi, 2:61; Pausanias 1.21.3.

75. Casella and Pozzi, 2:58–59. On the obelisks, Flavio Biondo writes: "infra dicit duos ibi fuisse obeliscos quorum unus minor et loco altior, qui Pinciano nunc in colle prostatus cernitur, lunae, alter soli dictatus" (*Roma instaurata*, 2:76). The position between mountains is corroborated by Fulvio's description of the Mausoleum of Augustus: "tutto questo circuito, et spacio che e tra il Monte, e questa machina di Augusto, era gia da gli edificii fatti da Augusto per infino al Tevere"; cited in M. Calvesi, *Il sogno di Polifilo prenestino* (Rome, 1980), p. 110.

76. On *De mirabilibus*, see C. Frugoni, "L'antichità: dai Mirabilia alla propaganda politica," in *Memoria dell'antico nell'arte italiana*, ed. S. Settis (Turin, 1986), p. 6. *Dittamondo* comprised an imaginary dialogue between the author and the personified City

of Rome; see *Dittamondo,* ed. G. Corsi (Bari, 1952), I, II, cap. 31, vv. 25–28.

77. "Roma, spoliata d'ogni masta, giace prostata a guisa di gigantesco cadavere putrefatto e d'ogni parte corroso. Che cosa mai vide il mondo di più grande, degli innumerevoli edifici urbani, templi, portici, terme, teatri, acquidotti, porti artifatti, palazzi adesso abbattuti, e di tante magnificenze quasi niente o poco sopravivere?" (Poggio Bracciolini, *De varietate fortunae* 6.7; in *Latin Writings of the Italian Humanists,* ed. F. A. Gragg [New York, 1927], trans. M. M. McLaughlin in J. B. Ross and M. M. McLaughlin, *The Portable Renaissance Reader* [New York, 1953], p. 382). See A. Mazzoco, "Petrarca, Poggio, and Biondo: Humanism's Foremost Interpreters of Roman Ruins," in *Francis Petrarch, Six Centuries Later: A Symposium,* ed. A. Scaglione (Chapel Hill, N.C., 1975), pp. 354–363.

78. On Bracciolini, see C. R. Chiaro, "Studi antiquari e produzione delle immagini," in Settis, *Memoria dell'antico,* pp. 271–297. Chrysolaras's *Comparison* can be found in C. Smith, *Architecture in the Culture of Early Humanism: Ethics, Aesthetics, and Eloquence* (New York, 1992), pp. 199–215.

79. Pozzi and Ciapponi, 2:120–121.

80. On Biondo, see Pozzi and Ciapponi, 2:66, n. 2; on Ketcham, see 2:63. See also Calvesi, *Il sogno di Polifilo,* pp. 53–54.

81. F. Borsi, *Leon Battista Alberti* (New York, 1977), p. 334.

82. On measurements, see Casella and Pozzi, 1:77, n. 8. Pozzi has found approximately eighty passages from the *De re aedificatoria* echoed in the *Hypnerotomachia.* See Pozzi and Ciapponi, "Indice dei nomi di persona e di luogo nel commento," in *Hypnerotomachia,* s.v. "Alberti," 2:323.

83. First noted by Temanza, *Vite;* see also Popelin, introduction, p. cxxxiii.

84. Alberti, *De re aedificatoria,* VI.13. This is my own translation from the Latin. Pozzi and Ciapponi, 2:46.

85. This is pointed out in Pozzi and Ciapponi, 2:105, no. 4.

86. *Hypnerotomachia,* b iiii v; Pozzi and Ciapponi, 2:46.

87. The *Hypnerotomachia* reads: "(tempio costruito) cum piu subtile investigatione e sculptura che unque nel secolo nostro fare ne investigare si potesse; ne tale ad Api deo, Sannitico aegyptio construsse" (n5), and Alberti writes: "Mirum illud: Api deo aedem fecisse Sanniticum Aegyptium columnis et variis signis ornatissimam" (VII.13).

88. Popelin, *Le songe de Poliphile,* 1: intro. Calvesi, *Il sogno di Polifilo,* p. 33.

89. Kretsulesco-Quaranta, *Les jardins du songe*, p. 22. This hypothesis is further supported in A. G. Bonds, "Är Poliphilus' dröm avslöjad? Hypnerotomachia Poliphili i ny tolkning," *Biblis* 20 (1989), pp. 9–58. I thank Wolfgang Jung for this reference.

90. A. Khomentovskaia, in an article published in four parts, makes this attribution: see "Felice Feliciano da Verona come l'auteur de l'*Hypnerotomachia Poliphili*," *La Bibliofilia* 37 (1935), pp. 154–174, 200–212; 38 (1936), pp. 20–48, 92–102.

91. Christian Huelsen was the first; see his "Le illustrazioni del Hypnerotomachia." See also K. Giehlow, "Die Hieroglyphenkunde des Humanismus in der Allegorie der Renaissance, besonders der Ehrenforte Kaisers Maximilians I," *Jahrbuch der kunsthistorischen Sammlungen des Allerhöchsten Kaiserhauses* 32 (1915), pp. 46–79.

92. See Giehlow, "Die Hieroglyphenkunde," p. 57. See also Calvesi, *Il sogno di Polifilo*, p. 91, who refers to a description of Rome by B. Marliani, *Urbis Romae topographia* (Rome, 1544).

93. According to Master Gregorius (twelfth or thirteenth century), chap. 7, p. 18. See the edition of his *Narracio de mirabilibus Rome*, ed. R. B. C. Huygens (Leiden, 1970).

94. Huelsen, "Le illustrazioni della Hypnerotomachia," p. 162; Giehlow, "Die Hieroglyphenkunde," pp. 54–56; L. Volkmann, *Bildschriften der Renaissance* (Leipzig, 1923), pp. 16–17. Cited in Pozzi and Casella, 2:54–55.

95. Huelsen, "Le illustrazioni della Hypnerotomachia." Edgar Wind, in *Pagan Mysteries of the Renaissance* (Harmondsworth, 1958), p. 31, n. i, claims that Prospero Colonna owned a group of graces, citing a phrase of Fra Giocondo: "Erant olim in domo R. mi Car.lis de Columna cum subscriptio versibus. Nunc vero sunt in R.mi Car.lis Senensis (Enea Silvio Piccolomini) sine infrascritio carminibus." The verses existed in the Casa Colonna and formed an epigram beginning with the words "Sunt nudae charites" (there are three nude graces). See also E. Tae, "Le fonti delle grazie di Rafaello," *L'Arte* 17 (1914), pp. 41–48.

96. The hieroglyphics on the base of the obelisk in the *Hypnerotomachia* reproduces the inscription of the Vatican obelisk, which reads in Latin: "Divo Iulio Caesari semper Augusto." See Giehlow, "die Hieroglyphenkunde," 52–53.

97. Calvesi, *Il sogno di Polifilo*, p. 162.

98. L. Donati, "Poliphilo a Roma: Il Mausoleo di S. Constanza," *La Bibliofilia* 46 (1968), pp. 1–37. Actually the building was erected at the beginning of the fourth century as a mausoleum for the sons of Constantine and Eleni. See Calvesi, *Il sogno di Polifilo*, p. 208.

99. Calvesi, *Il sogno di Polifilo*, p. 162.

100. Kretsulesco-Quaranta, *Les jardins du songe*, p. 177.

101. Calvesi, *Il sogno di Polifilo*, p. 115.

102. Ibid., pp. 210–211, 213–214.

103. Ibid., p. 212.

104. Kretsulesco-Quaranta, *Les jardins du songe*, p. 209.

105. Giehlow, "Die Hieroglyphenkunde," p. 53.

106. Modena, Bibl. Estense, a.L. 5.15, lat. 992; Pozzi and Ciapponi, 2:98. In fact this is incorrect. The octagonal structure in the Palace of Diocletian was not baths but the emperor's mausoleum, standing on an eleven-foot podium and externally octagonal within a peristyle of Corinthian columns on isolated pedestals. The massive walls are reduced internally by deep niches alternately round and rectangular; between the niches, Corinthian columns on a circular plan carry the projections of an engaged entablature and are surmounted by smaller columns, alternately Corinthian and composite. The dome, of elaborate brickwork, is round internally and an octagonal pyramid externally. See M. Wheeler, *Roman Art and Architecture* (New York, 1964), pp. 144–145.

107. Popelin, *Le songe de Poliphile*, 1:50; W. S. Heckscher, "Bernini's Elephant and Obelisk," *Art Bulletin* 29 (1947), pp. 154–182.

108. Heckscher, "Bernini's Elephant," p. 176, n. 115.

109. J. Burckhardt, *The Architecture of the Italian Renaissance* (Harmondsworth, 1987), p. 32.

110. Ilg, *Ueber den kunsthistorischen Werth*, p. 26.

111. C. Mitchell, "Archaeology and Romance in Renaissance Italy," in *Italian Renaissance Studies*, ed. Mitchell (London, 1960), pp. 455–483.

112. Ibid., pp. 468–474, 481–482. See also B. Ashmole, "Cyriac of Ancona and the Temple of Hadrian at Cyzicus," *Journal of the Warburg and Courtauld Institutes* 19 (1956), 179–191. Pozzi and Ciapponi, 2:61–62 write that: "Il motivo della gorgone sugli edifici è comune nell'antiquità classica (cfr. per esempio Pausanias I,21,3 su l'enorme medusa sulla scarpata dell'Acropoli di Atene). Una Gorgone grandissima posta sulla parete del tempio di Adriano a Cizico è in un disegno di Ciriaco d'Ancona."

113. Casella and Pozzi, 2:139.

114. Popelin, 1:350.

115. See Pozzi and Ciapponi, 2:122–125.

116. See Leidinger, "Albrecht Dürer und die Hypnerotomachia Poliphili"; G. P. Clerici, "Tiziano e la Hypnerotomachia Poliphili," *La Bibliofilia* 20 (1918), pp. 182–203; Heckscher, "Bernini's Elephant"; F. Saxl, "A Scene from the *Hypnerotomachia*

in a painting by Garofolo," *Journal of the Warburg Institute* 1 (1938–1939), pp. 169–171; and R. Schneider, "Notes sur l'influence artistique du Songe de Poliphile," *Etudes italiennes* 2 (1920), pp. 1–6. For the *Hypnerotomachia's* general importance as an iconographical source for Italian Renaissance artists, see Wind, *Pagan Mysteries of the Renaissance;* and J. Seznec, *The Survival of the Pagan Gods: The Mythological Tradition and Its Place in Renaissance Humanism and Art,* trans. B. F. Sessions (New York, 1953).

117. Bibl. vat. Stampi Chig., 2:610. Ref. in Heckscher, "Bernini's Elephant," p. 163.

118. Popelin, 1:50, n. 2. See also Heckscher, "Bernini's Elephant."

119. On the sculptures in the Palazzo del Tè, see Popelin, 1:45, n. 1. On those in Sacro Bosco, see Battisti, *L'antirinascimento,* pp. 139–152. See also M. Praz, "I mostri di Bomarzo," *Illustrazione Italiana,* no. 8, (1953), pp. 48–51, 81; M. Calvesi, "Il sacro bosco di Bomarzo," in *Scritti di storia dell'arte in onore di L. Venturi* (Rome, 1956), 1:369–402; A. Bruschi "Il problema storico di Bomarzo," *Palladio* 13.1–4 (1963), pp. 85–114. Bruschi writes: "Così l'elefante, il drago, la porta dell'Orco, il gusto per le iscrizioni e gli obelischi, ecc. del bizzarro giardino orsiniano possono avere le loro corrispondenza in altrettanti temi del Poliphilo" (p. 87).

120. E. Battisti, *L'antirinascimento,* 2nd ed. (Rome, 1989), pp. 138–256.

121. A. Bruschi "Nota introduttiva," in *Scritti rinascimentali di architettura* (Milan, 1978), pp. 148–180.

122. Calvesi, *Il sogno di Polifilo,* p. 167.

123. E. H. Gombrich, "Hypnerotomachiana," *Journal of the Warburg and Courtauld Institutes* 16 (1951), pp. 119–122. On the Cortile, see also Calvesi, *Il sogno di Polifilo,* pp. 63–64 (who mentions Pico della Mirandola), and D. Coffin, *Gardens and Gardening in Papal Rome* (Princeton, 1991), pp. 32–35.

124. J. Ackerman, "The Belvedere as a Classical Villa" (1951), in *Distance Points* (Cambridge, Mass., 1991), pp. 325–356.

125. Evidence that Peruzzi was familiar with the *Hypnerotomachia* is in Heckscher, "Bernini's Elephant," p. 157, n. 14.

126. R. Wittkower, *Art and Architecture in Italy, 1600–1750* (Harmondsworth, 1958), p. 292.

127. Temanza, "Vita di Poliphilo," in *Vite,* p. 20.

128. G. Hautecoeur, *L'Architecture classique en France* (Paris, 1963), 1:149–504; Blunt, "The Hypnerotomachia Poliphili," pp. 117–137.

129. See next chapter for a fuller description of the spherical chamber. See E. Kaufmann, *Architecture in the Age of Reason* (New York, 1955), pp. 161–166, for an exposition of the work of Boullée and Ledoux.

130. The quotations are respectively from Huelsen, "Le illustrazioni della Hypnerotomachia," p. 176; Ephrussi, *Étude sur le Songe,* p. 306; and S. Battaglia, *La letteratura italiana: Medioeve umanesimo* (Florence, 1971), reproduced in Calvesi, *Il sogno di Polifilo,* p. 314.

2. The Unread *Hypnerotomachia*, or Design as Dreamwork and Thought Experiment

1. This is not the received opinion among scholars. Maurizio Calvesi, *Il sogno di Polifilo prenestino* (Rome, 1980), sees the *Hypnerotomachia* as an exercise in antiquarianism: "La stretta relazione tra lingua e costruzione architettonica, sarà mesa a fuoco ed elaborata nel Polifilo, divenendo addirittura fondante: sia cioè per il già detto scambio tra il sacrario linguistico dei classici e il santuario prenestino, sia per le trasposizioni linguistiche delle architetture, ed insieme archeologiche e quasi architettoniche della lingua. . . . [I]l volgare, il cui uso sembra ormai irreversibile, diventa il supporto di una accanita e totallizante ricognizione filologica, il ponte di una nuova conoscenza e communicazione che riscopre in sè l'antica" (p. 71). Similarly, Salvatore Battaglia writes, "Le parole che Francesco Colonna riesuma hanno la stessa funzione delle loro colonne spezzate e rovesciate, che sono antichissime ma riacquistano un nuovo linguaggio non appena siano reintegrate nel loro contesto. Il lessico di cui si vale il Sogno di Polifilo nasce dallo stesso sentimento archeologico, che mira a riattualizzare come un rito perenne dello spirito le vestigia dell'età remota" (qtd. in ibid.).

   An exception is Arnaldo Bruschi, who describes the first, gigantic building—part pyramid, part temple, part obelisk—of the *Hypnerotomachia Poliphili* as an "elucubrazione fantastica." See "Nota introduttiva," *Scritti rinascimentali di architettura* (Milan, 1978), p. 148–149.

2. S. Freud, *The Interpretation of Dreams,* trans. J. Strachey (New York, 1965), pp. 353, 351. The passage on p. 353 is: "the way in which dreams treat the category of contraries and contradictions is highly remarkable. It is simply disregarded. 'No' seems not to exist so far as dreams are concerned."

3. T. Kuhn, "A Function for Thought Experimentation," in *Essential Tension* (Cambridge, Mass., 1977), pp. 240–265; and K. J. Holyoak and P. Thagard, *Mental Leaps: Analogy in Creative Thought* (Cambridge, Mass., 1995).

4. A. Tzonis, *Creative Design* (Cambridge, Mass., forthcoming).

5. The height of the pyramid of Cheops is about 480 feet, or a bit under one-tenth of a mile. The buildings of the Renaissance, such as St. Peter's in Rome or Westminster Abbey in London, could easily fit inside it.

6. C. Popelin, ed., *Le songe de Poliphile, ou Hypnerotomachia* (1883; reprint, Geneva, 1882), 1:34; hereafter cited as Popelin.

7. Diodorus, *De Sic.* 2.34; qtd. in Popelin, 21.

8. Pliny, *Natural History,* trans. D. E. Eichholtz (Cambridge, Mass., 1971), 10:36, 73.

9. See Popelin, 1:366, n. 1.

10. See the passages on *architecture parlante* in E. Kaufmann's *Architecture in the Age of Reason: Baroque and Postbaroque in England, Italy, and France* (New York, 1955), pp. 102, 130, 134–154, 165.

11. This is according to A. Khomentovskaia, who writes ("Felice Feliciano da Verona come l'auteur de l'*Hypnerotomachia Poliphili*," *La Bibliofilia* 38 [1936], p. 47): "On doit s'arrêter sur la porte magnétique du temple de Venus, d'autant plus que ni L. B. Alberti dans ses 'Ludi matematici,' ni les ouvrages modernes sur l'histoire du magnétisme et l'histoire de la technique ne connaissent pas d'application de ce genre." She cites P. Fleury Mottelay, *Bibliographical History of Electricity and Magnetism* (London, 1920); F. M. Feldhaus, *Die Technik der Antike und Mittelalters* (Potsdam, 1931). See *Hypnerotomachia*, n6v.

12. See G. Scaglia, "Alberti e la meccanica della tecnologia descritta nel 'De Re aedificatoria' e nei 'Ludi Matematici,'" in *Leon Battista Alberti*, ed. J. Rykwert and A. Engel (Milan, 1994), pp. 316–329.

13. Hero of Alexandria's *Pneumatics* describes a small sphere placed in a circular hole in the partition between two halves of a transparent sphere of glass, but it is not used to project moving images onto surroundings surfaces.

14. I feel justified in taking this liberty here because of the exceptional character of the *Hypnerotomachia*. I will also be using the term *furore*, whose introduction is usually associated with Ficino's translation in 1487 of Plato's work on the nature of poetic inspiration, *Ion*. However, as Martin Kemp has noted, the author of the *Hypnerotomachia Poliphili* is in general "the odd man out" in quattrocento aesthetic writings, idiosyncratically breaking all the rules; see "From Mimesis to Fantasia: The Quattrocento Vocabulary of Creation, Inspiration, and Genius in the Visual Arts," *Viator* 8 (1977), pp. 347–398. Furthermore, if the author was Leon Battista Alberti, as I believe, then he would have been familiar with the notion: Alberti was one of the greatest polymaths and most inventive minds of the Renaissance. In particular he was a great admirer of Lucian, who can be seen as one of the creators of *extravaganza*. And we know that Alberti knew the writings of Plato. In the *Ion*, both poet and critic are described as possessed by a frenzy, unable consciously to control their words. The author of the *Hypnerotomachia* has a very clear theory and similar of artistic creation: it is the result of "ingiegnio," which is in turn the result of "tanta iaxtantia e tanta ardente libidine di choacervare coagmentando petre ad tanto congesto? Heu me, gli spiriti fessi et lo intellecto per tanta assidua varietate confuso et gli sensi disordinati, non aptamente patiscono non solum il tutto narare, ma parte cum integritate di cosi depolita lithoglyphia exprimere non valeno" (bii v).

15. See G. Pozzi and L. A. Ciapponi, eds. *Hypnerotomachia Poliphili,* by Francesco Colonna, 2 vols. (Padua, 1980); hereafter cited as Pozzi and Ciapponi. Other scholars before them pursued a more piecemeal approach. See, e.g., the philological studies of C. Ephrussi, *Étude sur le Songe de Poliphile* (Paris, 1888); F. Fabbrini, "Indagini sul Poliphilo," *Giornale Storico della Letteratura Italiana* 35 (1900), pp. 1–33; and Popelin.

16. Pozzi and Ciapponi, 2:53–55.

17. See ibid., "Indice dei nomi di persona e di luogo del commento," 2:323–338.

18. From the first translation into English of the *Trionfi,* Lord Morley's *Tryumphes of Fraunces Petrarcke,* ed. D. D. Carnicelli (Cambridge, Mass., 1971), p. 80.

19. D. Gnoli, "Il sogno di Poliphilo," *La Bibliofilia* 1 (1899–1900), p. 268.

20. Ephrussi, "Étude sur le Songe," p. 403.

21. Ibid., p. 407.

22. Dante, *Inferno,* trans. J. D. Sinclair with Italian text (New York, 1961), pp. 22–23.

23. See Ephrussi, "Étude sur le Songe," p. 424.

24. Ibid., p. 414.

25. Popelin, introduction, 1: clxxxvii; Pozzi and Ciapponi, 2:138.

26. Gnoli, "Il sogno di Poliphilo," pp. 200–201.

27. E. H. Wilkins, *A History of Italian Literature* (Cambridge, Mass., 1954), pp. 104–105.

28. Popelin, introduction, 1:clxxxvii.

29. Cited in Popelin, 1:clxxxvii: "E poiche ha molte volte con la fetida boca non bacciata ma scombravata la mia."

30. Ibid.

31. G. Boccaccio, *The Elegy of Lady Fiammetta,* ed. and trans. M. Causa-Steindler and T. Mauch (Chicago, 1990), p. 3.

32. J. Schlosser, *La letteratura artistica* (1924; rpt. Florence, 1979), p. 352.

33. Gnoli, "Il sogno di Poliphilo," p. 201.

34. M. Calvesi has drawn attention to Poliphilo's pacificism combined with eroticism. See *Il sogno di Poliphilo* (Rome, 1983), p. 52.

35. See M. Bakhtin, "Forms of Time and Chronotope in the Novel," in *The Dialogic Imagination* (Austin, Tex., 1983), pp. 84–258, esp. p. 87. He argues that one of the traits of the heroes of novels descending from Hellenistic prototypes is that they are "exceptionally chaste."

36. Ruth Kelso is among the first to have pointed out this development in the construction of female sexuality in the Renaissance. See *The Doctrine of the Lady in the Renaissance* (Urbana, Ill., 1956), p. 97: "Next to simple obedience, simple chastity is probably the most frequently mentioned requirement of a wife and is often given first place." See also J. C. Caron, "Les noms de l'honneur feminin à la renaissance," *Poétique,* no. 67 (1986), pp. 34–53.

37. L. Donati, "Il mito di Francesco Colonna," *La Bibliofilia* 69 (1962), pp. 247–270.

38. Quintilian, *Institutio oratoria,* trans. H. E. Butler, 4 vols. (Cambridge, Mass., 1920–1922), 8.6.44; cited in A. Fletcher, *Allegory: The Theory of a Symbolic Mode* (Ithaca, 1964), p. 74.

39. The first scholar to have noticed that the hero is erotically moved by the architecture in the *Hypnerotomachia* was Anthony Blunt in "The Hypnerotomachia Poliphili in Seventeenth-Century France," *Journal of the Warburg Institute* 1 (1937–1938), p. 136, n. 2. But this is a passing mention, in a footnote at the end of his article: "Cf. the description of the ceremonial in the temple of Venus on the Island of Cythera, particularly the passage in which Poliphilus tears the veil inscribed IMHN with the arrow Cupid hands him." This type of symbolism, in Blunt's words, would have been "too strong meat" for subsequent readers, whom he saw as "more refined and less full-blooded" than was the author of the *Hypnerotomachia.* George Hersey briefly examined the passionate attachment of the hero to Neoplatonic geometry in his *Pythagorean Palaces: Magic and Architecture in the Italian Renaissance* (Ithaca, 1976), pp. 100–103. Subsequently this erotic attachment to architecture became the theme of Alberto Pérez-Gómez's *Polyphilo, or, The Dark Forest Revisited* (Cambridge, Mass., 1992). I believe that I am the first to have noticed that the hero makes love to architecture: see "Eros, Architecture, and the *Hypnerotomachia Poliphili,*" *Design Book Review,* no. 18 (1990), pp. 17–20.

3. THE HARD *HYPNEROTOMACHIA*, OR THE CODE OF RECOMBINATION

1. J. Martins, "Aux lecteurs," in *Le songe de Poliphile* (Paris, 1546), aiii.

2. E. R. Curtius, *European Literature and the Latin Middle Ages,* trans. W. Trask (New York, 1953), p. 125.

3. E. H. Wilkins, *A History of Italian Literature* (Cambridge, Mass., 1954), p. 102.

4. Ibid., pp. 37–40.

5. Qtd. in A. Blunt, "The Hypnerotomachia Poliphili in Seventeenth-Century France," *Journal of the Warburg Institute* 1 (1937–1938), p. 121.

6. A. Furetière, *Le roman . . .* (Paris 1868) 2:99; referred to in Blunt, "The Hypnerotomachia Poliphili," p. 123. One of the very earliest readers saw the text as encoded in a shorthand, cryptographic, a roman à clef. Many readers have tried like detectives to reconstruct the meaning.

7. Blunt, "The Hypnerotomachia Poliphili," p. 121.

8. Qtd. in ibid., p. 123.

9. B. de Verville, *Le tableau . . .* (Paris, 1547), p. 3.

10. E. Wind, *Pagan Mysteries of the Renaissance* (Harmondsworth, 1958); M. Calvesi, *Il sogno di Polifilo prenestino* (Rome, 1980), p. 77, writes that Poliphilo is not so "notturne" as Pico; V. Zabughin "Una fonte ignota dell'Hypnerotomachia Poliphili," *Giornale Storico della Letteratura Italiana* 74 (1919), pp. 41–49; E. Kretsulesco-Quaranta, *Les jardins du songe: Poliphile et la mystique de la Renaissance* (Paris, 1976), p. 20; L. Fierz-David, *The Dream of Poliphilo: The Soul in Love* (Dallas, 1987); S. Battaglia, "Francesco Colonna e il romanzo eterodosso," published in his *Le letterature italiana: Medioevo e umanesimo* (Florence, 1971), pp. 428–436, reproduced in Calvesi, pp. 314–320.

11. See A. Burgess, *Joysprick: An Introduction to the Language of James Joyce* (London, 1973).

12. G. Pozzi and L. A. Ciapponi, "Glossario," in *Hypnerotomachia Poliphili,* by Francesco Colonna (Padua, 1980), 2: 269–308. Hereafter cited as Pozzi and Ciapponi.

13. M. T. Cassella and G. Pozzi, *Francesco Colonna: Biografia e opera* (Padua, 1959), 2: 80–98. Hereafter cited as Casella and Pozzi.

14. P. Pedraza, ed. and trans., *Francesco Colonna: Sueño de Poliphilo* (Murcia, 1981), 1: 40, cites Pozzi's opinion that these neologisms, "extravagant and ponderous, advance slowly, flanked by cohorts of invented adjectives, centaurs and sirens, winding heavily throughout innumerable long lines until, at the end, a verb has been placed in the sentence that had previously seemed deprived of one." See also Cassella and Pozzi, 2: 103.

15. Casella and Pozzi, 2: 78.

16. See M. Lowry, *The World of Aldus Manutius* (Ithaca, 1976), p. 112.

17. N. Villani, *Discorso sulla poesia giocosa* (1631), p. 85; cited in F. Fabbrini, "Indagini sul Poliphilo," *Giornale Storico della Letteratura Italiana* 35 (1900), p. 26, n. 1. P. Marchand, *Dictionnaire historique* (1758; rpt. Paris, 1958), 1: 200.

18. "Così si vede in essa . . . uno stranissimo accozzamento di voci greche, latine, lombarde, ebraiche, caldee . . . che felice non dico che già giunse ad intenderla, ma solo chi si sa dire in che lingua esse sia!" G. Tiraboschi, *Storia della letteratura italiana* (Modena, 1772–1795), 4: 95.

19. Casella and Pozzi, 2: 78: "L'ingrediente di base è sicuramente il volgare: 'cum nostrati lingua loquatur': volgare è tutto il fondo della lingua puramente discorsiva o communicativa; volgare le forme morphologiche (desinenze, forme verbali ecc.); volgari i vocaboli non direttamente significativi ma che servono all'organizzazione sintattica e logica della frase (preposizioni, congiunzioni, avverbi) colle eccezioni abituali alla prosa umanistica d'introdurre certe formule latine: 'cum, tantum, solum, circa ecc.'"

20. L. Crasso: "Res una in eo miranda est, quod cum nostrati lingua loquatur, non minus ad eum cognoscendum opus sit graeca et romana quam tusca et vernacula" (p. iv), in his prologue to the original *Hypnerotomachia*.

21. Pozzi and Ciapponi, "Glossario," 2: 269–308.

22. Casella and Pozzi, 2: 118.

23. R. Dallington, trans., *The Strife of Love in a Dreame* (London, 1592), p. B.

24. Martin, "Aux lecteurs," a.

25. Casella and Pozzi, p. 119. It is worth looking at an example of Casella and Pozzi's masterful philological analysis. Take the following passage of the *Hypnerotomachia*: "O me che non per altro modo una venustissima nympha, insigne di forma, di florente aetate, piu che dire si pote decorata de angelici costumi et de praecipua honestate celebre, nel conspecto degli ochii meie eximiamente praesentata, la visitatione de la quale omni exquisito et delectabile contento humano excedeva, et io allato suo; piena di omni cosa che solatiosamente vale ad amare et appetire provocabonda et da qualunque altra operatione lo intellecto astrahendo, solo in se cumulantilo, non succureva percio ad lo anhelante et voluptabondo desio" (i8v). They comment: "Here Poliphilo is Tantalus, Polia the desired object. But the members of the antithesis are names, not definite; more simply, they are simply juxtaposed one in front of the other, not effectively opposed to one another: in fact the verb that is necessary for the antithesis is missing. The absence of this logical formula is made evident by the adverb *percio* (this is why), which is falsely conclusive, upon which an adversative, as for example 'yet,' should have, although tardily, created the antithesis wished for in the exemplum that dominates the sentence" (2: 119).

26. Ibid., 2: 120, 122.

27. L. Donati, "Studio esegetico sul Poliphilo," *La Bibliofilia* 52 (1950), p. 138.

28. P. Hofer, "Variant Copies of the 1499 Poliphilus," *Bulletin of the New York Public Library* 35 (1932), pp. 475–486.

29. See ibid., also G. Painter, introduction to *The Hypnerotomachia Poliphili of 1499: An Introduction to the Dream, the Dreamer, the Artist, and the Printer* (London, 1963), pp. 20–21.

30. To be sure, some pages are more straightforward than others; the more complex contain descriptive passages. See Casella and Pozzi, 2: 124.

31. Martin, "Aux lecteurs," iii v.

32. C. Popelin, introduction to *Le songe de Poliphile ou Hypnerotomachia* (1883; reprint, Geneva, 1982), 1: viii.

33. Pedraza, *Sueño de Poliphilo,* 1: 40.

34. C. Ripa, *Iconologia* (Padua, 1630).

35. G. Steiner, "On Difficulty" in *On Difficulty and Other Essays* (Oxford, 1978), pp. 18–47; quotation on p. 33.

36. Wind, *Pagan Mysteries,* pp. 103 ff.

37. This attribution was slipped into a poem at the beginning of the French edition of the book. "Here," it begins, "is the high Colonna [which translates as "column," except that here it is capitalized, as if it were a proper name] that holds up such a beautiful example of antique memory." The poem in its entirety reads:

Ecco l'alta Colonna che sostenne
quel bel typo de la memoria antica
Ogni figura, ogni mole, & fabrica,
et varie foggie che segni contenne.

Cio che mille occhi, & mille & mille penne
Veduto & scritto hanno con gran fatica,
In breve sogno tutto qui s'esplica,
In sogno intendo ch'a l'autor avenne.

[Here is the high column that sustains
such a beautiful example of antique memory,
Every figure, every plan and building
and various fragments that contain signs.

That which a thousand eyes and thousands and
    thousands of hands
have seen and written with great labor
in a brief dream is all explained
In a dream, that is, which occurs to the author.]

38. Casella and Pozzi are the major representatives of the first view, as biographers of the Dominican. There are two main partisans of the second view. One is Maurizio Calvesi. His "Identificato l'autore del Polifilo," *Europa Letteraria*, no. 35 (1965), pp. 9–20, was the first serious argument for attributing the book to Francesco Colonna the Colonna prince. This was followed by a book based on the article, *Il sogno di Polifilo prenestino*. Emanuela Kretsulesco-Quaranta's *Les jardins du songe*, based on Calvesi's hypotheses, was the first extensive work devoted to establishing the identity of Francesco Colonna as the heir of Palestrina and scion of the Colonna dynasty. In spite of occasional leaps to conclusions that lack a firm documentary basis, the book contains some valuable research, in particular related to the Colonna family, along the lines first suggested by Calvesi.

39. See G. Biadego, "Intorno al Sogno di Polifilo," *Atti dell'Istituto Veneto di Scienze, Lettere ed Arti* 40 (1900–1901), pp. 699–714.

40. See chapter 1 and M. Lowry, *The World of Aldus*, pp. 144–145, 162–163.

4. IMPLAUSIBLE AUTHORS

1. M. T. Casella and G. Pozzi, *Francesco Colonna: Biografia e opera,* 2 vols. (Padua, 1959), 1:12. Hereafter cited as Casella and Pozzi.

2. Ibid., pp. 23, 24.

3. Ibid., p. 24.

4. "Evagatorium in terrae Sanctae, Arabiae et Aegypti peregrinationem," ed. C. D. Hassler, *Bibliothek der literarischen* 4 (1849), p. 435; qtd. in G. Pozzi and L. A. Ciapponi, eds., *Hypnerotomachia Poliphili,* by Francesco Colonna (Padua, 1980), 1: 13–14.

5. See M. Sanudo, *Diarii* 55 (1900), p. 74; qtd. in Casella and Pozzi, 1: 25.

6. See M. Lowry *The World of Aldus Manutius* (Ithaca, 1976), pp. 121–2 and Casella and Pozzi, 1: 24.

7. This is claimed by D. M. Federici, an early biographer of Colonna (In *Memorie trevigiana sulle opere di disegno dal 1000 al 1800,* vol. 1 [Venice, 1803]), but refuted by Casella and Pozzi (see 1: 30).

8. Ibid., p. 33.

9. Ibid., p. 68.

10. The exact charge against Colonna was "sverginare una putta." See Lowry, *The World of Aldus*, p. 122,

n. 44. See also Casella and Pozzi, 1: 22, 33, and "Documenti," 17, p. 113; 25, p. 116.

11. Casella and Pozzi, 1: 50. See M. Bandello, *Novelliere,* in *Tutte le opere di Matteo Bandello,* ed. F. Flora (Milan, 1934). This is cited in Lowry, *The World of Aldus,* p. 122.

12. Casella and Pozzi, 1:14, 16–30.

13. See E. Kretsulesco-Quaranta, *Les jardins du songe: Poliphile et la mystique de la renaissance* (Paris, 1976), pp. 384–391; and M. Calvesi, *Il sogno di Polifilo prenestino* (Rome, 1980).

14. R. Krautheimer, *Rome: Profile of a City, 312–1308* (Princeton, 1980), p. 255.

15. D. R. Coffin, *Gardens and Gardening in Papal Rome* (Princeton, 1991), p. 182.

16. Ibid., p. 182. See also P. Litta, *Famiglie celebri italiane,* vol. 6, *I Colonna* (Milan, 1885); P. Colonna, *I Colonna* (Rome, 1927); A. Coppi, *Memorie colonesi* (Rome, 1855); P. Petrini, *Memorie Prenestine* (Rome, 1785); L. Rossi, *Die Colonna, Bilder aus Roms Vergangenheit* (Rome, 1912).

17. As I saw on a visit to the Palazzo Colonna, May 1993.

18. R. Weiss, *The Renaissance Discovery of Classical Antiquity* (Oxford, 1968), pp. 33–34.

19. See Calvesi, *Il sogno di Polifilo,* pp. 34–43.

20. Kretsulesco-Quaranta, *Les jardins du songe,* p. 377, n. 1.

21. Weiss, *Discovery of Classical Antiquity,* p. 108. He refers to A. Campagna, "Due note su Roberto Valturio," in *Studi riminesi e bibliografici in onore di Carlo Lucchesi* (Faenza, 1952), p. 15.

22. Weiss, *Discovery of Classical Antiquity,* p. 108; quoting from F. Biondo, *Italia illustrata,* in *Opera* (Basel, 1559), p. 311. On visiting the ruins of Antium, see Calvesi, *Il sogno di Polifilo,* p. 40.

23. See Weiss, *Discovery of Classical Antiquity,* p. 186. See also R. Lanciani, *Li scavi di Roma* (Roma, 1902), 1: 107, 82, 114.

24. Calvesi, *Il sogno di Polifilo,* pp. 136, 407.

25. E. Gombrich, "The Early Medicis as Patrons of Art: A Survey of Primary Sources" (1960), in *Norm and Form* (Edinburgh, 1966), pp. 35–57. See also F. Pintor, "Per la storia Libreria Medicea Rinascimentale Appunti d'Archivio," *Italia Medieoevale* 3 (1960), pp. 190 ff.

26. Vespasiano da Bisticci, *Commentario della vita di Papa Nicola V,* in L. Muratori, *Rerum italicarum scriptores* (Milan, 1751), 25: 271–272.

27. Girolamo Mancini, *Vita di Lorenzo Valla* (Florence, 1881).

28. J. Hankins, "The Popes and Humanism" in *Rome Reborn,* ed. A. Grafton (Washington, D.C., New

Haven, and Vatican City, 1993), p. 57; Calvesi, *Il sogno di Polifilo*, p. 408.

29. On G. Manetti, see Mancini, *Vita di Leon Battista Alberti* (1882; rpt. Florence, 1911), p. 275. See also E. Müntz, *La bibliothèque du Vatican sous Nicolas V* (Paris, 1887). On Nicholas of Cusa, see E. Wind, *Pagan Mysteries of the Renaissance* (Harmondsworth, 1958), 220–247.

30. Calvesi, *Il sogno di Polifilo*, p. 41.

31. M. Calvesi, "Hypnerotomachia Poliphili: Nuovi riscontri e nuove evidenze documentarie per Francesco Colonna Signore di Preneste," *Storia dell'Arte* 60 (1987), pp. 108–109, 116.

32. Calvesi, *Il sogno di Polifilo*, pp. 40, 42.

33. Calvesi, "Hypnerotomachia."

34. C. Burroughs, "Alberti e Roma," in *Leon Battista Alberti*, ed. J. Rykwert and A. Engel (Milan, 1994), pp. 141–143.

35. L. Heydenreich, "Der Palazzo baronale der Colonna in Palestrina," in *W. Friedländer zum 90 Geburtstag* (Berlin, 1985), pp. 85–91; rpt. in Calvesi, *Il sogno di Polifilo*, pp. 58–60.

36. Calvesi, *Il sogno di Polifilo*, p. 62. He sees the presence of many references to Palestrina in the *Hypnerotomachia* as the strongest argument that Colonna was the book's author.

37. See his biography: V. Zabughin, *Guilio Pomponio Leto*, 2 vols., (Grottaferrata, 1910).

38. J. Burckhardt, *The Civilization of the Renaissance*, trans. S. G. Middlemore (New York, 1944; German ed. 1860), pp. 168–169.

39. See A. Grafton, "The Ancient City Restored: Archaeology, Ecclesiastical History, and Egyptology," in Grafton, *Rome Reborn*, pp. 87–124, esp. 94–95. See also A. J. Dunston, "Paul II and the Humanists," *Journal of Religious History* 7, no. 4 (1973), pp. 287–306, esp. p. 288.

40. Coffin, *Gardens and Gardening*, p. 182. His reference is G. B. de Rossi, "L'Accademia di Pomponio Leto e le sue memorie scritte sulle pareti delle catacombi romane," *Bulletino di Archeologia Cristiana*, ser. 5, 1 (1890), pp. 81–94.

41. Calvesi, *Il sogno di Polifilo*, p. 41. See also L. Pastor, *Storia dei papi* (Rome, 1911), 7: 314.

42. The entire episode dealing with the Accademia Romana is to be found in L. Pastor, *Storia dei papi* (Rome, 1911), 2: 304–365. See also A. Reynolds, "The Classical Continuum in Roman Humanism: The Festival of Pasquino, the Robigaglia, and Satire," *Bibliothèque d'Humanisme et Renaissance*, no. 49 (1987), pp. 289–307.

43. See Dunston, "Paul II."

44. Ibid., p. 301. See also J. Delz, "Ein unbekannter Brief von Pomponius Laetus," *Italia Medioevalia et Umanistica* 9 (1966), pp. 417–440; R. J. Palermino, "The Roman Academy, the Catacombs, and the Conspiracy of 1468," *Archivium Historiae Pontificae* 18 (1980), pp. 117–155. These titles are cited in J. D'Amico, *Renaissance Humanism in Papal Rome: Humanists and Churchmen on the Eve of the Reformation* (Baltimore, 1983). See also J. Hankins, *Plato in the Italian Renaissance* (Leiden, New York, and Copenhagen, 1990), 1: 211.

45. Dunston, "Paul II," pp. 300, 299, 287–288.

46. Burckhardt, *The Renaissance*, pp. 23, 22, 33.

47. Quoted in ibid., p. 72.

48. Burckhardt, *The Renaissance*, pp. 72–73.

49. Kretsulesco-Quaranta, *Les jardins du songe*, p. 39.

50. Burckhardt, *The Renaissance*, pp. 69–70. See also Kretsulesco-Quaranta, *Les jardins du songe*, pp. 378–390; Calvesi, *Il sogno di Polifilo*, pp. 52–53.

51. Muratori, *Rerum italiorum scriptores* III, 2a, 877. The decree of 18.1.1432 written by Eugene IV against the Colonnas; referred to in Calvesi, *Il sogno di Polifilo*, p. 38.

52. See Burckhardt, *The Renaissance*, p. 77.

53. Mancini, *Vita di Alberti*, p. 278.

54. Prospero Colonna, *Columnensium Procerum Icones et memoriae, s.n.t.*; cited by Kretsulesco-Quaranta, *Les jardins du songe*, p. 38.

55. See Burckhardt, *The Renaissance*, pp. 69–70.

56. D'Amico, *Renaissance Humanism in Papal Rome*, p. 49.

57. Calvesi, *Il sogno di Polifilo*, 1980.

58. A. Grafton, "The Ancient City Restored: Archaeology, Ecclesiastical History, and Egyptology," in Grafton, *Rome Reborn*, pp. 87–125; quote from p. 90.

59. See W. S. Heckscher, "Relics of Pagan Antiquity in Mediaeval Settings," *Journal of the Warburg Institute* 1 (1937–1938), pp. 204–220, for a full account.

60. The work is cited in ibid.

61. The work is discussed in T. Buddensieg, "Gregory the Great, the Destroyer of Pagan Idols: The History of a Medieval Legend concerning the Decline of Ancient Art and Literature," *Journal of the Warburg and Courtault Institutes*, 28 (1965), pp. 44–65. It is mentioned in C. Frugoni, "L'antiquità: dai Mirabilia alla propaganda politica," in *Memoria dell'antico nell'arte italiana*, ed. S. Settis (Turin, 1986), p. 7. In *De mirabilis civitatis Romae*, another text of the fourteenth century, the destruction of the Colossus of the Colosseum is attributed not to Pope Gregory but to Pope Sylvester. See R. Valentini and G. Zucchetti, *Codice topographico della città di Roma* (Rome, 1953).

62. See Anonimo Romano, *Chronica,* ed. G. Porta (Milan, 1979), p. 143.

63. See Calvesi, "Hypnerotomachia," pp. 85–136.

64. See Kretsulesco-Quaranta, *Les jardins du songe,* p 385.

65. Ibid., p. 388.

66. The poems read:

Ad Francescum Columnam

Quis iam Pythagoram recte sensisse negarit,
    Qui remeare animas in nova membra putat?
Quin nova non tantum remeant in membra, sed
    unum
    In corpus geminae saepe redire solent.
Carmina, et illa modis tua verba soluta, reversam
    In te Arpinatis Virgiliique probant.
Tu quoque cognosces, si pauca haec legeris, in me,
    France, animam Mevi vivere vel Bavii.

De Eodem

Olim Roma duos habuit clarissima linguae
    Lumina, verum humili natus uterque domo
    est.
Ambo aliam stirpem a patria traxere deditque
    Arpinum huic, illi Mantua clara genus.
Nunc proprios priscoque ortos de sanguine in
    uno
    Hos habet: in verbis Franciscus utrumque
    refert.

They are from the epigrams published by B. Ziliotto, *Raffaele Zovenzoni: La viata, i carmi* (Trieste, 1950). The volume contains an edition of Zovenzoni's *Istrias* that includes the poems in question. In an attempt to enhance this Francesco's claim to authorship of the *Hypnerotomachia;* other equally unconvincing documents have been unearthed that are also addressed to him, by even very minor literary figures. In particular, there is a letter in the form of a long, lamenting, extremely conventional poem by an aristocratic childhood friend of Francesco's. See S. D. Squarzina, "Francesco Colonna, principe, letterato, e la sua cerchia," *Storia dell'Arte* 60 (1987), pp. 137–157. For the attribution of the *Hypnerotomachia Poliphili* to Francesco Colonna, see Calvesi, *Il sogno di Polifilo;* more recently, see also his "Hypnerotomachia."

5. THE REAL POLIPHILO

1. For example, Alberti is studied as a Platonist in R. Wittkower, *Architectural Principles in the Age of Humanism* (London, 1949), and in H. Muehlmann, *L. B. Alberti: Aesthetische Theorie der Renaissance* (Bonn, 1982); as a humanist in M. Tafuri, *L'architettura dell'umanesimo* (Bari, 1969), and an ironic critic of humanism in his *Ricerca del rinascimento* (Turin, 1992). C. Smith's passages on Alberti in her *Architecture in the Culture of Early Humanism: Ethics, Aesthetics, and Eloquence* (Oxford, 1992) concentrate on his early writings on aesthetics; G. Santinello, *L. B. Alberti: una visione estetica del mondo e della vita* (Florence, 1962), is also preoccupied with Alberti's aesthetics. F. Borsi, *Leon Battista Alberti,* trans. R. G. Carpianini (New York, 1977), is an in-depth analysis of his architecture; C. W. Westfall, *In This Most Perfect Paradise: Alberti, Nicholas V, and the Invention of Conscious Urban Planning in Rome, 1447–1455* (University Park, Pa., 1974), is a study whose title speaks for itself; M. Jarzombek, *On Leon Baptista Alberti: His Literary and Aesthetic Theories* (Cambridge, Mass., 1989) is devoted mostly to Alberti's *Intercenales* and his early literary works.

2. G. Mancini, *Vita di L. B. Alberti* (Florence, 1882; rpt. 1911, and 1967); Rome, the 1911 edition is cited here. This book is a classic and has served as a compendium of facts and as a biographical narrative framework whose traces are detected in all subsequent comprehensive studies of Alberti; for example, P. H. Michel, *Un idéal humain au XVe siècle: la pensée de L. B. Alberti* (Paris, 1930).

3. Joan Gadol's *Leon Battista Alberti: Universal Man of the Early Renaissance* (Chicago, 1969) adds much new evidence about Alberti's visual and scientific thinking to Mancini's framework. *Leon Battista Alberti,* ed. J. Rykwert and A. Engel (Milan, 1994), also contributes new knowledge about Alberti and presents many new attributions.

4. L. B. Alberti, *Vita di Leon Battista Alberti,* in *Opera volgari,* ed. A. Bonucci (Florence, 1843–1849), 1: lxxxix ff.

5. L. B. Alberti, *De commodis litterarum atque incommodis,* ed. G. Farris (Milan, 1971), p. 48; trans. in M. Jarzombek, *On Leon Baptista Alberti* (Cambridge, Mass., 1989), p. 8.

6. See G. Ponte, *Leon Battista Alberti, umanista e scrittore* (Genoa, 1981).

7. Mancini, *Vita di Alberti,* p. 232.

8. See Alberti, *Della famiglia,* in *Opere volgari,* ed. Bonucci, 2: 146; qtd. in Mancini, *Vita di Alberti,* p. 323.

9. C. Landino, *Apologia di Dante,* qtd. in Mancini, *Vita di Alberti,* p. 442.

10. Cecil Grayson is responsible for the dating. See Alberti's *Opere volgari,* ed. C. Grayson, vol. 3 (Bari, 1973).

11. See R. Fubini and A. M. Gallorini, "L'autobiografia di Leon Battista Alberti: Studio e edizione," *Rinascimento* 12 (1972), 21–78, esp. p. 70.

12. See Alberti, *Opere volgari*, 5 vols., ed. Bonucci. See Bonucci's introduction to *Deifira*, vol. 3.

13. See G. Gorni, "Storia del Certame Coronario," *Rinascimento* 12 (1972), pp. 135–181; and Ponte, *Alberti*, pp. 182–183. On his poetic oeuvre as a whole, see L. B. Alberti, *Rime e versioni poetiche*, G. Gorni, (Florence, 1954).

14. See Mancini, *Vita di Alberti*, pp. 40–44.

15. L. B. Alberti, *Vita di Leon Battista Alberti*, vol. 1 of *Opra volgari*, ed. A. Bonucci (Florence, 1843), pp. lxxxix ff.

16. Lapo di Castiglionchio, "Lettera dedicatoria dei 'sacrifizi' di Luciano all'Alberti," in Mancini, *Vita di Alberti*, p.

17. This list is based on a comparison of the indexes of G. Orlandi and P. Portoghesi's edition of Leon Battista Alberti's *L'architettura (De re aedificatoria)*, 2 vols. (Milan, 1966); the edition of J. Rykwert, N. Leach, and R. Tavernor of Alberti's *On the Art of Building in Ten Books* (Cambridge, Mass., 1991); and the edition of the *Hypnerotomachia Poliphili* by G. Pozzi and L. A. Ciapponi (Padua, 1980), hereafter cited as Pozzi and Ciapponi.

18. See index of Francesco di Giorgio's *Trattati d'architettura*, ed. C. Maltesi (Milan, 1966). The index of Filarete's *Trattato* compiled by John R. Spencer indicates that that author most often refers to Alberti (sixty-seven times). Although this index, like that of Alberti's *De re aedificatoria*, does contain Pliny, it does not include Hesiod, Homer, or Demosthenes. In addition, Filarete makes Biblical references—to Adam, Abraham, and Isaac—which Alberti does not. See the index to *Filarete's Treatise on Architecture*, trans. by J. R. Spencer (New Haven, 1965), 1: 333–339.

19. See J. R. Hays, ed., *The Genius of Arab Civilization: Source of Renaissance* (Cambridge, Mass., 1983). For the influence of the Hebrew Cabalistic writings and Arabic writings on European culture in the Renaissance, see E. Wind, *Pagan Mysteries of the Renaissance* (Harmondsworth, 1958).

20. See P. Watts, *Nicolas Cusanus: A Fifteenth-Century Vision of Man* (Leiden, 1982). See also Wind, *Pagan Mysteries*.

21. See A. Hamilton, "Eastern Churches and Western Scholarship," in *Rome Reborn*, ed. A. Grafton (Washington, D.C., New Haven, and Vatican City, 1993), pp. 225–291.

22. See Wind, *Pagan Mysteries*, pp. 256–257.

23. A. Burgess, *Joysprick: An Introduction to the Language of James Joyce* (London, 1973).

24. C. Landino, "Commento sopra la 'commedia'"; referred to in Mancini, *Vita di Alberti*, p. 326. Cf. R. Cardini, *La critica del Landino* (Florence, 1973), p. 130.

25. L. B. Alberti, *Dinner Pieces*, ed. and trans. D. Marsh (Binghampton, 1987), p. 3.

26. Ibid., p. 11.

27. This is true particularly of the passage depicting the rape of Praise by Momus, disguised as a climbing ivy. See A. Perosa, "Considerazioni sul testo e lingua nel 'Momus' dell'Alberti," in *The Language of Literature in Renaissance Italy: For Cecil Grayson*, ed. P. Hainsworth et al. (Oxford, 1988), pp. 45–62. See also the introduction by A. di Grado to L. B. Alberti, *Momo o del principe*, trans. R. Consolo (Genoa, 1986).

28. Alberti, *On the Art of Building*, trans. Rykwert et al., II.11, p. 3; see also VI.2. This edition will hereafter be cited parenthetically in the text.

29. See the editorial comments by R. Rinaldi in his edition of Alberti's *Ludi matematici* (Milan, 1980), p. 47. He traces the influence of Hero on Alberti's inventions. For a more detailed treatment of the texts with which Alberti would have been familiar, see G. Scaglia, "Alberti e la meccanica della tecnologia descritta nel 'De Re aedificatoria' e nei 'Ludi Matematici,'" in Rykwert and Engel, *Leon Battista Alberti*, pp. 316–329.

30. See Scaglia, "Alberti e la meccanica."

31. Scaglia, "Alberti e la meccanica," p. 324.

32. See A. Khomentovskaia, "Felice Feliciano da Verona come l'auteur de l'*Hypnerotomachia Poliphili*," *La Bibliofilia* 37 (1935), pp. 154–174, 200–212; 38 (1936), pp. 20–48, 92–102. She quotes P. Fleury Mottelay, *Bibliographical History of Electricity and Magnetism* (London, 1920), and F. M. Feldhaus, *Die Technik des Antike und Mittelalters* (Potsdam, 1935).

33. In 1535, Francesco de Marchi made an attempt to examine them. He designed a special diving suit: a wooden bell reinforced by metal hoops, suspended from a boat on the surface and covering the upper half of the diver. De Marchi suffered a nosebleed and got tangled up in his harness. In addition his view through a small window was hampered by the murkiness of the water. Worst of all, fish were attracted by the sandwich he had brought down with him and nibbled his exposed flesh in spite of his efforts to shoo them away. This endeavor is described in L. Sprague de Camp, *Ancient Engineers* (Cambridge, Mass., 1960), pp. 153–159.

34. See Mancini, *Vita di Alberti*, pp. 278–280.

35. Gadol, *Alberti*, p. 94.

36. See Biondo's account in *Roma illustrata*; qtd. in R. Weiss, *The Renaissance Discovery of Classical Antiquity* (Oxford, 1968), p. 113.

37. "Cum quale temerario dunque invento di arte? Cum quale virtute et humane forcie et ordine et incredibile impensa, cum coelestae aemulatione tanto nell'aire tale pondo suggesto riportare? Cum quale ergate et cum quale orbiculate troclee et cum quale capre o polispasio et altre tractorie machine et tramate armature?" (b).

38. Mancini, *Vita di Alberti*, p. 278.

39. See u7. This was remarked on by Khomentovskaia, "Felice Feliciano," p.

40. This is pointed out by Pozzi and Ciapponi, 2: 225–226. The passage from the *Hypnerotomachia* reads: "Et questa per medio dille due prime correspondeva, per che omni figura dispare angulare uno angulo obvia nel mediano dell'intercalato aequilatero constituito et poscia dal centro una linea nel medio della linea sopra la circunferentia adiacente deducta, tanto e la septanaria divisione dilla dicta circulare figura" (y7v).

41. Pozzi and Ciapponi, 2: 201. See *De re aedificatoria*, V.2: "Decem angulorum aream item ex ciclo perficiemus. Nam duos cicli diametros sese mutuo ad pares utrimque angulos secantes perscribemus. Tum ex ipsis semidiametris, utrum velis, dividemus binas in partes coaequales. Inde a puncto istic divisionis ad sublime caput alterius diametri lineam rectam via obliqua aducemus. Hoc igitur ex linea sic ducta si ademeris quantum est quarta totius diametri pars, quod illic reliquum residebit, id erit areae latus decangulae."

42. There is some debate whether it was Brunelleschi or Alberti who formalized the rules of perspective. E. Panofsky, *Perspective as Symbolic Form*, trans. C. S. Wood (New York, 1991; German ed., 1927), and Gadol, *Alberti*, attribute the invention to Alberti, and I find this argument the most compelling. See also S. Edgerton, "Alberti's Perspective: A New Discovery and a New Interpretation," *Art Bulletin* 48 (1966), pp. 367–378, and his *Renaissance Rediscovery of Linear Perspective* (New York, 1975).

43. Panofsky, *Perspective as Symbolic Form*, p. 570. He deals with the protoperspectival painting of Duccio and Ambrozio Lorenzetti.

44. See Gadol, *Alberti*, p. 42.

45. L. B. Alberti, *On Painting*, trans. J. R. Spencer (London, 1956), p. 43.

46. Gadol, *Alberti*, p. 28.

47. Gadol, *Alberti*, p. 168.

48. Alberti, *On Painting*, p. 56.

49. See Filarete, *Treatise on Architecture*, 1: 5.

50. Gadol, *Alberti*, p. 29.

51. Alberti, *On Painting*, p. 46. I have amended Spencer's translation slightly.

52. Panofsky, *Perspective as Symbolic Form*, p. 57. Panofsky mentions the example of the Annunciation, although Lorenzetti's *Purification* of 1432, now in the Uffizi, is regarded as the better example of *pavimento*, as Professor Christian Klamt has kindly pointed out to me.

53. Gadol, *Alberti*, pp. 23–32.

54. Alberti, *On Painting*, p. 71.

55. Ibid., p. 48.

56. "[C]eollocare cum pensiculata distributione le promptissime figure sopra li iusti piani. Et come le linee dille fabriche allo obiecto trahevano. Et come dagli ochii alcuni lochi quasi se perdevano. Et le cose iprefecte reducte a poco al perfecto et cusi percontra, il suo indicio as gli chi concedendo. . . . Aque, fonti, monti, colli, oschetti, animali dipravato il coloramento cum la distantia & cum il lume opposito" (d1v). This example was found by Khomenstovskaia, "Felice Feliciano," p. 24.

57. "[E]ra la profunditate tanto artificiosamente dall' artifice ficta, che, per la coloratine quelle dimonstratione essere vere mentivano, et di videre una absorbentissima voragine, cum mirifica aemulatione di gli coloramenti et di symmetria lineale di perspecto et dille figure la elegantia et copioso onvento et artifica designatione et cum incredibile argutia, che Parrhasio ephesio, insigne pictore, unque primo di simile excogitato non pote gloriarse" (q1).

58. Panofsky, *Perspective as Symbolic Form*, pp. 52–53.

59. Alberti, *On Painting*, p. 67. I have amended the translation.

60. A. M. Hind, *An Introduction to a History of Woodcut, with a Detailed Study of Work Done in the Fifteenth Century* (1935; rpt. New York, 1963), 2:466.

61. Panofsky, *Perspective as Symbolic Form*, pp. 49–59.

62. Mancini, *Vita di Alberti*, p. 282: "Insegna a misurare le alteze, le distanze e profondità per mezzo di triangoli, i odi di fare orologi ad aria e ad acqua con semplici meccanismi, di adoperare le meridiane portalili, di conoscere le ore osservando il moto delle stelle."

63. Borsi, *Alberti*, p. 33.

64. Mancini, *Vita di Alberti*, p. 103; Alberti, *Opera inedita*, ed. G. Mancini (Florence, 1890), 36–46. See Gadol, *Alberti*, pp. 181–185.

65. Bernardo Rucellai, qtd. in Mancini, *Vita di Alberti*, p. 103, from Oricellarii, *De urbe*, p. 1099.

66. Gadol, *Alberti*, p. 114. See also Weiss, *Discovery of Classical Antiquity*, p. 91, referring to D. Gnoli, "Di alcune piante topographice di Roma ignote o poco

note" *Bulletino della Commissione Archaeologica Communale* 13 (1885), p. 66: "As was explained by Gnoli, Alberti's instructions were to draw a circle, which was to be called the horizon and would be divided into forty-eight degrees, each degree in turn subdivided into four. Then from the center, which was the Capitol, a mobile radius divided into fifty degrees, each degree being in turn subdivided into four, was made so as to reach the horizon. . . . The plan resulted from these instructions and a vertical projection."

67. For references, see chapter 1.

68. See Sprague de Camp, *The Ancient Engineers*, pp. 154–155.

69. Alberti, *On Painting*, p. 49.

70. Ibid., pp. 49, 67.

71. Biondo, *Italia illustrata* (Brescia, 1482), p. 305; qtd. in Mancini, *Vita di Alberti*, p. 277. For Manetti, see p. 346.

72. Giorgio Vasari, *Lives of the Painters, Sculptors, and Architects* trans. A. B. Hinds, ed. W. Gaunt (New York, 1963), 1:350: "As we see from some sheets of his in our book, containing a drawing of the Ponte S. Agnolo, and of the roof made there from his design for the Loggia . . ."

73. Ibid., 1:350, cited by Mancini, *Vita di Alberti*, pp. 289–291.

74. Qtd. by Spencer, p. 21, n. 21, in his edition of Alberti, *On Painting*.

75. "In painting Alberti achieved nothing of any great importance or beauty. The very few paintings of his that are far from perfect, but this is not surprising since he devoted himself more to his studies than to draughtsmanship"; Vasari, *Lives of the Painters*, 1:350.

76. Ibid., p. 346.

77. Cristoforo Landino, *Chomento di Christoforo Landino Fiorentino sopra la comedia di Dante Alighieri poeta fiorentino* (1481), qtd. in Borsi, *Alberti*, p. 365.

78. Qtd. in Alberti, *On the Art of Building*, p. 1.

79. Vasari does mention Francesco di Giorgio, but only as a sculptor and an architect-engineer. See *Lives of the Painters*, 2:26.

80. See Borsi, *Alberti*, pp. 19–20; Mancini, *Vita di Alberti*, pp. 172 ff.

81. H. W. Janson, *Sculpture of Donatello* (Princeton, 1957), 2:65–72, 129–131.

82. Keith Christiansen, "The Art of Andrea Mantegna," in *Andrea Mantegna*, ed. J. Martineau (New York and London, 1992), pp. 32–42, esp. p. 34.

83. Ibid., p. 35.

84. J. Greenstein, *Mantegna and Painting as Historical Narrative* (Chicago, 1992) p. 12.

85. A. Petrucci, "L'Alberti e la scrittura," in Rykwert and Engel, *Leon Battista Alberti*, pp. 276–281.

86. See H. Belting, "The New Role of Narrative in Public Painting of the Trecento: Historia and Allegory," in *Pictorial Narrative in Antiquity and the Middle Ages*, ed. H. L. Kessler and M. S. Simpson, Studies in the History of Art, vol. 16 (Washington, D.C., and Hanover, N.H., 1985), pp. 151–170.

87. Alberti, *On Painting*, p. 79.

88. Ibid., p. 77.

89. Ibid., p. 81. Spencer's translation is amended in part.

90. See E. Battisti and G. Saccaro Battisti, *Le macchine cifrate di Giovanni Fontana* (Milan, 1984), pp. 60–80.

91. Mancini, *Vita di Alberti*, p. 102: "Un applicazione della scoperta dell'Alberti si riscontra ne' teatrini di vedure ottiche matematiche, dove si mostrano porti di mare, combattimenti navali, etc. La luce è data attraverso di carte oliate e regolata a forza si specchi. Gli spettri mostrati ne' teatri sono un'altra applicazione dell'invenzione di Battista. Il fondamento rudimentale della cinematografia riposa sugli spettacoli moventisi." At the time he was writing, street theaters in Italy used similar boxes. See also J. and P. Remise, *La magie lumineuse* (Paris, 1978).

92. Vasari, *Lives of the Painters*, 1:347.

93. Q. de Quincy, *Histoire de la vie des plus célèbres architectes* (Paris, 1830), p. 85.

94. "Miracoli della pittura, quali diversi miei compagni videro da me fatti in Roma"; Alberti, *Opere volgari*, ed. Bonucci, 4:25, 34. See also Mancini, *Vita di Alberti*, p. 101.

95. Alberti, *Vita*, p. cii (my translation of the following passage): "Coll'arte di dipingere l'Alberti eseguì cose inaudite ed incredibili agli spettatori, le quali racchiuse in piccola cassa mostrava da stretto pertugio. Vi vedevi montagne altissime, vaste province, estesissimo golfo bagnato dal mare, ed in gran lontananza regioni tanto remote da scorgerle confusamente. Tali cose appellava dimostrazioni, ed erano così bene congegnate, che gli esperti e gl'inesperti dubitavano di osservare cose vere e naturali, non dipinte. Le dimostrazioni erano di due specie, e le denominava diurne e notturne. In queste vedevi Arturo, le Pleiade, Orione e simili scintellanti costellazioni, risplendeva la luna nescente dalle vette di dirupati monti e le stelle mattutine. Nelle diurne sfolgoreggiava ed ampiamente illuminava l'immense orbe terraqueo, l'estro che, per dirlo con Omero, rifulge dopo l'Aurora madre della luce. Fecesi ammirare da certi mangati greci pratici del mare, poichè mostrando loro questo finto mondo attraverso il piccolo foro e domandando

loro che cosa vedevano, risposero:—scorgiamo una flotta in alto mare, prima di messodi approdera, se non glielo impedirà il turbine e la violenta tempesta che s'avanza da levante. Quindi il mare ingrossa e da segni minacciosi col riflettere troppo vivamente i raggi del sole—Peraltro poneva maggiore industria nell'investigare tali cose che nel divulgarle, e si studiava maggiormente d'esercitare l'ingegno che di cercar fama."

96. See Spencer's commentary in his English translation of Alberti's *De pictura, On Painting,* p. 106: "According to Manetti, Brunelleschi painted a small panel about 12 inches square of the baptistry of Florence. The observer looked through a whole from the back of the panel, placed at what we now call the vanishing point, into a mirror held at arm's length. Thus both viewing point and the distance were established."

97. See A. di Tuccio Manetti, *Vita di Filippo Brunelleschi* (Milan, 1976). For a reconstruction of Brunelleschi's demonstration, see L. Vagnetti, *De naturali et artificiali perspectiva* (Florence, 1979), pp. 200–202.

98. Alberti, *On Painting,* p. 83.

99. See Smith, *Architecture in the Culture of Early Renaissance Humanism,* pp. 98–117. "The actual experience of the urban fabric is optical rather than mathematical, dynamic rather than static, and unfolds in a temporal sequence determined by the spectators's physical movement" (p. 117).

100. C. Pedretti, *Leonardo Architect* (London, 1986), p. 309.

101. R. Wittkower, *Architectural Principles in the Age of Humanism,* p. 63.

102. Doni is quoted by Pedretti, *Leonardo Architect,* p. 120.

103. See A. Cazona, "Ludovico Gonzaga, Leon Battista Alberti, Luca Fancelli e il problema della cripta di San Sebastiano," in Rykwert and Engel, *Leon Battista Alberti,* pp. 252–275.

104. See J. Pieper, "Un ritratto di Leon Battista Alberti architetto: osservazioni su due capitelli emblematici nel duomo di Pienza," in Rykwert and Engel, *Leon Battista Alberti,* pp. 54–63.

105. See Borsi, *Alberti,* pp. 193–199, for the hypothesis that Alberti designed the palace, with Laurana as the engineer who supervised the project.

106. Giovanni Rucellai, *Zibaldone quaresimale* (London, 1960), pp. 118–122.

107. Vasari, *Lives of the Painters,* 1:346; Gadol, *Alberti,* p. 12.

108. Gadol, *Alberti,* p. 12.

109. Alberti, *Opere volgari,* ed. Bonucci, 1:48, *Della tranquillità dell'animo:* "Oh! dolce cosa quella gloria quale acquistiamo con nostra fatica. Degne fatiche le nostre, per quali possiamo a quei che non sono in vita con noi, mostrare d'essere vivuti con altro indizio che colla età, e a quelli che verranno lasciargli di nostra vita altra cognizione e nome che solo un sasso a nostra sepoltura inscritto e consignato! Dicea Ennio poeta: non mi piangete, non mi fate esequie, ch'io volo vivo fra le parole degli uomini doti."

110. Alberti, *Vita,* trans. in Borsi, *Alberti,* p. 360.

111. J. Burckhardt, *The Civilization of the Renaissance,* trans. S. G. Middlemore (New York, 1944; German ed. 1860), p. 86.

112. Quoted in Borsi, *Alberti,* p. 360.

113. My translation of "Tu me chiedesti molte volte, piu tempo fa, questi libri, *De profugiis aerumnarum* quali a noi erano perduti, per buono rispetto non diron come, ma tu conosca la natura di Messer battista mio fratello, ei non sa negare a persone cosa la quale gli sia chiesta: non diro piu. Un certo suo domestico . . . chi chiese questi libri subito che furono compiuti, gia passati anni circa anni trenta; ed ebbe la prima copia originale. Poi diede scuse e negolla avere, e noi non sapevano onde recuperarla. Ora la ritroviamo"; Alberti, *Opere volgari,* ed. Bonucci, 1:5, qtd. in Mancini, *Vita di Alberti,* p. 185.

114. See the "nota sul testo" by Alberti's Italian translator, Giovanni Orlandi, in *L'architettura,* pp. 1005–1013; see also Orlandi's "Le primi fasi nella diffusione del trattato architettonico albertiano," in Rykwert and Engel, *Leon Battista Alberti,* pp. 96–106. He quotes, in turn, the pioneering work on the manuscript by Cecil Grayson. See C. Grayson, "Un codice del *De re aedificatoria* posseduto da Bernardo Bembo," in *Studi letterari: Miscellania in onore di Emilio Santini* (Palermo, 1956), pp. 181–188.

115. See Orlandi, "Le primi fasi."

116. On the discovery by C. Colombo Pasinetti, see ibid.

117. Leonardo, "On Movements;—to know how much a ship advances in an hour," in *On Moving in Water,* in *The Notebooks of Leonardo da Vinci* (New York, 1970), pp. 173–174: "The ancients used various devices to ascertain the distance gone by a ship each hour, among which Vitruvius gives one in his work on Architecture. . . . There is another method tried by experiment with a known distance between one island and another; and this is done by a board or under the pressure of wind which strikes on it with more swiftness. This is in Battista Alberti."

118. Alberti, *Opere volgari,* ed. Bonucci, 3:5.

119. Macrobius, *Saturnalia* 7.2.2–3: "Ut aliud sonet, aliud intelligas." Quoted by Marsh in Alberti, *Dinner Pieces*, p. 5.

120. Ibid., pp. 210, 154.

121. See RL 12692 of the Windsor collection, and f. 80 r–a of the Codex Atlanticus.

122. E. H. Wilkins, *A History of Italian Literature* (Cambridge, Mass., 1954), p. 106.

123. E. H. Gombrich, "Hypnerotomachiana," *Journal of the Warburg and Courtauld Institutes* 16 (1951), pp. 119–22.

124. J. Bruner, *Actual Minds, Possible Worlds* (Cambridge, Mass., 1986), p. 46.

125. See Gadol, *Alberti*, pp. 207–208. The quotes are from Alberti's text.

126. Ibid., pp. 210–211, 208.

127. See C. L. Martinelli, "Philodoxeos Fabula Edizione Critica," *Rinascimento* 17 (1977), pp. 144–147, quotation on p. 147; qtd. in Jarzombek, *Alberti*, p. 17.

128. Bonucci, introduction in Alberti, *Opere volgari*, 3:246.

129. Ibid., p. 250.

130. Mancini, *Vita di Alberti*, pp. 26, 257, quoting Alberti's *Canis*, fol. 2.

131. See H. Klotz, "Forma der Anonymität," in *Essays in Honor of Sumner Crosbie* (New York, 1976), pp. 303–312. Quoted in Borsi, *Alberti*, p. 291.

132. Mancini, *Vita di Alberti*, p. 14. The paintings still exist.

133. Alberti, *Vita*, 1:93.

134. Alberti, *On the Art of Building*, VI.3, p. 158.

135. Alberti, *Vita* 1:1, 2:xcii; cited in Mancini, *Vita di Alberti*, p. 40.

136. Alberti, *Dinner Pieces*, p. 5.

137. Mancini, *Vita di Alberti*, pp. 233–245. The debate was settled once and for all in Pelegrini, "A. Pandolfini," *Giornale Storico della Letteratura Italiana* 8 (1886), pp. 36 ff.

138. D. H. Michel, *La pensée de L. B. Alberti* (Paris, 1930), p. 29.

139. On *Efebie*, see Mancini, *Vita di Alberti*, p. 59; on *Deifira*, see ibid.

140. Mancini, *Vita di Alberti*, pp. 277–278.

141. Two factors might explain why the *Hypnerotomachia* ends with a reference to the town of Treviso in early May 1467: "Tarvisii . . . M.CCCC.LXVII." First, Donatello was commissioned to paint a series of *trionfi*, completed in 1453. As one of Donatello's closest friends, who probably helped inspire his work, it is plausible that Alberti would have known the town of Treviso, as well as the members of the prominent Lelli family there. Second, it is known that Cardinal Lelli was in the papal curia, around 1464; see E. Kretsulesco-Quaranta, *Les jardins du songe: Poliphile et la mystique de la renaissance* (Paris, 1976), pp. 379 ff. We might then expect there to have been a visit to the Lelli family around 1467, when Alberti would have been finishing the book. See also M. Lowry, *The World of Aldus Manutius* (Ithaca, 1979), p. 122. Indeed the fictitious Polia introduces herself as belonging to the factual Lelli lineage. See also M. Billanovitch, "Francesco Colonna, il *Poliphilo* e la famiglia Lelli," *Italia Medioevale e Umanistica* 19 (1968), pp. 187–256; Pozzi and Ciapponi, 2:11–13. But we are here in the realm of pure speculation, which is thus best relegated to this footnote.

142. See C. Jordan, *Renaissance Feminism: Literary and Political Models* (New York, 1990), pp. 52–53. See also G. Mancini, *Vita*, pp. 78–79, about Alberti's misogyny.

143. "Architettura civile e militare," in Francesco di Giorgio, *Trattati*, 1:290 ff.

144. See "Indice dei nomi di persona e di luogo del commento," in Pozzi and Ciapponi, 2:323.

145. Gadol, *Alberti*, p. 186.

146. It is Pozzi who points to the similarity between the aquatic labyrinth of the *Hypnerotomachia* and the one described in Alberti's early work, "Fatum et Fortuna," from *Intercenales*, contained in *Opera inedita*, p. 36. See Pozzi and Ciapponi, 2:121.

147. For further reading on contemporary critical regionalism and historical roots, see L. Lefaivre and A. Tzonis, "Critical Regionalism," in *Critical Regionalism: The Pomona Meeting, Proceedings*, ed. S. Amourgis (Pomona, Calif., 1991), pp. 3–23. See R. Krautheimer, "Alberti's Templum Etruscum," in *Studies in Early Christian, Medieval, and Renaissance Art* (New York, 1963), pp. 333–339, for a parallel between Alberti's view of Etruscan architecture and his S. Andrea.

148. Alberti, *Opere volgari*, ed. Bonucci, 1:202. Christine Smith, *Architecture in the Culture*, pp. 5–6, first emphasized the importance of this passage.

149. According to Pozzi and Ciapponi, 2:156–157, n. 6. Alberti describes the round temple in VII.4, p. 196.

150. Borsi, *Alberti*, p. 50.

151. See H. Burns, "Quattrocento Architecture and the Antique: Some Problems," in R. R. Bolgar, ed., *Classical Influences on European Culture* (Cambridge, 1971), pp. 269–287, esp. p. 270.

152. T. Temanza, *Vite dei più celebre architetti e scultori veneziani che fiorirono nel secolo decimosesto* (Venice, 1778), p. 51, and L. Donati, "Studio esegetico sul Poliphilo," *La Bibliofilia* 52 (1950), p. 158.

153. I would like to thank Anne Engel for pointing this out to me in private conversation.

154. Bernardo Rucellai, *De urbe Roma*, in R. Valentini and G. Zucchetti, *Codice topografico della città di Roma* (Rome, 1953), p. 445.

155. See Mancini, *Vita di Alberti*, pp. 296–297. He mentions Milizia.

156. H. Burns, "A Drawing by L. B. Alberti," *Architectural Design* 49, nos. 5–6 (1979), pp. 45–56.

157. Mancini, *Vita di Alberti*, pp. 320, 471–473. Quasi-hemispheric domes had been built—Francesco di Giorgio's at S. Bernardino in Urbino, for example—but these were relatively small and simpler to construct.

158. Alberti, *On Painting*, p. 51.

159. This effect is often noted by scholars, and corresponds to my own experience. See Borsi, *Alberti*, p. 272. Wittkower's views on S. Andrea are found in *Architectural Principles in the Age of Humanism*," p. 56.

160. Jarzombek, *Alberti*, p. 104.

161. Quoted from Alberti's *Vita* by Borsi, p. 360.

162. Alberti, *Teogonio*; qtd. in Jarzombek, *Alberti*, p. 104.

163. C. Grayson, "Villa: un opusculo sconosciuto," *Rinascimento* 6 (1953), p. 45.

164. Cited in Mancini, *Vita di Alberti*, p. 278. See Biondo, *Romo instaurata*, in *Opera* (Basel, 1559), p. 240.

165. This aspect is what most interested, for example, Anthony Blunt, who saw in it the most influential feature of the book; see "The Hypnerotomachia Poliphili in Seventeenth-Century France," *Journal of the Warburg Institute* 1 (1937–1938), 117–137.

166. See C. Hussey, *The Picturesque* (London, 1925).

167. Alberti, *Della famiglia*, book 3, pp. 179–180; translated in Borsi, *Alberti*, p. 10.

168. Alberti mentions these artists by name in the prologue to *De pictura;* see *On Painting*, p. 39.

169. Mancini, *Vita di Alberti*, pp. 111 ff.

170. Oricellarii, *De urbe*, p. 1099 (see n. 65 above).

171. Quoted in Mancini, *Vita di Alberti*, pp. 156, 178, respectively.

172. P. Fiore and M. Tafuri, eds., *Francesco di Giorgio architetto*, (Milan, 1993). He was probably more prolific than Alberti in terms of built architectural designs.

173. *Filarete's Treatise on Architecture*, 1:16.

174. On S. Maria Novella, see Wittkower, *Architectural Principles in the Age of Humanism*, p. 35.

175. On the Tempio Malatestiano, see ibid., pp. 35, 39. See also Tafuri, *L'architettura dell'umanesimo*, p. 30.

176. This is according to R. Krautheimer, "Alberti's Templum Etruscum," in *Studies in Early Christian, Medieval, and Renaissance Art*, trans. A. Frazer et al. (New York, 1969), pp. 333 ff.

177. See M. Dezzi Bardeschi, "Nuove ricerche sul S. Sepolchro nella Capella Rucellai a Firenze," *Marmo*, no. 2 (1963), pp. 13–21. On the piazza of Pienza, see Smith, *Architecture in the Culture of Early Humanism*, pp. 98–129.

178. See Borsi, *Alberti*, pp. 20–25.

179. Wittkower, *Architecture in the Age of Humanism*, p. 56.

180. Cardinal Gonzaga is quoted in S. Davari, "Ancora della chiesa di S. Sebastiano in Mantova e Luca Fancelli," *Rassegna d'Arte*, no. 6 (1901), p. 183. Luca Fancelli's comments, referring to S. Andrea, are quoted in V. Braghirolli, "Luca Fancelli," *Archivio Storico Lombardo*, no. 3 (1876), pp. 21–22.

181. Alberti, *On Painting*, p. 43: "To make clear my exposition in writing this brief commentary on painting, I will first take from the mathematicians those things with which my subject is concerned. When they are understood, I will enlarge on the art of painting from its first principles in nature in so far as I am able. In all this disucssion, I beg you to consier me not as a mathematician but as a painter."

182. This is one of the themes of Gadol, *Alberti*.

183. Alberti, *On Painting*, pp. 92–93.

184. S. Freud, "Creative Writers and Day-Dreaming," in *The Standard Edition of the Complete Psychological Works of Sigmund Freud*, trans. J. Strachey (London, 1954), 9:141–153; quotation on p. 141.

185. M. Boden, *The Creative Mind: Myths and Mechanisms* (New York, 1990).

186. C. Smith, *Architecture in the Culture of Early Renaissance Humanism*, p. 240.

187. See ibid., p. 13. The cite is from Alberti, *Opere volgari*, vol. 2, book 3, p. 210: "Soglio, massime la notte, quando e' miei stimoli mi tengono sollecito e desto, per distormi da mie acerbe cure e triste sollicitudini, soglio fra me investigare e construere in mente qualche inaudita macchina da muovere e portare, da fermare e statuire cose grandissime e inestimabili. E qualche volta m'avenne che non solo me acquetai in mie agitazioni d'animo ma è ancora giusi cose rare e degnissime di memoria. E talora, mancandomi simili investigazioni, composi a mente e coedificai qualche compositissimo edificio, e desposivi più ordini e numeri di colonne con veri capitelli e base inusitate, e collecavi conveniente e nuova grazia cornici e tavolati."

188. T. Kuhn, "A Function for Thought Experiments," in *Essential Tension* (Cambridge, Mass., 1977), p. 263.

189. Alberti, *On Painting*, pp. 39–40.

190. Smith, *Architecture in the Culture of the Early Renaissance*, p. 70.

191. See L. Lefaivre, "Rethinking the Western Humanist Tradition in Architecture," *Design Book Review,* no. 34 (1994), pp. 1–3.

192. On this distinction, see A. Tzonis, *Creative Design* (Cambridge, Mass., forthcoming). See also A. Tzonis et al., *Les systèmes conceptuels de l'architecture* (Cambridge, Mass., 1975), where the view is also put forth.

193. E. R. Curtius, *European Literature and the Latin Middle Ages,* trans. W. Trask (New York, 1953), pp. 251–252.

194. The chief scholar to have taken a position in favor of an Aristotelian influence on the definition of *concinnitas* is Christine Smith. She sees it as a reconciliation of "the Aristotelian definition of beauty" as "that which gives pleasure through hearing and sight" with the Platonic (and Neoplatonic) notion that "beauty is a quality possessed by beautiful things." She continues, "This compromise, unsatisfactory from a philosophical point of view, must nonetheless have decribed Alberti's understanding of aesthetic experience. His formulation, I suggest, was much influenced by theological considerations. Perfect beauty, one of the attributes of the Divinity, was surely inherent in the Divine Nature and not in the eye of the beholder. . . . His view is consistent with Augustine's discussion of the knowledge of God examined earlier" (*Architecture in the Culture of the Early Renaissance,* p. 92). She complains that scholars have emphasized the Platonic aspect to the exclusion of the Aristotelian. Other authors have tended to attach the concept of concinnitas to individual sources. Wittkower in his *Architecture in the Age of Humanism* notably saw *concinnitas* as Neoplatonic, as did W. Tatarkiewicz. See his *History of Aesthetics,* ed. J. Harrell, 3 vols. (The Hague, 1970). V. Zoubov retraced its origins to medieval numerology; see "Leon Battista Alberti et les auteurs du moyen-age," *Medieval and Renaissance Studies* 4 (1958), pp. 245–266. P. von Naredi-Rainer links it to Boethius; see *Architektur und Harmonie* (Cologne, 1984).

195. The quotation is in H. Baron, *The Crisis of the Early Italian Renaissance* (Princeton, 1966), pp. 82–84.

196. J. Hankins, "The Popes and Humanism," in Grafton, *Rome Reborn,* p. 61.

197. N. Goodman, *Ways of Worldmaking* (New York, 1978).

198. Mancini, *Vita di Alberti,* pp. 165, 185. The book was written in the midst of political mutations; the Medicis became tyrants in 1434.

199. See J. Bialostocki, "The Power of Beauty: A Utopian Idea of Leon Battista Alberti," in *Studien zur Toskanischen Kunst: Festschrift für Ludwig H. Heydenreich* (Munich, 1964), pp. 13–19; cited in Tafuri, "Ricerca dei paradigmi," p. 79.

200. Smith, in *Architecture in the Culture of Early Humanism,* remarks on its appearance in *Profigiorum ab aerumna* (p. 88). L. Vagnetti, in "Concinnitas: Riflessione sul significato di un termine albertiano," *Studi e Documenti di Architettura* 2 (1973), pp. 139–161, noted its presence in *Pontifex,* where Alberti uses the term to refer to the equilibrium of virtue.

201. Alberti, "Letter," in *Opera inedita,* 258; qtd. in Mancini, *Vita di Alberti,* p. 360.

202. C. Stinger, *The Renaissance in Rome* (Bloomington, Ind., 1985), p. 251. See also L. Pastor, *Storia dei papi* (Rome, 1911), 2:304–365. The work in question is L. Valla, *De falso credita et emendita Constantini Donatione,* ed. W. Setz (Boehlau, 1976); translated by C. B. Coleman as *The Treatise of Lorenzo Valla on the Donation of Constantine* (New Haven, 1922). It still had the power to anger supporters of the papacy in the twentieth century, to judge from the tone of Pastor's account.

203. See Borsi, *Alberti,* for the best and clearest bibliographical documentation of Alberti's architectural and urbanistic projects since the classic article by G. Dehio, "Die Bauprojekte Nikolaüs des Fünften und L. B. Alberti," *Repertorium für Kunstwissenschaft* 3 (1880), pp. 241–275. But the historian of Renaissance architecture Manfredo Tafuri argued that Alberti was opposed to Nicholas and uninvolved with his projects, but the argument is speculative in nature and undocumented. See his "Niccolò V e Leon Battista Alberti," in *Ricerca del Rinascimento,* pp. 32–84. Finally, for a more scholarly and well documented assessment of Alberti's work in Rome as well as a good bibliography on the subject, see C. Burroughs, "Alberti e Roma," in J. Rykwert and A. Engel, *Leon Battisti Alberti,* pp. 134–157. See also the classic Westfall, *In This Most Perfect Paradise.*

204. See "Indice dei nomi," in Alberti, *L'Architettura,* ed. Orlandi and Portoghesi, 2:1053.

205. See Borsi, *Alberti,* pp. 42–49.

206. Mancini, *Vita di Alberti,* p. 298.

207. See Mancini, *Vita di Alberti,* passim. In the five years of his own life that remained, he was *persona non grata* in the city. At his death he was buried in an unmarked grave, and the meager inheritance he left to found a scholarship for the use of any Alberti who wished to study law was eventually confiscated by the papacy to pay for choir singing. See G. Mancini, "Il testamento di Leon Battista Alberti," *Archivio Storico Italiano* 72 (1914), p. 48, and idem, *Vita di Alberti,* p. 28; cited in Borsi, *Leon Battista Alberti,* p. 17.

208. See Alberti, *Opere volgari,* ed. Bonucci, 2:147.

209. This is quoted in D. Summers, *Michelangelo and the Language of Art* (Princeton, 1981), p. 90. The English translation by Spencer in *The Art of Painting* (p. 80) does not convey Alberti's meaning.

210. Tafuri, *L'architettura dell'umanesimo,* pp. 36–37.

211. E. Garin, *Portraits from the Quattrocento* (New York, 1972), p. 120.

212. See Alberti, "Dream," in *Dinner Pieces,* p. 66, and *Momo o del principe.*

213. Alberti, *On Painting,* p. 70.

214. M. Bakhtin, "The Problem of the Text, in Linguistics, Philology, and Human Sciences: An Experiment in Philosophical Analysis," in *Speech Genres and Other Late Essays,* ed. C. Emerson and M. Holquist, trans. V. W. McGee (Austin, 1986), pp. 103–131.

215. E. Panofsky, "Renaissance and Renascences," in *Renaissance and Renascences in Western Art* (New York, 1960), pp. 42–113.

6. RECONFIGURING THE ARCHITECTURAL BODY, CHANGING THE ARCHITECTURAL MIND

1. "Cold thinking" is based on Lévi-Strauss's notion of "cold society," defined as one where no change occurs, which is juxtaposed to "hot societies." See G. Charbonnier, ed., *Conversations with Claude Lévi-Strauss,* trans. J. and D. Weightman (London, 1969), pp. 32–34.

2. See H. Millon, ed., *The Architecture of the Renaissance from Brunelleschi to Michelangelo* (London, 1994).

3. Lévi-Strauss used the term "hot" to describe societies in which human associations multiply. By extension I am using the term to describe the same associative pattern in thinking.

4. See M. Bakhtin, *Rabelais and His World,* trans. H. Iswolsky (Cambridge, Mass., 1968).

5. L. Mumford, *Technics and Civilization* (1934; rpt. New York, 1963).

6. This world is to a high degree "archaic," to borrow Polanyi's term (see *Primitive, Archaic, and Modern Economies: Essays of Karl Polanyi,* ed. G. Dalton [Boston, 1968]); "gentile" or "tribal," to borrow Hick's (see J. Hicks, *Theory of Economic History* [1969; rpt. Oxford, 1977]); and "precapitalist," to borrow Marx's more widespread one. In this world there is hardly any surplus and only scarce circulation of goods. Private property is limited and hoarding practically absent.

   This view of medieval culture and of the place of architecture in it owes much to A. Tzonis, *Towards a Non-Oppressive Environment* (Cambridge, Mass., 1972). See especially "The Carrot of Cezanne," "The Divine Model," and "The Taxonomic Process," pp. 11–32.

7. Mumford, *Technics and Civilization;* E. J. Duijsterhuis, *The Mechanization of the World Picture* (Oxford, 1961); P. Duhem, *Les origines de la statique,* 2 vols. (Paris, 1905–1906); T. Kuhn, *The Structure of Scientific Revolutions,* 2nd ed. (Chicago, 1970).

8. M. Foucault, *Histoire de la sexualité,* 3 vols. (Paris, 1976–1984).

9. S. Freud, *Civilization and Its Discontents,* in *The Standard Edition of the Complete Psychological Works of Sigmund Freud,* trans. J. Strachey (London, 1956), 56:59ff. esp. 78.

10. Plutarch, *Non posse suaviter vivere secundum Epicurum* (On the fact that if one follows Epicurus one cannot live a pleasant life) 1104c; cited in M. Nussbaum, *The Fragility of Goodness* (1986; rpt., Cambridge, Mass., 1994).

11. On the role of the anti-*libidines* strictures in the early Christian tradition, see Foucault, *Histoire de la sexualité,* vol. 3; M. Foucault, "Le combat de la chasteté," *Communications,* numero spécial sur sexualités occidentales, no. 35 (1982), pp. 15–33; E. Pagels, *Adam, Eve, and the Serpent* (New York, 1988); J. Le Goff, "Le refus du plaisir," in *L'imaginaire médiéval: Essais* (Paris, 1985), pp. 137–148; J. Bugge, *Virginitas: An Essay in the History of a Medieval Ideal* (The Hague, 1975); C. W. Bynum, "The Female Body and Religious Practice in the Later Middle Ages," in *Fragments for a History of the Human Body,* ed. M. Feher, with R. Naddaff and N. Tazi (New York, 1989), 1:160–219; M. A. Williams, "Divine Image—Prison of Flesh: Perceptions of the Body in Ancient Gnosticism," in Feher, 1:128–147.

12. Lorenzo Valla's *De voluptate* was once titled *De vero bono;* trans. as *On Pleasure* by A. K. Hieatt and M. de Panizza Lorsch (New York, 1977). They read Valla as a "militant" Epicurean. See also E. Garin, *L'umanesimo italiano* (Rome-Bari, 1952), p. 63. For treatment of the medieval history of the body, see J. Le Goff, "Corps et idéologie dans l'Occident mediéval: La révolution corporelle," in *L'imaginaire médiéval,* pp. 123–127. Eugenio Garin is the only historian to my knowledge to have dealt with the rise of eroticism in the early Renaissance; he pays particular attention to the writings of Lorenzo Valla. See his *L'umanesimo italiano.*

13. R. Wittkower, *Architecture in the Age of Humanism* (London, 1949).

14. R. B. Onians, *Origins of European Thought about the Body, the Mind, the Soul, the World, Time, and Fate* (Cambridge, 1951); Feher, ed., *A History of the Human Body.*

15. C. Lévi-Strauss, *The Savage Mind* (Chicago, 1966), p. 149.

16. B. Stafford, *The Representations of the Body,* catalogue (Chicago, 1992).

17. L. B. Alberti, *On the Art of Building in Ten Books,* trans. J. Rykwert, N. Leach, and R. Tavernor (Cambridge, Mass., 1991), IX.5, p. 302: "When you make judgments on beauty, you do not follow mere fancy, but the workings of a reasoning faculty that is inborn in the mind."

18. M. Johnson, *The Body in the Mind: The Bodily Basis of Meaning, Imagination, and Reason* (Chicago, 1987). See also G. Lakoff, *Women, Fire, and Dangerous Things: What Categories Reveal about the Mind* (Chicago, 1987).

19. F. J. Varela, E. Thompson, and E. Rosch, *The Embodied Mind* (Cambridge, Mass., 1991).

20. The trichotomy—innatist, realist, and constructivist—comes from R. Shweder, *Thinking through Cultures: Expeditions in Cultural Psychology* (Cambridge, Mass., 1991), p. 156.

21. H. Putnam, "Meaning, Other People, and the World," in *Representation and Reality* (Cambridge, Mass., 1988), p. 25.

22. Feher, *A History of the Human Body.* See my review of the collection in *Design Book Review,* no. 25 (1992), pp. 35–38.

23. See Aristotle, *The Art of Rhetoric,* trans. J. H. Freese (Cambridge, Mass., 1926), esp. 1.2.8–11 for a discussion of the enthymeme.

24. Donald Schön, in his "Generative Metaphor: A Perspective on Problem-Setting in Social Policy" (in *Metaphor and Thought,* ed. A. Ortony [Cambridge, 1979], pp. 154–283); G. Lakoff and M. Johnson, *Metaphors We Live By* (Chicago, 1980), esp. p. 254.

25. Ibid., pp. 140, 10, 9.

26. A. Tzonis et al., *Les systèmes conceptuels de l'architecture de 1650 à 1800* (Cambridge, Mass., 1975).

27. M. Turner, "Categories and Analogies," in *Analogical Reasoning,* ed. D. Helman (Dordrecht, 1988), p. 3.

28. Lakoff and Johnson, *Metaphors We Live By,* p. 30.

29. Kuhn, *The Structure of Scientific Revolutions,* p. 101. He mentions the impact of the change from "geocentrism to heliocentrism, from phlogiston to oxygen or from corpuscles to waves" as metaphorical representations of physical phenomena.

30. Mumford, "The Monastery and the Clock," in *Technics and Civilization,* pp. 12–18; Lakoff and Johnson, *Metaphors We Live By,* p. 145.

31. See A. Tzonis and L. Lefaivre, "The Mechanical Body versus the Divine Body: The Rise of Modern Design Theory," *Journal of Architectural Education* 34, no. 1 (1975), pp. 4–7; Tzonis et al., *Les systèmes conceptuels de l'architecture;* and A. Tzonis, "City Planning Theories of the 19th and 20th Century," in *Villes en mutation, XIX–XX siècles,* Actes du 10e colloque international, Collection Histoire Pro Civitate no. 64 (Brussels, 1982), pp. 37–49.

32. Lakoff and Johnson, *Metaphors We Live By,* p. 25.

33. D. Davidson, "What Metaphors Mean" (1978), in *Inquiries into Truth and Interpretation* (Oxford, 1991), p. 26.

34. Turner, "Categories and Analogies," pp. 3–24, esp. p. 3.

35. Lakoff and Turner, *Metaphors We Live By,* p. 141.

36. Lévi-Strauss, *The Savage Mind,* p. 36.

37. Lakoff and Johnson, *Metaphors We Live By,* p. 145.

38. See Aristotle, *Art of Rhetoric.* Aristotle build his theory of rhetoric on the basis of the difference between enthymemic and apodeictic reasoning. See 1.2.8–11 for a discussion of the logical structure of apodeictic and enthymemic syllogisms.

This does not imply that metaphorical thinking is not as strictly syllogistically structured as apodeictic logic. In an unpublished paper, "The Games Metaphors Play" (1988), I have attempted to formalize the syllogistic reasoning created by the metaphor "the body of the building" in the *Hypnerotomachia Poliphili.* The technique combines notions from Tzonis et al., *Les systèmes conceptuels de l'architecture,* and C. Perelman and L. Olbrechts-Tyteca, *The New Rhetoric: A Treatise on Argumentation,* ed. J. Wilkins and P. Weaver (Notre Dame, Ind., 1969).

39. The example "Sally is a block of ice" is taken from J. Searle, "Metaphor," in Ortony, *Metaphor and Thought,* pp. 92–123.

40. J. Bruner, *Actual Minds, Possible Worlds* (Cambridge, Mass., 1986), p. 12.

41. Lakoff and Johnson, *Metaphors We Live By,* p. 10.

42. Bruner, *Actual Minds, Possible Worlds,* p. 11.

43. Ibid., pp. 51–52, 53.

44. Holyaok and Thagard, *Mental Leaps,* in particular the chapter on "The Construction of Similarity," pp. 101–137.

45. Mumford, *Technics and Civilization,* p. 3.

46. J. Huizinga, *The Waning of the Middle Ages,* trans. F. Hopman (Hardmondsworth, 1972; Dutch ed. 1924), p. 106.

47. See M. Bakhtin, "Discourse in Life and Discourse in Poetry," in *Mikhail Bakhtine, le principe dialogique,* ed. T. Todorov. See also K. Clark and M. Holquist, *Mikhail Bakhtin* (Cambridge, Mass., 1984), for a systematic exposition of the Bakhtinian notion of dialogue.

48. M. Bakhtin, "Discourse in the Novel," in *The Dialogic Imagination,* ed. M. Holquist, trans. C. Emerson and M. Holquist (Austin, Tex., 1981), pp. 342–343.

49. The notions of "masked" and "passwords" are Bakhtin's. See his "Discourse in Life," p. 192.

50. H. Baron, *The Crisis of the Early Italian Renaissance* (Princeton, 1966).

51. W. Sombart, *Luxury and Capitalism,* tr. W. R. Dittmar (Ann Arbor: 1967; German ed. 1923).

52. Freud, *Civilization and Its Discontents,* part IV.

7. THE DANGEROUS BODY

1. Gregory the Great, in *Patrologiae Cursus Completus, Series Latina,* ed. J.-P. Migne (Paris, 1844–1896), 77, col. 647 (hereafter cited parenthetically as *P.L.*) Peter Damian: *P.L.* 144, col. 313. All translations are my own. I am very grateful to Professor Arpad Orbàn for his help.

2. Petrus Cantor, *Verbum abbreviatum* (written 1187–1197), in *P.L.* 205, cols. 255, 256.

3. Hildebert of Lavardin, *Roma item de Roma* (ca. 1143), in *Kaiser, Rom und Renovatio,* ed. P. E. Schramm, 2 vols. (Leipzig, 1929), 1:300–304.

4. Alexander Neckham, *De naturis rerum* (late twelfth century), in V. Mortet and P. Deschamps, *Recueil des textes relatifs à l'histoire de l'architecture en France au Moyen Age* (Paris, 1929), 2:179. This work, along with vol. 1 (edited by Mortet only, 1911), will hereafter be cited as Mortet.

5. Ibid.

6. Mortet, 1:368.

7. Hildebert quoted in R. Krautheimer, *Rome: Profile of a City, 312–1308* (Princeton, 1980), p. 201.

8. *Analectica Divionensia* (1134), in Mortet, 2:32; *P.L.* 205, col. 256.

9. Savonarola, "Advent Sermon"; qtd. in P. Villari, *The Life and Time of Girolamo Savonarola* (London, 1896), p. 75.

10. Mortet, 2:285.

11. Quoted in H. Schüppert, *Kirchenkritik in der Lateinischen Lyrik des 12. und 13. Jahrhunderts* (Munich, 1972), p. 25. The citation is of Walter Map, "De presbytero et logico." Walter Map was born in 1140 in Herfordshire and studied with Girardus la Pucelle in Paris. In 1162 he returned to England to the court of Henry II.

12. Hugue de Fouilloi, *De claustro animae* (1019–1020), in Mortet, 2:92; Abelard, *Epistola prima ad amicum,* in Mortet, 2:43.

13. Mortet, 2:40.

14. Map, "De presbytero et logico," in Schüppert, *Kirchenkritik,* p. 30.

15. J. Taylor, introduction to *Didascalicon,* by Hugh of St. Victor (Chicago, 1961).

16. *Carmina Burana,* ed. A. Hilka and O. Schumann (Heidelberg, 1930–1941); qtd. in Schuppert, *Kirchenkritik,* p. 32.

17. J. Le Goff, "Le refus du plaisir," in *L'imaginaire médiéval: Essais* (Paris, 1985), pp. 136–148. (1985). The horror induced by the idea of eros and by the body has been amply documented by many historians of late antiquity. See P. Brown, *The Body and Society: Men, Women, and Sexual Renunciation in Early Christianity* (New York, 1988); E. Pagels, *Adam, Eve, and the Serpent* (New York, 1988).

18. See C. W. Bynum, "The Female Body and Religious Practice in the Later Middle Ages," in *Fragments for a History of the Human Body,* ed. M. Feher, with R. Naddaff and N. Tazi (Cambridge, Mass., 1989), 1:160–219.

19. See S. Tisseron et al., *La passion des étoffes chez un neuropsychiatre, Gaëtan Gatian de Clérambault* (Paris, 1990). See also G. Gatian de Clérambault, "La passion des étoffes chez la femme," in *Oeuvre psychiatrique* (Paris, 1942), pp. 439–452.

20. Mortet, 2:92.

21. See also Mortet, 2:157.

22. Mortet, 2:179: "How much human curiosity there is in the ostentation which consumes voluptuous expenses in glorious buildings."

23. Mortet, 2:93, 40.

24. Mortet, 1:157, 2:39.

25. Ibid., 1:367.

26. Ibid., 1:366, 367; 2:157.

27. Ibid., 2:157.

28. *Analecta Divionensia,* in Mortet, 35, 36, 38; *Statuta selecta capitulorum generalium ordinis Cisterciensis,* in 2:135–138.

29. Mortet, 2:39–40.

30. Ibid., 2:40.

8. THE MARVELOUS BODY

1. J. Le Goff, "Le christianisme et les rêves," *L'imaginaire médiéval: Essais* (Paris, 1985), pp. 265–316. p. 313.

2. For good documentation of architectural *mirabilia,* see L. Okken, *Das goldene Haus und die goldene Laube* (Amsterdam, 1987).

3. See G. Gatian de Clérambault, "La passion des étoffes chez la femme," in *Oeuvre psychiatrique* (Paris, 1942), pp. 440–445.

4. Einhard, untitled "Epistola 85," *Codex Carolingianus,* in J. Schlosser, *Schriftquellen zur Karolingischen Kunst* (Vienna, 1892), p. 6, ref. 15; Rabanus Maurus, *De universo* (ninth century), in ibid., p. 5.

5. From "Epistola 89," *Codex Carolingianus*, in Schlosser, *Schriftquellen zur Karolingischen Kunst*, p. 26.

6. From Schlosser, *Schriftquellen zur Karolingischen Kunst*, p. 17.

7. See Imad-ad-Din's description of the crusaders' defilement of the Dome of the Rock, quoted in F. Gabrielli, *Arab Historians of the Crusades* (Berkeley, 1969), p. 97.

8. Notker, *De Carolo Magno*, in *Einhard and Notker the Stammerer: Two Lives of Charlemagne*, trans. L. Pope (1971; rpt. Harmondsworth, 1981).

9. Quoted in Meyer Shapiro, "On the Aesthetic Attitude in Romanesque Art," in *Romanesque Art* (New York, 1977), p. 14.

10. See *Gesta pontificum anglorum*, ed. N. E. Hamilton (London, 1870), II.88, p. 193; quoted in Shapiro, p. 14.

11. See J. Taylor, introduction to *Didascalicon*, by Hugh of St. Victor (Chicago, 1961), p. 43.

12. See F. Pfister, introduction to *Kleine Texte zum Alexanderroman* (Heidelberg, 1910), pp. 1–9, esp. p. 6, n. 4.

13. See W. S. Heckscher, "Relics of Pagan Antiquity in Medieval Setting," *Journal of the Warburg Institute* 1 (1937–1938), pp. 204–220.

14. *Graphia aurea urbis Romae* (1143), in *Mirabilia urbis Romae*, trans. F. M. Nichols (London, 1889), pp. 3–10.

15. Fazio degli Uberti, *Dittamondo* II.3; see modern edition, ed. G. Corsi (Bari, 1952).

16. *Le voyage de Charlemagne à Jéruzalem et à Constantinople*, ed. P. Aebischer (Geneva, 1965), p. 27. See O. von Simson, *The Gothic Cathedral* (New York, 1962).

17. V. Mortet and P. Deschamps, *Recueil des textes relatifs à l'histoire de l'architecture en France au Moyen Age* (Paris, 1929), 2:192. This work, along with vol. 1 (edited by Mortet only, 1911), will hereafter be cited as Mortet.

18. Robert de Clari, "La conquête de Constantinople" (written ca. 1216), in *Historiens et chroniqueurs du Moyen Age*, ed. A. Pauphilet (Paris, 1952), p. 27.

19. Benjamin of Tudela: qtd. in C. Diehl, *Byzantine Empress*, trans. H. Bell and T. de Kerpely (London, 1964), p. 137; Odon de Deuil, "Croisade de Louis VII," in M. Guizot, ed., *Histoire des Croisades* (Paris, 1875–1890), 24:312.

20. Guillaume de Tyr, *Voyage*, in Guizot, *Histoire des Croisades*, 18:192–193.

21. Marco Polo, *The Travels of Marco Polo*, trans. R. Latham) (Harmondsworth, 1958), pp. 77–78.

22. Ibid., p. 96.

23. Ibid., p. 197.

24. Albrecht, *Der jüngere Titurel* (ca. 1270), in J. Schlosser, *Quellenbuch zur Kunstgeschichte des abendländischen Mittelalters* (Vienna, 1896), pp. 301, no. 14; 303, no. 37; 307, no. 75, respectively.

25. Ibid., p. 307, no. 75.

26. Ibid., pp. 305, no. 60; 307, no. 76; 303, no. 27.

27. Chrétien de Troyes, "Perceval le Gallois ou le conte du Graal," in *La légende arthurienne* (Paris, 1989), pp. 96–97.

28. Ibid., p. 97.

29. *Le livre de l'échelle de Mahomet*, trans. G. Besson and M. Brossard-Dandre (Paris, 1991). See also M. Akoun, J. Le Goff, T. Fahd, and M. Rodinson, eds., *L'étrange et le merveilleux dans l'Islam médiéval* (Paris, 1978).

30. Polo, *The Travels of Marco Polo*, 40.

31. *Le livre de l'échelle de Mahomet*, p. 33.

32. Chaucer, *House of Fame*, ll. 120–127, 1184–1186, in *The Complete Works of Geoffrey Chaucer*, ed. W. W. Skeat (Oxford, 1899). See Schlosser, *Quellenbuch zur Kunstgeschichte*, pp. 322–325.

33. Boccaccio is quoted in Schlosser, *Quellenbuch zur Kunstgeschichte* p. 352.

34. Quoted in D. Gnoli, "Il sogno di Poliphilo," *La Bibliofilia* 1 (1889–1990), p. 201.

35. Anonymous, "Terze rime in lode di Cosimo," quoted in R. Hatfield, "Some Unknown Descriptions of the Medici Palace in 1459," *Art Bulletin* 52 (1970), pp. 232–249.

36. Niccolò de' Carissimi da Parma, letter to Francesco Sforza (written 1459), reproduced in Hatfield, "Some Unknown Descriptions."

37. On Lincoln Cathedral, see *Vita metrica Hugonis* (ca. 1225), in *Metrical Life of St. Hugh*, ed. J. F. Dimock (Lincoln, 1868), p. 51. On Canterbury Cathedral, see *Chronica Gervasii* (1179–1184), in Mortet, 1:224.

38. From "Epistola 89," *Codex Carolingianus*, in Schlosser, *Quellenbuch zur Kunstgeschichte*, p. 26.

39. Abbot Suger, *Abbot Suger and the Abbot Church of St. Denis and Its Art Treasures*, ed. and trans. E. Panofsky (Princeton, 1960), pp. 104–106.

40. From *La légende arthurienne*, p. 91.

41. From G. Boccaccio, *Il decamerone* (written 1348–1353) (Bologna, 1977), Giornata Terza, p. 149.

42. Hatfield, "Some Unknown Descriptions," p. 233.

43. Suger, *Abbot Suger* (1946), pp. 61–63.

44. *Vita metrica Hugonis*, p. 27.

45. Ibid.

46. Gervase of Canterbury, *History of the Burning and Repair of the Church of Canterbury* (1185), in *A Documentary History of Art*, ed. E. Holt (New York, Doubleday, 1947), 1: 51–61; Albrecht, in Schlosser, *Quellenbuch zur Kunstgeschichte*, p. 307, no. 76.

47. See Chaucer, *House of Fame*, ll. 1187–1188.

48. See "Odoric of Pordenone," in *Cathay and the Way Thither: Being a Collection of Medieval Notices of China*, ed. and trans. H. Yule (London, 1866), 2:220–222.

49. See J.-C. Beaune, "The Classical Age of Automata: An Impressionistic Survey from the Sixteenth to the Nineteenth Century," in *Fragments for a History of Human Body*, ed. M. Feher, with R. Naddaff and N. Tazi (New York, 1989), 1: 431–480.

50. Polo, *The Travels of Marco Polo*, p. 51.

51. Albrecht, *Der jüngere Titurel*, p. 310; Polo, *The Travels of Marco Polo*, p. 50.

52. *La légende arthurienne*, pp. 97–98.

53. Ibid., pp. 79, 243, 1147.

54. Liutprand, *The Works of Liutprand of Cremona*, trans. F. A. Wright (London, 1930), p. 22.

55. *Le voyage de Charlemagne à Jéruzalem et à Constantinople*, p. 29.

56. *Recette générale* (1432–1433), in *Les ducs de Bourgogne: Etudes sur les lettres, les arts et l'industrie pendant le XVe siècle et plus particulièrement dans les Pays-Bas et le Duché de Bourgogne*, ed. le Comte de Laborde (Paris, 1849). 2:944–958; cited in Okken, *Das Goldene Haus*, p. 174.

57. See Le Goff, "Le merveilleux dans l'occident médiéval," in *L'imaginaire médiéval*, p. 20: "En revanche, au XIIe–XIIIe siècles, je crois voir une irruption du merveilleux dans la culture savante. Je ne tenterai pas ici de donner une appréciation et un essai d'explication du phénomène. D'une part je reprends les hypothèses d'Erich Köhler sur la littérature courtoise, liées aux intérêts de classe et de culture d'une couche sociale, en ascension et déjà menacée: la petite et la moyenne noblesse, la chevalerie. C'est son désir d'opposer à la culture ecclesiastique liée à l'aristocratie non pas une contre-culture mais une autre culture qui lui appartient davantage et dont elle puisse mieux faire ce qu'elle veut, qui l'a fait puiser dans un réservoir culturel existant, c'est à dire dans cette culture orale dont le merveilleux est un élément important" (pp. 20–21). See also E. Köhler, *Ideal und Wirklichkeit in der höfischen Epik* (Tübingen, 1956), and "Observations historiques et sociologiques sur la poésie des troubadours," in *Cahiers de Civilisation Médiévale* (1964); cited by Le Goff, "Le merveilleux," p. 21.

58. *Epistola Alexandri Macedonis ad Aristotelem magistrum suum*, from Pfister, *Kleine Texte zur Alexanderroman*, pp. 3–11; Albrecht: in Schlosser, *Quellenbuch zur Kunstgeschichte*, p. 307.

59. De Clari, *La conquête de Constantinople*, p. 17.

60. Guillaume de Tyr, in Guizot, *Histoire des Croisades*, 17: 378–379.

61. Ibid., 18: 192–193.

62. Mortet, 1: 206–228.

63. *La légende arthurienne*, pp. 91, 96–97.

64. Both quoted in Hatfield, "Some Unknown Descriptions," p. 248.

65. *Vita metrica Hugonis*, p. 9.

66. Gervase of Canterbury, *History of the Church of Canterbury*, p. 60.

67. Albrecht, in Schlosser, *Quellenbuch zur Kunstgeschichte*, p. 306.

68. Polo, *The Travels of Marco Polo*, pp. 17, 44.

69. *Epistola Alexandri Macedonis*, p. 8.

70. Maurus: see Schlosser, *Schriftquellen*, p. 5. For Albrecht, see Schlosser, *Quellenbuch zur Kunstgeschichte*, p. 307.

71. See de Clari, *La conquête de Constantinople*, p. 9.

9. THE DIVINE BODY

1. Sic habitat ut sit sacer ipse domorum
   Et situs et numerus sufficiensque sibi.
   Quadratam speciem structura domestica praefert,
   Atria bis binis inclyta porticibus,
   Quae tribus inclusae domibus, quas corporis usus
   Postulat, et quarta quae domus est Domini. . . .
   Quarum prima domus servat potumque cibumque,
   Ex quibus hos reficit juncta secunda domus,
   Tertia membra fovet vexata labore diurno,
   Quarta Dei laudes assidue resonat.

   From Geoffroy de Vendôme, *Laus vitae monasticae* (1093–1132), in V. Mortet, *Recueil des textes relatifs à l'histoire de l'architecture en France au Moyen Age* (Paris, 1971), 1: 285. This work, along with vol. 2 (edited by Mortet and P. Deschamps, 1929), will hereafter be cited as Mortet.

2. Honorius, in ibid., 2: 16.

3. From *Annali della fabrica del Duomo* (1400–1401), reproduced in J. Ackerman, "Ars sine scientia nihil est," *Art Bulletin* 31 (June 1949), pp. 84–111, esp. p. 100.

4. *Vita metrica Hugonis*, in *The Metrical Life of St. Hugh*, ed. J. F. Dimock (Lincoln, 1868), p. 00.

5. From Quicherat, *Mélanges* (Paris, 1896); qtd. in E. Mâle, *The Gothic Image: Religious Art of the Thirteenth Century*, trans. D. Nussey (1913; rpt. New York, 1973), p. 397, no. 1.

6. This summary of the description in the original was made by Haenisch; cited in R. Cornelius, "The Figurative Castle: A Study in the Medieval Allegory of the Edifice with Especial Reference to Religious

Writings" (Ph.D. diss., Bryn Mawr, 1930), pp. 46–47.

7. Joannes de Janduno, *De laudibus Parisis* (1323); qtd. in Mâle, *The Gothic Image,* p. 397, no. 1; Godfrey Admonensis, cited in Cornelius, "The Figurative Castle," p. 46.

8. Mortet, 2: 15.

9. Ibid.

10. Ibid.

11. On the influence of the pseudo-Dionysian theology of light see W. Tatarkiewicz, *History of Aesthetics,* ed. J. Harrell, 3 vols. (The Hague, 1970).

12. Abbot Suger, *Abbot Suger and the Abbey Church of St. Dennis and Its Art Treasures,* ed. and trans. E. Panofsky (Princeton, 1960), p. 60.

13. Ibid., p. 62.

14. From *Vita metrica Hugonis,* p. 27.

15. Robert Grosseteste, *Templum Domini,* reproduced in Cornelius, "The Figurative Castle," p. 129.

10. THE HUMANIST BODY

1. See primarily R. Wittkower, *Architecture in the Age of Humanism,* (London, 1949). It is the most influential study, and its impact can be sensed in many studies, most particularly in H. Muehlmann, *L. B. Alberti: Aesthetische Theorie der Renaissance* (Bonn, 1982) and more recently R. Tavernor, "Concinnitas o la formulazione della bellezza," and P. von Naredi-Rainer, "La bellezza numerabile: l'estetica architettonica di Leon Battista Alberti," in *Leon Battista Alberti,* ed. J. Rykwert and A. Engel (Milan, 1994), pp. 300–315 and 292–299, respectively.

2. L. B. Alberti, *On the Art of Building in Ten Books,* trans. J. Rykwert, N. Leach, and R. Tavernor (Cambridge, Mass., 1991), V.17, p. 146; VII.6, p. 201; VI.13, p. 186; VII.8, p. 206.

3. See G. C. Druce, "The Elephant in Medieval Legend and Art," *Archaeological Journal* 76 (1919), pp. 1–73.

BIBLIOGRAPHY

*

PRIMARY SOURCES

EDITIONS OF THE HYPNEROTOMACHIA POLIPHILI

Les amours de Polia ou le Songe de Polyphile traduit de l'italien. Paris, 1772.

Hypnerotomachia Poliphili. Venice, 1499. Rpt. Venice, 1545; London, 1969; New York, 1976.

Hypnerotomachia Poliphili, intro., ed., and notes by G. Pozzi and L. A. Ciapponi. 2 vols. Padua, 1980.

Hypnerotomachia: The Strife of Love in a Dreame. London, 1592. Rpt. 1976.

Le songe de Poliphile. Paris, 1546. Rpt. 1553, 1561, and 1963.

Le songe de Poliphile, trans., intro., and notes by C. Popelin. 2 vols. Paris, 1883. Rpt. Geneva, 1982.

The Strife of Love in a Dreame: Being the Elizabethan Version of the First Book of the Hypnerotomachia of F. Colonna. London, 1890.

Sueño de Poliphilo, trans., intro., and notes by P. Pedraza. 2 vols. Murcia, 1981.

Tableau des riches inventions couvertes du voile des feintes amoureuses, qui sont représentées dans le Songe de Poliphile, devoilées des ombres du songe, et subtilement exposées par Béroalde. Paris, 1600.

EDITIONS OF COLLECTED WORKS BY L. B. ALBERTI

Kleinere kunsthistorische Schriften, ed. H. Janitschek. Vienna, 1877. Contents: *De statua, Della pittura, I cinque ordini architettonici.*

Opera inedita et pauca separatim impresa, ed. G. Mancini. Florence, 1890. Contents: *Amator, Frottola, Madrigale, Psalmi, Descriptio urbis Romae, Elementa picturae* (in Latin and the vernacular), *De punctis e lineis apud pictores, Pontifex, Intercoenales* (books 1, 2, 4 and "Anuli"), *De amicitia, De equo animante, De porcaria conjuratione, Epistulae, Frottola, De lunarum quadratura, Nota de casu ad potentem Aelium, De cifra proemium, De B. Alberti quadam testimentaria voluntate.*

Opere volgari, ed. A. Bonucci. 5 vols. Florence, 1843–1849. Vol. 1: *Philodoxeus fabula, Della tranquillità dell'animo, La cena di famiglia, Avvertimenti matrimoniale, Intorno a tor donna, Sofrona; 2: Della famiglia, Sentenze pittoriche; 3: De iciarchia, Teogenio, Ecatonfilea, Ippolito a Leonora, Ippolito e Dianora; 4: Della pittura, Della prospettiva, Della statua, Dell'arte edificatoria, I cinque ordini architectonici, Lettera per il San Francesco di Rimini, Ludi matematici; 5: Tratatto del governo della famiglia, Epistola a Paolo Codagnello, Epistola consolatoria, Amiria, Ephebia, Lettere amatorie, Canzoni, Poesie.*

Opere volgari, ed. C. Grayson. 3 vols. Bari, 1960–1973. Vol. 1: *Libri della famiglia, Cena familiaris, Villa; 2: Rime, Teogenio, Profigiorum ab aerumna libri III, De iciarchia, Epistola consolatoria, Sentenze pittoriche, Uxoria, Naufragius; 3: De pictura, Elementi di pittura, Ludi rerum matematicarum, Grammatica della lingua toscana, Ecatonfilea, Deifira, De amore, a P. Condagnello, Sofrona, Istoriette amorose, Lettere.*

Opuscoli inediti, ed. C. Grayson. Florence, 1954. Contents: *Musca, Vita di S. Potiti.*

EDITIONS OF INDIVIDUAL WORKS BY
L. B. ALBERTI

L' autobiografia dì Leon Battista Alberti, trans. R. Fubini. Florence, 1972.

De commodis litterarum atque incommodis, Latin and Italian text, ed., trans., intro., and notes by Giovanni Farris. Milan, 1971.

Dello scrivere in cifra (De componendis cifris). Turin, 1994.

Il cavallo vivo (De equo animante), ed., trans., and intro. by A. Videtta. Naples, 1981.

The Albertis of Florence: Leon Battista Alberti's "Della famiglia," trans., intro., and notes by G. A. Guarino. Lewisburg, Pa., 1971.

The Family in Renaissance Florence, trans. and intro. R. Watkins. Columbia, S.C., 1969.

De pictura, English and Latin, ed. with trans., intro., and notes by C. Grayson. London, 1972.

On Painting, trans., intro., and notes by J. R. Spencer. London, 1956.

De Porcaria coniuratione, trans. in R. N. Watkins, *Humanism and Liberty: Writings on Freedom from Fifteenth Century Florence*, pp. 107–115. Columbia, S.C., 1978.

De re aedificatoria, Latin and Italian text, ed. and intro. by G. Orlandi. Milan, 1966.

On the Art of Building in Ten Books (*De re aedificatoria*), trans. J. Rykwert, N. Leach, and R. Tavernor. 1988. Rpt. Cambridge, Mass., 1991.

Intercoenali inedite, ed. E. Garin. Florence, 1965.

Dinner Pieces, trans. D. Marsh. Binghamton, 1987.

Intercoenali inedite, ed. E. Garin. In *Rinascimento* 4 (1964), pp. 125–258.

Una intercoenale inedita di L. B. Alberti: Uxoria, ed. C. Grayson. In *Italia Medievale e Umanistica* 3 (1960), pp. 291–307.

Ludi matematici (*Ludi rerum matematicarum*), ed. R. Rinaldi. Milan, 1980.

Momo o del principe, Italian and Latin, trans. R. Consolo, intro. A. Di Grado. Genoa, 1986.

Momus ou le Prince, trans. C. Laurens. Paris, 1993.

La prima grammatica della lingua volgare, ed. C. Grayson. Bologna, 1964.

Profigiorum ab aerumna, ed. G. Ponte. Genoa, 1988.

OTHER SOURCES

Albrecht. *Der jüngere Titurel* (ca. 1270). In J. Schlosser, *Quellenbuch*, pp. 301–313.

Bacon, R. *Opus majus*, ed. J. H. Bridges. 3 vols. London, 1900.

Boccaccio, G. *Il Decamerone*. Bologna, 1977.

Boccaccio, G. *The Elegy of Lady Fiammetta*, trans. M. Causa-Steindler and T. Mauch. Chicago, 1990.

Cavalcanti, G. *Istorie fiorentine*. Vol. 3 of *Scritti di Giovanni Cavalcanti*. Florence, 1839.

"La chanson du 'Pélerinage de Charlemagne,'" ed. G. Paris. In *Romania* 9, pp. 1 ff.

Chaucer, G. *The House of Fame*. In *The Complete Works of Geoffrey Chaucer*, ed. W. W. Skeat. Oxford, 1899. London, 1957.

Dante Alighieri. *Dante's Inferno, Dante's Purgatorio, Dante's Paradiso*, Italian and English, trans. J. D. Sinclair. 3 vols. New York, 1961.

Filarete. *Treatise on Architecture, Being the Treatise by Antonio Piero Averlino, Known as Filarete*, trans., intro., and annotated J. R. Spencer. 2 vols. New Haven, 1965.

Francesco di Giorgio Martini. *Trattati d'architettura civile e militare*, ed. C. Maltese. 2 vols. Milan, 1966.

Gesta Francorum et aliorum Hierosolimitanorum. Paris, 1924.

Giraldus Cambresis. "Speculum ecclesiae" (1220). In *The Latin Poems Commonly Attributed to Walter Mapes*, ed. T. Wright, pp. 37 ff. London, 1841.

Graphia aurea urbis Romae (ca. 1143). In *Mirabilia urbis Romae*, ed. F. M. Nichols. London, 1889.

Gregorius, Master. *Narracio de mirabilibus urbis Romae*, ed. R. B. C. Huygens. Leiden, 1970.

Guillaume de Loris and Jean de Meung. *Romance of the Rose*, trans. C. Dahlberg. 2nd ed. Hanover, N.H., 1983. *Le roman de la rose*, trans. A. Lanly. 3 vols. Paris, 1971–1976.

Histoire anonyme de la première croisade, ed. and trans. L. Bréhier. Paris, 1924.

La légende arthurienne, ed. D. Regnier-Bohler. Paris, 1989.

Liutprand of Cremona. *The Works of Liutprand of Cremona*, trans. F. A. Wright. London, 1930.

Le livre de l'échelle de Mahomet, trans. G. Besson and M. Brossard-Dandre. Paris, 1991.

Mortet, V. *Recueil des textes relatifs à l'histoire de l'architecture en France au Moyen Age*, vol. 1. Paris, 1911.

Mortet, V., and P. Deschamps. *Recueil des textes relatifs à l'histoire de l'architecture en France au Moyen Age*, vol. 2. Paris, 1929.

Odoric of Pordenone. In *Cathay and the Way Thither, Being a Collection of Medieval Notices of China*, trans. and ed. H. Yule. New York, 1913.

Patrologia Cursus Completus, Series Latina, ed. J.-P. Migne. 221 vols. Paris, 1844–1896.

Petrarch, F. *Tryumphes of Fraunces Petrarcke: The First English Translation of the Trionfi*, ed. D. D. Carnicelli. Cambridge, Mass., 1971.

Pfister, F., ed. *Kleine Texte zum Alexanderroman*. Heidelberg, 1910.

Polo, Marco. *Travels*, trans. R. Lantham. Harmondsworth, 1958.

Quicherat, J. E. J. *Mélanges*. Paris, 1886.

Robert de Clari. *La conquête de Constantinople* (ca. 1216). In *Historiens et chroniqueurs du Moyen-Age*, ed. A. Pauphilet, pp. 6–34. Paris, 1952.

Rucellai, G. *Zibaldone quaresimale*. London, 1960.

Schlosser, J. *Quellenbuch zur Kunstgeschichte des abendländischen Mittelalters*. Vienna, 1896.

———. *Schriftquellen zur Karolingischen Kunst*. Vienna, 1892.

Suger, Abbé. *Libellus alter: De consecratione ecclesiae Sancti Dionysii* (1144), and *De rebus in administratione sua gestis* (1144–1149). In *Abbot Suger on the Abbey Church of St. Denis*, ed. and trans. E. Panofsky. Princeton, 1960.

Uberti, Fazio degli. *Dittamondo*, ed. G. Corsi. Bari, 1952.

Valla, Lorenzo. *On Pleasure: De voluptate*, trans. A. K. Hieatt and M. de Panizza Lorch. New York, 1977.

Vasari, G. *Lives of Painters, Sculptors, and Architects*, trans. A. B. Hinds, ed. W. Faunt. 4 vols. New York, 1963.

Le voyage de Charlemagne à Jerusalem et à Constantinople, ed. P. Aebischer. Geneva, 1965.

Le voyage de Charlemagne à Jerusalem et à Constantinople, ed. M. Tyssens. Ghent, 1978.

SECONDARY SOURCES

Ackerman, J. "Alberti's Light." In *Distance Points: Essays in Theory and Renaissance Art and Architecture*, pp. 59–98. Cambridge, Mass., 1994.

———. "Ars sine scientia nihil est: Gothic Theory of Architecture at the Cathedral of Milan." *Art Bulletin* 31 (1949), pp. 84–111.

Ageno, F. "L'Hypnerotomachia Poliphili e un poemetto del primo Cinquecento." *Romance Philology* 15 (1962), p. 329.

Aiken, J. A. "Leon Battista Alberti's System of Human Proportions." *Journal of the Warburg and Courtauld Institutes* 43 (1980), pp. 71–80.

Akoun, M., J. Le Goff, T. Fahd, and M. Rodinson, eds. *L'étrange et le merveilleux dans l'Islam médiéval*. Paris, 1978.

Alatri, P., ed. *Federigo da Montefeltro: Lettere di stato e d'arte, 1470–1480*. Rome, 1949.

Appel, J. W. *The Dream of Poliphilus: Fac-similes of 168 Woodcuts in "Poliphili Hypnerotomachia."* London, 1888.

Argan, G. C. *Francesco Colonna e la critica d'arte veneta nel Quattrocento*. Turin, 1934.

Aristotle. *The Art of Rhetoric*, trans. J. H. Freese. Cambridge, Mass., 1926.

———. *The Poetics*, trans. W. Rhys Roberts. Cambridge, Mass., 1927; revised 1932.

Ashmole, B. "Cyriac of Ancona and the Temple of Hadrian at Cyzicus." *Journal of the Warburg and Courtauld Institutes* 19 (1956), pp. 179–191.

Bakhtin, M. *The Dialogic Imagination*, trans. C. Emerson and M. Holquist. Austin, Tex., 1981.

———. *Mikhail Bakhtin, le principe dialogique*, ed. T. Todorov. Paris, 1981.

———. *Rabelais and His World*, trans. Helen Iswolsky. Cambridge, Mass., 1968.

Balagna, J. *L'imprimerie arabe en occident*. Paris, 1984.

Barca, A. "Della geometria di Polifilo." *La Bibliofilia* 15 (1913–1914), pp. 21–29, 121–134, 186–195, 217–220.

Barker, N. *Aldus Manutius and the Development of Greek Script Type in the Fifteenth Century*. Sandy Hook, Conn., 1985.

Baron, H. *The Crisis of the Early Italian Renaissance*. Princeton, 1966.

———. *In Search of Florentine Civic Humanism: Essays on the Transition from Medieval to Modern Thought*. 2 vols. Princeton, 1988.

———. "The Querelle of Ancients and Moderns as a Problem for Renaissance Scholarship." *Journal of the History of Ideas* 20 (1959), pp. 3–22.

Barraud, R. "Essai de bibliographie du Songe de Poliphile." *La Bibliofilia* 15 (1913–1914), pp. 21–29, 121–134, 186–195, 217–220.

Battaglia, S. *La letteratura italiana: Medioevo e umanesimo*. Florence, 1971.

Battisti, E. *L'antirinascimento*. 2nd ed. Rome, 1989.

———. "Le arti figurative nella cultura di Venezia e in quella di Firenze e Roma nel '500." *Commentario* 4 (1955), pp. 241–253.

Battisti, E., and G. Saccaro Battisti. *Le macchine cifrate di Giovanni Fontana*. Milan, 1984.

Beardsley, M. C. "Metaphor." In *Encyclopedia of Philosophy*, ed. P. Edwards. s.v. New York, 1967.

Bédier, J. *Les légendes épiques: Recherches sur la formation des chansons de geste*. Paris, 1913.

Béguin, S. "A Lost Fresco of Niccolò dell'Abate at Bologna in Honour of Julius III." *Journal of the Warburg and Courtauld Institutes* 18 (1955), pp. 119–122.

Belting, Hans. "The New Role of Narrative in Public Painting of the Trecento: Historia and Allegory." In *Pictorial Narrative in Antiquity and the Middle Ages*, ed. H. L. Kessler and M. S. Simpson, pp. 151–170. Studies in the History of Art, vol. 16. Washington, D.C., and Hanover, N.H., 1985.

Biadego, G. "Intorno al Sogno di Poliphili: Dubbi e ricerche." *Atti dell'Istituto Veneto di Scienze, Lettere e Arti* 55 (1900–1901), pp. 699–714.

Bialostocki, J. "The Power of Beauty: A Utopian Idea of Leon Battista Alberti." In *Studien zur Toskanischen Kunst:*

Festschrift für Ludwig H. Heydenreich, pp. 13–19. Munich, 1964.

Bilodeau, D. *Precedents and Design Thinking in an Age of Relativization.* Delft, 1997.

Bisticci, V. da. *Renaissance Princes, Popes, and Prelates,* trans. W. George and E. Waters. New York, 1963.

Black, M. *Models and Metaphors.* Ithaca, 1962.

Bloch, R. H. *Medieval Misogyny and the Invention of Western Romantic Love.* Chicago, 1991.

Blunt, A. "The Hypnerotomachia Poliphili in Seventeenth-Century France." *Journal of the Warburg Institute* 1 (1937–1938), pp. 117–137.

Boden, M. *The Creative Mind: Myths and Mechanisms.* New York, 1990.

Bodnar, E. W. *Cyriacus of Ancona and Athens.* Brussels-Bechen, 1960.

Bolgar, R. R., ed. *Classical Influences in Western Culture,* A.D. *500–1500.* Cambridge, 1971.

Bonds, A. G. "Är Poliphilus' dröm avslöjad? Hypnerotomachia Poliphili i ny tolkning." *Biblis* 20 (1989), pp. 9–58.

Borsi, F. *Leon Battista Alberti.* New York, 1977.

Braham, R. B. *Unruly Eloquence: Lucian and the Comedy of Traditions.* Cambridge, Mass., 1989.

Branca, V. *Tradizione delle opere di Giovanni Boccaccio.* Rome, 1958.

Bréhier, E. *The Middle Ages and the Renaissance.* Chicago, 1965.

Brezzi, P., and M. de Panizza Lorch, eds. *Umanesimo a Roma nel Quattrocento.* Rome, 1984.

Briffault, R. *Les troubadours et le sentiment romanesque.* Paris, 1945.

Brown, B. *The Venetian Printing Press: A Historical Study Based upon Documents for the Most Part Hitherto Unpublished.* London, 1981.

Brown, J. C. "A Woman's Place Was in the Home: The Discourses on Sexual Difference in Early Modern Europe." In M. Ferguson et al., *Rewriting the Renaissance,* pp. 206–224.

Brown, P. *The Body and Society: Men, Women, and Sexual Renunciation in Early Christianity.* New York, 1988.

Bruner, J. *Actual Minds, Possible Worlds.* Cambridge, Mass., 1986.

Bruschi, A. "Hypnerotomachia Poliphili." In *Scritti rinascimentali di architettura,* pp. 147–180. Milan, 1976.

Bruschi, A. "Il problema storico di Bomarzo." *Palladio* 12 (1963), pp. 85–114.

Buddensieg, T. "Gregory the Great, the Destroyer of Pagan Idols: The History of a Medieval Legend Concerning the Decline of Ancient Art and Literature." *Journal of the Warburg and Courtauld Institutes* 28 (1965), pp. 44–65.

Bugge, J. *Virginitas: An Essay in the History of a Medieval Ideal.* The Hague, 1975.

Burckhardt, J. *The Civilization of the Renaissance,* trans. S. G. Middlemore. New York, 1944. First published in German as *Die Cultur der Renaissance in Italien: Ein Versuch* (1860).

Burgess, A. *Joysprick: An Introduction to the Language of James Joyce.* London, 1973.

Burns, H. "A Drawing by L. B. Alberti." *Architectural Design* 49, nos. 5–6 (1979), pp. 45–56.

———. "Quattrocento Architecture and the Antique: Some Problems." In Bolgar, *Classical Influences in Western Culture,* pp. 269–287.

Burroughs, C. "Alberti e Roma." In Rykwert and Engel, *Leon Battista Alberti,* pp. 134–157.

———. *From Signs to Design: Environmental Process and Reform in Early Renaissance Rome.* Cambridge, Mass., 1990.

———. "A Planned Myth and a Myth of Planning: Nicholas V and Rome." In *Rome in the Renaissance: The City and the Myth,* ed. P. A. Ramsay, pp. 197–207. New York, 1982.

Busch, A. F. *Die Bücherornamentik der Renaissance.* Leipzig, 1878.

Bynum, C. W. "The Female Body and Religious Practice in the Later Middle Ages." In Feher et al., *A History of the Human Body,* 160–219.

Calvesi, M. "Hypnerotomachia Poliphili: Nuovi riscontri e nuove evidenze documentarie per Francesco Colonna Signore di Preneste." *Storia dell'Arte* 60 (1987), pp. 85–136.

———. "Identificato l'autore del Polifilo." *Europa Letteraria,* no. 35 (1965), pp. 9–20.

———. *Il sogno di Polifilo prenestino.* Rome, 1980.

Camporeale, S. *Lorenzo Valla: Umanesimo e teologia.* Florence, 1972.

Caron, J.-C. "Les noms de l'honneur féminin à la renaissance." *Poetique* 67 (September 1986), pp. 34–53.

Casella, M. T., and G. Pozzi. *Francesco Colonna: Biographia e opere.* 2 vols. Padua, 1959.

Castelli, P. *I gieroglifici e il mito dell'Egitto nel rinascimento.* Florence, 1979.

Cavalcanti, D. *Istorie fiorentine*. Florence, 1839.

Cazona, A. "Ludovico Gonzaga, Leon Battista Alberti, Luca Fancelli e il problema della cripta di San Sebastiano." In Rykwert and Engels, *Leon Battista Alberti*, pp. 252–275.

Cessi, R. "Il soggiorno di Lorenzo e Leon Battista Alberti a Padova." *Archivio Storico Italiano* 5, no. 43 (1909), pp. 351–350.

Chiaro, C. R. "Studi antiquari e produzione delle imagini." In *Memoria dell'antico*, ed. S. Settis, pp. 271–297. Turin, 1986.

Christiansen, K. "The Art of Andrea Mantegna." In Martineau, *Andrea Mantegna*, pp. 32–42.

Ciaponni, L. "Francesco Colonna." *Archivio Storico Ticinese* 1 (1960), pp. 69–76.

Ciapponi, L., and G. Pozzi, eds. *Hypnerotomachia Poliphili*. 2 vols. Padua, 1980.

Cicognara, L. *Catalogo regionato dei libri d'arte*. Pisa, 1821.

Clair, C. *A History of European Printing*. London, 1976.

Clérambault, G. G. de. "La passion des étoffes chez la femme." In *Oeuvre psychiatrique*, pp. 439–452. Paris, 1942.

Clerici, G. P. "Tiziano e la Hypnerotomachia Poliphili." *La Bibliofilia* 20 (1918), pp. 182–203.

Coffin, David R. *Gardens and Gardening in Papal Rome*. Princeton, 1991.

Colin, J. *Cyriaque d'Ancone*. Paris, 1981.

Collins, P. *Architectural Judgement*. Montreal, 1971.

Colonna, P. *I Colonna*. Rome, 1927.

Concina, E. *Navis: L'umanesimo sul mare*. Turin, 1990.

Cornelius, R. "The Figurative Castle: A Study in the Medieval Allegory of the Edifice with Especial Reference to Religious Writing." Ph.D. diss., Bryn Mawr, 1930.

Croce, B. "La Hypnerotomachia Poliphili." *Quaderni della Critica* 6 (1950), pp. 46–54.

Curtius, E. R. *European Literature and the Latin Middle Ages*, trans. W. Trask. New York, 1953.

Dagron, G. *Constantinople imaginaire: Etude sur le recueil des patrias*. Paris, 1984.

D'Amico, J. F. *Renaissance Humanism in Papal Rome: Humanists and Churchmen on the Eve of the Reformation*. Baltimore, 1983.

Danesi Squarzina, S. "Francesco Colonna, principe, letterato, e la sua cerchia." *Storia dell'Arte* 60 (1987), pp. 137–157.

Davari, S. "Ancora della chiesa di S. Sebastiano in Mantova e Luca Fancelli." *Rassegna d'Arte*, no. 6 (1901), pp. 70–85.

Davidson, D. "What Metaphors Mean." In *Inquiries into Truth and Interpretation*, pp. 245–264. Oxford, 1991.

De Bruyne, E. *Etudes d'esthétique medievale*. 3 vols. Ghent, 1946.

Dehio, G. "Die Bauprojekte Nikolaus des Funften und L. B. Alberti." *Repertorium für Kunstwissenschaft* 3 (1880), pp. 241–275.

Delumeau, J. *Vie économique et sociale de Rome dans la première moitié du XVIe siècle*. Paris, 1959.

Delz, J. "Ein unbekannter Brief von Pomponius Laetius." *Italia Medioevale e Umanistica* 9 (1966), pp. 417–440.

Denomy, A. J. "Courtly Love and Courtliness." *Speculum* 28 (1953), pp. 44–63.

de Rossi, G. B. "L'accademia di Pomponio Leto e le sue memorie scritte sulle pareti delle catacombi romane." *Bulletino di archeologia cristiana* 1 (1890), pp. 81–94.

de Sanctis, F. *Saggio critico sul Petrarca*. Turin, 1952.

Dezzi Bardeschi, M. "Nuove ricerche sul S. Sepolchro nella Capella Rucellai a Firenze." *Marmo*, no. 2 (1963), pp. 13–21.

Diehl, C. *Byzantine Empresses*, trans. H. Bell and T. de Kerpely. London, 1964.

Di Grado, A. Introduction to *Momo o del Principe*, by L. B. Alberti, ed. R. Consolo. Genoa, 1986.

Dionisotti, C. "Per Francesco Colonna." *Italia Medioevale e Umanistica* 4 (1961), pp. 323–326.

Dodds, E. R. *Pagan and Christian in an Age of Anxiety*. Cambridge, 1965.

Donati, L. "Un altro relitto del Polifilo." *La Bibliofilia* 56 (1954), pp. 23–26.

————. "Appunti di bibliocronologia." In *Miscellanea di scritti di bibliografia ed erudizione in memoria di Luigi Ferrari*, pp. 261–262. Florence, 1952.

————. "Bibliografia Aldina." *La Bibliofilia* 52 (1950), pp. 199–203.

————. "Diciamo qualche cosa del Poliphilo!" *Maso Finiguerra* 3 (1938), pp. 70–96.

————. "Di una copia tra le figure del Polifilo (1499) ed altre osservazioni." *La Bibliofilia* 64 (1962), pp. 163–182.

————. "Una marca tipografica di Francesco Jacopo della Spera ed il problema del Polifilo." *Accademie e Biblioteche d'Italia* 25 (1957), pp. 246–261.

———. "Miscellenea bibliografica: Il mito di Francesco Colonna." *La Bibliofilia* 64 (1962), pp. 247–283.

———. "Polifilo a Roma: Il mausoleo di S. Costanza." *La Bibliofilia* 68 (1968), p. 30.

———. "Studio esegetico sul Polifilo." *La Bibliofilia* 52 (1950), pp. 128–162.

Dobiache-Rojdestvensky, O. *Les poésies des Goliards.* Paris, 1831.

Dorez, L. "Les origines et la diffusion du Songe de Poliphile." *Revue des Bibliothèques* 6 (1896), 239 ff.

Dragonetti, R. *La technique poetique des trouvères dans la chanson de geste.* Bruges, 1960.

Druce, G. C. "The Elephant in Medieval Legend and Art." *Archaeological Journal* 76 (1919), pp. 1–73.

Duhem, P. *Les origines de la statique.* 2 vols. Paris, 1905–1906.

Duijsterhuis, J. *The Mechanization of the World Picture.* Oxford, 1961.

Dunston, A. J. "Paul II and the Humanists." *Journal of Religious History* 7, no. 4 (1973), pp. 287–306.

Elias, N. *La civilisation des moeurs.* Paris, 1973.

Ephrussi, C. *Etude sur le Songe de Poliphile.* Paris, 1888.

Essling, Victor Massena, Prince d'. *Les livres à figures vénitiens.* 5 vols. Paris, 1907–1909.

Fabbrini, F. "Indagini sul Polifilo." *Giornale Storico della Letteratura Italiana* 35 (1900), pp. 1–33.

Faral, E. "Le merveilleux et ses sources dans les descriptions des romans français du XII siècle." In *Recherches sur les sources latines dans les contes courtois du Moyen-Age,* pp. 305–388. Paris, 1913.

Fasolo, F., and G. Giulini. *Il santuario della Fortuna Primigenia a Palestrina.* 2 vols. Rome, 1953.

Febvre, L., and H.-J. Martin. *The Coming of the Book: The Impact of Printing, 1450–1800,* trans. D. Gerard. London, 1990.

Federici, D. M. *Memorie trevigiane sulle opere di disegno dal 1100 al 1800.* Venice, 1803.

Feher, M., with R. Naddaff and N. Tazi, eds. *Fragments for a History of the Human Body.* 3 vols. New York, 1989.

Feldhaus, F. M. *Die Technik der Antike und Mittelalters.* Potsdam, 1931.

Ferguson, M. W., M. Quilligan, and N. J. Vickers, eds. *Rewriting the Renaissance: The Discourses of Sexual Difference in Modern Europe.* Chicago, 1986.

Festugière, A. J. *La philosophie de l'amour de Marsile Ficin et son influencè sur la littérature française au XVIe siècle.* Paris, 1941.

Fierz-David, L. *The Dream of Poliphilo: The Soul in Love.* Dallas, 1987.

Fillon, B. "Le Songe de Poliphile." *Gazette des Beaux-Arts* 21 (1879), pp. 536–548.

Fiore, P., and M. Tafuri. *Francesco di Giorgio architetto.* Milan, 1993.

Firmin-Didot, A. *Alde Manuce et l'hellénisme à Venise.* Paris, 1865.

———. *Essai typographique et bibliographique sur l'histoire de la gravure sur bois.* Paris, 1863.

Fleming, J. V. *The Roman de la Rose: A Study in Allegory and Iconography.* Princeton, 1969.

Fletcher, A. *Allegory: The Theory of a Symbolic Mode.* Ithaca, 1964.

Fleury Mottelay, P. *Bibliographical History of Electricity and Magnetism.* London, 1920.

Fokkema, D. W., and E. Ibsch. *Literatuur Wetenschap en Cultuuroverdracht.* Muyderberg, 1992.

Folena, G. "Bibliografia degli studi sul '400 (1950–1953): Francesco Colonna." *Giornale Storico della Letteratura Italiana* 132 (1955), p. 153.

———. "Noterelle lessicale albertiane." *Lingua Nostra* 18 (1957), pp. 6–10.

Foucault, M. "Le combat de la chasteté." *Communications,* numero spécial sur sexualités occidentales, no. 35 (1982), pp. 15–33.

———. *Histoire de la sexualité.* 3 vols. Paris, 1976–1984.

———. *L'usage des plaisirs.* Paris, 1983.

Frankl, P. *The Gothic: Literary Sources and Interpretations through Eight Centuries.* Princeton, 1960.

Freud, S. *Civilization and Its Discontents.* In *The Standard Edition of the Complete Works of Sigmund Freud,* trans. J. Strachey, 21: 59 ff. London, 1956.

———. "Creative Writers and Day-Dreaming." In *The Standard Edition of the Complete Work of Sigmund Freud,* trans. J. Strachey, 9:141–153. London, 1954.

———. *The Interpretations of Dreams,* trans. J. Strachey. New York, 1965.

Frugoni, C. "L'antiquità: dai Mirabilia alla propaganda politica." In *Memoria dell'antico,* ed. S. Settis, pp. 5–72. Turin, 1986.

————. *Distant City: Images of Urban Experience in the Medieval World,* trans. W. McCuaig. Princeton, 1991.

Fubini, R., and A. M. Gallorini. "L'autobiografia di Leon Battista Alberti: Studio e edizione." *Rinascimento* 12 (1972), pp. 21–78.

Gadol, J. *Leon Battista Alberti: Universal Man of the Early Renaissance.* Chicago, 1969.

Gaeta, F. *Lorenzo Valla.* Naples, 1955.

————. "Sull'idea di Roma nell'Umanesimo e nel Rinascimento: Appunti e spunti per una ricerca." *Studi Romani* 25 (1977), pp. 169–186.

Gargano, M. "Nicolo V: La mostra dell'acqua di Trevi." *Archivio della Società Romana di Storia Patria* 111 (1988), pp. 225–266.

Garin, E. *La cultura del rinascimento: Profilo storico.* Rome-Bari, 1957.

————. "Il pensiero di L. B. Alberti: Caratteri e contrasti." *Rinascimento,* ser. 2, 12 (1972), pp. 3–20.

————. *Rinascita e rivoluzione: Movimenti culturali dal XIV al XVIII secolo.* Rome-Bari, 1976.

Gerulaitis, L. V. *Printing and Publishing in Fifteenth-Century Venice.* Chicago, 1976.

Giatromanolakis, G. *Poleos soma: mia proimi elliniki metaphora kai prosopopoiia.* Athens, 1991.

Giehlow, K. "Die Hieroglyphenkunde des Humanismus in der Allegorie der Renaissance." *Jahrbuch der kunsthistorischen Sammlungen des Allerhöchsten Kaiserhauses* 32 (1915), pp. 1–232.

Givens, A. *La dottrina d'amore nel Boccaccio.* Florence, 1968.

Gnoli, D. "Il sogno di Poliphilo." *La Bibliofilia* 1 (1899–1900), pp. 189–212, 266–283.

Goldschmidt, E. P. *The Printed Book of the Renaissance.* Cambridge, 1950.

Gombrich, E. *Aby Warburg: An Intellectual Biography.* London, 1970.

————. "Hypnerotomachiana." *Journal of the Warburg and Courtauld Institutes* 16 (1951), pp. 119–122.

Goodman, N. *Languages of Art.* New York, 1968.

————. *Ways of Worldmaking.* New York, 1978.

Gorni, G. "Storia del Certame Coronario." *Rinascimento* 12 (1972), pp. 135–181.

Graf, A. *Attraverso il Cinquecento: I pedanti.* Turin, 1888.

Grafton, A. "The Vatican and Its Library." In Grafton, *Rome Reborn,* pp. 3–46.

————. ed. *Rome Reborn: The Vatican Library and Renaissance Culture.* Washington, D.C., New Haven, and Vatican City, 1993.

Grayson, C. "The Composition of L. B. Alberti's 'Decem libri de aedificatoria.'" *Münchner Jahrbuch der bildenden Kunst,* ser. 3, 11 (1960), pp. 152–161.

————. "The Text of Alberti's 'De Pictura.'" *Italian Studies* 34 (1968), pp. 71–92.

Greenstein, J. M. *Mantegna and Painting as Historical Narrative.* Chicago, 1992.

Grimal, P. *Les jardins romains à la fin de la republique et aux deux premiers siècles de l'empire.* Paris, 1943.

Hankins, J. *Plato in the Italian Renaissance.* 2 vols. Leiden, 1990.

————. "The Popes and Humanism." In Grafton, *Rome Reborn,* pp. 47–86.

Harvey, J. *The Gothic World, 1100–1600: A Survey of Architecture and Art.* New York, 1969.

Hatfield, R. "Some Unknown Descriptions of the Medici Palace in 1459." *Art Bulletin* 52 (1970), pp. 232–249.

Hautecoeur, G. *L'architecture classique en France.* Paris, 1963.

Hays, J. R. *The Genius of Arab Civilization: Source of Renaissance.* Cambridge, Mass., 1983.

Heckscher, W. S. "Bernini's Elephant and Obelisk." *Art Bulletin* 29 (1947), pp. 155–182.

————. "De Hypnerotomachia Poliphili: Een Italiaansch roman uit de Renaissance." *Op de Hoogte* 30 (1933), pp. 93–95.

————. "Relics of Pagan Antiquity in Medieval Settings." *Journal of the Warburg Institute* 1 (1937–1938), 204–220.

Hersey, G. *Pythagorean Palaces: Magic and Architecture in the Italian Renaissance.* Ithaca, 1976.

Heydenreich, L., and W. Lotz. *Architecture in Italy, 1400 to 1600.* Harmondsworth, 1974.

Heydenreich, L. "Der Palazzo Baronale der Colonna in Palestrina." In *W. Friedlander zum 90. Geburstag,* pp. 85–91. Berlin, 1965.

————. "Pio II als Bauherr von Pienza." *Zeitschrift für Kunstgeschichte* 4 (1937), pp. 119–124.

Hicks, J. *Theory of Economic History.* 1969. Rpt. Oxford, 1977.

Hind, A. M. *An Introduction to a History of Woodcut, with a Detailed Study of Work Done in the Fifteenth Century.* 2 vols. 1935. Rpt. New York, 1963.

Hofer, P. "Variant Copies of the 1499 Poliphilus." *Bulletin of the New York Public Library* 36 (1932), pp. 475–486.

Holyoak, K., and P. Thagard. *Mental Leaps: Analogy in Creative Thought.* Cambridge, Mass., 1995.

Huelsen, C. "Le illustrazioni della Hypnerotomachia Poliphili e le antichità di Roma." *La Bibliofilia* 12 (1910), pp. 161–176.

————. *La Roma di Ciriaco d'Ancona.* Rome, 1907.

Huizinga, J. *The Waning of the Middle Ages,* trans. F. Hopman. Harmondsworth, 1972.

Huper, M. S. *The Architectural Monuments of the Hypnerotomachia Poliphili.* Ann Arbor, 1956.

Hussey, C. *The Picturesque.* London, 1925.

Ilg, A. *Ueber den kunsthistorischen Werth der Hypnerotomachia Poliphili.* Vienna, 1872.

Ingersoll, R. "Dialogue with Joseph Rykwert on the Exhibition: Leon Battista Alberti." *Design Book Review,* no. 34 (1994), pp. 8–11.

————. *The Ritual Use of Public Space in Renaissance Rome.* Ann Arbor, 1985.

Ivins, W. "The Aldine Hypnerotomachia Poliphili of 1499." *Bulletin of the Metropolitan Museum of Art* 18 (1923), pp. 249–252, 273–277.

Jarzombek, M. *On Leon Baptista Alberti: His Literary and Aesthetic Theories.* Cambridge, Mass., 1989.

Jeanroy, A. *Les joies du gai-savoir.* Toulouse, 1914.

Johnson, M. *The Body in the Mind: The Bodily Basis of Meaning, Imagination, and Reason.* Chicago, 1987.

Jordan, C. *Renaissance Feminism: Literary and Political Models.* New York, 1990.

Kantorowicz, E. H. *The King's Two Bodies: A Study in Mediaeval Political Theology.* Princeton, 1957.

Kaufmann, E. *Architecture in the Age of Reason: Baroque and Postbaroque in England, Italy, and France.* New York, 1955.

Kelso, R. *The Doctrine of the Lady in the Renaissance.* Urbana, Ill., 1959.

Kemp, M. "From Mimesis to Fantasia: The Quattrocento Vocabulary of Creation, Inspiration, and Genius in the Visual Arts." *Viator* 8 (1977), pp. 347–398.

Kent, F. W. "The Making of a Renaissance Patron of the Arts." In *Giovanni Rucellai ed il suo Zibaldone,* 2:9 ff. London, 1982.

Khomentovskaia, A. "Felice Feliciano da Verona comme l'auteur de l'Hypnerotomachia Poliphili." *La Bibliofilia* 37 (1935), pp. 154–74, 200–212; 38 (1936), pp. 20–48, 92–102.

Kibre, P. "The Intellectual Interests Reflected in Libraries in the XIVth and XVth Centuries." *Journal of the History of Ideas* 3 (1946), pp. 257–297.

King, M. L. "The Patriciate and the Intellectuals: Power and Ideals in Quattrocento Venice." *Societas* 5, no. 4 (1975), pp. 295–312.

Klotz, H. "Forma der Anonymität." In *Essays in Honor of Sumner McKnight Crosby,* ed. P. Blum, pp. 303–312. Fort Tryon Park, N.Y., 1976.

Köhler, E. *Ideal und Wirklichkeit in der höfischen Epik.* Tübingen, 1956.

————. *Sociologia del fin'amore.* Padua, 1976.

————. *Trobadorlyrik und höfischer Roman.* Berlin, 1962.

————. *Zur Selbstauffassung des höfischen Dichters.* Hamburg, 1955.

Krautheimer, R. "Alberti's Templum Etruscum." In *Studies in Early Christian, Medieval, and Renaissance Art,* trans. A. Frazer et al., pp. 333 ff. New York, 1969.

————. *Rome: Profile of a City, 312–1308.* Princeton, 1980.

Kretsulesco-Quaranta, E. *Les jardins du songe: Poliphile et la mystique de la renaissance.* Paris, 1976.

Kristeller, P. *Andrea Mantegna.* London, 1901.

Kristeller, P. O. "The Language of Italian Prose." In *Renaissance Thought and the Arts.* Princeton, 1964.

————. *Renaissance Thought and Its Sources.* New York, 1979.

————. *Renaissance Thought: The Classic, Scholastic, and Humanist Strains.* New York, 1961.

Kruger, S. *Dreaming in the Middle Ages.* Cambridge, 1992.

Kuhn, T. "A Function for Thought Experiments." In *The Essential Tension,* pp. 240–265. Cambridge, Mass., 1977.

————. *The Structure of Scientific Revolutions.* 2nd ed. Chicago, 1970.

Lakoff, G. *Women, Fire, and Other Dangerous Things.* Chicago, 1987.

Lakoff, G., and M. Johnson. *Metaphors We Live By.* Chicago, 1980.

Lanciani, R. *Li scavi di Roma.* Rome, 1902.

Landau, D., and P. W. Parshall. *The Renaissance Print, 1470–1550.* New Haven, 1994.

Lecoq, A.-M., and J. Roubaud. "Les hieroglyphes du songe." *FMR*, May–June 1988, pp. 15–42.

Lefaivre, L. "Eros, Architecture, and the Hypnerotomachia Poliphili." *Design Book Review*, no. 18 (1990), pp. 17–20.

———. "Leon Battista Alberti: Some New Facets of the Polyhedron." *Design Book Review*, no. 34 (1994), pp. 12–17.

———. "Rethinking Western Humanist Tradition in Architecture." *Design Book Review*, no. 34 (1994), pp. 1–3.

Lefaivre, L., and A. Tzonis. *De Oorsprong van de Moderne Architectuur, 1000–1800.* 1984. Rpt. Nijmegen, 1990.

Le Goff, J. *L'imaginaire médiéval.* Paris, 1985.

Leidinger, G. "Albrecht Dürer und die Hypnerotomachia Poliphili." *Philobiblion* 4 (1931), pp. 146–180.

Lévi-Strauss, C. *Conversations with Claude Lévi-Strauss,* ed. G. Charbonnier. London, 1969.

———. *The Savage Mind.* Chicago, 1966.

Lewis, C. S. *The Allegory of Love.* 1936. Rpt. London, 1977.

Litta, P. *Famiglie celebri italiane.* Milan, 1819–1852.

Lorch, M. de Panizza. *A Defense of Life: L. Valla's Theory of Pleasure.* Munich, 1985.

———. Introduction to *On Pleasure: De voluptate,* by Lorenzo Valla, trans. A. K. Hieatt and Lorch. New York, 1977.

Lowry, M. *The World of Aldus Manutius: Business and Scholarship in Renaissance Venice.* Oxford, 1979.

Luecke, H.-K. "Alberti, Vitruvio e Cicerone." In Rykwert and Engel, *Leon Battista Alberti,* pp. 70–95.

Magnuson, T. "The Project of Nicolas V for Rebuilding the Borgo Leonino in Rome." *Art Bulletin* 36 (1954), pp. 89–115.

———. *Studies in Roman Quattrocento Architecture.* Rome, 1958.

Male, E. *The Gothic Image: Religious Art of the Thirteenth Century,* trans. D. Nussey. 1913. Rpt. New York, 1973.

Maltese, C. "Colore, luce e movimento nello spazio albertiano." *Commentari* 27 (1976), pp. 238–248.

Mancini, G. "Il testamento di Leone Battista Alberti." *Archivio Storico Italiana* 72 (1914).

———. *Vita di Leon Battista Alberti.* 1882. Rpt. Florence, 1911, 1967.

———. *Vita di Lorenzo Valla.* Florence, 1881.

Manoussakas, M., and C. Staikos, *L'attività editoriale dei Greci durante il rinascimento italiano (1469–1523).* Athens, 1986.

Marliani, B. *Urbis Romae topographia.* Rome, 1544.

Marolda, Paolo. *Crisi e conflitto in Leon Battista Alberti.* Rome, 1988.

———. "'Ragione' e 'follia' nel Theogenius di L. B. Alberti." *Rassegna della Letteratura Italiana* 85 (1981), pp. 78–92.

Martineau, J., ed. *Mantegna.* Milan, 1992.

Martinelli, C. L. "Philodoxeos fabula edizione critica." *Rinascimento* 17 (1977), pp. 144–147.

Marsh, D. "Poggio and Alberti: Three Notes." *Rinascimento* 23 (1983), pp. 189–215.

———. "Petrarch and Alberti." In *Renaissance Studies in Honor of Craig Smyth,* pp. 363–375. Florence, 1985.

Mazzocco, A. "Petrarch, Poggio, and Biondo: Humanism's Foremost Interpreters of Roman Ruins." In *Francesco Petrarca, Six Centuries Later: A Symposium,* ed. A. Scaglione, pp. 354–363. Chapel Hill, N.C., 1975.

Menegazzo, E. "Per la biografia di Francesco Colonna." *Italia Medioevale e Umanistica* 5 (1962), pp. 231–272.

Michel, P. M. *Un idéal humain au XVe siècle: La pensée de L. B. Alberti.* Paris, 1930.

Milizia, F. *Memorie degli architetti antichi e moderni.* Parma, 1781.

———. *Le vite dei più celebri architetti.* Rome, 1768.

Millon, H. "The Architectural Theory of Francesco di Giorgio Martini." *Art Bulletin* 40, no. 3 (1958), pp. 257–261.

———. ed. *The Architecture of the Renaissance from Brunelleschi to Michelangelo.* New York, 1994.

Mitchell, C. "Archaeology and Romance in Renaissance Italy." In *Italian Renaissance Studies,* ed. Mitchell, pp. 455–483. London, 1960.

Molmenti, P. "Alcuni documenti concernenti l'autore dell'Hypnerotomachia Poliphili." *Archivio Storico Italiano* 38 (1906), pp. 291–314.

Morison, S. "The Chancery Types of Italy and France." *The Fleuron* 3 (1925), pp. 23–51.

Morison, S. "Early Humanist Script and the First Roman Type." *The Library* 26 (1943), pp. 1–30.

Morison, S. *A Tally of Types.* 2nd ed. Cambridge, 1973.

Morison, S. "Towards an Ideal Type." *The Fleuron* 2 (1924), pp. 57–75.

Morison, S. "The Type of the Hypnerotomachia Poliphili." In *Gutenberg Festschrift zur Feier des 25 Jährigen Bestehens des Gutenberg Museums im Mainz*, pp. 254–258. Munich, 1925.

Mugnos, F. *Historia della augustissima famiglia Colonna.* Venice, 1658.

Mumford, L. *Technics and Civilization.* 1934. Rpt. New York, 1963.

Müntz, E. *La bibliothèque du Vatican au XVIème siècle.* Paris, 1887.

Neilson, W. A. *The Origins and Sources of the Court of Love.* Harvard Studies and Notes in Philology and Literature, vol. 6. Boston, 1899.

Nelli, R. *L'érotique des troubadours.* Paris, 1974.

Nolhac, P. de. *Pétrarque et l'humanisme.* Paris, 1907.

Nussbaum, M. *The Fragility of Goodness: Luck and Ethics in Greek Tragedy and Philosophy.* 1986. Rpt. Cambridge, Mass., 1994.

Okken, L. *Das goldene Haus und die goldene Laube.* Amsterdam, 1987.

Oleson, J. P. *Greek and Roman Mechanical Water-Lifting Devices: The History of a Technology.* Toronto, 1984.

Olschki, L. *Le livre illustré au XVe siècle.* Florence, 1875.

Onians, J. *The Origins of European Thought about the Body, the Mind, the Soul, the World, Time, and Fate.* Cambridge, 1951.

Orlandi, G. *Aldo Manuzio, editore.* 2 vols. Milan, 1976.

————. "Le prime fasi nella diffusione del trattato architettonico albertiano." In Rykwert and Engel, *Leon Battista Alberti*, pp. 96–105.

Ortony, A., ed. *Metaphor and Thought.* Cambridge, 1979.

Pagels, E. *Adam, Eve, and the Serpent.* New York, 1988.

Painter, G. *The Hypnerotomachia Poliphili of 1499: An Introduction to the Dream, the Dreamer, the Artist, and the Printer.* London, 1963.

Palermino, R. J. "The Roman Academy, the Catacombs, and the Conspiracy of 1468." *Archivum Historiae Pontificiae* 18 (1980), pp. 117–151.

Panizza, M. "Valla, Lactantius, and Oratorical Skepticism." *Journal of the Warburg and Courtauld Institutes* 41 (1978), pp. 35–50.

Panofsky, E. *Perspective as Symbolic Form*, trans. C. S. Wood. New York, 1991.

————. "Renaissance and Renascences." In *Renaissance and Renascences in Western Art*, pp. 42–113. New York, 1960.

Partner, P. *The Papal State under Martin V.* London, 1958.

Paschini, P. *I Colonna.* Rome, 1955.

————. *Roma nel Rinascimento.* Bologna, 1940.

Pastor, L. *La storia dei papi.* 6 vols. Rome, 1911.

Pedraza, P. *Sueño di Polifilo, traducción literal y directa del original.* Murcia, 1981.

Pedretti, C. *Leonardo Architect.* London, 1986.

Pelosi, O. *Il sogno di Poliphilo: Una quête dell'umanesimo.* Salerno, 1988.

Perelman, C., and L. Olbrechts-Tyteca. *The New Rhetoric: A Treatise on Argumentation*, trans. J. Wilkins and P. Weaver. Notre Dame, Ind., 1969.

Peretti, A. *Luciano: un intellettuale greco contra Roma.* Florence, 1946.

Perisauli. *De triumpho stultitiae*, trans. G. Fabbri. Florence, 1963.

Pérez-Gómez, A. *Polyphilo, or, The Dark Forest Revisited.* Cambridge, Mass., 1992.

Perosa, A. "Considerazioni su testo e lingua nel 'Momus' dell'Alberti." In *The Languages of Literature in Renaissance Italy: For Cecil Grayson*, ed. P. Hainsworth et al., pp. 45–62. London, 1988.

Petrucci, A. "L'Alberti e le scritture." In Rykwert and Engel, *Leon Battista Alberti*, pp. 276–281.

Piot, E. "Le maître aux dauphins." *Le Cabinet de l'Amateur* (1861–1862), pp. 252–265.

Polanyi, K. *Primitive, Archaic, and Modern Economies: Essays of Karl Polanyi*, ed. G. Dalton. Boston, 1968.

Ponte, G. *Leon Battista Alberti, umanista e scrittore.* Genoa, 1981.

Popelin, C., trans. *Le songe de Poliphile*, by F. Colonna. 2 vols. Paris, 1883.

Poppelreuter, J. *Der anonyme Meister des Poliphilo.* Strasbourg, 1904.

Pound, E. *Literary Essays*, ed. T. S. Eliot. New York, 1935.

Powell, C. L. "The Castle of the Body." *Studies in Philology* 16 (1949), pp. 197–205.

Pozzi, G. *Francesco Colonna e Aldo Manuzio.* Bern, 1962.

Proctor, R. *The Printing of Greek in the Fifteenth Century.* Oxford, 1900.

Putnam, H. "Meaning, Other People, and the World." In *Representation and Reality,* pp. 19–37. Cambridge, Mass., 1988.

Quilligan, M., and N. Vickers. *Rewriting the Renaissance: The Discourses of Sexual Difference in Early Modern Europe.* Chicago, 1986.

Quintilian. *Institutio oratoria,* trans. H. E. Butler. 4 vols. Cambridge, Mass., 1920–1922.

Ramsey, P. *Rome in the Renaissance: The City and the Myth.* Binghamton, N.Y., 1982.

Rava, E. C. *L'arte dell'illustrazione nel libro italiano del rinascimento.* Milan, 1945.

Renouard, A. A. *Annales de l'imprimerie des Aldes.* 3 vols. 2nd ed. Paris, 1925.

Richard, I. A. *The Philosophy of Rhetoric.* London, 1936.

Reidy, D. V., ed. *The Italian Book, 1465–1800: Studies Presented to Dennis E. Rhodeson on His 70th Birthday.* London, 1994.

Rivoli, Duc de. *Bibliographie des livres à figures vénitiens.* Paris, 1892.

———. "Notes supplementaires sur quelques livres à figures vénitiens de la fin du XVe siècle." *Gazette des Beaux-Arts,* ser. 3, 1 (1899).

Robertson, A. "Aldus Manutius, the Scholar Printer, 1450–1515." *Bulletin of the John Rylands Library* 33 (1950–1951), pp. 57–73.

Rodocanachi, E. *Histoire de Rome de 1354 à 1471: l'antagonisme entre les romains et le saint siège.* Paris, 1922.

Rodocanachi, E. *Les institutions communales de Rome sous la papauté.* Paris, 1901.

Romano, G. *Verso la maniera moderna: da Mantegna a Rafaello.* Turin, 1976.

Ronconi, G. *Le origini delle dispute umanistiche sulla poesia.* Rome, 1976.

Rossi, G. B. de. "L'accademia di Pomponio Leto e le sue memorie scritte sulle pareti delle catacombe romane." *Bulletino di Archeologia Cristiana,* ser. 5, 1 (1890), pp. 81–94.

Ruskin, J. Manuscript marginalia of 1880 in his copy of the *Hypnerotomachia Poliphili* (1545 edition). Houghton Library, Harvard University, Cambridge, Mass.

Sanctis, F. de *Storia della letteratura italiana,* vol. 1. Milan, 1946.

Sander, M. *Le livre à figures italien depuis 1467 jusqu à 1530.* 6 vols. New York, 1941.

Santinello, G. *Leon Battista Alberti: Una visione estetica del mondo e della vita.* Florence, 1962.

Sarton, G. *A History of Science.* 2 vols. Cambridge, Mass., 1952–1959.

Sauer, J. *Die Symbolik des Kirchengebäudes.* Freiburg, 1902.

Saxl, F. *Classical Antiquity in Renaissance Painting.* London, 1938.

———. "A Scene from the Hypnerotomachia in a Painting by Garofalo." *Journal of the Warburg Institute* 1 (1938–1939), pp. 169–171.

Scaglia, G. "Alberti e la meccanica della tecnologia descritta nel 'De re aedificatoria' e nei 'Ludi matematici.'" In Rykwert and Engel, *Leon Battista Alberti,* pp. 316–329.

Scaglione, A. D. *Nature and Love in the Middle Ages.* Berkeley, 1963.

Schianatico, G. "L'esperienza della follia nella letteratura umanistica: Note su Leon Battista Alberti." *Lavoro critico* 31–32 (1984), pp. 173–213.

Schine Gold, P. *The Lady and the Virgin.* Chicago, 1985.

Schlosser, J. *La letteratura artistica: Manuale delle fonti della storia dell'arte moderna.* 1924. Rpt. Florence, 1979.

Schön, D. "Generative Metaphor: A Perspective on Problem-Setting in Social Policy." In Ortony, *Metaphor and Thought,* pp. 254–283.

Schneider, R. "Notes sur l'influence artistique du Songe de Poliphile." *Etudes Italiennes* 2 (1920), pp. 1–16, 65–73.

Schramm, P. *Kaiser, Rom und Renovatio.* 2 vols. Studien der Bibliotheek Warburg, 17. Leipzig, 1929.

Schuppert, H. *Kirchenkritik in der Lateinischen Lyrik des 12. und 13. Jahrhunderts.* Munich, 1972.

Searle, J. "Metaphor." In Ortony, *Metaphor and Thought,* pp. 92–123.

Settis, S., ed. *Memoria dell'antico nell'arte italiana.* Turin, 1986.

Seznec, J. *The Survival of the Pagan Gods: The Mythological Tradition and Its Place in Renaissance Humanism and Art,* trans. B. F. Sessions. New York, 1953.

Shapiro, M. "On the Aesthetic Attitude in Romanesque Art." In *Romanesque Art,* pp. 1–27. New York, 1977.

Shweder, R. *Thinking through Cultures: Expeditions in Cultural Psychology.* Cambridge, Mass., 1991.

Simson, O. von *The Gothic Cathedral: Origins of Gothic Architecture and the Medieval Concept of Order.* Princeton, 1974.

Smith, C. *Architecture in the Culture of Early Humanism: Ethics, Aesthetics, and Eloquence, 1400–1470.* Oxford, 1992.

Sombart, W. *Luxury and Capitalism*, trans. W. R. Dittmar. Ann Arbor, 1967.

Southern, R. W. *Robert Grosseteste: The Growth of an English Mind in Medieval Europe.* Oxford and New York, 1986.

Sprague de Camp, L. *Ancient Engineers..* Cambridge, Mass., 1960.

Squarzina, S. D. "Francesco Colonna, principe, letterato, e la sua cerchia." *Storia dell'Arte* 60 (1987), pp. 137–157.

Stafford, B. *Representations of the Body.* Chicago, 1992.

Steiner, G. *On Difficulty and Other Essays.* Oxford, 1978.

Stinger, C. *The Renaissance in Rome.* Bloomington, Ind., 1985.

Tae, E. "Le fonti delle grazie di Rafaello." *L'Arte* 17 (1914), pp. 41–48.

Tafuri, M. *L'architettura dell'umanesimo.* Bari, 1969.

———. *Ricerca del rinascimento: Principi, città, architetti.* Turin, 1992.

Tatarkiewicz, W. *History of Aesthetics*, ed. J. Harrell. 3 vols. The Hague, 1970.

Tateo, F. *Alberti, Leonardo e la crisi dell'umanesimo.* Bari, 1971.

Tavernor, R. "Concinnitas, o la formulazione della bellezza." In Rykwert and Engel, *Leon Battista Alberti,* pp. 300–315.

Temanza, T. *Vite dei più celebri architetti e scultori veneziani che fiorirono nel secolo decimosesto.* Venice, 1778.

Tenenti, A. "Il Momus nell'opera di Leon Battista Alberti." *Il Pensiero Politico* 7 (1974), pp. 321–333.

Thoenes, C. "Studien zur Geschichte des Petersplatzes." *Zeitschrift für Kunstgeschichte* 26 (1963), pp. 97 ff.

Thorndike, L. *A History of Magic and Experimental Science,* vol. 1. New York, 1923.

Tietze-Conrat, E. "Notes on Hercules at the Crossroads." *Journal of the Warburg and Courtauld Institutes* 15 (1951), pp. 305–310.

Tiraboschi, G. *Storia della letteratura italiana.* 4 vols. Modena, 1772–1795.

Tisseron, S., et al. *La passion des étoffes chez un neuropsychiatre, Gaetan Gatian de Clérambault.* Paris, 1990.

Tobin, R. *Leon Battista Alberti: Ancient Sources and Structure in the Treatises on Art.* Bryn Mawr, Pa., 1979.

Tomei, P. *L'architettura a Roma nel Quattrocento.* Rome, 1924.

Topsfield, L. T. *Troubadours and Love.* Cambridge, 1975.

Turner, M. "Categories and Analogies." In *Analogical Reasoning,* ed. D. Helman, pp. 3–23. Dordrecht, 1988.

———. *Death Is the Mother of Beauty: Mind, Metaphor, Criticism.* Chicago, 1987.

Tzonis, A. *Creative Design.* Cambridge, Mass., forthcoming.

———. "Huts, Ships, and Bottleracks: Design by Analogy for Architects and/or Machines." In *Research in Design Thinking,* ed. N. Cross, K. Drost, and N. Roozenburg, pp. 130–165. Delft, 1992.

Tzonis, A. *Towards a Non-Oppressive Environment.* Cambridge, Mass., 1972.

Tzonis, A., M. Freeman, L. Lefaivre, O. Salama, R. Berwick, and E. de Cointet. *Les systèmes conceptuels de l'architecture de 1650 à 1800.* Cambridge, Mass., 1976.

Tzonis, A., and L. Lefaivre. "Critical Regionalism." In *Critical Regionalism: The Pomona Meeting Proceedings,* ed. S. Amourgis, pp. 3–23. Pomona, Calif., 1991.

Tzonis, A., and L. Lefaivre. "The Mechanical Body versus the Divine Body: The Rise of Modern Design Theory." *Journal of Architectural Education* 24 (1975), pp. 4–8.

Ullmann, R. *The Origin and Development of Humanistic Script.* Rome, 1960.

Vagnetti, L. "La 'Descriptio urbis Romae': uno scritto poco noto di Leon Battista Alberti." *Quaderno: Università degli studi di Genova, Facoltà di Architettura* 1 (1967), pp. 110–150.

Valentini, R., and G. Zucchetti. *Codice topographico della città di Roma.* Rome, 1953.

Valla, Lorenzo. *The Treatise of Lorenzo Valla on the Donation of Constantine,* trans. and ed. C. B. Coleman. New Haven, 1922.

van der Vin, J. P. A. *Travellers to Greece and Constantinople: Ancient Monuments and Old Traditions in Medieval Travellers' Tales.* 2 vols. Istanbul, 1980.

van Gemert, A. F. *Marinos Falieros en zijn biede liefdesroman.* Amsterdam, 1973.

Varela, F. J., E. Thompson, and E. Rosch. *The Embodied Mind.* Cambridge, Mass., 1991.

Vico, G. *The New Science,* trans. T. G. Bergin and M. H. Fisch. Ithaca, 1948.

Volkmann, L. *Bilderschriften der Renaissance: Hieroglyphik und Emblematik in ihren Beziehungen und Fortwirkungen.* Leipzig, 1923.

Walsh, J. E. *A Catalogue of the Fifteenth-Century Printed Books in the Harvard University Library.* Vol. 2, *Books Printed in Rome and Venice.* Binghamton, N.Y., 1992.

Warburg, A. *Sandro Boticellis "Geburt der Venus" und "Frühling": Eine Versuchung über die Vorstellung von der Antike in der italienischen Frührenaissance.* Hamburg and Leipzig, 1893.

Warburg, A. *La rinascità del paganismo antico.* Florence, 1966.

Watkins, R. "The Authorship of the Vita Anonyma of Leon Battista Alberti." *Studies in the Renaissance* 4 (1957), pp. 101–112.

———. *Humanism and Liberty: Writings on Freedom from Fifteenth-Century Florence.* Columbia, S.C., 1978.

———. "L. B. Alberti's Emblem, the Winged Eye, and His Name Leo." *Mitteilungen des kunsthistorischen Instituts in Florenz* 9 (1960), pp. 256–258.

Watts, P. *Nicolaus Cusanus: A Fifteenth-Century Vision of Man.* Leiden, 1982.

Weinberger, A. "The First Facade of the Cathedral of Florence." *Journal of the Warburg and Courtauld Institutes* 4–5 (1941–1942), p. 79.

Weiss, A. "A New Francesco Colonna." *Italian Studies* 16 (1961), pp. 78–83.

Weiss, R. *The Renaissance Discovery of Classical Antiquity.* Oxford, 1969.

Westfall, C. *In This Most Perfect Paradise: Alberti, Nicholas V, and the Invention of Conscious Urban Planning in Rome, 1447–1455.* University Park, Pa., 1974.

Wheeler, M. *Roman Art and Architecture.* New York, 1964.

Wilkins, E. H. *A History of Italian Literature.* Cambridge, Mass., 1954.

Williams, M. A. "Divine Image—Prison of Flesh: Perceptions of the Body in Ancient Gnosticism." In Feher et al., *A History of the Human Body,* 1:128–147.

Wilson, N. G. *From Byzantium to Italy: Greek Studies in the Italian Renaissance.* London, 1992.

Wind, E. *Pagan Mysteries of the Renaissance.* Harmondsworth, 1958.

Wittkower, R. *Architectural Principles in the Age of Humanism.* London, 1949.

———. "Marvels of the East." *Journal of the Warburg and Courtauld Institutes* 5 (1942), pp. 191 ff.

Yu, Li. *Number-based Design Reasoning Systems.* Delft, 1994.

Zabughin, V. "Una fonte ignota dell'Hypnerotomachia Poliphili." *Giornale Storico della Letteratura Italiana* 74 (1919), pp. 41–49.

———. *Giulio Pomponio Leto.* 2 vols. Grottaferrata, 1910.

Zarncke, F. "Der Graltempel: Vorstudie zu einer Ausgabe des jüngeren Titurel." *Abhandlungen der Kgl. Sächsischen Akademie der Wissenschaften, Leipzig* 17 (1879), pp. 373 ff.

Ziliotto, B. *Rafaelle Zovenzoni: La vita, i carmi.* Trieste, 1950.

Zorzi, A. "Dürer's Bibliothek." *Beiblatt der Zeitschrift für Bücherfreunde* 21 (1920), pp. 18 ff.

INDEX

*